HISTORY OF PRUSSIA

BY

HERBERT TUTTLE

VOLUME I. — (1134–1740)

AMS PRESS
NEW YORK

HISTORY OF PRUSSIA TO THE ACCESSION OF FREDERIC THE GREAT

1134—1740

By HERBERT TUTTLE

PROFESSOR IN CORNELL UNIVERSITY

SECOND EDITION

BOSTON
HOUGHTON, MIFFLIN AND COMPANY
New York : 11 East Seventeenth Street
The Riverside Press, Cambridge
1884

Reprinted from the edition of 1884, Boston
First AMS EDITION published 1971
Manufactured in the United States of America

International Standard Book Number:
Complete Set 0-404-06670-4
Volume One 0-404-06671-2

Library of Congress Number: 76-140031

AMS PRESS INC.
NEW YORK, N.Y. 10003

PREFACE.

—◆—

IN the volume which is herewith submitted to the judgment of the public, it has been my purpose to describe the political development of Prussia from the earliest times down to the death of the second king. At that point even the general reader will strike comparatively familiar ground. The nature of my plan has led me to make somewhat minute researches into the early institutions of Brandenburg; and throughout the work the development of the constitution has received more attention, and is elucidated by more copious references, than wars or treaties, than dynastic intrigues or territorial conquests. These have not been neglected, but they have been made of secondary importance.

It has seemed to me that even readers who are not Prussians have an interest in knowing what was the origin and what the early history of the political system which first came into universal notice through the victories of Frederic, and after a period of eclipse again astonished the world in the second half of the present century. The importance of the subject is therefore a sufficient excuse for the task which I have undertaken, though not for the defects in its execution.

ITHACA, N. Y., *October*, 1883.

CONTENTS.

CHAPTER I.

PRIMITIVE AND MEDIÆVAL BRANDENBURG.

CHAPTER II.

EARLY SOCIETY AND INSTITUTIONS.

vi CONTENTS.

CHAPTER III.

THE HOHENZOLLERNS TO THE SEVENTEENTH CENTURY.

CHAPTER IV.

THE SEVENTEENTH CENTURY TO THE PEACE OF WESTPHALIA.

viii CONTENTS.

CHAPTER V.

FROM THE PEACE OF WESTPHALIA TO THE DEATH OF THE GREAT ELECTOR.

CONTENTS.

CHAPTER VI.

STATE OF THE COUNTRY UNDER THE GREAT ELECTOR.

CHAPTER VII.

FROM THE ACCESSION OF FREDERIC III. TO THE ACQUISITION OF THE CROWN.

CHAPTER VIII.

EARLY YEARS OF THE NEW KINGDOM.

CHAPTER IX.

FOREIGN POLICY OF FREDERIC WILLIAM I.

CONTENTS. xiii

CHAPTER X.

FREDERIC WILLIAM'S ADMINISTRATIVE REFORMS.

CHAPTER XI.

SOCIAL AND DOMESTIC RELATIONS UNDER THE SECOND KING.

HISTORY OF PRUSSIA.

CHAPTER I.

PRIMITIVE AND MEDIÆVAL BRANDENBURG.

THE common and not incorrect designation of Prussia
as essentially a modern state assigns to a work
on the history of Prussia certain natural and Introduction.
obvious limitations, on which the critical reader will insist more or less warmly, according to the extent of his
special knowledge and the rigor of his literary canons.
A writer on this subject ought, therefore, to respect such
a prejudice, for it is founded in the reason of things.
But only the general truth can be conceded, only a
loose and elastic limit can be observed ; since opinions
vary widely as to the exact line along which the division
should be drawn, as to the precise point at which the
state began to take form and character, to be a factor in
European politics, to deserve the notice of the statesman,
the publicist, and the historian. Inquirers who are fond
of even dates and sharp divisions take the beginning of
the last century, and the acquisition of the crown, as a
convenient point from which to make the survey. The
Great Elector, Frederic William, is not only a picturesque character, such as history delights to study, but his
career, so full of significance for the institutions of the
country, has also the advantage of starting near the close
of the Thirty Years' War, and shaping itself by the Peace
of Westphalia. And even to go farther back, and begin
with the advent of the Hohenzollerns upon the stage,

would gratify all who feel an interest in the fortunes of
that remarkable house, without necessarily frightening
those who dislike the darkness and disorder of mediæval
story.

Yet it must be confessed that no one of these periods
falls within the sphere of what the world has hitherto
agreed to call Prussian history. Under the influence especially of an original and powerful work, all readers
except Prussians settled, apparently, a few years ago, in
the firm conviction that the reign of Frederic the Great
was the ultimate field of necessary research; that Frederic
alone gave the state a national form and an international
position.

This belief rests, in the first place, on an exaggerated
view of Frederic's achievements. But even without that, it is a fundamental error to ignore the
long course of development and preparation, of
which Frederic and his works were the legitimate outcome.
The childhood of Prussia preceded its manhood; and in
the natural dispositions, the surroundings, the early im-
pressions, the education of the child will be found the key
to the character and achievements of the man. The history of the state reveals a course of organic growth, turned
indeed, at intervals, in one direction or another by great
men, but wholly caused or wholly arrested by none of
them. It may be necessary, perhaps, to assume this principle of life and growth. It evades the touch in the state,
as in the man; but it can be traced through its effects in
political phenomena, and the longer the line over which
observation extends, the more copious and certain will be
the results. The practical limits of Prussian history are,
therefore, not those which are drawn arbitrarily at any
fixed point, but those which are imposed by the law of literary proportion according to the resources at its command. Even the state of Frederic himself cannot be fully
understood without at least an introductory sketch of the

Importance of early Prussian history.

elements and processes out of which it grew. It is the
purpose of the following volume to furnish such an introduction.

As a concession, however, to just scruples, the period
which closes with the accession of the Great Scope of this
Elector ought to be treated in literature accord- volume.
ing to the part which it played in history, as a period of
growth and preparation, not of action and achievement.
It is true that the founders of the state were not all unfitted for the work either of the cabinet or the field. The
primitive records are lighted up here and there with bright
touches of real statesmanship, and with triumphs of no
mean order on the busy stage of feudal warfare. And
even that final series of blunders and disasters which
brought the early colony nearly to the point of ruin was
an efficient though mysterious cause of subsequent progress, since it opened the way for the Hohenzollerns, and
ushered in a new era of prosperity under a manly and
energetic race. But this period and these events lead
merely up to the door of actual history, and they will be
used only so long as their guidance seems indispensable.

The first historical character is undoubtedly Albert the
Bear, who received the Mark of Brandenburg, or, as it
was then called, the North Mark, as a fief from the Emperor Lothair II. in 1134. Between him and his predecessors lies an interregnum of two centuries. An unbroken line of margraves had kept up, indeed, a nominal
succession, and *in partibus*, as it were, had maintained the
the imperial claim; but the Slavs were actually again in
possession, and the traces of German civilization had been
carefully effaced. This period is, therefore, practically a
blank. And since the earlier German occupation was not
complete in a political or a military sense, its annals are
too obscure, its bonds of connection with the more successful enterprise of Albert too few and frail, to give it much
historical value. That the original possession of the coun-

try by a Teutonic tribe, for which Tacitus is the chief authority, justified its reconquest in the name of the Empire is a conceit which may please the Prussian patriot, but has not proved conclusive to serious publicists.[1]

It may, however, be said briefly that, according to the The original Roman author, and to legend and tradition probable enough in themselves, the whole present territory of Prussia, north to the Baltic and east as far as the river Vistula, was originally occupied by the Germans. The region about Berlin — or the Mark — was the domicile of the Semnones. Tacitus has left a description of this people;[2] and as his facts were derived from the reports of his countrymen, who had felt their prowess in battle, it is not unreasonable to believe that they were distinguished above their neighbors for the antiquity of their origin, the nobility of their blood, and the preëminence of their military valor. But the irresistible migrations from the east swept them out of their ancient country, and into that stream which poured like a flood over the frontiers of The Slavs. the Roman Empire. A Slavonic tribe usurped the place of the Suevi; to the Wends fell the specific domain of the Semnones. One barbarism succeeded another; for the differences of degree, which have been detected by antiquaries, are not uniformly favorable to the Germans, and cannot be shown to have much affected the subsequent course of historical events. And it is not clear that the character of the early society was greatly influenced by the German invasions of the ninth and tenth centuries, which as has been said were brief episodes, and failed to establish a durable possession. The enemy awaited a more vigorous attempt under a more skillful and energetic leader.

In the mean time the dispossessed Germans were pushing their way into the very heart of the Roman Empire.

---

[1] See, for instance, Pierson, *Preussische Geschichte* (Berlin, 1865), p. 1.

[2] *De Mor. Germ.* 38–39.

They acquired an early contact with a civilized, an inquiring and a literary people, who opened up many of the secrets of their domestic, their civil, and their military polity; and this fact gives them an importance which the Slavonic intruders never obtained. A brief sketch of early Germanic society is therefore possible, and seems to be required. The inquiry, too, will cover the initial difficulties of our subject; for if the general obscurity common to all the German tribes, in all the countries that they settled, can be even partially removed, the natural changes which their institutions underwent, and the positive ordinances into which they grew, in the province of Brandenburg, will be far more easily understood.

The members or organs of that society admit of several orders of classification, according to the point of view from which they are to be examined. A natural or social division is that of the race into tribes, and these into families or branches.[1] Thus the Semnones were a family of the tribe of the Suevi and the race of the Germans. The civil or administrative scale, to which the military also corresponded, includes in a descending order the tribe, the family, the hundred, and the tithing. But it is probable that this is in part a formal and arbitrary division.[2] On the continent the hundred and tithing seem early to have lost the importance which they so long retained among the Anglo-Saxons; and the organic political divisions may be reduced to tribes, families, and households. These represent, again, the country which the tribe might possess or occupy; the gau or shire, at once a territorial and an administrative factor;[3] and the manor, which was the unit and spring of the system.

The Germanic polity.

---

[1] Volk, Stämme, and Völkerschaften.

[2] Comp. Waitz, *Deutsche Verf. Geschichte*, vol. i. (Kiel, 1844), p. 48.

[3] Eichhorn, *Deutsche Staats & Rechtsgeschichte*, 4th ed. 1 Th. § 14 b; Waitz, i. 49.

The manor was the domestic and social stronghold of the freeman, within which his will was supreme; the gau was presided over by a graf,[1] or some similar officer ; the tribe acknowledged a military king, or a council of military chiefs. Thus democracy, aristocracy, and royalty were all present in the system at once ; and if the kings were originally elected, the historian must still assume a process by which they became hereditary. At the time of the invasions there were recognized royal families, if there was not a fixed order of succession.[2] But the term democracy describes a sense or feeling of equality which pervaded the great body of freemen, not an institution or form of society, not the basis of a political structure. Political rights were confined to a few ;[3] and since the authority, original or delegated, of the magistrates was so slight, the aristocratic principle in the end prevailed, and the real power was lodged in the assembly of patrician warriors. A second principle which follows at once is that of personal liberty. Among the freemen this right or privilege was forfeited by no crime, however grave or odious,[4] and it is impossible to ignore the part it played in shaping the crude machinery of state. But if the principle of personal liberty was strong, so also was that of respect for military talent; and the two were able to produce a system in which the chief enjoyed the authority due to his rank and character, without usurping the powers reserved by a society of freemen.

This simple polity had satisfied all the wants of the barbarians for unknown centuries, until they issued from the

[1] Savigny, *Gesch. des röm. Rechts* (Heidelberg, 1843–51), i. 187.

[2] Waitz, i. 67–70; Guizot, *Histoire de la Civilisation*, passim.

[3] That is excluding the liti or coloni and the servi. It is maintained by Guizot, *Hist. de la Civ.* lect. 3, and by Eichhorn, Th. i. § 15, that these two inferior classes were the victims of war and conquest. Another theory makes them freemen, who had been degraded for crime, but I cannot regard it as fully established.

[4] Grimm, *D. Rechtsalterthümer*, says not even by regicide.

plains of Germany and began to confront, as a conquering force, the old and complex civilization of Rome. New influences then began to press them ; moral forces checked them even in the hour of military triumph. Germans and Romans. Their career was first arrested, not by the skill of the Roman generals, or the valor of the Roman soldiers, which were both traditions of the past; but rather by the Christian Church, which dazzled them with the pomp and splendor of her ceremonial, while she wooed them with the soft persuasion of her lessons ; and which by her arts no less than by her virtues baffled the schemes of unknown gods, and welcomed the invaders to the joys of her mysterious faith. The codification of the barbarian laws was a victory at least for the method of Roman jurisprudence, and revealed an early, not to say premature, progress in enlightenment. A still more important event was the revival of the imperial idea under the patronage of the church. But not even the authority of the church, the influence of Roman law, or the example of a universal monarchy could permanently obstruct a process which was encouraged by all the conditions of the time, and of which the centuries of disorder that followed the death of Charlemagne were perhaps a necessary part.

As a natural result of the new situation the barbarian kings, in the character of victorious leaders, were permitted to acquire powers which had once belonged to the patrician assemblies — the first step in a momentous social revolution. It did not indeed at once extend to the great body of free proprietors. These rather assumed on their new estates — whether acquired by lot, by royal grant, or by partition — a position not unlike that which their fathers had enjoyed in Germany. But the case was different with the counts and dukes.[1] After the invasion and conquest it was still necessary to Feudalism.

[1] On the previous position and character of these officials see Eichhorn, i. 14. b.

employ them in services adequate to their rank; but the powers of the king had been so much increased that it was impossible for them to resume their former character as the chosen magistrates of a free people. Accordingly they exchanged their many constituents for one master; the delegates of the people became servants of the crown.[1] But the Teutonic idea of the union between land and authority had been strengthened rather than weakened by the invasions, and the kings saw themselves confronted by the danger that the endowment of the nobles with large estates might place them entirely beyond its control. In this dilemma the Roman law supplied a convenient fiction. The nobles were distributed throughout the country on ample domains, which were the measure and support of their dignity; but they received their land *per beneficium*,[2] and accepted in return certain feudal duties, at court, and in civil and military administration, or a general obligation of fealty and service. By such a device the ultimate rights of the king were believed to be saved.

If these benefices were ever revocable at pleasure, they soon became valid for life, and then hereditary, though the latter quality grew up by prescription long before it was formally proclaimed.[3] In the mean time, however, a change took place in the relation of the fief to the office. At first the estate was treated as the property of the office, but in time the office came to be derived from the fief; who held the one, exercised the duties and enjoyed the honors of the other. But this movement, which began under the Merovingian kings, and was hardly arrested by Charlemagne, did not end until the conditions of land

[1] Savigny, i. 265–6.

[2] Waitz, ii. 208 et seq.; he describes the process but rejects the term. Huellmann, *Geschichte des Ursprungs der Stände*, 2d ed. (Berlin, 1830), p. 52, defends it.

[3] It was enacted in an edict of the Emperor Conrad II. at Milan in 1037.

tenure had been completely revolutionized.[1] The lord of the country with his vassals, the former allodialists, who by " commendation " had exchanged their allodial for feudal titles, organized a state within a state. The forms of homage to the king were indeed observed, but the royal power rapidly declined before the aggressions of men whose fathers had been docile servants of Charlemagne.

The other members of feudal society were developed in a similar way, and some of them from original Teutonic stock. Thus in the knights or gentry of the Middle Ages it is not difficult to recognize the ancient German freemen,[2] or in the peasantry, villein and free, the modified principle of the servi and liberti. In these, as in the nobles, the German predominates over the Latin element. But when we examine the cities and the church we detect at once a prevailing Roman influence, which in a society penetrated by the Gothic idea of classes kept alive the tradition of municipal freedom and of universal spiritual authority. It would be incorrect, however, to describe these as hostile forces, fixed in the midst yet plotting the overthrow of feudal institutions. They aided, on the contrary, in giving them form, as in nature friction and resistance affect the shape of a body ; and they in turn received from this attrition the impress of the common type, and learned to work as members of a common system.

No sooner was feudalism firmly settled over a large part of Europe than it began a comprehensive career of conquest. The Norman invasions of England and Italy, the Crusades, the conquest of the Slavonic lands on the Baltic, and finally the second oc-

Feudal conquests.

---

[1] See Montesquieu, *Esprit des Lois*, liv. 31, ch. 8 ; Hallam, *Middle Ages* (ed. London, 1872), i. 163.

[2] Vollgraf, *Die teutschen Standesherren* (Mayence, 1851), i. 46 and 55.

cupation of the North Mark seem to be movements inspired by a common impulse. In some cases the pretended motive was religious, as with the great armies that went to the rescue of the Holy Sepulchre, or those that carried the cross among the heathen of the North.[1] In others love of war and conquest was the controlling passion. But during two or three centuries feudal Europe was surging restlessly against its barriers on every side, and seeking outlets for an energy that without foreign employment would turn and rend the system on which it had been nourished. This impetus carried Albert the Bear into the Mark of Brandenburg.

His feudal seat was Ballenstädt, a petty settlement on the eastern fringe of the Harz Mountains, but Albert the Bear. the more common family name, that of the "Ascanians," was taken from the castle of Aschersleben,[2] which was also an ancestral possession. In a wider sense he belonged to the great division of the Saxons. The contemporary chronicles, reflecting, of course, local usage, give Albert the descriptive title of Beautiful — Der Schöne — in addition to that of the Bear, which was not descriptive either of his person or his manners, but arose from a device that figured on his shield. His fine features were improved by a graceful figure, by a noble carriage, by a supple and powerful frame. Wanting neither courage, nor enterprise, nor audacity, he was one of the most renowned and successful warriors in Germany, and made several campaigns under the standard of the Empire. He appears to have had, too, what was unusual in those days, a certain sense of German patriotism, rising above the formal obligations of fealty, and suppressing at times the impulses of personal resentment. His patron, Lothair,

[1] Slavos aut christianiæ religioni subderent aut omnino delerent, said a pious chronicler quoted by Gercken, *Stiftshistorie von Brandenburg*, p. 78.

[2] Latin Ascaria, corrupted into Ascania.

owed the imperial dignity in a measure to Albert's forbearance, and paid the debt according to the practice of the times by the gift of the North Mark.

1134.

A more exacting creditor than the Count of Ballenstädt would perhaps have scrutinized the equivalent somewhat closely. It had first to be conquered by the sword; and although that task could not alarm an active soldier, prudence might justly inquire whether the prize was worth the effort. It comprised, loosely speaking, a district lying along the west side of the Elbe, opposite the basin of the Havel. The territory was inconsiderable in extent, but in the grant was implied the permission, not to say the command, to enlarge it indefinitely by further conquests toward the Baltic. But the dullness of the landscape and the poverty of the soil would throw grave suspicion upon the bounty of a person less august than the head of the Holy Roman Empire. Long sandy plains stretch from one sluggish stream to another. Even to-day, with all the efforts of skilled husbandry, the peasants lead but a sorry life, and in its age of virgin freshness the land could not have been rich in promise. Vast and impassable swamps were a derisive relief from the monotony of the deserts. The rivers, indeed, were liberally stocked with fish; but the forests were mostly pine, and harbored bears, wolves, and wild boar. Wendish towns were scattered about along the Havel at points easy of defence, and in the brief intervals when border warfare was suspended a crude and irregular traffic was maintained between the Christian and the heathen. The church frowned on such intercourse, but her humane precepts were disregarded. In the contested region between the two peoples the habits of life gradually approached a common standard ; an occasional Wendish chieftain embraced the cross; intermarriages were not unknown. But the general relation was one of permanent hostility, embittered by religious difference.

The North Mark.

If the new acquisition had first to be won by the sword, and was of little value when won except as a nucleus for further political growth, it is no less true that the conditions of that growth were strictly subject to the feudal constitution of the Empire. Facts did not indeed always correspond to principles in the Middle Ages. The reality and efficiency of political relations were largely determined not by formal law, but by the comparative resources and opportunities of suzerain and vassal, and the spirit in which each interpreted the tie between them. There were princes strong in treasure and in retainers who served the Emperor mechanically from a sense of duty. There were others who essayed hopeless resistance out of willful insubordination. And there was a third class who practiced a discriminating obedience ; who presumed neither on their strength nor their weakness ; who performed their duties without renouncing their rights, and thus, when met by similar intelligence in the suzerain, brought their own interests into harmony with those of the Empire. Albert is assigned to this class by common consent. And the more tact was required of him, since in the relation of margrave he was liable to a double subordination, — that of a vassal to his lord, and that of an official to his superior. In a sense which would shock a modern prince he was theoretically only a servant in his own state. His political functions were defined by the title itself. He commanded on a frontier which was the limit of the imperial authority ; and since the hostile or unknown lands beyond were to be conquered in the name of the Emperor, the "Markgraf" was simply his representative, subject in many ways to his orders and dispositions.[1] It is true that in practice no emperor could

Margrave and emperor.

---

[1] See Droysen, *Gesch. der pr. Politik*, i. 21 ; Heeren, *Kleine Historische Schriften* (Goettingen 1808), i. 112. Heeren says of the margraves, . . . sie waren doch so wenig eigentliche Landesherren als blosse Beamte ; sie waren ein Mittelding zwischen Beiden, das

assert this theory to its full extent against a spirited and resolute vassal. It survived in law because it was ignored in fact, or, what is the same thing, because it was observed in petty forms and ceremonies, which were but feeble restraints upon real power. But to accept the Mark with this condition was nevertheless to accept a burden, even if one of those burdens which flatter the bearer by their weight and responsibility, and encourage him by their promised compensations.

Finally Albert had to enforce his claim against jealous neighbors of his own race and religion. Adventurers like Henry the Lion, of Saxony, moved by a similar ambition, obtained similar favors of the Emperor; and as geographical limits were ill-defined in the patents, disputes of priority and jurisdiction easily arose ; and the rivalries of the imperial court were revived on the remote plains of the north. Powerful prelates set up counter-claims to one district and another, and defended them with the allied resources of church and state. Albert himself was indeed an abrupt disputant, averse to trifling, but his successors inherited an annoying fund of litigation. *Albert's rivals.*

Of the military measures taken by Albert to secure possession of his estate, few details have survived. He appears to have led a considerable army into the country, and to have taken every precaution to make his triumph both prompt and sure. But force was employed only as a last resort; for Albert was a statesman as well as a soldier, and by a politic liberality insinuated first his religion, and then his authority, upon many of the most influential Wends. Arms and diplomacy thus composed a hostile and refractory people into a body of sympathetic subjects. At the same time he fixed the conditions of his social polity on such a firm and yet prudent *His policy.*

schwer zu beschreiben ist. . . . I should be reluctant to undertake a task from which Heeren shrank in dismay.

basis that even before his death the prosperity of the Mark had begun to excite the envy of its neighbors. He acquired the title of Arch-Treasurer of the Empire, one of the four great honorary offices of state.

Albert did not wait, however, for death to terminate his rule, but voluntarily gave it up in 1168, and re-

Otho I.   tired to Ballenstädt. His son Otho succeeded him in the Mark. In 1170, as it would appear, the name of Brandenburg was substituted for that of North Mark, which had ceased to describe more than the original nucleus of the colony, now one of the several districts into which it was divided.[1] The city and territory of Brandenburg were not probably included in the imperial grant, but were inherited from the Wendish prince, Pribislaw, whom Albert had converted to Christianity and taught some useful Christian principles of testamentary conveyance. The localities known as Glien, Bellin, Rhinow, and Friesack were also, it is believed, acquired by treaty with the Wends. Priegnitz was the fruit of a successful cam-

Pomerania.   paign. Albert even made an expedition into Pomerania, but accomplished little, although several bishops took part in the scheme, and gave it the special sanction of the church. If this enterprise was of doubtful legality owing to the claim of Henry the Lion to Pomerania, Otho's right was made more clear by the act of Frederic Barbarossa, who, on the death of Henry, formally conferred it, or rather the expectancy to it, upon the House of Brandenburg, and thus founded a relation which in later years gave rise to the most obscure and intricate disputes. The Danes also had pretensions to Pomerania, and defended them obstinately with the sword.

Under Otho II., brother of the preceding, the family inheritance was sorely mismanaged. The Mar-

Otho II.   grave becoming involved in some quarrel with the See of Madgeburg, the Archbishop placed him under

1 Comp. chap. ii. p. 38–39.

the ban; and as the price of release Otho was required to accept the suzerainty of the prelate for the older and better part of his dominions. His brother and successor, Albert II., was also unfortunate in the beginning of his career; but recovered the favor of the Emperor, and restored the prestige of his house before his death. He left two sons, both minors, and a widow, Mathilda, who approved herself an energetic and sagacious regent.

Albert II.

Very important acquisitions were made during the reign of these two princes. The preoccupations of the King of Denmark gave them a secure foothold in Pomerania, which the native nobility acknowledged; the frontiers were pushed eastward to the Oder, where the New Mark was organized, and the town of Frankfort was laid out; purchase put them in possession of the district of Lebus; and the bride of Otho III., a Bohemian princess, brought him as her dowry an extensive region on the upper Spree with several thriving villages, — all this in spite of the division of power and authority. The precedent was regarded as auspicious. Otho III. died in 1267, John one year later; and a new partition of the estate was made between their several sons, the oldest, Otho IV., receiving, however, the title and prerogatives of head of the house. Otho made some acquisitions, but also suffered some reverses. The practical disintegration of the state began to work its natural effects. Divided councils paralyzed the common forces. A course of decay and dissolution was setting in.

Fresh acquisitions.

In view of the condition into which these later margraves brought the Mark, it is difficult to accept as just, or even sincere, the praises that have been lavished upon them. Their ardent eulogists were perhaps more often charmed by the romantic virtues of the knight, which their heroes undoubtedly possessed, than by the sober practical qualities of the statesman, which were conspicuous by their

absence. And in the Middle Ages even the effusive loyalty of the courtier might conceal but a small amount of
real affection. How, in fact, could intense feeling be con-
centrated on a throne which was shared between a dozen
owners? The spirit of loyalty in the subject is personal;
and if it extends to all the members of a ruling house it is
not diffused equally over them all, but is rather transmitted with just gradations of force through the chief object
to the partners of his name and heirs of his authority.

In Brandenburg the fashion of the thirteenth century
spared the vassals this useful distinction. Not
only were all the brothers seen reigning together,
but even their sons were commonly called margraves at about the age at which a modern prince receives his first uniform as lieutenant in the army. And as
their number increased it is quite possible that a score of
them once met on a hill near Rathenow, as an old legend
relates, to deplore the poverty of the land and its failure
to support them in the appropriate style of their rank.[1]

Decline of the Ascanians.

The complete extinction of this family in 1319 is therefore a puzzling circumstance. Since the process of reduction seemed for a time to stop at Waldemar, the
last margrave,[2] it is possible that the people of
the Mark did not regard it with that keen sorrow which
the following years taught them to feel. Waldemar was a
brave, accomplished, and popular prince.[3] As he reunited
under one sceptre all the various provinces of the Mark,

Waldemar.

[1] Even Ranke, *Pr. Gesch.* i. 15, relates this story, and apparently in
good faith.

[2] His cousin and only heir, Henry, was a minor, and survived him but
a year. Stenzel, *Gesch. des Pr. Staats* (Hamburg, 1830), i. 102, says
that after Waldemar's death the land was treated "als wäre kein
rechtmässigner Erbe. . . . vorhanden."

[3] Stenzel, i. 64 ; Buchholtz, *Gesch. der Churmark Brandenburg*
(Berlin, 1765–75), ii. 271, and the historians generally, who, however
merely reproduce the judgment of local chroniclers. In reality little is known of Waldemar except his wars.

he came into possession of a more liberal income than his
predecessors had enjoyed, and was thus enabled to give
more lustre and dignity to his government. He would
perhaps have recovered even the revenues which they had
sold, and thus in time have restored order to the public
treasury; but these and all other hopes were frustrated by
his death. How unwillingly his countrymen and subjects
parted from him is shown by the credit which,
years afterwards, they gave to a report that he
was still alive, and the welcome which they of- End of the Ascanians, 1319.
fered to an obscure pretender who claimed to be the true
Waldemar.

The House of Anhalt had thus ruled in Brandenburg two
hundred years. During this period and under
their rule the principality had traversed the va- Their work.
rious stages of conquest, pacification, aggrandizement, and
dissolution ; and the course of reunion and reconstruction
under Waldemar was only a promise which never reached
fulfilment. But at the close of the dynasty under this
last prince there still remained a large and distinct gain
in all the elements of social and political well-being. The
undisputed territory was greater than in the time of Albert. The Wends were subdued, converted, assimilated;
the towns were larger and more numerous ; the aggregate wealth was greater, the revenues, if properly administered, would have been far more productive; the laws
were more systematic and better understood; the church,
though more greedy and arrogant, wielded an influence
often favorable to order and morality, and taught branches
of learning in the monasteries and parish schools which
were unknown to the rude warriors that followed the first
Ascanian across the Elbe. In short, in most of those
social interests whose successful conduct seldom calls for
the direct action of the prince, and depends therefore but
little on his personal character, the subjects of Waldemar
were probably more favored than those of Albert. And

2

this class of interests was relatively larger in the four-teenth century than in the twelfth, as would naturally result from the development of political forms, and the growth of governmental machinery.

On the death of Waldemar, or, more correctly speak-
The inter-   ing, of his cousin, a host of claimants arose for
regnum.   the whole or parts of the Mark. The estates showed at first a gallant devotion to the widow, and in-trusted the reins of authority to her; but she repaid this fidelity by hastily espousing the Duke of Brunswick, and transferring her rights to him. The transaction was not, however, ratified by the estates, and the Duke failed to enforce it by arms. Pomerania threw off the yoke which it had once unwillingly accepted; Bohemia reclaimed the wedding portion of Otho's bride; the Duke of Liegnitz sought to recover Lebus, although it had once been reg-ularly sold; and in the general scramble the church, through its local representatives, fought with all the en-ergy of mere worldly robbers.

But in this crisis the Emperor forgot neither the duties of his station nor the interests of his house. Louis II. of
The Bava-   Bavaria then wore the purple. By feudal law
rian line.   a vacant fief reverted to its suzerain; and Bran-denburg being a fief of the Empire, the disposition of it, on the extinction of the Ascanian house, fell to the reign-ing Emperor. It was not therefore contrary to law, nor did it shock the moral sense of the age, when Louis drew the Mark practically into his own possession by conferring it nominally upon his minor son. The motives which gov-erned the bestowal of such benefices were generally those of self-interest. Compensation for actual benefits, the pressure of debt, the desire of winning allies or disarming foes, and baser considerations of dynastic advantage, — such are the causes to which more than one of the reigning houses of Europe owes the good fortune that piety, or ser-vility, or hypocrisy now ascribes to divine favor. Bran-

denburg was exposed for a century to this flippant and brutal caprice.

During the minority of Louis the Margrave, the province was administered by Louis the Emperor, and with some show of vigor. His campaigns and his negotiations were alike promising. The integrity of the Mark might have been fully restored, and an orderly population handed over to the young Elector, if more menacing troubles had not called the Emperor into other parts of Germany, and thus checked the unfinished work of reconstruction. But the Margrave, when he took possession of his appanage, proved wholly and ludicrously incompetent. He bought off the Pomeranians indeed; but he neither bought nor drove off the Poles, and learned from their invasion how fierce was the resentment, how unscrupulous were the tactics of the church.

Margrave Louis I.

This pious enterprise took place in 1325. The Emperor having provoked the wrath of Rome, and spiritual censures proving insufficient, Pope John XXII. called the secular power to his aid ; and the King of Poland was inspired by the zeal of a Catholic or the ambition of a prince to invade the Mark, not the least vulnerable of Louis' possessions. His army marched into the New Mark ; sacked and burned several towns ; and ravaged a wide extent of country along the Oder. The Margrave watched the devastation in helpless dismay, and his father, fighting desperately in the South for his own existence, could afford no relief. The local population was therefore driven to self-defence ; and in the Middle Ages the self-defence of resolute burghers showed in many a desperate crisis an untaught military skill, an astounding energy, and a valor against which neither numbers nor tactics could prevail. The young city of Frankfort was the leader in the tardy but successful uprising. The Poles were expelled ; the citizens had for the time saved the Mark. But they were keen though

Branden-burg and the church.

rude politicians, and could reason from near events to remote causes. Believing that the Bishop of Lebus was the real author of their troubles, they seized that unscrupulous prelate, threw him into prison, and kept him there two years in contempt of all the edicts fulminated against them by the church.

The Margrave finally wearied even of the forms of authority, and sold his unhappy dominions to his two brothers, another Louis and Otho. In the mean time his father had died. The Electors — or five of them — had already deposed him, and chosen in his place Charles of Moravia, a prince of the house of Luxemburg, as his successor. He became respectably and even cred-itably known in history as Charles IV. If not a brilliant and successful warrior, he was a most astute politician ; and although he failed in the attempt to subdue by arms the Margrave of Brandenburg, who had naturally espoused his father's cause, he was persistent and ingenious in diplomatic schemes for overthrowing the House of Bavaria and bringing the Mark under his own sceptre. The device of the false Waldemar is ascribed to him, and in 1356 he raised Brandenburg, as an act of policy, to the rank of an Electorate. From Louis he procured, in return, a treaty of succession, by which he should acquire Brandenburg in case of the death of that Margrave and his brother Otho without heirs. His intrigues were finally crowned with complete success. Louis died suddenly in 1365. Otho, thenceforth alone in the charge, vacillated between weak submission to the Emperor's will and spurts of petulant but feeble resistance ; until Charles put an end to the farce by invading the Mark, crushing the army of the Margrave, and forcing him to an abject capitulation.

In 1371, after a nominal rule of half a century, and for the price of a meagre annuity, the Bavarian line transferred all its rights to the family of Charles IV.

Louis II. and Otho V.

Expulsion of the Bavarians, 1371.

As long as Charles personally governed the Mark, — a task which fell upon him during the minority of his son Wenzel, — it was governed, as even his enemies admit, with vigor, justice, and intelligence. The period was indeed brief, for he died in 1378. But during that time he succeeded in winning the respect and obedience of his vassals, brought order out of chaos, stimulated every form of industry by wise and liberal measures, and especially gave a secure basis to fiscal and agrarian relations by preparing a systematic survey and register of real property throughout a large part of the Mark.[1] The picture was gloomy enough, and presumably, therefore, did not flatter.

Line of Luxemburg. Wenzel.

Wenzel, for whom the Mark had been destined in the plans of Charles, acquired, meanwhile, the crown of Bohemia, a richer prize, and Brandenburg passed to t˴ next son, Sigismond. The change was a disastrous one. The new Margrave, though a man of some light and showy accomplishments, had, as a ruler, neither his father's firm, clear eye nor his practical sense of duty ; and the abrupt termination of the regent's regular visits, of the brilliant yet solemn and useful assemblies which Charles had been accustomed to hold at the quaint old town of Tangermünde, on the Elbe, was followed by the revival of social and political disorder. The next step was to pawn the Mark, as Sigismond did in 1388, to his kinsman of ·Moravia ; and Jobst or Jodocus renewed an experiment in which so many had al-

Sigismond.

Jobst.

[1] The Landbuch of 1374, which is the earliest recognized authority on the tenures and the revenues of the Mark. Mr. Carlyle treats this sagacious Kaiser with ludicrous injustice. True he was called the "Pfaffenkaiser" because he understood the use of diplomacy and pacific reform better than war, a fact which would of course condemn him in Mr. Carlyle's judgment; but the author of the Brandenburg Domesday Book and the Golden Bull cannot have been wholly a contemptible person. Stenzel is eloquent in the description of his statesmanlike virtues.

ready failed. The estates were not asked, it appears, to approve this transaction. It was simply notified to them, with the benevolent assurance that it had been effected " in order, with God's help, so to dispose all matters, that a summary end may be put to all wars and dissensions, and peace and order be everywhere restored."

But the result did not quite correspond to Sigismond's noble intentions. Abstention and indifference, which with the other margraves had been a vice, became with Jobst a policy; and it is difficult to say whether during the next twenty years the Mark suffered most from the rapacity of his deputies, from the unrestrained license of its own gentry, or from the forays of neighboring lords. Professional brigands, like the noble Quitzows, scoured the country with their followers, leaving desolation in their path. The Archbishop of Magdeburg and congenial allies invaded the Mark, pillaged the district of Brandenburg, penetrated even to Rathenow, and levied heavy contributions upon the dismayed and helpless people. The Margrave's officials could make but a feeble resistance, and generally hastened to compromise with the robbers.

Imperial affairs during this period were in scarcely less confusion. Wenzel of Bohemia had been chosen emperor, and then deposed for obvious unfitness. Rupert, Count Palatine, had next been elected, and had died. Again the post was vacant, and Sigismond, still the real Elector of Brandenburg, and the only one who ever acquired the purple, issued successful from the contest.

His good fortune was due in a conspicuous degree to the influence and the money of Frederic, Burggrave of Nuremberg; and it is to the credit of Sigismond that he did not add ingratitude to his other vices, but on his election as emperor hastened to make his patron statthalter, or viceroy, of the Mark. This is the customary loyal account of the transaction. That

Anarchy.

First glimpse of the Hohenzollerns.

the Burggrave had in fact secured his bond, like a prudent capitalist, before loaning his money, and simply enforced it when it became due, is a theory which, it is hardly necessary to add, ought to be rejected by every dutiful subject of the House of Prussia.

CHAPTER II.

EARLY SOCIETY AND INSTITUTIONS.

IT is important, before introducing the Hohenzollerns, to give some account of society and government as organized by their predecessors, as modified during the years of their rule, and as transmitted in the fifteenth century to the new incumbents. The task is of course little more in effect than an examination of the feudal system for the same period. But although the general outlines of that system were the same throughout Europe, various local peculiarities nevertheless arose; and those of Brandenburg, during at least the first century of the Ascanians, will be found, I believe, more often favorable than unfavorable to justice, liberty, and progress.[1]

And first it must be remarked that the singular constitution of the Empire gave to the distinction between nobles and knights, or between knights who were barons and those who were not, a meaning somewhat different in a political sense from that which it had, for instance, in England. In Germany there were many rulers and intricate gradations of feudal rank; in England, where the Norman kings exacted allegiance from every freeman, there was in fact, as in theory, but a single sovereign.[2] It is indeed a truism to say that the political art

Nobles and knights.

---

[1] I throw this out, not as a thesis to be defended, but as an opinion drawn from a considerable course of reading. Some of the reasons for the opinion will appear, however, in the progress of the chapter.

[2] The reader will recall the remark of De Lolme, that the power of

was raised above the level of ignoble social intrigues much later in the one country than in the other. But it is indispensable to bear in mind that in Brandenburg, as in every other German principality, feudal rank and political influence were often convertible terms, so that such nobles as held directly of the Emperor acquired with their titles certain high powers, like justice or coinage, and exercised them even in domains which they owed to the partiality of a territorial superior. The knights, on the other hand, though personally free, could hold land only as the military vassals of their local prince. Hence the former had privileges ; the latter, only rights. But it does not appear that the nobles in any great number shared in the enterprise of Albert.[1] Jealousy of the leader, or contempt for the cause, held them back. But the politic Margrave knew that they were essential to the prestige of his court; and after some years, when his power was more firmly settled, a few adventurous barons were attracted to his standard. They became burggraves in the fortified towns, and governed counties in the name of their accepted lord ;[2] while others who attached themselves to the person of the prince, and filled the so-called ministerial offices,[3] acquired more power with less dignity. But the knights formed by far the largest class of military retainers. As the warriors of mediæval society they were indispensable ; and the margraves, as they pushed farther and farther into the country of the Wends, and opened yearly new regions to German civilization, laid broad and deep the foundations of the Prussian gentry.

the Norman kings is the explanation of English liberty. Compare also Vollgraf, *Die teutschen Standesherren*, i. 42.

[1] Heinemann, *Albrecht der Bär* (Darmstadt, 1864), pp. 234-5.

[2] Ibid. pp. 224-5.

[3] The " domestici " of the Franks, who now and then produced a Pepin. It has indeed been denied that they could be free or noble, in spite of the expressions " liberi ministeriales " and " nobiles ministeriales," which now and then occur.

The spiritual nobility must have played an active part, and have enjoyed great respect and influence, in an enterprise which was a species of crusade.

The clergy.

Their cathedrals and cloisters wanted, indeed, the rich endowments by which the ampler wealth of southern countries showed its devotion to the church; but in the division of spoils they were always liberally remembered. In every village which was laid out, the priest received a section of land as the support of his pious labors. This was prescribed by mediæval usage, it is true, but the reputation of the Ascanians for generosity toward the church rests upon other and voluntary contributions, which amounted to wanton prodigality.[1] At the same time they seem to have maintained a sharp line between spiritual and temporal functions. In the domain of religion and morals the clergy practised freely their elevated zeal; from the domain of secular affairs they were jealously, and it would appear successfully, excluded. And this arrangement the clergy for their part wisely accepted. In spite of the feudal privileges which they might exercise and did, in spite of their high social rank, the bishops long continued to show a proper deference to the civil power, and were hardly accounted a formidable element in the state before the fourteenth century.[2]

In the early municipal system no less than three sorts of cities may be distinguished. There were first a few old towns, like Brandenburg and Havelberg, which were Wendish by origin, and were in a thriving condition when Albert appeared in the Mark. They readily took on a German dress, and became royal residences. Their size, their importance in trade, and the

The towns.

[1] "Welche die Gränzen der Staatsklugheit überschritte," dryly observes Moehsen, *Geschichte der Wissenschaften in der Mark Brandenburg* (Berlin, 1781), p. 118.

[2] Muelverstedt, *Die ältere Verfassung der Landstände in der Mark Brandenburg* (Berlin, 1858), pp. 25, 31; also Stenzel, i. 90.

resolution of their free citizens, early conquered special privileges for them; and they could even become the patrons of smaller towns. The second class arose from the necessity, which survived the conquest by many years, of assuring the safety of the Mark by a series of fortresses, or " burgs," around the frontier and at all exposed points. Each burg was naturally the centre of the adjacent agricultural district;[1] and on the reduction of the Wends, which put an end to the danger of hostile forays, they were thrown open to trade and the peaceful arts. The colonies which had grown up around the walls were then organized into municipalities. Many of these towns were, however, long afflicted with a military spirit, which was difficult to exorcise, and maliciously obstructed the course of their progress. A third class finally was formed, either out of peasant settlements which had outgrown their village institutions and were accorded the name and character of municipalities,[2] or from such as having chosen the banks of a navigable stream, or for various reasons being more favorable to other industries than to agriculture, never passed through this preliminary stage, but were recognized as cities from the first. They were chiefly peopled by artisans, and among these the very best were Flemish exiles, whom the frequent inundations and the great distress in the Low Countries had driven abroad for homes. This was a singular case of reëmigration. In the eighth century Charlemagne, as the easiest way of checking the aggressions of the restless Saxons, had colonized large numbers of them in Flanders. Four centuries later their descendants returned to help the Saxons colonize the land of the Wends.

In respect to the physiognomy of the towns it has been

[1] Compare for a strikingly similar system that of the primitive Italian towns in Marquardt, *Römische Staatsverwaltung*, vol. i. 4 (Leipsic, 1873).

[2] Comp. Eichhorn, ii. § 263.

much disputed whether they were mainly settled and built up by free traders and free mechanics, or by nobles with their vassals and villeins.[1] That many of the earlier ones were founded as manorial boroughs is not indeed pretended,[2] but it is known that some of them were governed by burggraves, who were commonly also " ministerials " and courtiers, who naturally gathered about them knights and barons, and thus laid the basis of aristocracies, not to say oligarchies. Others which had acquired privileges, but were too feeble to maintain them, fell an easy prey, in times of disorder, to lawless and powerful nobles. But the older and stronger ones, like Stendal and Brandenburg, which had solid bases of prosperity, which were the homes of hardy and intelligent burghers, and which were commended by their large public contributions to the special favor of the prince, added privilege after privilege to the charters of their freedom, until their part in the general system was determined almost by their own will and interests. The long roll of their achievements may be read in the archives of the thirteenth and fourteenth centuries. It will show that in a humble way they were no mean representatives of the general spirit of municipal freedom, which in that age re-awoke and began to make itself felt in Europe. Modest in size and modest in aspirations though they were, they resembled their older sisters at least in the sturdy vigor with which they asserted their virgin rights ; and the prudence of the margraves, obeying if not anticipating the spirit of the age, formed them by a liberal policy to be the light and support of the rising commonwealth.

The peasantry were not originally treated as an order or an estate in a political sense, but their condition at any time may testify for or against the

The peasants.

---

[1] On this subject see Lambert, *Entwickelungen der deutschen Städteverfassungen im Mittelalter.*

[2] Riedel, *Die Mark Brand. in 1250* (Berlin, 1831), ii. 77; Stenzel, i. 78.

prosperity of a country. Because they are free and flourishing, it is not of course to be assumed that the government is just. It may be only weak. Nor is it necessarily weak; it may be strong by rallying the peasants to its support against the other orders. But it is obvious enough as a general truth, that a government under which the petty cultivators of the soil — the most numerous and yet most helpless class — are prosperous and contented, cannot be wholly bad; that some of its dispositions are wise, if not generous; and that at least one principle of sound administration is understood.

The Ascanian dynasty left no complete picture of peasant life in the Mark. Its outlines, its leading features, the ratio of light and shade, can now be drawn only from fugitive and obscure documents of the time. Fortunately these are interpreted in but one sense. It is held with rare unanimity by German historical scholars, that in nearly all the conditions of social and material well-being the peasants of Brandenburg were favored beyond their brethren in other parts of Europe. Even the barrenness of the soil was at first their ally. It enabled them to exact better terms for the labor and skill which alone could bring the sandy plains under the discipline of the plow and reclaim the treacherous swamps to the uses of the husbandman.

To such advantages as they acquired, again, the method of colonization gave a determinate form, and the sanction of a solemn compact. This sys- Colonization. tem was not indeed peculiar to Brandenburg. It was already quite common in other Teutonic settlements; it enjoyed the favor of the church; it had been encouraged by laws and decrees of the Empire. But under Albert and his successors it found such a wise, loyal, and liberal application that its beneficent workings may be traced for a century.[1] The immediate agent in the process was the

[1] Heinemann pp. 215, 225–6 ; Droysen, i. 41 et seq.

contractor or " locater." [1] The contractor bought or otherwise acquired from the margrave or some lesser proprietor — it might be an abbot or a baron — a tract of land,
on which he undertook to lay out and organize a rural
commune, or Landgemeinde.   He first set aside one
tenth of the land for himself, which he held in a species
of knight's fee, even if he were not of gentle birth.[2] That
is to say it was free from taxes and other pecuniary burdens, but the holder was required to furnish a mounted
soldier in time of war.[3] The church next received her portion, and the rest was parcelled out among peasants on the
"three field" system.[4] The little community was thus organized.   The burdens of the peasants were light and for
the greater part fixed ; and these being the leading features of English socage tenure, they were not unlike the
Sochemanni.[5] Their annual ground tax was a species of
interest on mortgage, or, still better, of rent on a perpet-
ual lease.   Military service could not be required of them
except in case of invasion ; and even the irregular services which they might be summoned to perform, such as
purveyance for the prince's journey, labor on the walls of

---

[1] Locator or Unternehmer.   Usage has unfortunately robbed the
English word "undertaker" of the general signification to which it is
etymologically entitled, and which its equivalents in other tongues
still enjoy.

[2] The Locatores were, as a rule, plebeians, and Riedel has found but
a few instances in which they were knights.

[3] This military condition was not personal, but was associated with
the land as its contribution to the public service.   Yet at the epoch
which I am now discussing this distinction was a real privilege and
an honor ; and it shows that the contractors were held in some estimation.

[4] On the Dreifelderwirthschaft see the treatises of G. L. von Maurer.

[5] There were still lower classes of common laborers, without land,
and often without independent domiciles, but Riedel, ii. 274–7, thinks
there was no actual serfdom except on the estates of a few Wendish
nobles.   I can find no class corresponding as such to the "servi" of
Domesday Book.   Comp. Stenzel, i. 75.

the burg, and, if necessary, their defence, were at least localized, and in a territorial sense, therefore, fixed. It is probable, too, that the greater part of these peasant settlements were made upon land ceded directly by the margraves. The nobles were too few, the estates of the knights too small, for the early development of manorial villages.[1] In this fact is to be found one evident advantage for those primitive husbandmen. A great prince is more likely than a petty landlord to affect a splendid generosity, and remote tyranny cannot, even if it will, practise the more direct and vexatious forms of oppression. So long, therefore, as the margraves retained their authority unimpaired in form or spirit, so long the peasants retained the two cardinal rights of freemen, the disposition of their persons and of their estates. In other parts of Germany, at the same epoch, villenage, often hardly distinguishable from bodily servitude, was the common rule.[2]

Such were the factors of that early society. In passing, next, to the political system in which they all had a place, it may be convenient to divide the inquiry into three topics : first, the source and operation of authority ; second, the method of public finance; and third, the administration of justice.

I. It has already been stated that as the term " Mark " meant, not perhaps originally but at the time of Albert, a frontier military district, the markgraf, or commander of the district, was in strict usage a subordinate official as well as a vassal of the Emperor, and bound to obedience in the one character, as he was to homage and fealty in the other. This relation had an amazing vitality in law. Probably no precise date can

<small>Administration.</small>

---

[1] I have some doubts about the best usage to adopt, but it can seldom cause confusion if the suzerainty of the Emperor be practically ignored, and the immediate vassals of the margrave be regarded as tenants *in capite*.

[2] For instance, in Mecklenburg, which had been conquered by Henry the Lion, Albert's rival. Comp. Droysen, i. 41.

be named at which, in respect to Brandenburg at least, it formally and absolutely ceased, at which the margraves began to rule wholly as independent princes. Some traces of the feudal tie, and thus of the Emperor's final supremacy, even remained after the Elector of Brandenburg became King of Prussia. The change was slow, irregular, invisible; and the course of reform in the interior administration coincides at many points with the movement which released the state from bondage to this pernicious fiction.

It was not simply from above, moreover, that the margraves were exposed to feudal restraints. In their own dominions, in the treatment of the several estates, in the organization of the government, their freedom of action was far from complete; and solemn prescriptions dictated their general policy, if not all of their particular acts. Thus the rights and privileges of an ecclesiastic had a more powerful sanction than the piety or justice of his secular prince. The position of the nobles on their manors, and accordingly the extent to which the Elector might interfere in them, were defined by the written law of the Empire, or the more general unwritten law of the feudal system. Even the contractor of a peasant village could obtain the office of schulze by virtue of a positive enactment.[1] But an administrative system, strictly understood, will be sought in vain in an age of great disorder and a society with which self-preservation was the chief end of civil government. There was not even an efficient adaptation of means to this end, for where public duties are not clearly distinguished from private rights the strength of a state can be only partially and irregularly displayed. Progress itself was an organic growth, owing but little to

[1] In an imperial decree of the year 1319, for instance, it is reaffirmed. . . . qui ejusdem villæ locator esse debet et scultetus. . . . Schulze is abbreviated from Schultheiss. In Latin the form Sculdais also occurs. The official corresponds, apparently, to the Anglo-Saxon tungerefa, or tithingman.

conscious human aid ; and the people were still far enough from that point in political experience where the jealous distinction between the power that makes, the power that executes, and the power that interprets the law, laid the foundation of modern civil liberty. In other words, the aggregation was better understood than the distribution of functions.

Hence it is not surprising that the office of schulze — to begin at the bottom of the scale — should combine the duties of constable and judge. As local magistrate, the schulze presided in his petty court; but he was also guardian of the public peace, having charge of what is known as the police of the neighborhood ; received the taxes due from land and crops ; and was in all things the intermediary between the peasants and their prince or their landlord.

The schulze.

In the cities which were laid out by contract the contractor acquired also the title and general functions of the schulze. But the more important ones were originally governed, as has been said, by burggraves, who both as civil and as military officials were immediate deputies of the margrave, and could apparently be removed at will. They became, however, in time serious burdens to the community, or at least objects of strong popular dislike, for, in the course of the thirteenth century the office was abolished throughout the Mark.[1] About the same time the municipal councils, or councillors, — the " consules " of the public records, — appear on the scene. It would seem that after ·the disappearance of the burggraves their powers were divided between the schulzen, who received the purely judicial functions, and

Burggraves.

[1] In Stendal, for instance, by Margrave Albert II. in 1215. . . . ad petitionem dilectorum nostrorum civium Stendaliensium. . . . According to Riedel, *Mark Brand. in 1250*, ii. 129, no traces of burggraves can be found after the middle of the thirteenth century. Comp. also Gercken, *Cod. Dip. Brand.* v. No. LV., and the accompanying note.

councils, which were the executive agents, — a change that begins the movement of the cities toward municipal freedom.

But such a revolution could not be made at a blow. The rights of the crown in general administration

Vogts.

were guarded from that time by a set of functionaries called "vogts,"[1] who, succeeding the burggraves as commanders in the fortified towns,[2] also represented the tardy triumph of the civil over the military interest. The leading authorities are indeed more explicit about the fact than about the explanation. It is difficult to see in what respect the vogts differed originally from their predecessors, — whether their supposed superiority was the cause or the effect of the introduction of the vogtey system. In a general sense they were probably carried along by the same process which the burgs underwent; that is to say, as fast as the growth of peace and security allowed the burgs to exchange their military for a civil character, the surrounding districts were naturally erected into administrative divisions, and the lieutenants of the margraves became governors of shires. If this be true, it would follow that even the vogteys — in appearance the most artificial feature of the Ascanian system — were really a natural growth, not an arbitrary creation. Some of the Prussian writers are not free from careless language in treating this subject. Thus, Droysen says "the remaining territory" — that is, after eliminating the church lands —

---

[1] Advocatus, originally an official appointed for the civil administration of an ecclesiastical estate. In English the term may be rendered by provost, i. e. Stadvogt, and sometimes sheriff, sometimes bailiff, i. e. Landvogt. It will be more convenient, however, to transfer than to translate this term, and some others, but I shall occasionally take the liberty of anglicizing the plural.

[2] Gercken, *Cod. Dip.* v. 55, note, maintains, in opposition to Lenz and others, that vogts were known in the Mark before the disappearance of the burggraves. The change was probably not unlike that by which in England the sheriff displaced the ealdorman.

"was divided into some thirty vogteys." [1] But nobody knows better than this writer that a geographical or mechanical division, like that which produced the French departments or the American counties, never actually took place ; that such a system of political arithmetic was unknown to the experience or reason of the Middle Ages ; that the boundaries of the vogteys were adjusted to the natural, historical, and indivisible wants of land and people.

The subject of legislation is closely connected with that of administration in every society which has not learned the fundamental and organic distinction between them ; yet it is evident that what is called the separation of powers in a modern constitutional state can never be quite complete. There are certain inevitable points where one function will reach over into the others, sometimes as a vicious encroachment, but often as a wise and salutary coöperation. At least this interdependence is not necessarily an evil ; and a prudent statesman will strive to surround it by exact though flexible limitations, and make it a wholesome principle to serve the cause of good government.

Now the Middle Ages had this principle without its proper safeguards. An author who was unlikely to yield any of the rights of the crown lays it down as a general truth, that no German prince was an absolute ruler in his own land.[2] This is especially the case in respect to that form of arbitrary power which extends to the making or changing the laws. Like their brethren, the margraves of Brandenburg had the aid and support of their estates ; and this participation was a right which, having its source in the earliest instincts of Germanic society, had survived the vicissitudes of many eventful centuries.[3] But since the members of the estates were

Restraints upon the prince.

---

[1] *Gesch. der Pr. Politik*, i. 34. Comp. Riedel, *Mark Brand.* ii. 86–87.

[2] Lancizolle, *Rechtsquellen*, p. xii. (Berlin, 1847).

[3] It was affirmed in imperial decrees, for instance by Frederic II.

in a measure the creation of his own will, since, in other words, a feudal conqueror like Albert could in theory distribute his land and thus organize the landed aristocracy, endow the church, and incorporate towns according to his own pleasure, his power asserted itself unmistakably even in the machinery set up to control it. On the employment of this machinery, too, in legislation the initiative of the prince was awaited at nearly every stage. He issued the summons, fixed the occasions, and introduced the business of the public councils ; and thereby retained, it is clear, a great influence over their deliberations and resolutions. The protocols record only achieved results, indeed, but if in the earlier times the refusal of the vassals was often given, the evidence of such disloyal conduct was ingeniously suppressed.

In respect to the first point, the composition of the councils, the discretion of the margrave was sub-
The estates.
ject to the personal claims which might presume on his needs or his weakness, and the natural respect that would be paid to the demands of a class or a locality. There being no statutes which defined their rights, the barons and knights would be consulted in general legislation, the clergy on church matters, the towns on municipal questions. The natural divisions of the land and its inhabitants fixed in the same way an easy order of geographical classification. But if in case of any supposed grievance an individual or a town had appealed to the law of the Empire, a margrave might have pleaded its vague and obscure language. Who were the prudent elders of the land, — the meliores et majores terræ, — without whose consent the laws could not be changed? If they had been a determinate class, organized as a political corporation, a

in 1231. . . . Ut neque principes neque alii quilibet constitutiones vel nova jura facere possint, nisi meliorum et majorum terræ consensus primitus habeatur. Comp. Campe, *Lehre von den Landständen*, 2 ed. p. 70 (Lemgo, 1841).

general summons, or their own initiative, would have called
them at any time to the exercise of their parliamentary
rights.   But the estates of Brandenburg do not answer to
such a description until a much later period.[1]   Up to the
time of the first Hohenzollerns they were turbulent and
undisciplined forces, which when united were indeed irresistible, but which were sometimes more ready to tear one
another into pieces from mutual jealousy, than to combine
for constitutional resistance to the will of their lord.

And yet although the power of creating peers and en-
franchising towns gave the margrave no little *Composition
of the Diets.* influence on the composition of the Diet, it was
a power which could be used only in respect to individuals,
personal or corporate, not to classes.   The rise of an estate,
or its recognition as a political factor, was due to forces
and principles in feudal society.   And this was scarcely
more true of the landed gentry, whose position was as old
as the Germanic polity itself, than of the other two chief
orders, the clergy and the towns, which had been admitted
after the invasions, and through the force of circumstances
that the territorial princes had but little controlled.

In regard to the prelates it may be assumed that their
recognition as peers was not long subsequent to *The spiritual peers.* the conversion of the barbarians, for their participation in the national councils, at least of the Franks, is
distinctly mentioned as early as Clothaire II. in the year
615.   But further details are lost in obscurity.   It would
be interesting to have full records of all the stages in this
important innovation, — to know whether they were many
and gradual, or few and abrupt; whether the political
character of the clergy flowed merely from their spiritual
functions, from respect for their religious mission and dependence on the learning which they alone enjoyed, or was
conditional, as under the theory of feudal law, on secular

[1] On this matter comp. Stenzel, i. 68 ; Droysen, i. 64; Roenne, *Pr.
Staatsrecht* (Leipsic, 1856–63), i. 7; and Campe, p. 71.

proprietorship as landlords and vassals. It would be interesting, but the point has little practical value. In the
earlier, as in the later, ages the bishops were certainly acknowledged as a class or order, and the possession of land
by no means placed them, even in a political sense, on a
level with the secular peers. Their estates were not less
essential to their dignity as prelates than to their claim
for admission into the Diets. The uncertainty is practically confined to the time, therefore, at which the great
change was operated; but even this doubt is largely removed when we pass to the communes. The date of their
The com-   enfranchisement in the various principalities of
mons.   Europe can now be ascertained with considerable precision. In Brandenburg they appear in the records as early as 1280; but the general recognition of
their place as an order in the state, and a constituent part
of every Diet, was hardly established before the first half
of the next century. The law, too, of their enfranchisement is no less clear. The qualities of a free corporation,
subject to no seigneur lower than the prince of the land,
were indispensable to a city of the Mark which claimed
the right of parliamentary representation.

Previous to the year 1170 there is no evidence of a leg-
             islative council of the estates. It is true that
Early Diets.
             both before and after that date nearly every offi-
cial instrument contains the names of nobles, knights, and
ministerials, in number and rank according to the gravity
of the occasion, who, in the language of the time, " certi-
fied " to the reality of the transaction; [1] and when they
gave advice the conclusion could even be called that
of the country. But the act of 1170, by which the name
of Brandenburg was formally given to the Mark, seems to
have issued more strictly from a parliamentary process.
It was in the " Placitum which is commonly called Bot-

[1] They were called testes, and their part in the proceedings was the
testimonium.

ting" that the margrave invited the barons to designate the
city most deserving of a certain compliment; whereupon
one of them rose, and, in behalf of the assembly,[1] declared
that Brandenburg was the most famous and most glorious
town. In the opinion of the best authorities this is the
first recorded instance of a legislative council in the Mark.[2]
Hints of similar gatherings appear again for the first time
in 1224, but the annals of the following years are full of
them. The list of vassals who attend and give advice
grows longer and more imposing. The vogts, the prelates, and in necessary cases the delegates of the larger
towns are all present. As yet, however, they had not outgrown their semi-military character. The nameless many
of the "placita" — the wise, the prudent, the discreet, as
they are variously called — whose counsel was such an important factor, may be safely conjectured to have been
knights with weapons in their hands, and not the plebeian
deputies of town and village. There being no complete
representation of the whole land, or of all the orders, two
features of a national parliament were wanting.

In the year 1280 there was very striking and significant progress. A subject of the keenest prac-
tical interest called together for legislative action   1280.
the representatives of every province and of every order;
but although the Bede compromise was wrested from the
crown by a revolt of the vassals, it was a political not a
military revolt, and made use only of the ordinary governmental machinery to obtain its ends. No clash of arms,
no show of martial strength, no Runnymede would seem to
have ushered in the slower process of legal forms; no
swords were used to fashion the novel ordinance. This is

---

[1] . . . pro omnibus et præ omnibus circumsedentibus. . . .

[2] Muelverstedt, p. 3; G. W. von Raumer, *Ueber die ältere Verfassung der Churmark Brand.* (Zerbst, 1830) p. 17. The document itself is published in the appendix to Buchholtz, *Gesch. Brand.* iv. 17,
and by Gercken, *Fragmenta Marchica* (Wolfenbüttel, 1755–63), part 3,
No. I. It is proper to add that its genuineness has been questioned.

indeed only an inference drawn from the absence of proof to the contrary. But though the history of the treaty will never be known, its origin, if violent, would not have been wholly neglected by contemporary writers. Their silence eulogizes the moderation or the prudence, or both, of the Margrave.

The documents which are evidence in the case bear the dates of 1280, 1281, and 1282, were all issued by the margraves of the Stendal line, and are evidently different versions of the same transaction, or different proclamations of the same principle. Gercken even charges the text and date of the third to a blunder of Lenz. This may be unjust; but there is one fact which strongly supports his opinion, and throws doubt upon the common theory as adopted in later works. In the version of 1282 a certain payment is fixed for Michaelmas, 1281. But it was not common, even in mediæval contracts, to affront the calendar in that way; and unless a clerical error be assumed, the provision can only be explained by a previous agreement, of which this was the tardy or the renewed promulgation. Even if two distinct parliaments were held they form but a single stage or landmark in constitutional history. In their operation and effects they were general, and the compact to which they agreed was clearly applied to the whole Mark.[1]

The earliest of these protocols shows that in 1280 the margrave or margraves were driven to renounce a practice which had become altogether too common. The language of the act leaves no doubt upon this point. It is singularly clear and explicit; and when the margraves declare that thenceforth " throughout their entire dominions every sort of extraordinary exaction, except by the consent of their vassals, shall be forever abolished," [2] the inference is strong that the burden of such ex-

Revolt of the barons.

---

[1] Gercken, *Cod. Dip. Brand.* i. 354, note; Muelverstedt, p. 187.

[2] . . . omne genus exactionis precarie et parangarie per totam ter-

actions had become intolerable, and that the estates had
demanded a general reform.   By thus laying new emphasis on their rights, they reëstablished the ancient principle that special tributes issued from the bounty of the
Diet, not from the prerogative of the crown.   The document is further made peculiarly interesting by a long list
of the vassals and others who attended and took part in
the proceedings.   It begins with the august name of the
Bishop of Brandenburg, the only spiritual peer who was
present, or at least the only one who is expressly mentioned.   The great nobles of the Mark were more nu-
mĕrous, although even they, like their brethren in other
feudal states, doubtless regarded attendance on the councils as a burden rather than a privilege.   Those who fill
the largest place in the parliamentary roll are evidently
knights, but there are many names in which the absence of
the nobiliary particle and other signs suggest the deputies
of the towns.   And from the " aliis quam pluribus nostris
militibus et vassalis," the fancy of the reader may construct that great reserve of silent and modest members
who were not the less deserving because their names were
not proclaimed in the official catalogue.

The compact, or compacts, of 1281 and 1282 would seem
to be complementary to the act of 1280.   It gave Magna
as it were practical form and efficiency to a pur- Charta.
pose, or a pledge, which had been announced in abstract
general terms.

To this end it contained some novel and ingenious provisions.   So slight, apparently, was the confidence which
the margraves could command, that they were obliged to
appoint a permanent council of four knights to decide
when the danger of war, or other sudden crisis,[1] required

ram nostram omnimodo esse mortuum et deletum preterquam si de
consilio nostrorum vassalorum. . . . Gercken, *Cod. Dip. Brand.* i.
353-6.

[1] . . . legitima necessitas aut guerrarum periculum. . . .

a resort to extraordinary measures, as well as what form
of character such measures should take ; [1] and even their
proposals were to be submitted for the approval or revision
of a larger committee of the whole land.[2] Thus in a way
far from contemptible was provided a species of ministry
which should be responsible for the demands made by the
crown upon the purse of the vassals.   And in order that
this board should be permanent, it was further declared
that if one of the members died and a new one equally
good was not appointed within a month, the vassals might
seize and hold the fortress of Tangermünde until the
vacancy was filled.

Such was the simple parliamentary system of mediæval
Brandenburg.[3] Such was the Magna Charta which the
Saxons of the Elbe, instinctively following the more famous precedent set, half a century earlier, by the vassals
of King John of England, interposed as a barrier between
their constitutional rights and the innovations attempted
by an ambitious dynasty. For two reasons it seemed
proper to refer thus in detail to the incident. It is interesting as a contribution to the useful science of comparative politics, and a contribution drawn, too, from a field
which scholars have long neglected. It will serve as a
convenient key to the subsequent fortunes of the Prussian
people, and the later development of the Prussian monarchy.   At this epoch — the thirteenth century — the
rights of the people were as clearly understood, and perhaps as securely guarded, as anywhere in Europe ; and it
follows that only ignorance or servility can attempt to derive the absolute Prussian kings of later times legiti-
ately and organically from their ancestors.   The Freder-

[1] . . . quicquid iidem ordinaverint ad commodum et utilitatem
terre. . . .

[2] . . . auditis potioribus et senioribus terre. . . .

[3] The purely financial or fiscal provisions of the charter belong
properly, and will be treated, under the next division of the subject.

ics and Frederic Williams have been faithfully served by
both these busy and officious allies.   The very fervor of
their zeal has been efficient in deception ; and when the
Prussian people themselves seemed to accept phrases like
" the historic rights of the crown " and " the peculiar development of the Berlin monarchy" as the just foundations of
the despotism under which they languished, foreigners could
hardly be expected to know that the rights of the people
were as ancient as those of the crown, or that the development of the monarchical principle had been violently
twisted out of its original course.

II. Under a system which makes no distinction between
the state and the head of the state, the control of the public revenues may have some vigor, but is likely to have little method.   The general treasury is the private
purse of the prince.   Of the disbursement of the   *Finance.*
funds no account is rendered to those who furnish and
replenish them; and even a margrave of Brandenburg
might reward from the same source the hardy warriors who
fought his battles and the frail companions of his secret
joys.   But political forms are determined more by the
nature of the revenues than by the manner of their outlay.
The amount and, even more, the method of his exactions
make the tyrant; while it is only in an educated society,
enjoying a constitutional government, that the jealous tax-
payer scrutinizes the use made of his contributions.[1]

The revenues of the Ascanian counts may be ranged under two general descriptions.   They were feudal, permanent, and regular; or they were special and public.   In the
former class are included all the tributes regu-   *The reve-*
larly due under mediæval law or usage from   *nues.*
vassals to their lord, and all perquisites which under any
name or by any process perpetually accrue to the crown.
In the latter are reckoned the levies made by the prince,
or granted by his subjects, on special occasions and in lim-

[1] Mr. Hallam, *Middle Ages*, i. 67, seems to hold a view somewhat
different from this.

ited amounts.   The distinction is practically the same, therefore, as that drawn by Blackstone between ordinary and extraordinary revenues.   The several sources of income that made up these two classes were also not materially different from those which were enjoyed by feudal princes in all parts of Europe ; and one of these classes, the ordinary revenues, is capable in Brandenburg, as elsewhere, of a further subdivision, which though not used at the time, or even perceived, is of some importance in political thought.

Among the more productive of the permanent revenues were the proceeds of justice, the fees from forests and fisheries, the so-called market tax, which, however, was often surrendered to the cities, and the tolls of highway and river.   The exactions from the Jews were enormous, though they hardly enter into the description of regular revenue.   But all the others which have been enumerated, though personal in theory, and derived from the personal distinctions of feudal law, are nevertheless such as might be admitted into a sound scheme of finance under any form of government.   For feudal prince, put the state ; for vassals, subjects ; for tributes, taxes, — and all the claims of political economy are satisfied.   Not so, however, with the feudal incidents proper.   Relief, escheat, wardship, marriage, the three aids, and others, — these were wholly anomalous, and expired with the system under which alone they were possible.   A partial exception ought, perhaps, to be made also in behalf of the direct revenues of the crown domains, since on these the margrave was landlord as well as sovereign, and acquired their profits like any proprietor.[1]   But by a singular practice, which

---

[1] The German renders this distinction better by " Landesherr " and "Grundherr," two terms which correspond respectively to the relation of a prince over subjects and a proprietor over tenants.   On the domains the margrave would receive the ground rent, the dime where it had not been acquired by the church, and he would also have the profits from such manors as were cultivated under the direct charge of his stewards.

survived until recent times, the tenants on the domains were alone called subjects.[1]

All these revenues failed, however, to satisfy the needs of the margraves. The conduct of petty feudal Farming the revenues. wars, and the participation in greater ones, the support of the court establishment, the gifts to the church and to favorites were burdens which the household officials increased by wasteful and corrupt administration. Even these expenses might not have impoverished one margrave. But when in contempt of primogeniture the inheritance was divided among a number of equal rulers, having similar wants to satisfy, the situation became intolerable. Then, too, the margraves relieved it in a way which in the end only made it more acute. They adopted the vicious habit of the times, and farmed out their revenues for ready money. Whoever could bring relief was welcome; every salable privilege — even the profits of justice, and thereby justice itself — was sold. And in the course of time this policy began to bear its fruits. The original feudal tributes had passed into other hands — to the towns, the barons, and the clergy; — the tolls were pawned for years in advance; and the money raised by these measures had also disappeared. From such a situation there was but one escape. The prince who had sold the fixed income of a feudal lord could only supplicate the people to relieve the common necessities of the state.[2]

In this way the margraves were driven to the Bede. As the term implies,[3] and under a principle as The Bede.

---

[1] Unterthanen ; see Lancizolle, p. xii.

[2] I am describing the logical, which was not necessarily the chronological order. In respect to time, special subsidies were, of course, demanded and granted long before all of the regular tributes had been sold, and some of these even survived the alienation of the permanent subsidy, which is mentioned later. But the logical order is that which I have given.

[2] Bede = Bitte, prayer or request, and, by extension, that which was given in response to a prayer or request.

clear and indisputable as any in the experience of society, this was a voluntary grant, which could only be required of the land when authorized by the estates.[1] A
city, a vogtey, a province could be invited to make a contribution; and it does not much affect the principle that a
request in the mildest terms was seldom denied. Doubtless this formality was not always observed in its full extent. The peasants, upon whom fell a good share of the
burdens, had no voice in public deliberations,[2] and were
but indifferently represented by the other orders; while
the cities were better able to bear extortion, and from policy were willing by liberal subsidies to purchase the good
will of their only masters.[3] But the principle was never
quite ignored that all special grants to the purse of the
margrave, all taxes beyond the ordinary feudal tributes,
required the assent of the estates.

This is strikingly illustrated in the proceedings of 1281
and 1282, by which the vassals and the margrave reorganized the system of public contributions, and not only fixed the rate of a permanent Bede,[4]
but also defined more strictly the occasions when in addition to that an extraordinary subsidy might be demanded. This compact is known as the Bede-Vertrag.
It gave positive form to a species of exaction, which, as

Bede-Com-
pact.

[1] Compare Stenzel, i. 68; Roenne, *Staatsrecht*, i. 7; Huellmann,
Deutsche Finanz-Geschichte, p. 116 et seq. According to the last named
author the word Bede owes itself to the church, which set the example
of borrowing from the Roman jurisprudence, practices and principles
that, under the influence of feudal society, were soon metamorphosed
into other and less agreeable forms. See, also, Muelverstedt, pp. 186–7.

[2] They were, in other words, Hintersassen (or Unterthanen) and not
Landsassen. Comp. Campe, p. 77, and the remark of Niebuhr there
quoted.

[3] For instance, Stendal in 1282; Salzwedel in 1282; and Prenzlau
in 1305.

[4] This tribute is commonly called a tax on land, but the text of the
" treaty " seems to indicate that it was rather a personal tax levied on
the actual or estimated products of land.

subject only to the most general rules, was capricious in its demands, had often been abused, and easily became a hardship and an evil. Above all it established by law the duty of the nobles toward the public treasury. The amount and nature of their contributions, beyond the ordinary feudal incidents, cannot now be ascertained; it is the opinion of Dr. Riedel that they were very moderate. For their own manors they of course rendered knight's service instead of money tributes, and were alike free from the hidage of the peasants and the tallage of the towns. But the extraordinary Bede was probably levied on every person according to his means. Such is at least the most reasonable inference from the terms of the treaty. By that instrument the vassals — that is those who held by knight's fee — agreed like the other orders to pay an annual tax, on part at least of their estates, in place of the Bede, petitionem sive precariam, which had been formerly exacted by the margraves. But this reformed tribute was also a compensation to the prince for renouncing the habit of extraordinary levies; and this was evidently the point about which the nobles were most concerned. If they had not before been liable to the extraordinary Bede their solicitude would have therefore little meaning. The new system was the result of a species of revolution, — a revolt of the vassals against burdens which they could not, or would not, longer endure. The language and spirit of the compact show that it was a concession wrested from the crown, or at least the recovery of rights which had been too long neglected, and too often infringed.

The sources of the margraves' income are not difficult to discover. They are found in the great universal code of feudalism, are announced more or less vaguely in the early chronicles, and may be extracted from the records of the local Diets. But the aggregate or average amounts realized from these sources, during any period, by any prince of the Ascanian line, are hidden in an obscurity which no diligence can pierce. Neither of the profits which accrued to the margrave as a landlord, nor of the royalties which belonged to the lord paramount, nor of the subsidies which were voted by the Diet, does history or tradition reveal any details that could lead the inquirer even to a reasonable conjecture. I shall, therefore, make no apology for the defects of this part of the subject.

III. In passing to the judicial system of this period one is struck by its evident superiority to the other branches of civil administration. It was more liberal and enlightened in spirit, more highly developed as an efficient organ, more sacred and awful in its antiquity; and by the peasants especially it was cherished with a tender and picturesque affection. To them it was not a mere series of functions which by a long, circuitous, and difficult route led finally up to the head of the commonwealth. It afforded, rather, at the simplest stage the protection of a personal sovereign. So long as the village schulze held court and gave judgment in the name of the margraves, so long as there existed the right of appeal, even if seldom exercised, to the tribunal of the vogt, so long, in short, as the judicial system was independent of the knights and nobles, it was no unworthy agent of the lower jurisprudence, no feeble guardian of local equity and justice.

Justice.

The confidence of the peasants is in part explained by the checks which their own participation in the trial of suits put upon their hereditary judges. The "schoeppen" do not correspond in all respects to the modern jurors, but they issue perhaps from the comparison without too much dishonor.[1] They represented at least the precious right of freemen to be judged by their

The jury.

---

[1] Scabini = assessores. Schoeppen and Schoeffen are both used in Germany, and seem to have about equal authority. On the difference between these assessors and the modern jury compare Zachariæ, *Das moderne Schöffengericht* (Berlin, 1872). Savigny denies, of course, that the institution is Teutonic in its origin or its principle.

peers; and if the form of the representation was somewhat faulty, if its action was crude and clumsy, it grew logically out of the spirit and necessities of the age, and was not adopted from a society radically different.

The courts of the burggraves in the three cities of Stendal, Salzwedel, and Brandenburg, which had original jurisdiction for the burgess, were at first courts of appeal from the village magistrate.[1] But after the institution of the vogts, the appellate jurisdiction for the peasants was transferred to them. The schulzen of the county, judges in their own courts, then became schoeppen, or jurors, in the court of the vogt,[2] an arrangement which would seem to be just and ingenious. There was still a final appeal to the privy court of the margrave. Disputes among the nobles were heard in first instance by the margrave himself,[3] and the appeal was to the High Chamber of the Empire. In the cities the judiciary varied with their own characters, as they were "immediate" or manorial cities, and again as they were or were not within the jurisdiction of the vogt; but the larger ones were both immediate and self-governing, and the courts of their elective judges were equal in dignity to those of the vogtey. The burgesses could appeal directly to the margrave.

In early times the lower courts were restricted to civil causes, or criminal causes of a trivial nature. The power of corporal penalties and the punishment of capital crimes — the so-called "Blutbann" — was regarded as a sovereign privilege, which even a margrave could exercise only in the name of the emperor.[4]

Courts of appeal.

Capital punishment.

---

[1] Buchholtz, ii. 316.

[2] Stenzel, i. 75 ; Raumer, *Cod. Dip. Brand. Con.* ii. 118.

[3] Comp. Isaacsohn, *Gesch. des pr. Beamtenthums*, i. 192–4 (Berlin, 1873).

[4] Stenzel, i. 75 ; Raumer, *Cod.* ii. 107.

Und unter offnem Himmel, schlicht und klar,
Sprach er das Recht, und ohne Furcht der Menschen.

4

But in the thirteenth century a more liberal view began to prevail. The margraves became strong enough both to preserve their tribunals from the supervision of a remote authority, and even to endow them with the awful power of life and death. At first this privilege was intrusted only to the vogts, but eventually many cities acquired it by purchase; and then, as a symbol of its possession, the Roland statue, which is preserved to the present day in many German towns, was set up in front of the Rathhaus, whence it brandished its retributory sword, and glared through its sightless eyes, — hideous enough in art to appall the hardest malefactor.

The private law of Germany reflected, during the early

The law.   Middle Ages, the general confusion of society. A shapeless mass of customs, precedents, and traditions, of Germanic principles which had developed with little training or method, and of local ordinances which faintly caricatured the municipal life of Rome, — it might have seemed almost by its very nature to defy order and system. Logical and geographical harmony were alike wanting. In the first place, there was a separate set of laws for each order or estate. The church was firmly intrenched behind the bulwarks of canon law, and as the mistress of all learning kept alive also the traditions of Roman law long after the Dark Ages had spread their obscurity over that magnificent structure.[1] The nobles were subject only to feudal justice. The cities were favored or burdened with a body of municipal statutes, in which neither a German of the army of Clovis, nor a Roman of the time of the Antonines, would have found his familiar institutions.[2] What was called the Landrecht,

---

[1] See F. von Raumer, *Gesch. der Hohenstauffen* (Leipsic, 1823–25), v. 221; also, G. W. von Raumer, *Cod. Dip.* ii. 115, and Ledebur's *Archiv.*

[2] Magdeburg was held to have the best law, and the keenest desire of all growing towns was to receive " Magdeburgisches Recht."

or common law, was contemptuously banished to the petty village court of the peasants. In a territorial sense there was the same disorder, and the different states or provinces seemed to agree only in the wisdom of eternal variety. The law itself was thus less simple, less systematic, and above all less favorable to the interests of the humbler classes, than the courts which interpreted and applied it.[1]

At length, in the thirteenth century, a successful attempt was made to reduce these vagrant prescriptions to the sobriety and dignity of a code. The Sachsenspiegel. In Saxony, the Sachsenspiegel; in Suabia, the Schwabenspiegel; and in Franconia, the so-called Fraenkisches Recht, were completed about the same time. Brandenburg was a Saxon colony, and to the common people Saxon law was a privileged inheritance.[2] The measure of the relations of peasant to peasant, it also defined in its own way the relations of peasant toward noble, priest, town, and prince. It contained the schedule of his rights in his courts, and the assertion of his modest claims to civil recognition. The perpetuation of this in a written code might promise to place the peasant or the laborer above the reach of the most powerful and the most aggressive of his many foes. But such, unhappily, was not the case. As will be shown in another place, neither the independence of the hereditary schulzen, nor the exact guaranties of a formal code, were able to preserve the freedom of these classes as it flourished in the twelfth and thirteenth centuries.

In the foregoing sketch I have spoken of the crown, of the royal power, of the prince. These synonyms General conclusion. were convenient in use, and, if taken in the sense for which even the least informed reader ought to be pre-

[1] Comp. Gneist, *Eng. Verfassungsrecht*, i. 169 (Berlin, 1857–60).

[2] Comp. Raumer, *Cod.* ii. 114; Eichhorn, ii. § 277 et seq.; Daniels, *Alter und Ursprung des Sachsenspiegels* (Berlin, 1853).

pared, can have caused no confusion. I have also attempted
a survey of the system of finance, of justice, and of civil
administration. Such terms may certainly be applied to
any society where revenue is collected and disbursed,
where the laws are administered by courts, and where the
domestic interests of the commonwealth are watched over
by the agents of a central authority. But as it is impossible to describe these as systems in the modern sense, so
it would be folly to look for a modern prince in the margraves of Brandenburg. The ominous idea of prerogative
had not yet found its way into their lexicons or their practice. In place of this they had had only the rights and
privileges of a seigneur as against his vassals. The difference is, perhaps, indeed only relative. Prerogative is a
more elevated and exclusive privilege, — one which shot
out as it were beyond its fellows, drew new conceptions
around it, and became a leading element in royalty. But
this was long after the margraves of the House of Anhalt
had passed into history. During the two centuries that
their family held the government of the Mark, and in
spite of some unusual powers that they owed to their character and situation, the feudal principle, which was the
seasoning virtue of their foreign policy, likewise penetrated
all the agents and institutions of civil authority. It aided
or determined their form, hampered their efficient action,
and obstructed, where it did not mislead, their development.
Above all, it gave to the organization of the public powers
and relations in the state a character which was vague and
anomalous, which modern political language fails to describe, and which can be learned only in its most general
outlines.

The curiosity of zealous research, the inquiries of the
special historian, reach, indeed, far beyond this point. It
would be gratifying in studying that remote society to
learn in detail, and more exactly, about education, for instance, and the schools; about the position of woman;

about the distribution of land and the methods of industry ; about the wealth and population of the towns ; about
the records of justice, the returns of revenue, and many
other data, without which generalization is difficult and
hazardous. Unfortunately the dignity of mediæval chronicles seldom trifled with such details. One can trace out
the campaigns by which year after year, and inch by inch,
the reluctant Wends were driven out of the land of their
fathers ; but the details of that more arduous struggle,
which wrested fertile fields and thriving towns from the
hostile forces of nature, are irrecoverably lost. Even the
official papers that were preserved, through the care or the
carelessness of contemporaries, though many in number,
are limited in scope and variety. The gifts to bishops and
abbots, the bestowal of municipal charters, the bargains
with vassals for subsidies, — the copious records of such
transactions throw light upon the practical machinery of
state, but very little. on the humbler social relations which,
in the end, make up its life and strength.[1]

During the hundred years between the Ascanians and
the Hohenzollerns, and facilitated by the miscon- Social
duct of weak and profligate princes, the elements changes.
of Brandenburg society passed through serious vicissitudes,
and suffered the most violent readjustments. But, even
without the aid of weak princes, the times were abundantly
ripe for constitutional changes. A movement which profoundly agitated Europe for two centuries had drawn to
a close ; and a current of new feelings, habits, ideas was
gurgling through all the arteries of society.

The historians have always taken delight in expounding
the real, or supposed, influence of the Crusades. Influence
Among their various effects, near and remote, of the Crusades.

---

[1] The excellent Moehsen, *Gesch. der Wissenschaften*, p. 153, suggests,
and throughout his works employs, an ingenious method of repairing
this deficiency. Even a century ago, it appears, the art of *a priori*
historical writing was not unknown in Germany.

there are perhaps few that can be called unmixed evils,
and many that were undisguised blessings. They gave
the warriors experience of men and manners, and thus
loosened the sway of feudal forms; they opened new high-
ways of trade and intercourse, and thus widened the beneficent sway of commerce ; they tapped the great reservoirs
of Eastern science and learning, and allowed the refresh-
ing stream to flow over Europe. Such general propositions as these are hardly open to dispute. But a graver
difficulty arises, if one takes the form and measure of these
benefits by a comparison with other effects which were not
benefits ; if one attempts to strike an average between the
wholly good and the partly bad, between the salutary and
the doubtful or the vicious, and thus to ascertain the permanent changes left by those marvellous displays of fanaticism.   This subject deserved the prize of the French
Academy, and produced the admirable essay of Heeren.

It is evident that such vast popular migrations — for
the Crusades were nothing else — could not fail to work
changes in the character of the different social orders, and
in their relations to one another ; and that the end might
show an unexpected balance of gain or loss. An order or
an institution might issue weakened from an enterprise
which its own selfish ambition had encouraged. Thus, if
a king should lead an army into Palestine his unruly kingdom might go to pieces in his absence, while if he remained
at home to save his crown he would draw down upon himself the censures of the Pope and the contempt of the people. The cities, again, might rejoice at the departure of
their ancient foes, the nobles, and yet in the interval be
harassed by a higher power. Finally, the glory that awaited
the knights in the Holy Land often required the sacrifice
of fortune and position at home.[1]

Yet in spite of many unequal and inconstant effects,

[1] See Heeren, *Folgen der Kreuzzüge,* p. 169; also Robertson's *View
of the State of Europe.*

a certain loose order of progress may perhaps be discovered. The first to profit, while the enthusiasm was
fresh and sincere, was clearly the papacy. In the thirteenth century, which called not only the great nobles but
kings and emperors to the Cross, the cities were relieved
of many burdens, and under the impulse of freedom set
out upon a new and glorious career.[1] But when, at length,
the Crusades came to an end, and the royal and aristocratic powers reinstated themselves at the head of society,
they not only reconquered the ground which had been lost,
but through the martial habits acquired in two centuries
of warfare, and the ingenious arts learned in Eastern
schools of despotism, were even enabled to wrest new
privileges from peasant, burgess, and priest.

In respect to the Mark of Brandenburg, the period of
highest municipal prosperity nearly coincides with the last
century of the Ascanian margraves, and is covered by the
foregoing pages.

During the next century the cities were on the defensive.
Their trade was almost ruined by the noble banditti; and
although they were strong enough to resist direct attacks,
this was at best a negative advantage. When shut up
within their walls the hardy burghers derived little profit
from their independence. The forms, like the Fate of the
phases of political progress, depend on the con- towns.
tact and coöperation of societies, on the reciprocity of
complex intercourse, and on all the schemes and combinations which bind communities efficiently together. A city
confined within its own streets is like a man isolated from
his fellows, — it is outside the ordinary standard of political measurement.

This consideration is not much affeċted by the fact that,
during the interregnum, — as the interval from Waldemar
to Frederic may be called, — unions for mutual defence

[1] M. Blanqui has an interesting chapter on this subject: *Histoire
de l'Economie Politique*, c. xiv.

were often formed between the cities themselves, and between the cities and factions of the nobles.[1] These were
temporary, even revolutionary, leagues, and they left no
durable impress on institutions. They ceased with the
danger which called them into being.

Some of them are, nevertheless, interesting, whether as
mirrors in which are reflected the fierce disorder of the
times, or as examples of the service that the towns ren-
Municipal dered to Brandenburg in the darkest hour of her
leagues. history. The practice was begun even under
the later Ascanians, perhaps with prophetic foresight of
coming danger. Thus, in 1308 there was a "union" of the
cities in the jurisdiction of Margrave John, and the object
is set forth with sufficient clearness.[2] In the next year,
which seems to have been one of great insecurity, a number of such leagues, though more modest and restricted in
scope, may be found recorded.[3] But in 1321, before the
successor of Waldemar had begun to put even his feeble
restraint on the license of the barons, the whole Mark
was apparently divided into factions, and organized into
leagues.[4] 1344 is another dark year in the calendar,[5]
and throughout the century similar instances occur.

The leadership seems to have been conceded to the cities
in the alliances of which the nobles were also members.
Stendal, Brandenburg, and the other great towns were, of

[1] "Einigungen," they were called, and they are to be distinguished
from "Conventions," which were voluntary meetings of all the estates for the whole territory.

[2] If any violence should be done to one of them then, it was declared, nos eidem civitati pro nostra possibilitate astare volumus con-
siliis pariter et expensis. . . . Lenz, *Brand. Urkunden*, No. 78.

[3] For instance, in Gercken, *Frag. March.* part iii. No. 12 ; ibid. part
vi. No. 3, b.

[4] Lenz, Nos. 107 and 108; Gercken, parts v. 8, and vi. 4, etc.

[5] Lenz, No. 131. Some of the cities also joined at different times
the Hanseatic League, — a step which argues a considerable degree
of independence of their territorial prince.

course, willing to throw their protection around the " honest " or " honorable " knights, as they were called ; and these, for their part, were even more willing to be protected from their lawless brethren. Many nobles even took up their residence within the cities, became burgesses, and thus founded the patrician families.

Within the cities themselves all was not, however, peace and harmony. About the time that the wealth and power of the patricians began to excite discontent, a less noble but no less rigid oligarchy arose in the guilds and corporations. But even in these the extravagant regard paid in the Middle Ages to the claims of *Guilds and corporations.* birth was expressed. They formed a caste rudely based on descent. The shoemaker stuck to his last until he relinquished it to his son ; the offspring of the draper sold cloths ; and throughout the trades the law of hereditary privilege was faithfully observed. If this custom had been derived from the natural preference on the part of the son for the profession and the professional ties of the father, it would have deserved nothing but sympathy and respect. But there is no doubt that it had a less respectable origin, — that an innocent greed first taught the traders to unite for mutual support, that union made them exclusive and intolerant, and that the power of extorting special privileges from the prince of the land became a facile instrument of tyranny over their fellow-citizens. From the organization of the tradesmen and artisans into guilds, which were close monopolies, to the demand for political power as a corporate right was but a single step. With the older cities of the Mark this process began early in the thirteenth century. During the next hundred years, in the absence of a strong central power which alone could have held them in check, and profiting from the lax vigilance which in times of external danger is commonly applied to domestic affairs, the guilds pushed their pretensions to extreme lengths of intolerance, and became the most restless, if not the most discreet, actors in municipal life.[1] But their practical energy, their sturdy civic virtue, and their martial valor were equal to their intolerance, and carried the towns triumphantly through a grave and protracted crisis.[2]

The nobles and cities were not, however, the only belligerents during this period. With a scent no less acute, and an audacity learned from the Holy See itself, the clergy, too, rushed into the fray, and claimed their share of the spoils.

No slight tribute to the influence and authority of the clergy was paid by the Emperor Charles IV., when that politic prince made the Bishops of Lebus and Brandenburg guardians of his two sons, the appointed successors of Margrave Otho.[3] A prelate of still greater dignity — though a neighbor, not a subject of the margrave — was the Archbishop of Magdeburg. The See was a powerful one; and its successive incumbents seem to have pursued uninterruptedly the same policy of ambition and aggrandizement, supported, indeed, in the case of the Old or North Mark, by a certain claim to the succession after the extinction of the Ascanian line.[4] It is unnecessary here to examine into the merits of that claim. But the tone in which, in 1374, the Archbishop summoned the cities of the Old Mark to do homage to the Emperor at Berlin[5] was that of a lawful if not an actual master;

Power of the clergy.

[1] Comp. Zimmermann, *Gesch. des Bauernkrieges* (Stuttgart, 1843), i. 43.

[2] Some just observations on this subject may be found in the prize essay of Victor Boehmert, *Beiträge zur Geschichte des Zunftwesens*, p. 27 et seq. The leading authorities in general are Wilda, *Das Gildewesen im Mittelalter* (Halle, 1831), and Brentano, *On the History*, etc. *Gilds and Trade-Unions* (London, 1870).

[3] Stenzel, i. 128.

[4] See, for details, Fix, *Territorial-Geschichte*, p. 15 (Berlin, 1869). The claim was formally relinquished in 1449. Gercken, *Cod. Dip. Brand.* v. No. 192.

[5] Gercken, *Dip. Vet. Marchiæ*, i. No. 146 ; and for other instances, Gercken, *Cod. Dip. Brand.* i. Nos. 363 and 367.

and similar arrogance was displayed on other occasions. That he could command ample military aid for the execution of his schemes has already been shown. The pretensions of the church were in fact seldom higher, its measures seldom more violent, than during the fourteenth century. The subtle energy of the Guelphs, pushing itself into the most distant parts of the Empire, awoke the twin evils of political strife and religious strife in towns which had just risen from the desert or the swamp, and renewed the battles of the Danube and the Po along the pine-clad valleys of the Havel. But this was the energy and the violence of despair. The rise of the papal power, which culminated under Innocent III., gave place under Boniface VIII. to a decline, less rapid, indeed, but no less sure; and although the church in Germany could still utilize the feuds of persons and factions, there was a general purpose on the part of the more powerful nobles no longer to submit to her dictation.

The fate of the peasants has been foreshadowed, as it were, in the history of the other and rival classes. In such an unhappy age the fittest element might not survive, but the weakest could hardly hope to prevail.

The fall of the peasantry began with the financial difficulties of the later Ascanians, or rather with their imprudent measures of relief; but it was *Decline of the peasantry.* rapidly completed during the fourteenth century.[1] This was in effect the heavy price at which the crown averted bankruptcy. By the process of farming their revenues, or pledging them as security for loans and advances, the margraves not only alienated a large part of their income, but they also surrendered with that income and its sources the political, or rather civil authority which was associated with them. We have already seen that the fiscal connection, which carried with it judicial relations, of the peasants with the crown was an unmistakable

[1] Comp. Moehsen, *Gesch. der Wissenschaften*, p. 227.

privilege. The course of their public contributions, as in every scheme of organized society, marked out the channel within which went on the reciprocal play of their rights and duties as subjects. With the transfer of their fiscal obligations were also transferred all their immediate relations in civil society.

It is true that the legal status of a peasant was not necessarily changed by a change of landlord. His relations were simply transferred, in whole or in part, from one master to another; and even when he passed from the margrave himself to the petty lord of a manor the change was not inevitably a misfortune. But it was made a misfortune by the evils and opportunities of the age.

The only precaution which the margraves took against the evil consequences of their conduct was to prevent the acquisition of all the revenues of a township by a single person. The dime would be assigned to one ; the profits of justice to a second ; the rents to a third. The regular tribute, too, of 1281, which had been solemnly declared inalienable, came early upon the market like the other revenues, and like them was bought by noble or ignoble speculators.[1] Thus the peasants were harassed by claims from many different persons ; but the jealousy of those persons, though it led to fiscal anarchy, was an obstacle to complete and systematic oppression. But this dissipation of their forces was intolerable to the proprietors, and a course of bargains and exchanges by which they should concentrate their perquisites and consolidate their power was a natural or a necessary policy. The disorder of the interregnum enabled force and fraud to assist the process.

It was less easy at first to subvert the institutions of justice, the last refuge of peasant freedom. The lord of a

[1] Stenzel, i. 69 ; Droysen, i. 49 and 65. According to the Landbook of Charles IV., the Bede remained in the hands of the crown only in a ludicrously small number of communes, e. g. in 6 out of 104 in the Zauche, in 3 out of 104 in Havelland, etc.

village, even when in possession of all its tributes, did not thereby acquire in law, and would seldom Manorial courts. usurp by force, the control of the local court; but he could purchase the rights of the hereditary schulze, or — what was more common — claim the reversion to the office on the failure of heirs. In this way the independence of those tribunals was lost. The hereditary magistrates, who had administered justice in the name of the margrave over free peasants, gave way to creatures of the proprietary landlords holding their office by favor and administering it iniquitously.

Only a single right now remained to the peasants. They were not yet adscripti glebæ; they were Predial servitude. still masters of their own movements. But by a series of vexatious regulations — some of them faintly veiled by a show of equity, others the open injustice of brute force — the landlords managed to throw obstacles, which were almost prohibitive, even around the exercise of this last privilege. By withholding their sanction, which came to be a recognized condition of every transfer of peasant land; by requiring the seller to become responsible for tributes which the buyer might fail to render; by demanding indemnification for various losses which were alleged to follow a change of owner; — in short by imposing a great variety of annoying delays in the legal forms of a sale, they could effectually prevent what no law forbade. The next step was to claim the return, as absconding debtors or fugitives from justice, of peasants who, in spite of these obstacles, sold or abandoned their land. Such a demand might have been indignantly resented in the thirteenth century. But during the interregnum the law of generosity had been supplanted by the law of self-preservation; and the cities, already menaced by dangers on every side, were reluctant to make new enemies by harboring refugees. It was at once a measure of fear and of policy to surrender them to their masters.

As precedents multiplied, a rule and a legal principle, if
not a law, grew out of this unhappy practice; and little
more was then needed to complete the ruin of the peasants.

While the nobles were thus bringing into their own
hands the revenues of the crown, they had likewise been
shaking off the public burdens to which they themselves
were bound. The Diet of 1281 had fixed a limit
to the amount of untaxed land which they might
have under cultivation, — a compact which was a
species of compromise between rival claims.[1] But even the
compromise was a restraint; and although the knights were
sure to throw it off on the first opportunity, it is doubtful
if even they foresaw that within fifty years their success
would be complete. Such was at least the case in the Old
Mark, where, in 1319, they procured a declaration that
thenceforth they might have under the plow as much land
as they wished exempt from taxes; and a score of years
later they are described as holding on these easy terms
from eight to thirty hides each.[2] In the land-book of
1374 this inequality has nearly become the rule throughout the Mark.

Exemptions of the nobles.

One important class of social relations was thus slowly
revolutionized, and a new element or force was thrown
into political life. But to describe this interesting process
in detail, to recapitulate all the results, direct and indirect,
which it produced, in short to give a complete account of
the manorial system as it existed in Brandenburg at the
end of the fourteenth century, would carry me too far
beyond the point at which it ceases to have a necessary
connection with the subject. I shall therefore compress
into a paragraph the effect which these changes had on
the development of parliamentary forms.

---

[1] The Bede-Vertrag above described.

[2] The Hufe, if it equalled the English hide, was probably about
thirty acres. Comp. Kemble, *The Saxons in England* (London, 1849),
i. 101, and the learned note in the Appendix.

Since the peasants had no political rights to lose it might at first seem that any change in their condition need not disturb the adjustment of political power in the state. The effects were indeed slow and indirect. But since social position was the chief measure _{Results.} of political authority, so that even the prelates and cities were admitted to the Diets only in virtue of free and immediate proprietorship, it follows that the acquisition of the revenues and the civil jurisdiction in the villages, by increasing the wealth and dignity, would also increase the power and influence of the landed gentry. As it manifested itself in the fourteenth century, this gain of political prestige was torn violently from the crown. With the rise of the nobles the central power for a time declined. But the remaining orders — the prelates and the cities — came forward during the same period, less violently, indeed, but no less surely, and fixed themselves in secure and eligible positions. The division or classification of the estates took a permanent form during this century. General parliaments for the whole Mark, as left by Waldemar, were of course impossible, since large sections of it had been seized by hostile neighbors: by the Dukes of Brunswick, of Pomerania, and Saxony, by the Poles and Bohemians, and by the no less rapacious princes of the church. In their weakness, or indifference, the margraves could only hold local and irregular assemblies. But this state of things was not unfavorable to the growth of the estates. They learned confidence, if not discipline ; they had power, if without method and system ; and when the Hohenzollerns came upon the scene they found their title disputed by jealous, haughty, and resolute opponents.

CHAPTER III.

THE HOHENZOLLERNS TO THE SEVENTEENTH CENTURY.

THE name of the Hohenzollerns, or rather the family which afterward received the name, first appears in positive history about the time that the Emperor Henry IV. was waiting barefoot and a penitent at the doors of the papal palace. The term, like so many other noble patronymics, was derived not from a common ancestor but from an ancestral seat, — the heights of Zollern, in the Suabian Alps. There they possessed a formidable castle, and from thence they were no doubt accustomed, in the style of the Middle Ages, to levy toll in the undefended passes, and as occasion offered to plunder the settlements in the plain below. But this antiquity and this origin are not sufficient for the more devout friends of the family. Such a pedigree might be the pedigree of any mediæval brigand, who afterwards gave up the practice of highway robbery, bought a title from some needy prince, built a castle on a rock, and founded one of the ancient and aristocratic houses of Europe. Genealogical research aided by etymological ingenuity has, therefore, feigned to trace the name beyond the times of Charlemagne, through Lombardy, and back to the noble race of Colonna.[1] And Albert Achilles, the third Elector, familiar with the legend but little read in the books of her-

The Hohenzollerns in fable.

---

[1] See, for instance, Cernitius, *Decem e Familia Burggraviorum Nurenberg* pp. 5–8 (Wittenberg, 1626). The latest serious researches on the subject are those of Schmid, *Die Geschichte der Grafen von Zollern-Hohenberg* (Stuttgart, 1862).

aldry, made an abrupt settlement of the question by placing his ancestors among the fugitives from Troy and the
founders of Rome.

The historian who dares to ignore these ambitious myths
can follow the family down with reasonable safety
from about the middle of the eleventh century.
Count Burchard of Zollern, the contemporary
of Henry IV. and Hildebrand, was a friend of the Counts
of Stauffen; and this early relation being afterwards
strengthened by the ties of political interest, the heirs of
Burchard became known as strenuous supporters of the
most illustrious dynasty in the annals of the German Empire. In 1192 the Burggraviate of Nuremberg fell to
Count Frederic III. of Hohenzollern, as the consort of the
nearest heir. Other possessions in Austria and Franconia
were acquired through the same happy marriage; and the
family was recognized as one of the most powerful in Germany. But the integrity of this vast estate was not long
preserved. An amicable partition was made by Frederic's
two sons, — Frederic, the elder, keeping Nuremberg and
the title of burggrave; Conrad, the younger, resuming the
family possessions of Zollern. Both of these branches
survive to the present day. From Conrad is derived the
cadet line which still has its seat in Suabia, and has furnished candidates, successful or unsuccessful, for more
than one of the lesser thrones of Europe. The elder
branch expanded into the House of Prussia.

The career of Frederic's descendants during the next
two centuries differs little except in detail from
that of other leading families of the Empire.
The burggraves seem, as a rule, to have been
brave and skilful, rather than enterprising warriors; conservative in their views of imperial politics and favorable
to the regular as against factional emperors; rich withal
and adroit in making the best use of their riches; orthodox though not bigoted churchmen; and cultivated beyond

*The Hohen-
zollerns in
history.*

*Imperial
politics of
the family.*

5

most laymen of their own times.   Although they had no
voice in the electoral college their influence was not inconsiderable, and was eagerly courted by candidates.   Frederic III., not to be confounded with the other of the same
name, supported Rudolph, the first Hapsburg Emperor,
in his successful contest.   Frederic V. and Albert adhered
to Louis of Bavaria through all his troubles with the
Pope and with secular rivals ; and in consequence of this
fidelity their relations with Charles IV. were at first not a
little embarrassing.   But that Emperor never sacrificed
the interests of his house to merely sentimental feuds, and
eventually offered a reasonable accommodation, which the
Hohenzollerns as readily accepted.   It should be added
that they on one occasion sent a force to the aid of Margrave Louis in the Mark, and thus made their first acquaintance with that turbulent province.   No sooner had
Charles established friendly relations with the Burggraves
of Nuremberg than he began, characteristically, to turn
them to his own profit.   An imperial patent made them
grandees of the Empire ; and their thrifty policy of pecuniary accumulation was willingly encouraged ; for the
betrothal of Wenzel with the daughter of Frederic, to
whom, in default of male heirs, the inheritance of Nuremberg had been secured, promised Charles a large addition
to the wealth and prestige of his family.   But the Burggrave's wife finally gave him not one son alone but two,
and frustrated all these ingenious schemes.   The elder of
these sons eventually entered the imperial family by espousing the Princess Margaret.   The younger, afterwards
Frederic VI., found a more exalted career as Frederic I.
of Brandenburg.

On the 1st of May, 1411, there was a noteworthy gath-
Sigismond and Burg-grave Fred-eric VI. ering at the imperial residence in Ofen, opposite Pesth.   Jobst was dead ; Sigismond had
resumed possession of the Mark ; and the estates were summoned to repeat the ceremony of homage

to their truant lord. The towns were well represented, and in graphic language once more rehearsed the story of their wrongs, once more called urgently for relief. The other orders sent but a single delegate, a knight, and even he could pledge only his own personal fealty. The Emperor was affable and sympathetic. He regretted that he could not himself visit the province, but he had selected a representative who would faithfully carry out his benevolent plans, and with whom his loyal vassals would be well satisfied. This was the sixth Frederic Burggrave of Nuremberg. The delegates promptly assented; Frederic, who was present, signed the protocol of the proceedings; and, a little later, Sigismond issued to him a full patent or commission as governor-general in the Mark. He acquired, practically, all the powers and rights of the margrave, except the electoral vote; and the honor was made hereditary in his family until the territory should be redeemed by the payment of the debt due from Sigismond.

Frederic seems to have been not unfitted for his delicate and difficult task. One of the first soldiers, Character of one of the richest nobles, and one of the best Frederic. scholars of Germany, he enjoyed great authority among the princes of the Empire, and great popularity among all classes of people with whom he came in contact. On his assignment to the Mark, it acquired a new importance in the imperial system. And if in the interior the new ruler did not at once seem to inspire much respect, if he did not at once restore the order and harmony and happiness of the thirteenth century, it must be remembered that a hundred years of anarchy had taught the nobles to despise restraint, and especially the restraint of intruding aliens. This feeling, too, Frederic unwisely encouraged by the preference which he always showed for his earlier possessions in Franconia. He came seldom into the Mark, but spent the greater part of his time at Nu-

remberg, which was certainly a more attractive home, and
was endeared to him by the associations of his youth.

As often, however, as he did visit Brandenburg, the
nobles felt the iron hand of a master if they
neglected to yield to the persuasive tact of the
politician. He always assumed the pacific character first, for he was averse to unnecessary strife. It
is certain that the more powerful among his own vassals
and his neighbors, such as the family of Bredow, the
Archbishop of Magdeburg, and the Duke of Saxony,
were early secured by his diplomatic skill for an active
friendship, or a sympathetic neutrality.[1] But this left
him free to reduce by force the Putlitzs, the Rochows,
the Quitzows, and their confederates, who refused to do
homage, scoured the country with their bands, and when
pursued shut themselves up in their stubborn castles.
The fortress of Friesack was their favorite stronghold.
All attempts to reduce it by the ordinary methods failed,
and Frederic was compelled to resort to extraordinary
methods, which happily were within his reach. Fire-arms
had lately been introduced, and the margrave, borrowing
a small cannon from a neighbor and ally, easily battered
down the walls of Friesack, and put an end to rebellion.[2]
This was the earliest use of artillery in Brandenburg,—
a species of weapon in which the successors of Frederic
have since shown some proficiency.[3]

His policy as governor of the Mark.

[1] Walter, *Sing. Magdbg.* p. 59; Raumer, *Cod. Dip. Brand. Cont.*
i. 58; Droysen, i. 211–12; Pauli, *Allg. Pr. Staatsgeschichte*, ii. 96
(Halle, 1760–67).

[2] G. W. von Raumer, *Codex*, i. 35, advances the paradoxical theory that the nobles instead of being mere banditti were really only
practising the lawful private warfare of their class. But it is the
theory alone which affords them any excuse. All practical considerations not only condemn them, but make a vast distinction between
their revolt and the lawful parliamentary action of the assembled
estates.

[3] This particular cannon is Mr. Carlyle's "Heavy Peg," which is

The severest struggle between Frederic and the insurgents took place during the few years that Frederic is he held the Mark as administrator under a kind made Margrave and of mortgage, as above explained. This mort- Elector. gage was foreclosed in 1415; the formal investiture took place two years later. After that, the resistance of the malcontents was for a time suspended. 1417. One after another the Rochows and Holtzendorfs laid down their arms and acknowledged their new seigneur; their allies, the Dukes of Pomerania and Stettin, recalled their troops from the Mark; and in 1421 the Elector was in the full enjoyment of his authority.

The clergy had been well disposed toward Frederic from the first, and the towns were only too willing to support him against the nobles. The list of cities which did homage in 1412 includes nearly all that are known to have existed at the time.[1] For his own part, too, the Elector was careful to foster this spirit; and after the general declaration of fealty, which took place at an assembly of the estates in Berlin, he made a tour through the Mark, visited the leading towns, and by the confirmation of old and the bestowal of new privileges secured one class of firm and useful subjects.

Before his death Frederic made, or essayed to make, provision for the future of his family. In de- Frederic's fiance of the Golden Bull and of primogeniture, will. he arranged by his will, which was proclaimed before a Diet at Tangermünde in 1438, that the Mark should be divided after his death between his second son Frederic, who was also to have the electoral dignity, and the fourth son, also called Frederic; while the Franconian territory was to be shared in a similar manner by the first and third sons, John and Albert Achilles. But the self-ab-

made to do more arduous service in the pages of his *Frederic* than it did at the siege of Friesack.

[1] Raumer, *Cod.* i. No. 28.

negation of the sons themselves fortunately averted the worst effects which might have followed this scheme. John relinquished the principality of Bayreuth to Albert, who thus reunited the Franconian possessions. In Branenburg, Frederic the younger, seeing the necessity of keeping the Electorate undivided, consented to hold his part under the superior authority of his brother.[1] When he died in 1463 without heirs, this relation was still further simplified. The death of Frederic II., also without heirs, left Albert, in 1471, sole ruler both in the Mark and in Franconia.

In his treatment of the estates, Frederic II. continued the work begun by his father. The latter humbled the knights ; the former disciplined the towns.[2] It was a measure of prudence on the part of the elder Frederic, since he was engaged in a quarrel with the nobles, to overlook for a time the pretensions of the cities ; but this forbearance, which often passed into a real partiality, only stimulated the spirit of independence. Even during his reign some of them, apprehending perhaps that their turn would come after the knights, had begun again openly to coquet with the Hanseatic League. To meet this Frederic II. soon after his accession formed a counter alliance with several northern princes.[3] The city of Berlin, in the assertion of a sturdy municipal independence, having once refused his father some petty favor, Frederic II. undertook to punish the affront and prevent its repetition ; and to this end seized what might at first be taken for the innocent opportunity

Elector Frederic II. 1440.

[1] This is the common story, but Pauli seems to be doubtful about its authenticity.

[2] Raumer, *Cod.* i. 155; Moehsen, p. 319.

[3] With the King of Denmark and the Duke of Mecklenburg; Gundling, *Leben Fried. II.* p. 71 (Potsdam, 1725). It is unfortunate that Gundling did not pay more attention to Frederic's relations with his own people, and less to his relations with the Pope and the Emperor.

of a quarrel between the magistracy and the burghers to come forward as an arbitrator.[1] But his arbitration was that of the crafty fox in the fable. The better part of the privileges in dispute was simply added to his own prerogative. He acquired the right of confirming the magistrates in their office, of controlling the administration of justice, of levying and collecting various taxes ; and he exercised the power, though he could hardly claim the right, of building a fortified castle in the heart of the city.[2] This last achievement gave the Elector the key to the situation. The burghers tried by petition and by force to interrupt or delay the execution of the scheme, but Frederic was inexorable. The completed castle commanded the city. Parts of the walls, as originally laid by Frederic, are said still to remain, though half hidden by later additions, in the present royal castle.[3] But it would seem that in spite of this striking display of force the Elector did not feel strong enough wholly to neglect the authority of precedents, and the appearance of legality, for he summoned a special court composed of clerical and municipal dignitaries, and procured from it a formal confirmation of his claims.[4]

It will not be imagined, however, that the spirit of the nobles or of the towns was crushed by the energetic measures of the two Frederics. On the contrary, the first impression recorded of Albert Achilles, the next Elector, when he came to Berlin to receive the homage of the estates, was one of great impatience at

Albert Achilles. 1471.

---

[1] The two adjoining cities, Berlin and Cölln, had been united in 1432 as a single corporation, and their union was one cause of the dispute (Gercken, *Cod. Dip. V.* No. 78).

[2] Raumer, *Cod.* i. Nos. 67 and 70.

[3] The details of the controversy are graphically given, though with too much partiality for Frederic, by Helwing, *Brand. Geschichte*, ii. 499 et seq. (Lemgo, 1834). Even Lancizolle does not attempt to defend the proceeding.

[4] Raumer, *Cod.* i. 68.

the lawlessness of the nobles, and one not less strong at
the arrogance of the towns.[1] Albert was one of the most
brilliant cavaliers of the age. The epithet of Achilles,
which general usage added to his name, was a tribute to
his martial qualities, but prepares one to believe that even
in politics the rough vigor of the soldier prevailed over
the moderation of the statesman.[2]

The estates had not long to wait before learning the will
and temper of their new seigneur. At a Diet held at Berlin
in 1472, Albert laid before them a statement of the debts
His violent left by his brother, and demanded for their liqui-
measures. dation the revenue from a beer tax. This the
estates refused. But they agreed to a subsidy of one hundred thousand guldens, payable in four years, on condition
that the Elector himself would furnish a fifth of the
amount as the contribution of the crown lands. Of the
remainder the prelates and nobles promised to pay thirty
thousand.[3] As soon, however, as this had been concluded
the Elector demanded a special tax to raise his own contingent; and when it was refused he sent his troopers
abroad and collected it by force from the dismayed people.
But the most important act of Albert was the so-called
"House-Ordinance." By this he separated permanently
The House- the two parts of his dominions, Franconia and
Ordinance. Brandenburg, and introduced in both the law of
primogeniture to regulate for the future the succession to
the government.[4]

[1] Raumer, *Cod.* ii. No. I.; also in the same connection the proceedings of the Diet of 1479, ibid. ii. No. 42. Compare Helwing, ii. 528.

[2] Cujus tot victoriæ fuerunt, quot prœlia, was the modest tribute
of a contemporary eulogist. But Professor Helwing tries to give the
Teutonic Achilles a better character for statesmanship than most
writers are willing to concede.

[3] Mylius, *Corpus Constitutionum Marchicarum IV.* Abth. I. No. 8.
By the same act the feudal Landbede, or rural land-tax, was abolished.

[4] The act is given by Pauli, ii. 301–12. Mr. Hallam says this was
the earliest incorporation of the principle into the public law of a
European state.

In the enjoyment of his ample domains in Franconia, and of all the pomp and luxury which his taste demanded, Albert passed the closing years of his life, while his son John, as governor in the Mark, too often felt the bitter edge of poverty. The disputed subsidy of 1472 had been assigned to him for settlement, and in 1480 the state of the privy purse was again laid before a general Diet.[1] A beer tax was again rejected, and the subsidy was renewed. But the Old Mark at first refused the payment of its quota, and an acrimonious controversy ensued. John wrote angry letters, to which a postscript from Albert often lent serious emphasis,[2] until finally, when the resistance was reduced to seven cities, the matter was referred to an extraordinary Diet organized as a court of arbitration. The judgment was in favor of the Elector.[3]

Albert died in 1486, and John became Elector of Brandenburg. He was called John Cicero in honor of his copious and ornate eloquence, and perhaps in contempt of his military qualities. But if he wanted the robust nature of his three predecessors, and preferred the soft delights of poetry to the costly triumphs of the battlefield, it does not appear that he was a weak prince, or that the prerogative suffered in his hands. In a dispute with the Chapter of Lebus he defended successfully the rights of the state.[4] He kept the nobles in fair subjection without permitting the towns to carry too high their own pretensions. In 1488 he even procured from the estates the grant of a beer tax for the payment

Elector John. 1486.

Introduction of the excise.

---

[1] Raumer, *Cod.* ii. No. 50.

[2] Thus in a communication to the recusant estates of the Old Mark he summons them "peremptorie" to fulfil their obligations like the other vassals, "unser Notturfst halben," etc. (Raumer, *Cod.* ii. No. 57). In a subsequent letter he threatens them with the interposition of Albert, whom their conduct had "nicht unbillich befremdet" (Raumer, ii. No. 61).

[3] Raumer, ii. No. 63.

[4] Wohlbrueck, *Gesch. Lebus* (Berlin, 1829), i. 248.

of his debts ; and when the cities of the Old Mark — the
spoiled favorites of three centuries — resisted its collection,
he promptly occupied them with soldiers, and reduced
them to obedience.   Originally conceded for seven years,
this excise came afterwards to be voted at the beginning
of each reign for the life of the elector, and eventually
became a permanent and hereditary impost.[1]   The towns
favored it for the sensible reason that, being an indirect
tax, it would fall upon all consumers of beer, and therefore
upon many classes, — such as strangers, temporary tenants, and common laborers, — who owning no land, practically escaped taxation.   For the same reason the project
doubtless had also its enemies.

From the time of John the power of the cities began to
decline, or at least ceased to advance.   The Hus-
site and other wars had deranged their trade,
and put heavy burdens on their productive industry ; and with the means of resistance the spirit of resistance naturally fell.   In the method of war the introduction of mercenaries was a blow to the rude military art of
the burghers, and improved the fortunes of the class which,
in a monarchical country, commonly enjoys the fruits of
military patronage.   To this neither policy nor prejudice
made the margraves averse.   As soon as the nobles ceased
to be troublesome rivals, and acknowledged their own
general authority, the Hohenzollerns were not slow to display their sympathy for the order with which they were
connected by the ties of blood, and which was the natural
support of a monarchical government.

Upon the internal organization of the cities the effect
was wholly favorable to the patricians or Geschlechter.
If they were not openly and exclusively patronized by the
Elector, — which indeed would have been contrary to
sound policy, — there is a strong tendency apparent in the
latter half of the century to espouse their side of the many

*Political de-
cline of the
towns.*

[1] The act itself is in Mylius, *Corp. Const. March.* iv. IV. No. I.

quarrels that arose. With the power of confirming the nominations to the councils, the margraves acquired in a sense the control of those bodies.[1] This power of control enabled them again to bring the magistracy into the hands of the patricians ;[2] and the judges, too, would naturally be taken from the ranks of those who had a further source of authority in their wealth and social standing. In the mean time the cities where the democratic spirit was strongest, where the guilds formed a haughty political caste, where the populace was turbulent and formidable, — such cities as Stendal, Berlin, Prenzlau, — were made to feel repeatedly the stern displeasure of their prince, and discovered, after the loss of many of their privileges, that a new era had dawned upon the Mark.

In the course of time even the term "privileges" had almost acquired a new sense. Three centuries earlier the exemption from certain public burdens, or the bestowal of certain positive rights, had been a judicious and even necessary means of furthering the settlement of a new country. Even the surrender to a growing town of some measure of self-government was an encouragement to education in the political art ; and without being a menace to the central power, it trained the resolute and spirited citizens to act as a check upon the other orders. But power once enjoyed is impatient even of reasonable limits. During the fourteenth century the cities, facilitated by the absence of a restraining lord, and by the universal disorder in society, began, as has been already shown, to act like petty republics, to form leagues among themselves, and to set all superior control at defiance. Already, therefore, the municipal privileges, which had issued from the bounty or the necessities of the prince, had become, through abuse, hostile to the interests of a consolidating state.

Spirit of the towns.

[1] Isaacsohn, *Gesch. des pr. Beamtenthums,* i. 176.
[2] Stenzel, i. 262; Eichhorn, ii. § 311.

But the evil carried with it its own cure. As soon as the power of the towns became an object of envy, it became also an object of strife ; and from that moment its decay might have been foreseen. This third period coincides in general with the appearance of the Hohenzollerns on the scene. They found the cities outwardly still strong, resolute, and ambitious, but torn by factions and feuds within their walls, and ready, as it were, to become the prey of any politic mediator. The common burghers were jealous of the patrician families. The trading companies were arrayed against both these classes, and were fiercely demanding the enlargement of privileges which were already grotesquely excessive and unjust. The magistrates and the councils disputed about their respective powers; and different sections of a city often quarrelled for no apparent cause whatever. Beneath all this noisy partisan violence lay, indeed, a spirit which in its nature and possibilities was thoroughly wholesome, and which, if it had appeared two or three centuries later for organized resistance to the schemes of military despots, would have been a beneficent force in civil and political life. But when the municipal spirit was most needed it could no longer be found.

It must be kept in mind, finally, that that particular act of grace called " confirmation of privileges," by which each margrave signified his accession to power, and which, repeated from time to time, secured the affection of the cities, was in no sense a recognition of the general principle of municipal independence. The principle was hardly implied in the privileges when they were granted. They expressed rather the favor or the weakness of the prince ; not even a Tribonian could have codified them into a uniform scheme. In some cases, it is true, the franchises, especially those of the thirteenth century, were liberal and intelligent, and comprehended most of the necessary subjects of a charter.[1] But these

Internal dissensions.

Municipal charters.

[1] Comp. Eichhorn, ii. § 310.

were afterwards buried under a mass of special orders and concessions, and the confusion was aggravated by the circumstance that the court seldom kept a record even of its own prodigality. But this negligence was in a measure repaired by the towns themselves. In their archives and their traditions the evidence of their rights was carefully, though not systematically, preserved. Each knew the tolls and taxes from which it had been specially released; the particular jurisdictions from which it was by " treaty " exempt; what it might claim from a neighboring lord or village; what power it had over refugees; how it might build its walls; when it might hold market; and in short the entire sum of its rights and duties as a civic corporation. Thus an unwieldy mass of petty dispensations, accumulated during several hundred years, and now become self-conflicting and obscure, made up the fundamental law or " privileges " of a city of the Mark; is it strange that they were viewed with impatience by princes like the Hohenzollerns?

It was perhaps not so much the extravagance of these privileges as their perplexing variety which made them mischievous. They had a habit of obtruding themselves at the most critical moment, barring a river here and a road there, thwarting the leader of armies in his campaigns, and shutting out the tax-gatherer to the injury of the privy purse; in short, embarrassing the operations of state with capricious uncertainty, and at an endless number of points. As they existed and acted, each of them seemed a distinct encroachment upon the prerogative, and was therefore hateful to a strong prince.

The Elector Joachim was in general well-disposed toward the towns. When he succeeded his father Joachim I. in 1499 they seemed tranquil and docile, and 1499. quite ready to repay by good conduct the protection which he alone could afford against the renewed lawlessness of the nobles. This lawlessness he suppressed with a vigor, and punished with a severity that the Mark had never known. But for the aggressions of the towns, when such was attempted, the Elector had an eye no less keen, and a retribution no less swift. Berlin, Frankfort, Stendal, all incurred his displeasure, and for offences of various kinds were made to surrender ancient rights and accept new burdens.

The measure which most distinguished the reign of Joachim I., and which may explain or excuse the epithet of " Nestor," [1] was the institution of the Chamber, or court of highest jurisdiction for the entire Mark.[2] This reform nearly coincides with, and was in a measure a consequence of, the transfer of the official residence from Tangermünde to Berlin.

Reform of the judiciary.

We have already seen that the courts of the Mark were of three kinds and three degrees. There were the courts of first instance in the villages and the towns; the county or land courts of the vogts; and the privy tribunal, the aula regis, of the margrave But during the fifteenth century this system had undergone some modifications. As the vogt had been shuffled aside by a more important officer, the provincial governor, or " landeshauptmann," who commanded not one vogtey but several, so the tribunals of the vogts had been fused into the land-tribunals, of which one was formed for each province. At the same time the accumulation of business in the privy court made it extremely inconvenient for suitors to follow their prince about in his frequent journeys. Various expedients of relief were tried. A number of provincial courts were endowed also with the character of royal or privy courts; but either because they

The Chamber. 1516.

---

[1] Il reçut le surnom de Nestor, comme Louis XIV. celui de Juste, c'est-à-dire sans que l'on en pénétre la raison, dryly observes Frederic the Great, *Mémoires pour servir à l'histoire de la Maison de Brandebourg* (ed. Berlin, 1758), part I. p. 17.

[2] Mylius, ii. 1, has the act of incorporation, which was with the assent of the estates.

lacked the necessary dignity in the absence of the margrave or for some other reason, the nobles refused ·to acknowledge their jurisdiction, and they failed to meet the needs of the situation. It was therefore determined that there should be one court of highest appeal, that it should be permanently fixed, and that being at the capital it should be theoretically near the royal person.[1] Hence the conversion of the Land-Tribunal of the Middle Mark into the Chamber at Berlin. In origin and history like the other land-tribunals, the Chamber was elevated by its union with the privy court one degree above them all. In the organization of the college of judges, four were named by the Elector, and two each by the prelates and nobles, by the knights, and by the towns. Sessions were appointed four times a year, three at Berlin and one at Tangermünde. The prescriptions in regard to the presidency, the records, the fees, the procedure, the law and its interpretation, — all were elaborate and precise; and although in the course of the century some reforms and modifications were found necessary,[2] the essential features of the Chamber were long ʻpreserved as a monument to the foresight and statesmanship of Joachim.

It is a remark of Blackstone, reporting indeed only a notorious fact, that the location of the Common Pleas at Westminster drew around that court the great body of professional jurists, and made a powerful bulwark against

[1] The reader will recall the circumstances in which the English Court of Common Pleas was fixed at Westminster; the Parliament of Paris and the imperial Chamber had just received permanent seats.

[2] For instance, in 1534, 1538, and 1540. It is even a theory of Köhler, the author of an unpublished history of the Chamber, that the earlier scheme of 1516 was only put forth by Joachim tentatively, and that the court was not really constituted before 1540. Isaacsohn seems to adopt this view. The ̓ reader is also referred to Kühns, *Gesch. der märk. Gerichtsverfassung* (2 vols. Berlin, 1865–67), passim.

the intrusion of the civil and canon law. As the world knows, this bulwark did its work singularly well. But the little band of English civilians who deplore this result will take pleasure in learning that the Brandenburg Chamber was fixed at Berlin for quite a different purpose, — for aiding rather than resisting the introduction of Roman law. This was a scheme to which Joachim was warmly devoted, and which he supported with measures of rare sagacity. It was for this reason he founded the Uni-

Roman law introduced. versity at Frankfort on the Oder, and filled the chairs of jurisprudence with scholars who had walked barefoot to Bologna, and sat reverently about the shrines of Baldus and Bartolus. The institution had indeed but a brief prosperity, and is now almost forgotten. But during its life it did great service in raising the standard of general culture,[1] as well as in furthering more especially the study of that law which Joachim was resolved should become the basis of the Brandenburg judicial system.

The mission of the Chamber was to apply in practice what the University taught as a science. But at this point we come upon a controversy which has long divided the jurists and historians of Prussia, and on which the opinion of a layman and a stranger ought to be expressed with some diffidence. Did the reform of Joachim extend the Roman law over the whole field of jurisprudence, or only over certain special departments?

If the answer to this question were to be found in a lit-

The measure examined. eral interpretation of the charter it would be comparatively easy. The application of the new law seems to have been expressly made only to the subject

[1] Before this Joachim is said to have declared that "learned men were as scarce in the Mark as white ravens." Comp. Moehsen, *Gesch. der W.* pp. 394–6. The school won questionable distinction by giving a degree to the notorious Tetzel, and in general for its hostility to the Reformation.

of inheritance.[1] Originally regulated by the principles
of Teutonic law which, for Brandenburg, were found in
the Sachsenspiegel, but which had been gradually modified by the cities each to suit its own wants or desires,
this important charge had fallen into a state of perplexing confusion, not to say anarchy. Joachim's attention
was called to the evil during a tour which he made through
the larger towns. He found it a grave obstacle even in
the real estate transactions of a single city; but on account
of the variety of systems, inter-municipal testaments and
descents must have .been the fruitful seed of litigation.
A century earlier the burghers would have tolerated the
abuse rather than give the central authority the power to
correct it. But in the age of Joachim different conceptions began to prevail, and while the spirit of order deplored the want of a systematic jurisprudence, political
reason was not averse to the reforming intervention of the
crown. That a codification of the existing rules would
have been wiser, even if more difficult, is a proposition
which could perhaps be defended. But it has now only
a speculative interest. It suited the purposes of the Elector to adopt bodily the Roman practices, and in the act
incorporating the Chamber to give them exclusive authority over the descent of property. This act had the assent, and presumably, therefore, the approval of the Diet.

Since now the descent and distribution of property is
the earliest and latest process in which the jur- Scope of the
ist, if not the philosopher, observes the relation reform.
of person to things, and since the principle of this process
determines in harmony with itself the minor incidents of
ownership, it follows that the Elector Joachim prepared
an actual revolution in some of the most sensitive interests

---

[1] The Roman law treated this interest much more elaborately than
the Teutonic, yet Blackstone says, with rather careless English, that
"the doctrine of descents, or law of inheritance in fee simple, . . .
is the principal object of the laws of real property in England."

of social life.   After he had once opened the door to Roman law it was out of his power to say how far it should
enter.   It seems to me, therefore, that Raumer is quite justified in refusing to believe that the intruding system
would halt before a restricting clause in a judicial charter; and that the attempt of the Elector to divide that
vigorous body and select from its parts was hopeless from
the first.[1]   It not only had a fund of vitality in itself,
but its revival and growth were singularly encouraged by
contemporary circumstances.   The art of printing had
just been discovered, and multiplied the ease with which
the codes could be disseminated.   The institution of new
universities, and the general revival of learning, is an influence to which allusion has already been made.   More
important, perhaps, than all these forces was, finally, the
example of the imperial Chamber, which as perfected by
Maximilian was almost exclusively governed by the maxims of the civil law and enjoyed the highest authority
throughout Germany.   The clergy,[2] the jurists, and the
court favored the innovation; there is no evidence that the
towns heartily opposed it; and by the end of the century
its success was complete.   Roman law was made common
law, and Saxon law provincial.   In no other part of Germany, not even in the ecclesiastical electorates, was this
great revolution more rapid, more thorough, more far-
reaching in its effects.[3]

It is observed by Stahl[4] that the Roman law displaced
the Teutonic only in the sphere of those relations which
regard men as individuals without organic connection,
but that the ancient rules and usages continued to gov-

[1] See his various writings on the subject, and especially an article
" Ueber die Einführung des röm. Rechts in der Churmark Brandenburg," in Ledebur's *Archiv*, vol. v.

[2] Even Popes did not consider the Sachsenspiegel beneath their
hostile notice.

[3] Compare Raumer, ubi supra.

[4] *Phil. des Rechts*, ii. 400, ed. 1845.

ern the operations of society taken as a corporate body. This is a pedantic way of saying merely that the private law of Prussia was Romanized ; the public law, not. But self-evident as this distinction seems, it is not absolutely accurate. In Prussia, as in every other state, private law and public law are not two completely independent structures, as they are sometimes conveniently treated by jurists. They are rather members of an organic whole, are mutually influenced by each other, and have a natural tendency to modify and adjust themselves according to a common principle of life. It follows, also, that the stronger of the two will infuse its own vitality into the whole, and give direction to its growth. When one reflects, therefore, on the characteristic features of Roman law, and especially on the fact that it had to be administered by trained and permanent officials who, referring their authority to a central source, were ignorant of local feeling and indifferent to liberal impulses, one has a clue to certain changes which its introduction would inevi- *Its effects.* tably make in the spirit and temper of a people. I shall have many other occasions to refer to this subject. At present it is enough to say that great as were the advantages of the Roman law to the scientific jurist, its adoption in Brandenburg was a hardship for the common people because, among other reasons, it was unfamiliar ; because its procedure was largely written and secret, instead of oral and public, and therefore slow, technical, and costly ; because it created the two professional classes of advocates and judges, with interests too often allied against those of suitors ; and because it introduced a set of penalties invented by despotism, and hostile to the manly spirit of Germanic society.

In the mean time a new and ominous movement had begun to puzzle the faculties of the German Nes- *The Reformation.* tor. An audacious Saxon monk was in open revolt against the church of Rome ; and the swift contagion

of the struggle soon carried its passions and its violence
into the Mark of Brandenburg.

The hostility of Joachim to this great religious event
Is opposed by was early, active, and uncompromising. But it
Joachim I. was political rather than theological. Like
many less intelligent and less independent rulers, he associated reform in the church with revolution in the state,
and feared that the fall of the Catholic establishment
would subvert all the institutions of social and civil order.
His sons were suspected of a secret preference for the
reformed faith. His wife Elizabeth openly embraced it,
and was banished to Saxony for her insubordination.
The sympathy of the people followed the Electress in her
exile, and encouraged her children in their slower conversion. Even a considerable part of the clergy, headed by
the Bishop of Brandenburg, readily exchanged the vest-
ments, ritual, and discipline of Rome for the simpler
habits and purer belief of Luther. The Elector alone
held to the religion of his fathers.[1]

Yet this fidelity was clearly not inspired by the soundest
considerations even of political expediency. No
His error. other proposition is more fairly warranted by the
experience of history, and none ought to have commended
itself more strongly to the foresight of the sixteenth century, than this, that the Reformation, being aimed at the
authority and pretensions of the Pope, was wholly favorable to the rival supremacy of the state.[2] And it does not

[1] Comp. Schmidt, *Brand. Kirchen und Reform-Gesch.* p. 151. The
reader will find in this pious work an account of many striking man-
ifestations of the divine power, intended, though in vain, to frighten
the obstinate Elector. Of course only malice could suggest that
Joachim was at all influenced by regard for his brother, Albert,
Archbishop of Mayence, who was making such a handsome thing out
of the traffic in indulgences.

[2] On the political bearings of the Reformation, see, among other
writings, Dr. Baumgarten's pamphlet, *Der Protestantismus als poli-
tisches Prinzip im Deutschen Reiche* (Berlin, 1872); also the reflections
of Wachsmuth, *Europ. Sittengeschichte,* vol. v. (Leipsic, 1838).

affect the proposition that the royal power increased quite as rapidly in certain countries where the Reformation was crushed as in others where it triumphed; that the Catholic Charles V. was the contemporary of the Protestant Henry VIII. For the political results of the Reformation spread far beyond the narrow field within which it worked religious change. Even a state like France, which put down heresy with unsparing rigor, was ultimately obliged to conceal under the specious term "rights of the Gallican church" a degree of independence, in what concerned its relations to Rome, but little lower than that openly claimed and defended by Protestantism. But in Germany the House of Austria was not prepared to attempt the part either of the Tudors or of the Bourbons. It repelled with strange vehemence the advances of the Protestant religion. It refused even to assert that degree of political independence which in France has been found consistent with the most loyal devotion to the spiritual authority of Rome. Those powers which wished to shake off the supremacy of Austria in the Empire were therefore driven by reason and by circumstances first to shake off the yoke of the church; [1] and of no other power was this more true than of Brandenburg. The prompt conversion of his own people, and the tempting blindness of Austria, offered Joachim a task far simpler than that of Henry of Navarre.

The social and political changes which followed the Reformation were inviting facilities to a prince who could foresee and properly use them. Among them Heeren has mentioned three as the most important: the power of the crown was vastly enlarged; religion was made the formal basis of the state; and the clergy were deprived of their political authority.[2] Some degree of the first two effects was also

Political effects of the Reformation.

---

[1] See the reflections of Schiller, *Gesch. des dreissigjährigen Krieges*, book I.

[2] *Kleine Schriften*, i. pp. 82–96; *Handbuch*, p. 78.

felt in Catholic countries; but the third, chiefly in those
countries which accepted the Reformation. But it is still
a subject of dispute among scholars to what extent, if at
all, they were foreseen and approved by Luther.   His
own writings alone furnish no clear answer. They are
well supplied with the common maxims of civic prudence,
and contain here and there hints of the more abstruse
topics of political speculation, but the student will not
find in them a complete treatise either on the art or the
science of government. The truth seems to be that
Luther's political opinions varied greatly during the vicissitudes of his career. They would naturally, if unconsciously, be made subordinate to the interests of his
religious mission; but these interests, it is clear, would
take different shapes according to the changing phases of
the reform itself, or at least to the attitude of the secular
princes. The friendless monk of Wittenberg, struggling
to arouse the people of Germany, taught in a radical
form the right of private judgment. The successful
reformer, at the head of a new church, and courted by
scores of powerful rulers, wrote of the authority of the
state in the style of Hobbes or Filmer. When he thought
of George, Duke of Saxony, or Joachim, Margrave of
Brandenburg, he did not hesitate to declare that "if the
temporal power presumes to give law to the conscience it
trespasses on the domain of God;" or, on another occasion,
that "princes are made not by God, but by men." When,
on the other hand, he recollected the Elector Frederic,
and other illustrious friends, he told the insurrectionary
peasants that they "had no right to resist authority even
when it was cruel and unjust." Now it is possible, in
thought, to reconcile the right of private judgment in
religious matters with the denial of that right in the
relations of civil and political society, — to grant it to the
inquiring Christian, yet refuse it to the loyal subject.
But this distinction was hardly perceived in the six-

teenth century. Luther at least failed to grasp it. The essential principle, the characteristic watchword of the Reformation, was freedom, as Luther was never weary of repeating, sometimes with grotesque emphasis; and he had extreme difficulty in restricting the work of emancipation to the operations of the religious conscience. Again and again he found himself, in his zeal for religious freedom, striking also at the bonds of civil obedience. This was in his younger and more impetuous years, it is true. But his indiscretions seem rather those of a faulty logic than of political immaturity. He fell lower and lower into theories of absolutism in the state as his own cause and fortunes flourished, as he grew arrogant and despotic in his views of ecclesiastical authority. The two interests were so closely allied, and, one might add, so indispensably allied, according to the conceptions of the age, that the march of thought in regard to them proceeded, even when directed by the clearest intellect, in a single narrow path.[1]

The insurrection of the peasants and other social disorders did not shake Luther's faith in the Reformation, which was in effect their proximate cause; they simply led him to distinguish more sharply religious agitation and political anarchy. But this qualified conservatism was not enough for Joachim of Brandenburg. He saw in Luther a rebel against political as well as against spiritual authority, and refused to be conciliated by the theories of passive obedience which the reformer hurled at the insurrectionary Suabians. And even Joachim II., when he became Elector, suffered a sense of responsibility to temper and guide his zeal. It suited his theories of political prudence, or his disputatious and refining mind, to ascertain the exact articles which ought to compose the new creed; the modifications which would be required in the clerical body, and in its relations to

Joachim II. 1535.

[1] Compare on this subject the observations of Eichhorn, iv. § 405, and the notes.

the secular power; and the course or order in which the steps of the reform should succeed one another, before he would consent to adopt Protestantism as the recognized official religion of the state. The preliminaries being completed in 1539, and ratified by the estates the same year,[1] the Reformation was formally proclaimed. Very little violence, or even excitement, social or ecclesiastical, seems to have accompanied the momentous change. It can hardly be called a revolution from above, like the Reformation in England, for the new faith, though not previously established in law, was already very generally held, so that Joachim II. simply gave unity and settled shape to an accomplished fact.[2] But in another sense his intervention was of vast significance. It established the character of the regent as " summus episcopus," as head of the church, a relation which in Prussia is not a mere constitutional fiction, but an exceedingly substantial and vigorous fact, at once political and ecclesiastical, and which has left marks of its influence on every stage of the church's progress.[3]

Proclaims the Reformation.

This was the first step in the conversion of the church into a subordinate institution of the state. But another was needed to complete the work. If the clergy as an order, as an estate, had been permitted to retain their position and influence in the Diet they would have continued to control in no slight degree, through political machinery, both the doctrinal and the administrative interests of the church. They would even have kept up

[1] They were embodied in the so-called " Kirchenordnung im Churfürstenthum der Marcken zu Brandenburg," printed in 1542. Schmidt adds that to each of the two parts into which the ordinance was divided there was prefixed an explanatory and justificatory introduction, composed by the Elector, and written out in his own hand. *Reform. Gesch.* p. 194.

[2] See Stenzel's general reflections on the course of the Reformation in Germany, i. 285.

[3] Roenne, *Pr. Staatsrecht,* i. 639.

their restless and not always salutary interference in purely secular affairs. Logic and policy agreed, therefore, in requiring another measure which should complete the unfinished revolution. The establishment of the church was followed by the disfranchisement of the clergy.

The reader will recollect the pretended inquiry with which Henry VIII. preceded the confiscation of monastic property in England, and the elaborate attempt of Edmund Burke to show that by that formality the measure was essentially distinguished from the spoliation of the church in France. Joachim was no less circumspect, and at a time when he could hardly have been a mere imitator of the Tudor king.[1] The visitation of the English cloisters took place in 1536; the report of the visitors seems to have been published, or at least rendered, the same year. In the Mark the inquiry began a little later, but whether in 1539 or in 1541, that is whether before or after the Elector had adopted the reformed faith, is still undetermined.[2]

The commissioners are described as men of intelligence, impartiality, and independence.[3] They were required to investigate not only the monasteries, but also the parishes and schools; and while they detected abuses with a keen eye they redressed them with a strong hand.[4] Some of the revenues of the monks and clergy, especially such as issued from the discarded practices of the Church of Rome,

Confiscation of monastic property.

[1] Dr. Lingard even pretends that Henry learned the device from Germany, not, of course, the visitation itself, but the art of procuring from the visitors an *ex parte* report, which should cover an intended act of pillage with a show of deliberation and justice.

[2] Schmidt (page 207) favors the latter date. The question is of little practical importance except to those who believe that pending the result, and up to the year 1540, the decision of the Elector was held in suspense, — a theory which requires of those who accept it an uncommon degree of credulity or — loyalty.

[3] Helwing, ii. 713.

[4] Schmidt, 208 et seq.

were at once confiscated. Their landed possessions were
gradually sequestrated, with or without the forms of law.
Harassed in this way even the cloisters, which for a time
escaped summary dissolution, heard the signal of their
inevitable fate ; and many of them hastened to purchase
mild treatment by an early accommodation with the state.
Their wealth was diverted through various channels into
the treasuries of the cities, into funds of parishes and
schools, but the larger part into the purse of the Elector
himself.[1]

This endowment would alone have worked the practical
exclusion of the prelates thenceforth from the
Diet. With the loss of their landed estates,
the episcopal and monastic foundations lost what,
according to feudal or mediæval law, was a leading condition of their representation as a political element in
the united estates. But there was a further consideration,
which in the sixteenth century was perhaps not neglected.
In the sixteenth century political thought, and even political usage, had begun to relax somewhat the stern maxim
which associated public authority exclusively with the possession of land. Personal merit gave personal dignity,
and was consulted for its own sake. It might not, therefore, have shocked the conceptions and susceptibilities of
the age if Joachim or any other German prince, while
secularizing the domains of the church,[2] had left the

Conse-
quences of
the measure.

[1] Comp. Stenzel, i. 208. It is worthy of note that Luther, himself
a member of the regular clergy, was opposed to the secularization of
church property, and refused to regard it as a logical consequence of
the Reformation. Frederic the Great did not scruple to ascribe his
ancestors' conversion to mercenary motives.

[2] In the case of the three episcopal sees of the Mark the process of
secularization was not fully completed until the year 1598, under
Joachim Frederic. The plan adopted was the simple one of putting
the sees, as they became vacant, into the hands of princes of the
electoral house, as secular administrators. Then, through the fiction
of inheritance, these estates gradually came into permanent possession
of the crown, which thus escaped the odium of direct confiscation.

bishops and abbots their seats in the Diet on account of the loftiness of their mission, the dignity of their social position, and the presumed excellence of their private virtues. But in fact, even this title was in great part swept away by the reforms which were made in the internal organization of the church. Abbots and bishops alike had no place in the modified system. The abbots naturally fell with the fall of the orders to which they belonged, and either laid off their clerical character or carried it with them into countries not yet invaded by Protestantism.[1] The dioceses were converted into mere administrative divisions,[2] over which presided not powerful episcopal magnates, but simple colleges or boards of government, not picturesque in themselves, and not inviting any special deference on the part of the prince who created them. A partial representation was still granted to the church, but on a new basis, which is to be explained by other considerations.[3]

Yet this change did not visibly impair, at least immediately, the constitutional vigor of the Diets. If one looks back over their history during the sixteenth century one finds them displaying as much energy after as The Diets in before the Reformation, taking on gradually a the six-teenth cen-better organization, becoming more highly dis-tury. ciplined, and, above all, learning to adjust and use their own forces. For this opinion there may be offered the testimony of a great historian, whose judgment is never swayed by enthusiasm for liberal ideas. Above all, says Professor von Ranke, "however strongly the Hohenzol-

[1] Helwing, ii. 723.

[2] Roenne, *Staatsrecht*, i. 641.

[3] The chapters of Brandenburg and Havelberg, the cathedral of Stendal, and a convent in Priegnitz were alone thus favored. The chapters were represented in the Diet by their canons ; the convent by its bailiff, — in all cases, however, not as personal members of the first estate, but as mere delegates of an ecclesiastical authority. Comp. Muelverstedt, p. 33.

lerns asserted their claim to supreme power, their most important measures were carried through only by the assent of the estates. With the approval of the estates the peace of 1414 was proclaimed; the assembled estates constrained the city of Berlin to submit to the Elector; when later another revolt was attempted in the Old Mark the majority of the estates organized themselves into a court, and summoned the insurgents to obedience; the estates provided the means for repurchasing the New Mark, and supported with all their strength the claim to Pomerania; with the consent of the estates the Chamber was founded; . . . on their advice the secularization was begun, and, although this was also an advantage to them, it gave above all a broader basis to the central authority." From this active participation in public affairs "it could not fail to follow," continues Ranke, "that the estates had great influence, and came, as it were, to share the power of the state. Since they granted the required taxes from loyalty and good will, and not from mere duty, the administration of the same, including both their collection and their disbursement, was left to them. In the executive councils the landraths from the nobility sat as adjuncts of the crown officials. . . . Under John George, prince and estates, nobility and towns, the spiritual and the temporal, were in an admirable equilibrium." [1]

This equilibrium had not been reached by any violent readjustment of power in the state, but was rather the result of an equality of progress between the two leading public forces. The authority of the estates was undoubtedly greater in the sixteenth than in the fourteenth century. But the authority of Joachim was also greater than that of Jobst or

Harmony of the public powers.

---

[1] *Neun Bücher Pr. Geschichte*, 1st ed. i. 25–27. Comp. Lancizolle, *Königthum und Landstände* (Berlin, 1846), pp. 4 and 279; Campe, p. 104.

Sigismond. Both the crown and the orders had added to their functions, and in consequence to their powers; but the ratio of accretions had been so well preserved that their aggregate relations remained nearly unchanged. The title of the Elector was no longer disputed. The taxes were collected, justice was spoken, leagues and alliances were concluded, and other prerogatives of the prince were exercised without any organized resistance on the part of his subjects. But the rights of the estates were no less frankly respected by the Elector. If his authority had become firmer, their forces had become more flexible and efficient; if his functions had a range far beyond the sphere of a mediæval prince, their Diets were more imposing assemblies than the feudal " placita," and legislated on a greater variety of subjects. And it is not difficult to point out the chief influences which affected these parallel lines of development. The estates lost their appellate jurisdiction by the introduction of professional judges and written law; their direct influence on military affairs was lessened by the formation of a paid soldiery; the Reformation robbed them of the powerful aid of the church; — and yet their proper legislative powers continued to grow with the institutions of the country, and in harmony with that process of development which made the modern state out of the shapeless elements of feudal society.

It would accordingly be inexact to say that the rights of the Diet reposed in the end only on the negative Scope of legislation. power of refusing taxes. This power, which in the sixteenth century had almost become a general control over the public purse, was an undoubted means of coercion upon the crown, but in law and in fact it was only one of many attributes, all of which issued from the same source, and enjoyed in principle the same constitutional sanctions. One has only to read for proof of this statement the protocols collected by Mylius and other antiqua-

ries.[1] The very earliest Diet whose proceedings are recorded with any fulness in a journal, that of 1445, under
Frederic II., was summoned to settle an old dispute about
the limits of ecclesiastical jurisdiction, which had been
gradually and unreasonably extended.[2] A number of similar instances are mentioned by Ranke in the passage above
quoted; and Muelverstedt, who, it will be remembered, is no
radical, has drawn up a considerable schedule of subjects
on which the Diet acted by direct legislation. He mentions ecclesiastical affairs, which comprised education as
as well as religion; the more important domestic or dynastic events within the electoral family; foreign relations;
civil and criminal law; the administration of justice; trade
and industry; the preservation of public order and peace;
military organization; and finally, as only one of many
interests, taxation and revenue. This is certainly not a
very contracted field of parliamentary labor. Religion,
justice, diplomacy, commerce, police, finance, — the scheme
includes the most delicate and most momentous interests
with which civil government is concerned, and omits
scarcely one to which a modern legislature would lay
claim.

It is true that fiscal affairs formed the most common excuse for convoking the estates, and claimed the most time
in their deliberations. But for this there is an easy explanation. It was the fashion in that age to invite Diets
to pronounce only upon matters of principle or of general

---

[1] The principle seldom failed to be asserted in the rescripts with
which the Diets were closed. Thus, for example, in 1602 (Mylius, vi. I.
No. 58) . . . wollen wir auch keinewichtige Sachen, daran des Lande
Gedey oder Verderb gelegen, ohne unser gemeinen, — i. e. allgemeinen
— Landstände wissen und Rathschlüsse vornehmen, und auch in keine
Verbündniss, dazu unsere Unterthanen und Landsassen sollten oder
müssen gebraucht werden, ohne Rath und Bewilligung gemeiner
Landräthe begeben. . . . This formula with but slight variations will
be found repeated by the Elector to nearly every Diet.

[2] See Buchholtz, iii. 154.

policy, and seldom upon administrative details. Now except when a proposition of the Elector threatened the country with some new pecuniary burden, it was difficult to procure an adequate attendance. If the higher nobles, for instance, had no interest in the subject to be discussed they wholly abstained.[1] It might be a question exclusively affecting the landed gentry when the towns would send no delegates; or it might have only a local interest for the Middle Mark, and the Old Mark would make default. Examples of all these classes of abstention are frequent. Hence arose the question whether the resolutions of a Diet thus imperfectly constituted, through the non-representation of an order or a province, were of binding force; it was often discussed, and never, it appears, absolutely settled.[2]

In contrast to the indifference shown on other occasions was the natural and lively interest felt in schemes of general taxation. These affected all classes and all sections, indirectly if not directly; and they more easily overcame what seems to us the strange reluctance of the estates to exercise their undoubted rights. And in the latter part of the fifteenth, and during the whole of the sixteenth century, there was a further special reason for the prominence which fiscal questions have in the quaint parliamentary records. The crown was heavily in debt, and in spite of repeated measures of relief was often threatened with bankruptcy, until John George put the finances in better order and restored the solvency of his house. It is significant that soon after

The Diet and the public purse.

---

[1] They and the prelates were the worst truants, and for reasons which suggest themselves. See Raumer, *Cod. Dip.* ii. 227, where the complaints of the other legislators are formulated against the unfaithful colleagues; also Muelverstedt, p. 83. The barons and prelates had a personal right to appear, while the deputies of knights and towns had also the obligation to obey their prince's summons.

[2] In general, it appears, the electors took the affirmative, and the estates the negative, of this question.

this reform the power of the estates began to decline. Their own apathy, which had learned to withstand almost everything except a request for new taxes, was easily punished through a reform, that by lessening the needs of the Elector lessened his dependence on the Diet, and thus invited a fatal disaster as soon as the strong prince should appear.

The two conclusions, then, to which the foregoing inquiry leads, are these : That the estates in their corporate union as a Diet had a controlling voice in all public affairs which were to be regulated by general laws ; and that this right rested on no favor of the prince, but was as ancient, as sacred, and as unquestionable as his own prerogative.[1]

It has already been observed that the records of the Diets are confined to results themselves ; that they throw but little light on the preliminary debates. This was the case, too, not simply during the earlier and cruder ages, when the written tongue was the Latin, and even that was written only by priests, but also after the Reformation had ennobled the language of the people, and an archaic German might have saved for posterity the patriotic harangues of a More, a Pym, or a Somers. For the historical student this is a double privation. It baffles that just curiosity which seeks to learn from the deliberations of the Diets the degree of firmness needed by them to assert their rights, the sort of pressure by which the Elector influenced their judgments, — in short, that minute picture of motives, interests, passions, of action followed by reaction, of protest and defiance responding to prayer, exhortation, and menace, — the incidents and elements of parliamentary life. It reduces our knowledge of legislative organization and legislative forms to a frail basis of speculation.

[1] " Wie von alters her " is the proud phrase in which the estates caused their immemorial rights to be recognized in so many parliamentary protocols. Comp. Lancizolle, *Königthum und Landstände*, p. 272.

These two problems have not been neglected by Prussian writers, nor have they been satisfactorily solved.

In regard to the first, one thing is clear: the golden age of the Diets was the sixteenth century, or, more accurately speaking, the hundred years from John Cicero to John George. The former obtained the grant of an indirect tax, which had been repeatedly refused to his predecessors. If the records do not deceive, this and other favors were freely conceded to him because the estates knew that his character as a man of firmness was not incompatible with the most scrupulous respect for their rights and the country's laws. But the enormous subsidy which John George procured in 1572 was accompanied by a vigorous though ineffectual protest. As given by Leuthinger it was a vehement dissertation on the true conception of a prince, and on the duty of the estates as representatives of the land. The Elector is told that princes are the guardians but not the owners of their subjects' goods. For them arbitrarily to dispose of such goods is therefore tyranny. Who can remain indifferent, the Diet asks, when rulers do whatever happens to please their fancy? When they waste their time and the people's money in the chase, in spectacles, and in all manner of licentious orgies? When in order to fill their treasuries at the cost of the land they deceive the Diet with false promises, or coerce it by threats and violence? The prodigality of private persons, it is added, is punishable by law, — how much more demoralizing is it in the head of the State! [1] The same Elector also ordained by his will, and without consulting the estates, a new division of the Mark, but his successor insisted firmly on the law of the family, which forbade such a transaction.

Golden age of the Diet.

---

[1] The authenticity of this interesting paper is not fully established, and it is possible that Leuthinger only summarized in his own words complaints which were freely uttered but never formally entered in writing.

7

Under Joachim Frederic and the two following electors there were many Diets. Some of them showed now and then enough independence to refuse their assent to schemes and requests of the crown, especially during the time of George William and the Thirty Years' War. But a change was nevertheless coming over the spirit and temper of the estates. One must go back to the reigns of John and the two Joachims for the finest displays both of parliamentary courage and of parliamentary discipline, for the most cordial coöperation of the different social orders in the defence of the common cause, for the most harmonious relations, based on mutual respect, between the executive and the legislative. In the seventeenth century no Diet in Brandenburg held the language of the Long Parliament; but in the century before no elector addressed the estates in the style of the Tudors.

It is not possible or desirable, in a work of this kind, to avoid frequent reference to the example of England. In architecture everything is compared to the Parthenon; in constitutional history all progress is measured by the stately and triumphant march of English freedom. And the test is useful not only in ascertaining the nature and the sanctions of parliamentary rights in Brandenburg, but also in the search for the more mechanical secrets of the Diets themselves, their composition and practical action, to which latter task a paragraph must now be devoted.

The great model will nevertheless serve only for the most general comparison, and during the earlier periods. In passing from the origin to the development, from the object to the organization of feudal legislatures, and from the Middle Ages to the later centuries, a parallel for Prussia will be found not in England but in Scotland, and a parallel strikingly close. Here as in Scotland the estates formed a single assembly, not two. The presidency was intrusted to a minister of the margrave, or some official like the Scotch chancellor,

Parliamentary organization.

not to an elective chairman. Even the Lords of Articles had their counterpart in the Ausschuss.[1] But in one important respect the estates of Brandenburg depart from the example both of Scotland and of England. In Scotland the knights or lesser barons seem to have formed, after they were admitted to Parliament, a separate and distinct body, having their special representatives in the Lords of Articles. In England, on the other hand, liberty owes an incalculable debt to the prudence which reduced the knights of the shire to the rank of commoners, and gave them seats with the delegates of the towns. As in both these countries, so also in Brandenburg, four social classes were recognized, and the writs of invitation to Parliament specify, in an order which was seldom essentially varied, lords spiritual, lords temporal, knights, and burgesses.[2] This classification Muelverstedt extends beyond the composition even to the practice or action of the Diet. Other authorities insist on a division into upper and lower estates, — the former comprising prelates, nobles, and knights; the latter only the towns. But a multitude of rescripts show beyond all doubt that in the deliberations of the Diets, and in the delivery of their responses, these divisions were lost in a third, viz. : that of prelates, that of noblesse, and that of towns. First the clergy, as the most exalted order, gave their answer ; then the Ritterschaft, which included both lords and knights ; and finally the cities through their delegates. For the purpose of deliberation each of these classes doubtless retired by itself, so that in a certain sense there were three assemblies ; and when a special committee was appointed for any purpose, whether by the estates or by the Elector, three classes of

[1] Comp. Robertson, *History of Scotland* (Basle, 1791), ii. 85, 86. We have already seen, in 1281, the appointment of a permanent committee of knights charged to examine and pass upon propositions of the margrave before they were submitted to the Diet.

[2] Prelaten, Herrn (Freiherren), Grafen, Manne, and Stete.

members, corresponding to the above division, are almost invariably discovered.[1] But in form and in principle the estates were gathered as a single body about their lord.

In regard to the composition of the Diets under the Hohenzollerns, but little is to be added to what was said in the second chapter. The changes introduced by the Reformation have already been discussed. If any very striking movement or tendency is to be observed it will be found in the growing frequency with which the knights of the open country chose and dispatched delegates to the Diets instead of appearing in a body. But the evidence of this practice is not abundant, and it hardly became systematized until late in the sixteenth century.

No sooner had it taken the character of a system, however, than it began, by lessening the necessity for general Diets, to have a mischievous effect on the relations of the estates to the Elector. The Ausschuss began to supersede the Landtag, and next led the way to the provincial and county Diets.

The Ausschuss, or general committee, was a species of mutilated Diet, composed of representatives of each of the estates. Their number is not essential, though it is believed that from each province or division of the Mark the prelates sent one, the landed gentry two, and the towns two;[2] but it is essential to bear in mind that these delegates were not charged with the general mission of acting according to their own reason and conscience, but received special instructions, from which they were not suffered to depart. Since the writs of summons were accompanied by the questions to be submitted this precaution could easily be taken. Such a body would naturally want the dignity and authority of a full Diet; and being for this reason commended to the preference of the

[1] See, for instance, the proceedings of the Diet of 1522, in Raumer, *Cod. Dip.* ii. No. 54.

[2] Muelverstedt, p. 104.

electors, it was encouraged by them to the prejudice of their legal parliaments.[1] The next downward step was from this Ausschuss itself to the local organizations of whose delegates it was composed. If the committee could do the work of the Diet, why could not the primary assemblies — the electoral colleges as it were — do the work of the committee? It was only necessary to combine the several local orders into a single body, instead of having them meet separately as for the choice of delegates, and the result was a petty Diet of the Old Mark, or of Priegnitz, or even of some lesser political fraction, as a county. For the transaction of purely local business these bodies had always been in the habit of meeting, the intervention of the national Diet being reserved for occasions when a general reform was contemplated, or a general tax was to be demanded; and the policy of the margraves from the middle of the sixteenth century was to depress the Diet by exalting the local assemblies. These latter were less democratic, were more easily swayed by the crown officials, and could not command for a given object so much political momentum. Many of the smaller towns were not represented in them, or only imperfectly represented by proxy; and both class and sectional jealousy were abroad, unconsciously doing the work of that central power which ought to have been resisted by all the estates as their common foe. The policy of the electors in patronizing these petty councils was, therefore, from their point of view, apparently correct.[2]

The successor of Joachim II., his son John George, was a prince of a different stamp from his father. Joachim had apparently no very firm views or convictions, and was, therefore, little inclined

John George. 1571.

---

[1] Comp. J. J. Moser, *Von der teutschen Reichstände Landen* (Frankfort, 1769), p. 887.

[2] Many details in regard to this subject may be found in Moser, ubi supra, lib. ii. cap. 18.

to severe measures either of usurpation or of reform. He accepted the Reformation as a fact against which, whatever may have been his first impulses, he had not sufficient energy to make an earnest struggle ; and because to the prayers of his people was joined the privileged persuasion of his wife and mother. The latter he had properly recalled from the exile to which, on account of her heresy, she had been condemned by the first Joachim. But her active schemes of benevolence, the less venial extravagance of his wife, his own taste for show and luxury, and his utter ignorance of systematic management, proved disastrous to the privy purse, and left the crown, at Joachim's death, with a debt vastly larger than that which he had inherited with it.

All this was changed, with tempestuous violence, on the accession of John George in 1571. He removed the popular bur gomaster of Berlin, Thomas Mathias, and drove him by cruel persecution into a bankrupt's grave. An opulent Jew, whose purse had been a convenience to Joachim, was hanged and quartered. The favorite mistress of the father was imprisoned for life by the dutiful son. It was therefore natural that the new policy, or the method of its execution, should alarm the innocent scarcely less than the guilty, and fill all minds with gloomy apprehensions.

But after completing the work of destruction, in which his want of judgment and his temper led him into acts of gross injustice, after cleansing the official household, a task in which he too easily confounded the good and the bad, the Elector began to show more delibera-tion, and reconstructed affairs on a basis strictly and severely practical. He was then, indeed, accused of meanness, as he had before been accused of cruelty. But his meanness justified itself by its results. Peculation ceased in the public offices ; the court expenses were reduced ; thrift and industry were imposed upon the people by a series of useful though arbitrary enactments ; a Latin school and other educational institutions were founded ; and in recognition of John George's undeniable reforms the estates finally, though under protest, granted him a special subsidy of two and one half millions for the purpose of redeeming the crown domains and paying the debts of his predecessors.[1] In this reign, too, the New Mark was once again united with the Electorate, John of Cüstrin dying about the same time as his brother Joachim, and John George being the common heir of both.

Joachim Frederic, who acceded in 1597, has like his father a fine character in the standard text-books. He was honest, frugal, discreet, and pacific. The release of the crown estates through the bounty of the Diet gave him greater resources for such schemes as he attempted, and it does not appear that he purposely abused his power. He is, however, chiefly known for some reforms, and for a general policy of improvement, in the civil service ; and the order of topics now requires a brief discussion of this important interest.

Joachim Frederic. 1597.

Modern Prussia is a state, and a Latinized state, in which the principle of local self-government long since expired. The same treacherous hand struck down the legislative and the administrative rights of the estates. But if the writer has not made too careless inquiries, or drawn false conclusions from parallels which seem as exact as any in the moral world, the estates of Brandenburg guarded the one of these rights as jealously as the other, — the right of applying as jealously as the right of making the laws, — and thus kept the development of Saxon polity on the Elbe and the Oder abreast of that on the Thames, down to an epoch more recent than is commonly supposed.

The conversion of so many monastic estates into crown domains added, of course, largely to the territory over

[1] Comp. supra, pp. 95, 97.

which the Elector had control as a landlord. In the The domains. place of vogts, who as servants of ecclesiastical lords were no less independent than the stewards of the barons on their manors, came the officials [1] of the margrave, who collected rents, maintained the police, and even dispensed justice under the responsibility of a single and more august proprietor. But it is to be observed, on the other hand, that the confiscation of these estates had the approval of the Diet at a time when it scrutinized every measure with a sharp eye, and must, therefore, have weighed the political consequences of such a step. The principle that the Elector could not alienate any part of the domains without the consent of the estates was early established,[2] though often disregarded. But as the Diet seemed always ready to redeem such property, it was not strange that the Elector should treat the relief thus offered as a ratification of his prodigality, and gradually as the removal of every restraint upon his freedom of action. He was subject to but little more control in the administration of the other permanent revenues, the royalties.[3] Like the profits of the domains, they were levied directly by the personal servants of the margrave, and turned over to the treasury of the court,[4] which was originally exposed to no interference on the part of the estates. It was not until the debts of the crown became too heavy, and accordingly the applications to the people too frequent, that the Diet began to insist on more

[1] Amtmann = bailiff.

[2] Comp. Lancizolle *K. und L.* p. 279. The regularity is diverting with which year after year the Acts of the Diet contain first an enunciation of the above principle, and then the grant of money to redeem domains which had obviously been mortgaged in violation of the principle.

[3] The two classes of revenue — from the domains and from the ordinary feudal tributes, — confounded in one term by Blackstone, are commonly treated separately by German writers.

[4] The "Hofrentei."

exact accounts of the privy purse, and finally on a certain share in its control.

In more primitive times the practice of the vassals to levy and direct the taxes proper was made necessary by the absence of an organized civil service, radiating from the margrave ; and this was equally true of other charges which were imposed upon, not simply granted to the territorial gentry. But as soon as the electors began to consolidate their government these local powers ceased to be burdens, became rights, and were defended with great tenacity. All through the fifteenth and sixteenth centuries the estates had great influence in the appointment of the provincial governors,[1] who were generally local residents, and as such more devoted to their own districts than to the central administration. The lesser officials were no less imbued with the spirit of provincial patriotism. One by one their functions were usurped by the electors ; justice by the introduction of Roman law and professional judges ; the army by the introduction of a paid and permanent soldiery ; but the conduct of the finances was the last to be surrendered by the estates, and during the period now under discussion was even falling more completely into their hands.

The agents of the estates collected the taxes in their own way, and paid them with prudent indirec- *The fiscal* tion into the treasury of the Elector. Above *service.* them, as an intermediate instance, stood a board of audit and supervision,[2] which was expected to have some control over the expenditures, and to maintain some degree of order in the accounts of the court servants. Through

[1] Sometimes, it is true, the selection was made absolutely by the margrave, Raumer, *Cod. Dip.* i. p. 136, but often " mit Rate unser Rete," ibid. i. p. 141, or " mit Rate unser Rete und haubtstete."

[2] The "Landrentei," divided into three sections, viz.: one for the general land tax ; one for the house tax of the cities ; and one for the excise on beer. See Lancizolle, *K. und L.* p. 278.

this board, too, the estates acquired a modest voice in the management of the ordinary, personal revenues. The subsidies were properly regarded as supplementary credits. They came to the relief of the prince after his regular income was exhausted, or when its inadequacy to support the public charges was foreseen; and accordingly they were gauged to the actual or probable dimensions of the deficit. In regard to their form and amount there was no appeal from the decision of the Diet. Hence, while the estates recognized as a rule of public conduct the duty of supplying innocent deficiencies, the duty was not an unconditional one, but was accompanied, in each case, by the right to ascertain whether the emergency was real and unavoidable, or merely the result of careless prodigality. This came finally to mean the general right of inquisition into the state of the personal revenues, into the manner of their employment, and, in effect, into the ultimate secrets of fiscal administration.

The chief minister of the margraves, the chancellor, The chancellor. rises above his colleagues almost to the height of a viceroy or regent. It would seem as if the uncertainty of his powers over against the spirit of local independence made it necessary and easy for him to fix a firmer grasp on the prerogative of his master — to shoot out the more ambitiously in the one direction because his growth was arrested in the other. It is true that the personal qualities of prince and minister had much to do with fixing their relations. Not every elector was a Joachim II.; not every chancellor a Distelmeier. But even Distelmeier, whose personal character gave him unusual credit in the Diet, and who, with its assent, carried through a number of reforms, was often checked by its narrow obstinacy and forced to abandon schemes of great utility; while the powers that he derived from the Elector, and exercised without any interference from the estates, were apparently the least restricted in scope, and in his hands the most

usefully employed.[1] As justiciary of the Mark and president of the Chamber the chancellor was an important
member of the legal establishment. He was at the head
of diplomatic affairs, and in that position had opportunities for statesmanship. And he had a seat in the Privy
Council, where in the absence of the Elector he was
charged to represent the views and wishes of the palace.

The council itself was an ill-organized, unshapely body,
until the early part of the seventeenth century, The Privy
when Joachim Frederic undertook its reforma- Council.
tion. But he effected only a slight improvement. He modified somewhat the composition of the body by giving the
burgess element a place with the nobles ; and he defined
more clearly the sum of its functions.[2] The distribution
of these functions with a view to their efficient exercise
was, however, reserved for later reforms, — those of John
Sigismond, Frederic William, and their successors. They
divided the council into sections, each having its appointed
duties. The members were dispatched over the country
on regular or special missions, and collected materials for
their common use when reassembled as a college. In
short, as the Diets disappeared on the one hand, and
ministers arose on the other, the Privy Council acquired
an anomalous position, partly legislative, partly executive,
with great influence and little responsibility.

The system of land tenure and the distribution of real
property continued to have great influence in fixing the
scope and methods of administration. But they did not
apparently undergo any important change dur- Tenure of
ing this period, although there was a tendency to land.
treat the demesne lands less as private possessions of the
Elector and more as state property, in which the public

---

[1] Gundling's biography of Lambert Distelmeier is the best of the
many works of that industrious but much derided author.

[2] See the reform ordinance in Isaacsohn, *Gesch. des pr. Beamtenthums*, ii. p. 23 (Berlin, 1878).

had a legitimate interest. The peasants on the domains
were still the most prosperous; the freedom of private
manors from taxation was a settled principle ; and as yet
no law forbade the indefinite increase of those manors by
the acquisition of peasant land. The limitation, so carefully put upon this practice in 1280–82, and so recklessly
abolished a century later, had not yet been revived. But
personal servitude was not yet, according to Eichhorn,
legally adopted.[1]

Manorial lands, electoral and baronial, were held under
one species of tenure ; another was that of the peasants.
To the peasants the restoration of order and the progress
of society brought some relief from wanton robbery and
violence, but reduced rather than increased the
theoretical rights which they had against the proprietary landlords. Their ancient feudal duties
had been codified into a refined and cruel system. They
were compelled to perform a great amount of labor, honorable or menial, on the estate of their lord. They were
forbidden to sell their scanty acres without his consent,
and he had the right of preëmption. They alone paid the
taxes which the nobles generously granted to the margrave. The village judge was a creature of the lord;
while on the manor, in the court baron, he himself passed
sentence on his dependents. Even the household affairs
of the peasants were subject to various forms of interference and control, some of which grossly violated the sanc-
tity of the domestic relation, and all of which were contrary to sound principles of justice. This state of things
was but little improved before the beginning of the present century. As the central government grew strong,
and — to use Professor Stubbs's expression — became conscious of itself, the duty of the nobles toward the state

Hardships of the peasantry.

[1] As late as the sixteenth century, he says, *D. St. und R. Gesch.* iv.
§ 545, there prevailed the maxim, "tota marchia neminem habet servile conditione natum."

was indeed somewhat more sharply defined, and more rigorously exacted; but their authority over their unfortunate tenants suffered little mitigation until the time of
Stein and Hardenberg.

There was finally a special municipal tenure, not everywhere the same, though having the same general features,
by which real property was held in the towns.

To these three species of tenure corresponded, however,
not three but four administrative units. In the
government of the cities, and in their relations
to the central authority, there was much variety of system, but, as in the municipal tenures, a single
general type. The royal domains were beginning to be
called Aemter,[1] in administrative usage, and the bailiffs
had the double character of private stewards of the Elector
and public servants of the state. The manors, or personal
estates of the nobles, formed a third unit in the scale.
The fourth, finally, was the rural commune, where the
peasants trembled before the local magistrate. These four
different elements had as many different kinds of government, a fact which would alone have made administration
difficult, even if lines of division and separation had been
sharply drawn. But in reality the systems were inextri-
cably mixed up with one another. Landlords disputed
about the spoils of a commune. Jurisdictions trespassed
upon one another. Cities fought with bailiffs, and bailiffs
with landraths. All rights were questioned, all authority
was insecure; the cohesive forces of society were only
beginning to learn their own use. With slight local differences, the course of events was the same in all the provinces which were afterwards united under the sceptre of
Prussia.

Local administration.

[1] Bailiwick is perhaps the best English equivalent.

CHAPTER IV.

THE SEVENTEENTH CENTURY TO THE PEACE OF WEST-PHALIA.

THE two great and engrossing topics connected with the period, 1608–1648, to which I purpose to devote this chapter, are the territorial acquisitions made within that time by the House of Brandenburg, and its unfortunate part in the Thirty Years' War. The period begins and ends with the annexation of new lands; the interval is disgraceful, and nearly disastrous. This chronological order of events suggests, therefore, the logical order of treatment; but it will be convenient first briefly to review the territorial changes which had taken place since the accession of the Elector Frederic I.

The reader is aware that the dominions which the first Hohenzollern acquired were somewhat less extensive than those which were left by the last Ascanian. The process of dismemberment had indeed begun even before the time of Waldemar. But under the adventurers who controlled the Mark during the fourteenth century its integrity had not even been guarded by fictions; the fairest portions were lost one after another; until a little region about Berlin and a few cities in the Old Mark were the only undisputed remnants. The Hohenzollerns undertook, therefore, to restore the ancient boundaries, and then to extend them by new acquisitions. The recovery of the

Territorial growth.

right of reversion in Pomerania was rather a theoretical than a real advantage, though it was the result of a successful war, and naturally impressed other enemies by a wholesome display of resolution.[1] Not much more can be said for the compact of 1449 with the Archbishop of Magdeburg, under which Frederic II. rectified his frontiers in the west by giving up some unimportant towns between the Havel and the Elbe, while the prelate in return abandoned his claim to more valuable districts. The same Elector also acquired, by purchase and by force, considerable territory in Lausitz, between the upper Spree and the Oder. But a more important achievement than any of these was the reunion of the New Mark to the electoral dominions. The Teutonic Order had bought this province of Sigismond in the year 1402. It was repurchased in 1453 by Frederic II.; set off to a younger son by Joachim I.; and again and finally recovered by John George, as described in the preceding chapter.

In the Jülich-Cleve affair the Elector John Sigismond inherited a quarrel rather than an estate. The two houses of Saxony rested their claim to the *Jülich-Cleve.* duchies on an ancient, though authentic and undisputed decree of the Emperor. The Count Palatine of Neuburg had married a younger daughter of Duke William the Rich, and for the son of that marriage claimed the inheritance on the ground of the general preference of law and usage for male heirs. But William had executed a dynastic will before his death, and this complicated the issue. It gave the succession in the first place to the heirs of Mary Eleanor, the oldest daughter, in case her brother, John William, should die, as he did, without children, and after her, conditionally, to the other daughters. Mary Eleanor had no sons; but her daughter had married John Sigismond of Brandenburg, and it was natural that he, re-

[1] Besides the general histories, I have consulted for the facts in this digression the admirable though unfinished work of Lancizolle, *Geschichte der Bildung des pr. Staats* (Berlin, 1828), and the convenient manual of Fix, *Die Territorial-Geschichte des pr. Staats* (Berlin, 1869).

jecting any pretended superiority of male heirs, should rest the case simply on priority of birth, which gave the preference of course to his own wife. Finally, to complete the confusion, the Emperor put in a claim, and supported it with an invading army. By agreement of all the other parties Saxony was quietly eliminated from the dispute; but the efforts of Brandenburg and Neuburg for union against the Emperor, first by a joint occupation, and next by a marriage between the two houses, led only to fresh contention and bitterness. Religious difference was also thrown in to feed the strife. The Count Palatine went over to Rome, and thus won the imperialists for his cause. The Elector adopted the Swiss confession, and called in the Dutch. For a time the dispute was lost in the greater issues of the Thirty Years' War, but the Peace of Westphalia left it still unsettled; and it again revived with all its fierceness. By the final settlement of 1666 the territory was divided, each of the two contestants carrying away his share.[1]

If John Sigismond failed to realize all his expectations on the Rhine he found compensation for the disappointment in the final union of East Prussia with Brandenburg. This event took place in his reign, but as the result of a chain of circumstances which had been preparing for a century.

The rise and fall of the Knights of the Teutonic Order
The Teutonic Order.   is perhaps better known than any other event or series of events in the early history of Prussia. Through the whole course of their picturesque career, from that heroic age when their achievements in the Holy Land

---

[1] Carlyle gives, of course, the Prussian view of this controversy. The language of the will, rigorously interpreted, was indeed favorable to Brandenburg's claim, which Ranke calls " ein sehr gegründeter Anspruch," but the case of Neuburg was not unsupported by precedents and legal authority. The cautious Heeren abstains from any opinion.

filled the Christian world with pious delight, to their conquest and occupation of a remote province on the northeastern frontier of Germany, romance and history, the songs of poets, the prayers of the church, and the favor of the Empire were preparing them an enduring place in the affections of all future times. That their virtues are more famous than their vices, their triumphs than their failures, is an admission which the just historian is indeed compelled to make. But if he be liberal as well as just he will not follow the admission with too stern a censure of the ingenuous fervor, the hearty, sincere, and innocent, though often uninformed enthusiasm, which magnifies in such a way the heroes of mediæval story. The sentiment which underlies these generous illusions is not without a certain value. For since the primitive Germanic society was the germ at once of the civil institutions and the civil capacities, which though once common to a whole race were finally preserved and suffered to obey the law of natural growth, little disturbed by alien influence, only in England and England's colonies, the tendency to idealize the heroes of feudal Germany, to see only the grand, noble, and glorious, not the petty and pernicious in mediæval life, is on the part of Anglo-Saxons one form of fraternal interest in a kindred people who afterwards snapped the ties that bound them to their own past, and corrupted the sources of their own strength. And from this inoffensive näiveté the Teutonic Knights have received even better treatment than they deserve. They were not true representatives of all, or even the best, instincts of German society; and their last hours were passed not in the valiant use of the arts which had once won them renown, but in the abuse of cruel powers which had been tolerable in the past only because they were lighted up by resplendent military virtues. And yet they merit respect because they were Germans, and efficiently served, though from narrow motives, the cause of German civilization.

8

Prussia, or Po-Russia, is a term by which the Germans designated the country stretching from the Vistula north-eastward along the Baltic. The inhabitants were
Preussen.
the Po-Russians. It has been much disputed between ethnologists whether they were Slavs or Teutons by race; and although patriotism makes the Germans claim them for kinsmen, science, more diffident, has not yet reached that conclusion. But it is certain that they were obstinate heathen and desperate warriors, who for centuries successfully resisted the arms and the missionaries of the German church. For the church was not averse to using both these instruments of conversion. The first attempt on the Prussians was made toward the end of the tenth century, by Bishop Adalbert of Prague, supported by Duke Boleslaw of Poland; but it was fiercely resisted, and the bishop fell a martyr to his zeal. His bones may be seen to this day by the pious, or the credulous, in the cathedral church of Gnesen. Two hundred years elapsed and the enterprise was again taken up, this time under the leadership of a monk named Christian, from the convent of Oliva. Christian met with some success, and was appointed bishop; but, as afterwards appeared, quite prematurely. The natives again rose against the invaders, defeated the force of adventurers called by Christian to his aid, and drove them back with terrible loss over the Vistula. Then the bishop applied to the Teutonic Knights, who had their headquarters at Venice and were unemployed. The grand master was one Hermann von Salza; and in his zeal for the Christian cause he did not neglect to secure a political position in Preussen, but in 1226 obtained a treaty, ratified by the Emperor, giving the territory to the order as a hereditary fief. The serious work of conquest then began.

The Knights proceeded with caution, and according to
The conquest.
the strictest rules of the military art. They fortified their way as they proceeded, and when

repulsed could retreat along a line of formidable posts. Here and there, as at Königsberg, Thorn, and Marienburg, they erected stately castles, the original strength of which is attested by the excellent state in which they yet present themselves to the tourist. But although the stout hearts of these warriors never failed, and they stood up in battle year after year against multitudes of desperate enemies, there came moments when their literal extinction seemed near, and then the cry for help rang throughout Germany. Fortunately help was generally at hand, for the enterprise was regarded almost as a new crusade. In 1255 King Ottocar of Bohemia joined the little band with a numerous army. Otho III. of Brandenburg found time for the fraternal duties of chivalry. And through the aid of these and other allies, but above all by the indomitable courage and persistence of the Knights themselves, the task was in the end accomplished; the Prussians sullenly submitted; the Christian religion was proclaimed; and the sway of the order was recognized throughout the land.

During the two succeeding centuries the work of defending Preussen was nearly as arduous as had been that of conquering it, and called into constant exercise the same heroic qualities. But with the fifteenth century the decline of the order began. The manner of the endless wars with Poland, in which the Knights *Decline of the order.* showed neither the wisdom of the serpent nor the courage of the lion; the fatal treaties in which they signed away the fairest portions of their land; the homage abjectly rendered to a neighbor whom they had often defied and always despised; and especially the ease with which, at the time of the Reformation, they discarded their military character and their Catholic religion, — all these warrant the belief that but little remained of the spirit which had once led the order to the shores of the Baltic; that the virtues of the early pioneers, thrift, energy, fortitude, endurance, religious enthusiasm, and martial valor, were no

longer present in the hour of danger. And this was in
spite of or perhaps in consequence of the steady growth of
the province in population and material prosperity. The
towns were growing in size and multiplying in number.
Trade flourished in every harbor. The rough surface,
the coarse texture of society were touched with the refining influence of commerce, travel, and wealth; and by
the fifteenth century the unlettered plowman, the simple
burgher, essayed to stammer the dialect of polite Germany.
But at that critical moment the Knights, the rulers and
leaders of the people, began themselves to waver. They
relaxed that stern discipline which had bound them together as a wall of iron. Laying aside the armor of
Christian warriors, they clothed themselves and paraded
grotesquely in the soft garments of oriental luxury. The
vows of temperance, which had once nerved the order to
the performance of great deeds, gave way to an emulation
of lust, a rivalry of dissipation, a contest of prodigality and
waste; until in the early part of the sixteenth century,
the course of decay being nearly completed, Albert of Hohenzollern caught up the sinking reins of government.[1]

The dark and gloomy lines in this picture are nevertheless not without a compensating relief. The
Enfranchise-
ment of the   order as a governing caste lost indeed both
people.
military and civil capacity, but from its weakness the mass of the people, its subjects, snatched the
opportunity of enfranchisement. Down to the year 1411,
it may be said, the people, of whatever degree, had no
part in the government.[2] The nobles, who went thither to

[1] Baczko's account of the decline and fall of the order, *Gesch. Preussens* (Königsberg, 1792–1806), iii. c. 1, is graphic and at times eloquent.

[2] It will be understood that I am here speaking of the central government. In their local affairs both the municipal and the rural
communes enjoyed many privileges; and the peasants were protected against wanton cruelty; but these rights and privileges did
not include any participation in political affairs. Besides the elabo-

lay the basis of an aristocracy; the burghers, who founded the busy towns and gave such an impetus to trade; the peasants, who in their humble way diffused over the land a high level of agricultural prosperity; — all wanted one distinctive quality of German freemen. It mattered little how the order governed so long as its government was arbitrary. It was endured for so many years not because it was good but because it was invulnerable; and on the first show of weakness the complaints of the people of Preussen rose louder than the cries of the victorious Poles.

A reluctant concession by the order to the estates was made under the influence of a calamity, the battle of Tannenberg in 1410. It consisted in the organization of a so-called national council [1] of nobles and burgesses, who had full political rights as estates, and were to be consulted on every great measure of public policy. But this innovation was hateful to the great body of the Knights. If powerless against foreign foes they could still vex and retard the course of liberation at home; and they threw Henry von Plauen, the grand master of the order, and the enlightened author of the reform, into prison. The national council was then abolished, or at least paralyzed by the withdrawal of its most important functions.

The natural consequence of such a policy was that the people were driven to conquer by force what they had failed to obtain as a measure of peaceful justice. With their spirit rose also their demands. A scheme in 1430 to restore the national council, and give it control especially of the public purse, was now inadequate to the situation; for in the year 1440 the towns and nobles formed an alliance, the famous Preussischer Bund, *Internal dissensions.*

rate histories of Baczko and Voigt, see Nauwerk, *Urkundliches zur Gesch. und Verf. der Provinz Preussen*, especially p. 21 et seq.

[1] Landesrath; see Baczko, iii. 154, Beilage XVIII.

and matured a complete plan of action.[1] The order was
rapidly going to pieces. Petulant outbursts of spite at the
rival prosperity of its subjects were its rare and only displays of vigor. Confronted by the league the grand master
appealed to the Emperor; and Frederic III. issued an
edict of dissolution, which the confederates received with
open derision. Overtures to Poland were anticipated by
the patriots, who in negotiating with their powerful ally
made somewhat free indeed with the territorial integrity
of the province, but otherwise secured an efficient guaranty
for their new political rights. And when after the victory
dissensions arose, as was natural, among the victors, and
the Knights answered the favor conspicuously shown by
Poland to the Slav population by granting still greater
privileges to the Germans, the artifice was too late to be
effective. The seat of the grand master was transferred
to Königsberg. West Preussen, or the territory west of the
Vistula, had been ceded to Poland; East Preussen was
only retained under Polish suzerainty; and the struggle
between the hostile races in the land offered no point
where the order could interfere for the recovery of its
lost prestige and authority.

Albert, who became grand master in 1511,[2] quickly
saw the impossibility of reconstructing the order
on the old basis. The office had in fact become
so generally associated with the ideas of hard
work, much danger, and little honor, with the duty and
yet the difficulty of reëstablishing a position forfeited by
years of gross misconduct, that new candidates were reluctant to try the hazardous and thankless experiment.
And Albert himself failed so long as he adhered to the
old methods. Poland insisted on the formality of homage,

Albert of
Hohenzol-
lern grand
master.

---

[1] See the articles of union in Nauwerk, p. 28. The hero of the coalition was Hans von Baysen, a brave, adventurous, and sagacious man.
See Baczko, iii. 189 et seq.

[2] Son of Frederic of Anspach, and grandson of Albert Achilles.

which was the condition of East Preussen's possession by
the order; and when the grand master knocked at the
doors of the German states for aid he received only advice.   But while only the masters of legions could give
aid anybody could give advice, and that of Luther and
Melancthon proved to be the soundest.   The secularization of the order, and the introduction of Protestantism, which they counselled, were nearly   Secularization of the
equivalent measures.   Both were facilitated by   order.
the progress which the reformed religion had already made
in Preussen, for even many of the Knights had secretly
embraced its doctrines, and the lay population was still
farther advanced in the path of apostasy.   Everything was
ripe for the revolution which Albert proclaimed in 1525.

It is possible that the King of Poland had greater
hopes of succeeding to a secularized duchy, which had also
become Protestant, than to the control of an order, which
being originally German should also remain Catholic.
The Knights were long the wards of papal Germany.
They had, indeed, been left at a critical moment to fight
and lose their own battles; but Frederic III. was a weak
prince, and while the Empire might not deplore   Attitude of
an event which briefly reduced the pride and   Poland.
arrogance of the order, it would very unwillingly have
seen the Polish arms drive out the last representatives of
German culture in the northeast.   But the secularization
and the conversion of the Knights caused them to forfeit,
in a double sense, the sympathy of the church, and with
the sympathy of the church vanished the patronage and
protection of the Emperor.   Poland was left the favorite
Catholic power of northern Europe.   She had a right,
therefore, to expect for her diplomacy and for her arms,
and in spite of the alien or rival blood that flowed in the
veins of her people, the preference of that great commonwealth which, under the emperors of the time, had
but too often shown how much dearer to it were the for-

tunes of the Holy Roman Church than those of the Teutonic race and polity. Charles V. actually endeavored to
arrest the course of events in Preussen, and procured
from the Diet repeated condemnations of Albert. These
measures were impotent; but they show that, up to a certain point, Poland had reasoned well. She made friends
for herself among the orthodox by betraying her rival into
heresy.

The King of Poland, then, not only did not oppose, but
seems even to have encouraged the dissolution of the order.
His suzerainty was reasserted, though over a temporal
and Protestant duchy; but as all the hopes which he had
founded on his subtle policy proved delusive, the transaction was wholly and singularly advantageous to Albert.[1]

The circumstances in which they had been politically
organized were not without influence on the character and
career of the estates of the new Duchy. Fused into a
homogeneous mass, the disestablished fraternity and the
rest of the population — nobles, knights, and burgesses,
excluding only the peasants — were pervaded by a common sentiment of pride and independence, beyond what could probably be witnessed in any
other part of Germany. The shaping experi-
ences were different, but the visible results were the same.
The Knights, of course, preserved for generations the
traditions of the order to which their ancestors had belonged, and retained the spirit of command long after
they had laid aside its symbols, and, dissolved into the
system of civil society, were living under the sceptre of
Brandenburg. With these disendowed yet still haughty
pioneers was associated a body of freemen, whose fran-

The Duke
and the es-
tates.

---

[1] Robertson, *Charles V.* ii. 375–376 (ed. Basle, 1788), gives a singularly partial account, which might have been written by Walter von
Eronberg, of what he calls Albert's "usurpation." If Albert was
an usurper, how many of the contemporary dynasties of Germany
were legitimate?

chises, though recent, were prized as the trophies of a prolonged and heroic struggle. It mattered little that the struggle was against, and that their franchises had been won from the order itself. The erection of an hereditary secular duchy revolutionized all the relations of the state, — those of the several social classes to one another, and those of the whole society to the central organ ; and in a very short time the opposition between crown and people became so conspicuous that minor jealousies were dazzled by its glare, and ceased to assert their helpless petulance. The estates were united by the common necessity of resisting the common foe; and the history of their resistance to arbitrary power is not the least creditable chapter in the annals of the Prussian state.

It remains only to state briefly the course of events by which the Duchy of Preussen was added to the dominions of the House of Brandenburg.

Albert died in 1568, leaving but two male heirs through whom the succession could be perpetuated in his own, the Franconian, branch of the family; after them, and in the absence of further heirs, the Duchy would revert, under feudal law, to the crown of Poland. It was therefore the duty of Brandenburg to avert such a disaster. For a long time Poland stubbornly and brusquely refused to enter into any arrangement; but Joachim II., having the aid of his wife, a Polish princess, and of Distelmeier, the astute chancellor, finally carried his point, and the co-enfeoffment of the electors in Preussen was solemnly proclaimed. In case of the extinction of Albert's line, the Duchy was to pass to the kindred line of Brandenburg. This was in 1569, one year after the accession of Albert Frederic, Albert's son. The second duke was a poor imbecile, weak both in mind and in body ; and before he had reigned many years it was found necessary to ask Poland for the appointment of a regent. The choice fell upon George Frederic, Margrave of Jä-

Branden-
burg and
Preussen.

gerndorf. But he died in 1603, and the office was then reluctantly conceded by Poland to Joachim Frederic, Elector of Brandenburg, to whom, as to his son and successor, John Sigismond, the notables of Preussen had a most violent repugnance. Father and son had each espoused a daughter of Albert Frederic and his wife, the Mary Eleanor of Cleve, above described ; and a new title was thus added to their claim on the Duchy. The unfortunate Duke finally died in 1618, and John Sigismond entered upon his inheritance. Poland threw many obstacles in the way of this result and no little diplomacy was needed to overcome them ; but in the end the Republic consented that the Elector should become Duke of Preussen on the acknowledgment of its own suzerainty.

1618.

John Sigismond himself survived the event only one year ; and release from the trouble of asserting his authority over his new subjects may have been an advantage which measurably softened the pangs of death. For although his title was sound, according to the legal and political conceptions of the age, and although that method of disposing of Preussen doubtless saved it from a worse fate, the people protested, as two centuries earlier the people of the Mark had protested, against such simple and summary transactions. In modern Europe there is more respect, at least, for appearances. The process of acquisition is surrounded by ingenious forms or fictions, — treaties, conquest, congresses, the argument from nationalities, from the need of geographical symmetry, of lines of defence, of scientific frontiers ; now and then the people themselves are admitted to have rights, though they may be secretly betrayed or openly ignored in the end ; — by such devices modern civilization palliates acts of violence no less grave than those by which mediæval princes founded their houses and built up their territories. In principle there is therefore very little difference between the fate of Savoy or Alsace

John Sigismond.

in recent times, and the fate of Brandenburg or Preussen centuries ago. In the one case the victims are coolly trans-ferred as the spoils or the indemnity of war; in the other, they are bought or inherited like a farm, or a house, or a yoke of oxen. But between the two cases there are sev-eral differences of detail ,which ought not to be over-looked. The proceedings of the mediæval prince were justified not only by the law but also by the ethics of his time. If the church opposed him, it was from interest, not from principle. The philosophers were silent. He was condemned by no authoritative censor of morals ; and he doubtless proceeded with a clear conscience to occupy lands which had become his through purchase in the open market, through marriage, or through the death of some favorite uncle. But, on the other hand, the people of a modern province know that their annexation will be en-forced by vast armies, and completed by a subtle and om-nipresent political authority, in whose acts they can only acquiesce ; while the founder of a new dynasty in a terri-tory of the Middle Ages was sparely endowed with military or political resources, and often had to fight his way into his dominions foot by foot through weary years. The illegality of the transaction in the one case does not pre-vent a sullen submission ; its legality in the other did not prevent a violent and determined resistance. But the substantial injustice is the same in both methods, and is not affected by contemporary theories of ethics, or the varying facilities of political coercion.

It was the fortune of John Sigismond and his successor to acquire a title, which was sound according to feudal law, and was opposed according to feudal tactics. The nobles and burghers of Preussen were little acquainted with the maxims and syllogisms of speculative politics, but they conceived that they had certain rights and were disposed to maintain them. And the weakness of the intruder gave them an opportunity of resistance.

Resistance in Preussen.

Defiant resolutions of the Diet, the sullenness of powerful
nobles, outbreaks in the towns, intrigues with Poland, in-
flammatory sermons by the clergy, embassies to the Emperor, — such were the resources of the Duchy, and,
obstinately used, they harassed the House of Brandenburg
long after the death of John Sigismond.

It will of course be understood that the Diet of
Preussen remained an organization quite distinct
from the Diet of Brandenburg. Through all
the territorial changes of the fifteenth and sixteenth centuries the Kurmark was preserved as a political unit, from
which the margrave derived the electoral dignity, and
which in domestic affairs was a defined district, both for
the operation of the central authority and for the coöperation of the estates. But in Preussen the Elector was
not a margrave but a duke, and even this honor he held
only under the patronage of Poland. The attempt to combine this province with Brandenburg would, therefore, have
been contrary to reason and policy. It would have been
resisted, and probably defeated, by jealous neighbors.

The Diet of Preussen.

John Sigismond's reign is of no special importance in
the history of inner organization and development. He receives the unusual panegyric at
the hands of national writers; is pronounced
earnest, sagacious, moderate, and conscientious; the welfare of his country and people was his constant concern.
There is, indeed, no special reason for doubting that his
intentions were good. He was guilty of no deliberate
offence against the liberties of the state, and professed to
be willing to administer the government as he had received it from his fathers. But the discontent of a prince's
subjects is evidence that his policy, however well-meant, is
at least unpopular; and the latter half of John Sigismond's career was vexed by the united complaints of the
nobles, the clergy, and the people in general. The leading cause of these dissensions was apparently trivial

The Elector's change of faith.

enough, — the Elector's change from Lutheranism to Calvinism.[1] To the practical modern mind this step, if it proceeded from reasons of conviction and not of policy, and especially since it was only the substitution of one form of Protestantism for another, seems purely a private affair of the Elector, for which he was accountable only to his own conscience. But this is an inadequate view of the affair. It ignores both the circumstances in which the Reformation had been carried through in Brandenburg, and the nature of the relations between church and state in the seventeenth century.

The reader has already seen that in the Mark the Reformation was not the work of the prince alone, but of prince and people united and coöperating. It must also be observed that the movement was not a merely negative one, not a movement simply of hostility to Rome, but one which had positive aims, and which, after it had destroyed, proceeded to rebuild according to a plan deliberately chosen. That much dogmatic controversy, much balancing of creeds and liturgies, preceded the final act, is of course improbable. But as an act of state, the adoption of Luther's religion rather than Zwingle's was as binding upon the officials of the Elector as any other measure of regular legislation ; and the denial of its regularity, though perfectly consistent on the part of the Catholic church, would have been absurd in the mouths of Calvinists, who, where they had numbers and power, adopted the same policy. If, therefore, the Reformation was correct in form, its only legitimate offspring in the Mark was the Lutheran church.

Now the new position which the Reformation gave to the Elector in ecclesiastical affairs, and the not inconsiderable increase of political power *Examination of the step.* which he derived from that position, from the confiscation of the church lands, and from the secularization of so

[1] Comp. Stenzel, i. 387 et seq.

much clerical authority, imposed upon him in a correspondingly greater degree the obligation of constancy and fidelity. The accident of birth had put him in possession of an entailed estate. The coöperation of his ancestors with the ancestors of his subjects had made a certain religious polity the basis of one class of social relations; and it follows that any arbitrary attempt to overthrow that adjustment was a breach of trust and a species of revolution. That John Sigismond only claimed the right to exercise a personal discretion, which he granted in turn to the meanest of his subjects,[1] was creditable to his liberality or his indifference, but nothing more. His private views were one thing and his public policy was another; but his position as head of the church, and the vast patronage which he enjoyed in ecclesiastical affairs, made it extremely probable that the legal preponderance of Lutheranism in the official councils would cease, that the dissenting sect would begin to share the favors of the crown, and that the constitution would thus be essentially changed. This is the view which the Lutherans of the Mark might have taken. From their standpoint the Elector seemed to be guilty of perjury as well as of apostasy, and even the theological rancor which embittered the quarrel was neither new nor surprising.

Luther himself had given the example of an intolerance which stopped only short of the rack and the stake, and against which the gentler Melancthon was nearly powerless. The German Protestants were divided against themselves. In the south and along the Rhine Calvinism was popular and the Heidelberg Confession had been adopted. The pact of Augsburg, which founded a brief religious peace, and gave the Lutherans recognition in the Empire, was supported in the northern territories. But geographical lines were not

Lutheranism and Calvinism.

[1] See his declaration to that effect quoted by Pierson, *Pr. Gesch.* p. 80.

strictly observed, and Luther had found it expedient to
open a school at Halle as an additional barrier against
the encroachments of the rival though kindred sect.
Luther's bigotry and arrogance were transmitted by him
to his disciples, and thus perpetuated through many generations. They learned to pursue Calvinists as fiercely as
Catholics. It was owing to this spirit that the struggling
Protestants of France were denied the indispensable support of the most powerful sect of their brethren in Germany; and that Lutheranism and Calvinism, reluctant to
act together even in the most deadly crisis of the Thirty
Years' War, were nearly crushed one after the other under
the iron heel of Austria. The literature of the sixteenth
century will furnish the inquirer an edifying notion of the
tone in which controversy was carried on from the chairs
of the universities and the pulpits of the church.

The Catholic princes, some of whom had learned dialec-
tics in the Jesuit schools, made an adroit use of
the schisms in the evangelical party. At the _Catholics and Prot-estants._
imperial Diet of 1608 the Emperor's represen-
tative gave a gloomy hint of impending danger by asserting that the Augsburg Confession was no longer the creed
of the Protestants, and that since the religious truce had
been practically broken by the Lutherans, it was not binding on the Catholics. A common alarm seized both wings
of the Protestant party, and the famous Union was
formed. The Catholics responded with the League.
The forbearance which the Emperors Charles V. and Ferdinand I. had shown toward the Protestants was replaced
in their successors, Rudolph II., Matthias, and Ferdinand
II., by a vindictive fanaticism, encouraged and directed
by the agents of Rome. The counter-movement was begun in Bohemia, where the memory of Huss still survived.
Ferdinand, as King of Bohemia, having arrogantly violated the most solemn rights of the Protestants, an uprising followed, and the enraged people threw three of their

most active persecutors out of the historic castle window. Matthias, the Emperor, who was timid as well as cruel, offered but slight resistance. The Bohemians were joined by gallant allies from Protestant Germany, an army was organized, and the insurgents marched to the very gates of Vienna. The Thirty Years' War was begun.

In the midst of these stirring events John Sigismond died, and was succeeded by his son, George William. To the weakness, the vacillation, the duplicity of this prince is commonly ascribed the inglorious past which Brandenburg played in the great religious struggle.

The Thirty Years' War.

He was a Calvinist like his father. Like his father he joined the Union; but he gave it only a feeble and heartless support, which angered the Emperor without satisfying the Protestants. His subjects in the electorate were suspicious of the Union, which they regarded as a mere device of the Calvinists. The estates of Preussen refused homage to an apostate. Sigismond, King of Poland, was offended because the Elector's sister had espoused Gustavus Adolphus of Sweden, and the Swede was estranged by the refusal of his brother-in-law to form an alliance. In Cleve the Dutch and the Spaniards confronted each other; and while aliens thus disputed the fact of possession, the right of property, as between the original litigants, receded apparently farther and farther from the point of settlement. A strong prince might have risen above all these embarrassments, but George William could only temporize, expostulate, and dissemble.

George William. 1619.

The infatuation of the Brandenburg populace, the aggressive obstinacy of the Prussian estates were not without illustrious examples among the most powerful princes of the Lutheran faith. When the cause of Protestantism was in danger there ought to have been but one party and no hesitation in Saxony, the

Attitude of the Lutherans.

birthplace of the Reformation, and a state whose alliance could almost turn the scale one way or the other; but the Elector's jealousy of Calvinistic rivals, and the hope of substantial rewards from the Emperor, led him to a species of armed neutrality, scarcely less advantageous to the imperialists than an open alliance. A regiment of English soldiers, tardily sent by James I. to the aid of Bohemia, was suffered by George William, to the horror and alarm of his subjects, to traverse the Mark. The Saxons barred them the way on the upper Elbe. Brandenburg was accused of insincerity toward the Emperor; the Saxons invaded Lausitz and threatened the Old Mark. This policy was agreeable to the narrow and selfish view which the Lutherans took of the crisis, and the imperialists were left unopposed. Bohemia was crushed under an overwhelming force. The reformed religion disappeared in fire and blood. The Count Palatine,[1] who showed little nerve in the hour of trial, was robbed of his electoral dignity, and his vote conferred on Bavaria. Then at length the Saxon court and the Lutherans awoke to the supreme peril of the situation.

In Brandenburg three forces were at work in as many different directions. The great mass of the people and the estates as a corporation were less concerned, even after the bloody drama in Bohemia, about the aggressions of the Catholics, and the prospect of a reaction which should sweep away every form of dissent, than about the advantage which Calvinism might gain from a general league of all Protestants against the Emperor. The Privy Council, as reorganized by John Sigismond, was Calvinistic in tone, and favorable to prompt action. And the Elector's chief minister, Count Adam von Schwarzenberg,

---

[1] Son-in-law of James I. of England; he had been chosen King of Bohemia by the Protestant estates. John George of Jägerndorf (an appanage of the Brandenburg House) was also put under the ban, and the principality sequestrated.

was a Roman Catholic, and accounted a secret tool of the
Emperor. George William had known Schwarzenberg
in Cleve, where during the previous reign he had held an
administrative office, and had been promptly promoted, on
the accession of his new patron, to the highly honorable
and confidential post of chancellor.[1] The count was undoubtedly a man of no little talent. He was highly educated, prompt in decision, of a restless energy, polished,
elegant, adroit, insinuating; his ascendency over the Elector was complete. Widely as his policy differed from that
which was urged by the Privy Council, and which ought to
have been the policy of Brandenburg, it has never been
shown that he designed any actual treachery; since it was
possible for a true Catholic to believe that the interests of
the Mark lay in the line of a good understanding with the
Emperor. But an open alliance was at the time out of
the question, and the attitude of timid neutrality taken by
George William served the imperialists nearly as well.

The Privy Council was, therefore, driven to undertake
a scheme of secret diplomacy. One of its members, Bellin,
a stern Calvinist, was sent to Stockholm to sound Gustavus Adolphus, and found him ready for action on certain
conditions; thence to Copenhagen, where Christian IV.
was not less ready, though on conditions irreconcilable
with those of the Swede; and finally to Paris and London,
where much disinterested advice but no pledge of active
assistance was given.[2] At both the French and the English
courts the feeling was, however, more favorable to Denmark than to Sweden, and it became clear that until a
campaign should be tried under Christian the field would
not be ripe for Gustavus Adolphus.

The Danish King marched with 7,000 men through
Holstein and Mecklenburg to the Elbe. On the
Leading gen-
erals.   way he was joined by Duke Christian of Brunswick, one of the few clear-sighted and resolute Protestant

---

[1] See Stenzel, i. 444.   [2] Droysen, III. i. 33.

princes, and by the veteran Mansfield, whose fidelity could be shaken by no inequality of numbers, no amount of misfortune, no degree of ill-treatment. The united forces were not over 60,000 strong. Opposed to them stood Tilly and Wallenstein, — Tilly the conqueror and despoiler of Bohemia, fresh from the Rhine and the Palatinate, where he had crushed one after the other the armies of Mansfield and Brunswick, eager, unwearied, cruel, fanatical; Wallenstein, the new favorite of Kaiser and Pope, a scholar and a politician, fond of wealth and power, arrogant in his feelings, despotic in his manner, fearless and unscrupulous in his conduct, — two leaders who made the heart of the Emperor throb with exultation, and whom only the most reckless of his enemies dared to face. Europe was appalled, Catholic France no less than Protestant England, and in breathless anxiety awaited the clash of arms.

The storm was gathering at the very doors of Brandenburg, and Brandenburg remained — neutral. What had Protestantism, indeed, to expect from a state which was ruled by a timid and capricious prince, had a Roman Catholic for chief minister, estates bitterly hostile to Calvinism, a Privy Council destitute of systematic powers, a people enervated by a century of peace and impoverished by schemes of aggrandizement on the Rhine and on the Baltic? The Elector's appeals lacked the emphasis of a firm will guiding a clear policy, and carried no conviction to those to whom they were addressed. It was with difficulty that he could procure from the Diet a small subsidy for the equipment of 3,000 men; and even this grant the estates burdened with the condition that their "ultimate seigneur, the Emperor, be treated with proper respect" and that the guidance of Saxony be meekly accepted. Irresolution seemed to paralyze every enterprise of George William. Schwarzenberg was sent into Transylvania to explain why his master could not join the movement for reviving the Protestant Union; and the heroic Bethlen

Gabor, in natural disgust at such imbecility, thought for a moment of applying to the Turks for relief.[1] The Elector flitted between Berlin and Königsberg, finding only discord and despair. He complained that he was universally despised and insulted; the world, he said, must hold him to be a paltry coward, that he could only fold his arms and sit still in such a crisis. Of the estates he alleged that they had "delayed and hindered everything necessary for the land." And the estates retorted that they had "been left like sheep without a shepherd to destruction."

In the mean time the neutrality of the Mark, the acceptance of which by the belligerents had been made conditional on the seizure of the fords of the Elbe and the Havel by the Elector's troops, was repeatedly violated by one general after another as occasion required. Mansfield was the pioneer in this policy. The fords had not been guarded as the Elector had promised, and in February, 1626, Mansfield crossed to the right bank of the Elbe; swept across the Mark to Rathenow and Brandenburg, which he occupied; and levied contributions as from the subjects of an enemy. But to reach Bethlen Gabor, whom he aimed to join, he had to recross the Elbe, and Wallenstein was at Dessau with a powerful army commanding the bridge. Mansfield was more brave than prudent. He chafed under inaction, and attempting to storm the position of the imperialists he was completely defeated, and his army scattered to the four winds of heaven. Westward of the Elbe the coalition fared no better. Tilly carried out faithfully his part in the imperialist strategy, by moving around the Harz Mountains into Brunswick, and thus preventing any coöperation between the two wings of the Protestant army. The Danish king advanced to meet him, but refused an engagement. On the report of Mansfield's disaster Christian abandoned the field, and retreated ignominiously northward.

Mansfield and Wallenstein.

[1] Droysen, III. i. 37.

Neither of the belligerents now made even a show of respecting Brandenburg's neutrality. Mansfield, who had rallied his forces and found some new recruits, again broke into the Mark, and crossing the Oder bore down through Silesia and Moravia toward Bethlen Gabor. Wallenstein followed him closely, and as was his custom made the country through which he passed support his army. But a second engagement was not reached. The brave Mansfield died a fugitive in Bosnia ; his successor lived but a few days ; and Bethlen Gabor hastened to make peace with Wallenstein. The victor then retraced his steps ; again traversed Brandenburg in spite of the Elector's protests, leaving the marks of his progress in wasted fields and ruined households ; joined his forces to those of Tilly, who in the interval had overtaken and routed Christian ; and together the two pursued the fugitives to the very shores of the Baltic.

Invasions of the Mark.

The one redeeming event in this season of disaster was the defence of Stralsund. While the armies of the coalition were dissolving under the blows of the imperialists, and the great territorial lords were bowing in terror at the feet of Ferdinand, the rude burghers of Stralsund met Wallenstein with a courage and a confidence equal to his own, beat back with terrible slaughter the veterans whom he hurled against the walls, calmly endured month after month the thunders of his artillery, and forced him at last to abandon the task and take an unheroic revenge on the helpless towns of the neighborhood.[1]

Heroic defence of Stralsund.

With this exception, which was but an episode, though a glorious one, the triumph of the imperialists was complete. In the whole length and breadth of Germany no enemy opposed them ; and every electoral prince, every petty vassal, neutral or belligerent,

Triumph of the Emperor.

[1] The sequestration of Pomerania was decreed by the Emperor, and Brandenburg's right of expectancy coolly ignored.

awaited in anxious suspense the announcement of Ferdinand's terms. They proved to be as severe as the most timid Protestant had feared, or the malice of the Jesuits could suggest.

In March, 1628, appeared the famous imperial Edict of Edict of   Restitution. It first decreed that all church Restitution. property sequestered since the Treaty of Passau should be restored ; second, granted to every Catholic prince the right to impose his religion upon his people ; third, withdrew all concessions previously made to the Calvinists, and recognized only the Lutherans as entitled to toleration ; and, fourth, threatened with the ban of the Empire all who should oppose the edict. By one act, therefore, the most precious rights of the Protestants were swept away.

Tilly and Wallenstein were charged with the execution of the edict, — a congenial task, which they performed with their usual vigor. But the land was so exhausted, the names of the two Catholic soldiers were so formidable, that little resistance was offered except by the rich and Siege of   flourishing town of Magdeburg. The city fought Magdeburg. with a desperation equal to Stralsund's, but not with equal success ; and the story of the atrocities committed by Tilly's troops after its fall is still read with horror by the civilized world. In the great adjustment of accounts which followed the advent of calmer times the massacre and pillage at Magdeburg were charged by the House of Hapsburg upon the League of Catholic princes. Tilly was indeed their officer, and Tilly's brigands were their contingent ; while Wallenstein and his troops were the contribution of Austria. And even before Tilly's cruel achievement discord had arisen among the members of the august alliance, leading finally at the Diet of Regensburg in 1630 almost to an open rupture. The princes were apprehensive about the sudden growth of the imperial power, and saw in the arrogance of Ferdinand a spirit hostile to their own independence. Wallenstein lay outside the city with an army of 100,000 men. He was known to be ambitious, and the Diet was in his power. The League summoned Ferdinand, therefore, to dismiss his dangerous servant and Ferdinand complied, though with grave doubts about the result; but to the sur- Fall of prise and relief of the Diet the Emperor's order Wallenstein. was obeyed. The Friedlander laid down his command, took leave of his soldiers, and retired to his estates in Bohemia.

The restitution edict was as false in policy as it was inhuman in purpose.[1] It gratified three classes, the Spaniards, the Catholic princes, and the Jesuits of the imperial court; but it shocked and alarmed the Protestants all over the Empire, Lutherans scarcely less than Calvinists, and at once gave a new turn to diplomatic negotiations. Mansfield's invasions of the Mark Effect of the had for a time well served the purpose of Edict. Schwarzenberg. It is true that the imperialists had also shown no respect for Brandenburg's neutrality; but they, it was ingeniously explained, were the troops of the Elector's superior. The laws and constitution of the Empire were stretched to cover their offence, and Ferdinand sent a special ambassador to Berlin to apologize, to explain away the affront, to promise indemnity. In July, 1626, another insult had been offered to the Elector by the Protestant party. Gustavus Adolphus had landed at Pillau, seized the forts and fortresses of Preussen, and thus begun the war with Poland. George William was in despair. There seemed no alternative: "I must go over to the Emperor," declared he; "what interest have I in the common cause, if I am to lose all my honor and reputation?" Fear of the Emperor, who was threatening him with the ban, the restless intrigues of Schwarzen-

[1] In the Memoirs of Cardinal Richelieu, the Emperor's envoy is made to charge the edict upon the League.

berg and Dohna, the ambassador, and the contemptuous
conduct of the Swedes, had nearly led him to a positive decision, when the news of the edict spread through Germany, and threw the unfortunate prince once more into a
panic.

About the same time affairs on the Vistula took a more
Sweden and
Poland. favorable turn. The Poles had been routed in
every engagement which they had attempted
against Gustavus Adolphus, and a regiment of Brandenburg troops, sent to vindicate the neutrality of Preussen,
had thrown down their arms at the sight of the Swedes.[1]
As a last resort the Emperor sent an army toward the
scene of action, although there had been no declaration of
war against the Empire, and the King of the Swedes was
nominally in search only of the Poles. But the imperialist
demonstration gave him a convenient pretext for widening
the sphere of operations.

Against Austria, Poland, and Brandenburg, Gustavus
Gustavus
Adolphus.
1630. would, however, have had a difficult struggle,
and it did not suit the purpose of France to see
the gallant Swede crushed in such an unequal
contest. France undertook, therefore, to mediate, and
with success. Aided by England the French court
brought about, in October, 1629, an armistice for six years
between Sweden and Poland, thus leaving Gustavus Adolphus confronted only by Austria and the Catholic League.
He returned accordingly to his own country, raised and
equipped a small force, and in the following summer
landed again in Germany.[2] The imperial court and the
young officers made merry over the enterprise, and planned
the prompt annihilation of the invaders. Tilly alone was
wiser. He measured the danger with the eye of an experienced soldier, and the man who had faced death on so

[1] Stenzel, i. 452.
[2] On the 24th of June, 1630, the hundredth anniversary of the
Augsburg Confession.

many battle-fields could not imperil his reputation for courage by urging the need of prudence and circumspection.

In the mean time the Swedes pressed southward through Pomerania, easily brushing every obstacle out of their path, until at length they halted at the frontiers of Brandenburg. It was another crit- ical moment for George William. The Swedish King was in no humor for trifling even with his brother-in-law, and he pressed the Elector for a decision. Tilly was drawing his lines remorselessly about Magdeburg; the situation of the town was daily growing more desperate; Gustavus Adolphus was burning with anxiety to relieve the heroic garrison; and George William wasted precious time in timid deliberation. It was not until the King drew up before Berlin, and trained his guns upon the town, that he succeeded in carrying his point.[1] By a treaty with the Elector he secured his rear and his communications, and then he hastened upon his urgent mission. On the borders of Saxony he was met by further protests and further dissimulation, this time from the Elector John George, and during this delay the fall of Magdeburg was announced. The King justly charged the fate of the city to the disgraceful conduct of the two Protestant princes.[2]

Coerces Brandenburg and Saxony.

May, 1631.

In the end, however, the arguments and threats of Gustavus Adolphus prevailed, and both Saxony and Brandenburg were induced to promise a species of coöperation against the Emperor. And then began the Swedish campaign of 1631–32, a campaign which, in the nobility of its motives, the brilliancy of its

Swedish campaign in Germany.

[1] Comp. Carlyle, *History of Friedrich the Second* (ed. New York, 1874), i. 256.

[2] The Protestant administrator of Magdeburg, a Hohenzollern, and uncle of George William, was put under the ban for resisting the Edict of Restitution.

execution, the suddenness of its results, is surpassed by no
other in the annals of warfare, ancient or modern. The
combined armies of the two Electors entered Bohemia
and laid siege to Prague. Gustavus Adolphus chose the
scene of danger; saved Saxony by defeating Tilly at
Breitenfeld; swept in triumph through the heart of the
Empire to the Rhine; returned to meet Wallenstein, on
whom in his alarm the Emperor had again called; saved
Saxony from Wallenstein as before from Tilly;
and in the victory of Lützen gave up his own
life for the cause of Protestantism and religious freedom
in Germany.

November, 1632.

With the death of their great leader the grasp of the
Swedes upon the two electors sensibly relaxed.
Saxony fell away from the coalition, and drew
back within the lines of her original selfish
policy. The minister Schwarzenberg, who had wisely
fled from Berlin on the approach of Gustavus Adolphus,
returned to his master, recovered his subtle influence, and
proclaimed again the neutrality of the Mark. The action
of these two powers was hastened by the belief, which was
common to nearly all Germany, that the Protestant cause
was lost, and that the Emperor would soon be again triumphant. But the outlook proved deceptive. Although
Gustavus Adolphus was dead his political genius survived
in his chancellor, Oxenstiern, and his military genius, or
part of it, in generals like Banner and Wrangel; at least
one accomplished German soldier, Bernard of Weimar,
remained true; France paralyzed the efforts of Spain;
the imperialist hopes now centred in Wallenstein alone;
and the relations of this powerful leader with his employ-
ers were lamed by mutual distrust, jealousy, and hatred.

Defection
of Saxony
and Bran-
denburg.

In the war which was now resumed, and raged with
strange vicissitudes all over Germany, the participation of
Brandenburg was faint and uncertain, passed soon into a
suspicious neutrality, and at length into a complete change

of front. The Elector of Saxony had already made his peace with the Emperor in the Treaty of Prague, May, 1635. Some increase of territory was promised the traitor, and some concessions, more apparent than real, were made to the Lutheran Protestants. George William was likewise tempted with a petty bribe, the recognition of his right of succession in Pomerania. This the Swedes had contested. The Elector hesitated for a time; but in July followed the example of his Saxon ally, and gave in his adhesion to the Emperor. This was followed by active military coöperation, and Brandenburg troops took the field against the Swedes. The Diet having approved this course, the Elector's treachery was constitutionally correct; but there was a good deal of debate and controversy between the members, and the towns especially seem to have been not unfavorable to the Swedish alliance. For the charge that Schwarzenberg, who conducted the negotiations, anticipated his master's decision in signing the treaty, I cannot find sufficient authority.

The treaty between the Elector and Ferdinand contained no allusion either to the Duchy of Preussen or the possessions of George William on the Rhine; and while Swedes and imperialists are again devastating the Mark, one party after the other, as the fortunes of the war change, a brief paragraph must be given to the two outlying provinces.

The Treaty of Xanten, concluded in 1614, and renewed with slight modifications in 1630, had divided the contested territory between Brandenburg and Pfalz-Neuburg. But during the Thirty Years' War neither party obtained more than a nominal possession. The Emperor continued to assert his own claim; and for many years the country was the battle-ground of Spaniards and Dutch, while the theoretical rulers were hardly consulted or considered. Even after 1631, when the Spaniards were expelled, the Dutch remained in occupation, and the land was required to support their garrisons. The state in which these trials left the people themselves was naturally deplorable enough.

Preussen was somewhat more fortunate. It lay beyond
Issues in   the sphere of hostilities between Swedes and im-
Preussen.   perialists, and since the conclusion of peace be-
tween Sweden and Poland had been left in the enjoyment of an enviable tranquillity. The troubles which George William had in the Duchy were therefore chiefly domestic. They concerned the feudal connection with Poland, the powers and privileges of the estates, the exemptions of the cities, the prerogatives of the prince, the subjects of military service and fiscal contribution; matters perplexing enough in themselves, but local and to that extent, therefore, simple. Some of these relations, too, the Elector succeeded in modifying in a sense favorable to himself and his pretensions. Restrictions were put upon the right of appeal to Poland, of which the territorial gentry had made such frequent use in the past. Limits were drawn about the right of intervention and supervision claimed by the Diet of Warsaw. And the rivalry between the nobles and the towns was utilized by George William for increasing his own privileges at the cost of local autonomy, one of the few real achievements of his reign.

George William removed his court to Königsberg in Preussen in 1638, the impoverished Mark no longer affording the means for its support. Schwarzenberg remained behind as viceroy. But his tried and recognized fidelity to the Emperor was no security against the excesses of the Emperor's troops; and the Swedes, fallen from the stern discipline of Gustavus Adolphus, plundered as relentlessly as Pappenheim's dragoons. Every bond of unity between the Elector's different territories was broken; anarchy was present, and political dissolution seemed near.

At this threatening crisis George William died, and his

son Frederic William succeeded him as elector. A youth of twenty, his life had been spent in study rather than action, in watching the storms that swept over Europe, not in trying or tempting their fury; but the age was one which drilled the observant not less than the practical faculties, and the opportunities of the prince had been good. He had spent several years at the Hague, and might have drawn the inspiration of a just ruler from the history of Holland. The traditions of her war of independence, the memory of her patriots and heroes, the daily example of her civil and political virtues, — what could be better fitted to impress the mind of an ingenuous youth with the most liberal theories and the most upright maxims of public conduct?

Death of George William. 1640.

The prince electoral had never enjoyed the favor of Schwarzenberg. That astute politician had discovered in him early germs of insubordination; and although he approved the plan of his systematic isolation from the Berlin court, the choice of Holland for his residence was correctly held to be inauspicious for the Austrian party and policy in Brandenburg. Nor was the minister pleased with the influence which the prince's mother exercised over him. Both the wife and the mother of George William were devout Calvinists, and strong partisans of the Swedish alliance; and as often as the prince visited Berlin he was taught views of public policy which differed as widely in character from those of Schwarzenberg as they differed in intensity from those of the Elector. There were even rumors, which Droysen does not distinctly reject,[1] that the chancellor was concerned in plots to poison the zealous neophyte. Be that as it may, the prince began his task with clear notions of its nature, its limitations, its difficulties; and almost simultaneously with his accession gave a new impulse to public affairs.

Elector Frederic William.

The manner in which the young Elector played fast

[1] III. i. 131.

with his engagements to the Emperor, to the Swedes, to

His diplo-   Poland, could perhaps be justified by the ethics
macy.   of diplomacy as understood at the time. No
one ought to have excused such duplicity more readily
than Schwarzenberg, who was himself one of its earliest
victims. It being held desirable for a time to keep up
good relations with the imperial court, that intriguing
minister was tolerated in office until the secret negotiations with Sweden should be concluded, and the Elector's
plot be ripe for execution.

That the Mark needed time for rest and recuperation
was clear enough. After being for many years the common prey of friend and foe, of Austrian and Swede, it was
now suffering scarcely less from its own demoralized and
State of the   lawless soldiery. They too had caught the un-
Mark.   happy infection of the age.[1] They robbed and
burned and killed as cheerfully as the alien intruders,
making no distinction between their own people and their
enemies ; and yet as soldiers they were almost beneath
contempt. To reduce such freebooters to discipline and
obedience was impossible. To disarm, disband, and reorganize them was by no means easy, but it could be tried
as soon as actual hostilities with the Swedes should be
suspended. Fortunately for the Elector he had in this
policy the sympathy and coöperation of his estates, which
in the Diet adopted an address calling upon him in urgent
terms to put an end to the war, and rescue the Mark from
its own troopers. " Friend and foe," complained the municipal council of Berlin, " have made the land a desert.
The officers, who ought to protect it, levy vast tributes for
their own use, live luxuriously, refuse to pay the soldiers,
and force them to desert or starve. Against the electoral

---

[1] The poetry of Schiller describes the character of the weary struggle more graphically, and not less correctly, than his prose. See for
example, the inimitable soldiers' chorus at the end of " Wallenstein's
Lager."

dragoons neither property nor life is safe; and the fields of the peasants are abandoned. All industry is prostrate. Towns and villages are in ruins; for miles and miles one will find neither people nor cattle, not a dog or a cat. And yet the war contributions are rigorously exacted. From the people have been taken their houses, gardens, crops, vineyards, and given to the officers, who are free from taxes, while the owners are crushed by the burden of taxation. The officials, the clergy, the teachers cannot be paid. Many have been driven to end their own lives by drowning, by the halter, or by the knife; and the rest are preparing to leave their homes with wife and child and wander abroad in the bitterest want." [1] It is not probable that this picture is greatly overdrawn, or that it was true only of Berlin and the adjacent country.

That the estates themselves were in part responsible for this misery is a retort which, if inopportune, would have been at least logically just. Their own intolerance, their obstinate parsimony, their opposition even to the timid plans of George William, had paralyzed the energies of the Mark at a time when a frank and loyal adhesion to the cause of Protestantism might have decided the issue of the conflict, and saved not only Brandenburg but all Germany from a long course of devastation. To complain of their suffering in 1640 was, therefore, to accuse their own blindness and folly.

The estates.

It nevertheless cost the Elector no trouble to be gracious to the petitioners. Their reasons and ultimate objects were not his, but their immediate aim was one to which he himself was committed by policy and feeling; and at that time, according to a letter from the younger Schwarzenberg, he had not yet learned to despise such humble allies. Without consulting the estates, says the letter, "the Elector will undertake no affair of great importance." [2] This

---

[1] Quoted by Pierson, *Pr. Gesch.* p. 89.

[2] The German text is " vom Landtage werden alle weiteren Dis-

was correct practice, and had the Elector's obedience to the constitution been an act of sincere good faith and not a mere politic concession to the convenience of the hour, the historian would readily admit that the boy of twenty felt scruples which were unknown to the man of forty.

The declaration of the estates was adopted on the 8th

Representations of the Diet.

of January, 1641, about one month after the accession of Frederic William,[1] and it was sent to him at Königsberg, where he was negotiating for the investiture in Preussen. It was significant that the Diet had so far weakened in its imperialist sympathies as to call for the immediate cessation of hostilities against Sweden, "no matter in what form;" and that this action was taken in the very face of Schwarzenberg's protests and menaces. That minister was still, by the Elector's request, governor in the Mark, but he was such only in name. Even while he was outwardly in favor and was conducting the routine of such details as could not at the moment be transferred to new hands, the Elector was practically undermining his authority and undoing his work. The representations of the Diet embodied such a plan of action.

The three points were peace with the Swedes ; the reduction of the army ; and the personal assumption of the government by the Elector. These three make up essentially the sum of Frederic William's policy to the time of the Peace of Westphalia.

The need of some accommodation with Sweden was par-

Foreign policy.

ticularly urgent. Banner's troops were again at the gates of Berlin, and Schwarzenberg was stiffening the resolution of his own regiments by new oaths of allegiance to the Emperor. Fresh disasters seemed there-

segni und Nachrichtungen abhangen, denn der Churfürst will ohne Berathungen der Stände nichts von hoher Importanz oder von hauptsächlichen Sachen vornehmen."

[1] His father died December 1, 1640.

fore inevitable; when to the delight of the people and the amazement of the governor, an order came from Königsberg " to proceed cautiously in the matter," followed within twenty-four hours by another, still more peremptory, to suspend hostilities altogether. Corresponding instructions were sent to the Elector's envoys at the Diet of Regensburg; the Emperor in his turn was shocked and alarmed. The envoys, as Schwarzenberg's agents, were about to complete the triumph of his policy, and bind up the fortunes of Brandenburg indissolubly with those of Austria, by an alliance which guarantied indeed the Elector's claim on Pomerania, but was of no practical value so long as the Swedes were still in possession. The concession doubtless seemed to Frederic William to be wholly on his side. He had to furnish troops, to put them under the command of Austrian officers, and to offer the Mark as the stage of further campaigns; while in regard to Pomerania he felt bound to consider whether there were reasonable hopes of expelling the Swedes, and whether after they were expelled Ferdinand would keep his word. Accordingly he decided to let the matter rest for a time. The envoys were ordered, without Schwarzenberg's knowledge, to make no positive engagements, not to press the Pomeranian question in a way to provoke the Swedes, and to report the progress of negotiations directly to the Elector. At the same time commissioners were sent with propositions for an armistice to the several Swedish commanders and to the court of Stockholm.

The reduction and reform of the army were taken up with the same energy. Of the whole corps of officers only one, Colonel von Burgsdorf, the commandant at Cüstrin in the New Mark, was unreservedly devoted to the Elector and his policy; the others were mere tools of Schwarzenberg, and under the pretence of loyalty to the Emperor maintained themselves as a lawless oligarchy, defiant of all control. Such were the colo-

Reduction of the army.

10

nels Lüdicke and Goldacker who planned an open mutiny; such was Rochow at Spandau, who threatened to blow the fortress into the air rather than obey the Elector. It was necessary, therefore, to proceed with prudence, and prudence the chancellor mistook for indecision. Confident of his own power, of the fidelity of the officers, of the Emperor's support, he was reflecting not whether but how he should check this audacious stream, when to his amazement it struck and carried him hopelessly away. Goetze, his personal and political rival, was reinstated in the chancellorship; fresh vigor was put into the Privy Council; some of the regiments took the oath to their new master; and an officious gossip reported to Schwarzenberg that his fate had been already decreed. This series of humiliations proved too much for the infirm statesman. A sudden illness prostrated him and he died on the 14th of March, 1641.[1]

The death of Schwarzenberg, whether caused or not by a broken heart, was probably in view of the circumstances an embarrassment to Frederic William, but the reduction of the army was not interrupted. The Diet had suggested that only sixteen companies and two colonels be retained. This number was adopted. At the same time an investigation was ordered both into Schwarzenberg's accounts and into the general misconduct of the officers during the past, — a new affront to those gallant men and a new provocation to mutiny. The younger Schwarzenberg, a worthy son of his father, appeared in Berlin and put himself at the head of the malcontents. But affairs had passed beyond his control. His private correspondence fell into the Elector's hands; and its contents were so suspicious that the Diet began an impeachment for treason, which the

---

[1] See Ranke, *Neun Bücher Pr. Geschichte*, i. 42; Horn, *Leben Friedrich Wilhelms des Grossen* (Berlin, 1814), p. 24. The count was indeed old and feeble, but it is generally agreed that his death was hastened by a rebuke from the Elector.

count only escaped by sudden flight. Goldacker followed
with the remnant of his regiment. Rochow was placed
under arrest. And on the 14th of July the negotiations
at Stockholm came to a successful close, and an armistice
for two years was concluded. The Swedes gained, it is
true, some military advantage by the treaty, — the right to hold certain districts in the Mark, to pass through with their armies when necessary, *Armistice with Sweden.*
and other privileges of a similar kind, — but the neutrality
of the Elector was reëstablished in form and an interval
for indispensable work secured.

The remaining duty of Frederic William as enunciated
by the Diet and accepted by him — his personal presence
in the Mark — was subject at first to local necessities in
Preussen.

The authority of the electors in the Duchy had always
been a mere shadow. For practical purposes the province was a republic and governed itself. The chancellor
could refuse to affix the seal to the decrees of the duke;
local officials controlled the privy purse and the domains;
the Diet decided in all important matters; and *Government of Preussen.*
the suzerainty of Poland was a guaranty of the
independence of the estates, rather than a support of the
nominal ruler.[1] The nobles had not learned servility
during a century of practical autonomy. The municipal
spirit in the larger towns was well developed, resolute, and
even aggressive. It happened besides that the Diet which
had been summoned by his father was still in session
when Frederic William appeared at Königsberg;[2] and
without any delay it fearlessly challenged his plans and
dispositions.

Its long bill of grievances seemed to him a signal of re-

[1] So, in substance, Ranke, i. 52. See also Nauwerk, pp. 45, 46;
Baczko, iv. lib. II. p. 422.

[2] Pufendorf, *De Rebus gestis Frederici Wilhelmi magni, Electoris
Brandenburgici* (Leipsic and Berlin, 1733), i. 15.

volt. The estates complained that the Calvinist religion
The Prussian Diet. was insidiously making its way into the provinces, where it already boasted a number of private chapels and a cemetery. They required the exclusive employment of native born nobles for public offices.[1] They demanded that all sales of crown domains, all appointments to territorial governorships, and even all pardons should be ratified by the Diet before becoming valid. But even if the Elector had accepted all of these conditions without reserve he would not have removed the last embarrassment. He had not yet done homage in Warsaw, and received the investiture from the King of Poland; and that potentate began to make his offended dignity heard in the negotiations. The King maintained, and the Diet upheld him, that the investiture must precede not only the *de jure* but also the *de facto* assumption of the government. The problem called for the exertion of all of the Elector's powers. To yield to the threats of Poland and the demands of the Diet would make a grave precedent for the future, and yet he was not strong enough to carry his point with open force. He was driven therefore to a middle course, through which he steered with singular skill. Keeping Poland quiet with promises and postponements he succeeded by some judicious concessions in detaching the Prussian nobles from the alliance of the towns, and won them over to his own cause.[2] This was only a partial victory but it saved the form of things. Investiture in Preussen. When he repaired to Warsaw for the investiture the cities followed him with their delegates, but their protest had no effect. In fact the conditions of the

[1] This principle was conceded by Albert himself in 1542, and was repeatedly confirmed, for instance in 1617. The diploma is given by Nauwerk, p. 55.

[2] Baczko says, "blos dis drei städte Königsberg representirten eigentlich den Bürgerstand." There were a number of other towns like Memel and Tilsit which also had municipal charters, but followed in political matters the advice and example of Königsberg.

final infeoffment comprised many of the very provisions for which the estates had contended, and were the reverse of favorable to Frederic William.[1] The towns nevertheless refused to acknowledge the transaction even when the Elector returned from Warsaw. The nobles received him with every show of loyalty and obedience, and voted the required taxes, but the towns still remained irreconcilable; and a long course of negotiations was necessary before they would consent to accept and welcome their new seigneur.[2]

The estates of Cleve had even a greater freedom of action than those of Preussen. Not only were they far removed in a geographical sense from the retributory arm of the Elector, but the fortunes of the war and the patronage of the Netherlands even enabled them to assert a dangerous degree of political independence; and they formed a permanent league of defence and defiance among themselves. It was hazardous for any member to refuse to join this organization, and long impossible for Frederic William to interfere with it. The estates seem early to have become suspicious of their new lord; and this reunion, which was formed without his consent in 1645, continued to vindicate the ancient rights and privileges of the duchy in spite of the edicts of dissolution that were fulminated against it.[3] For a time, therefore, Frederic William was obliged to accept the situation.

Cleve.

[1] Pufendorf, i. 16, 17.

[2] "Ohne Prejudiz ihrer wohlhergebrachten Rechte und Freiheiten" was the saving clause on which the burghers successfully insisted. Even Orlich, *Gesch. des pr. Staatesim* 17 *Jahrhundert* (Berlin, 1838), i. 271, admits that the grants voted by the nobles bore chiefly upon the burgesses.

[3] See Droysen, III. i. 251 et seq. This right of the estates had even been confirmed by a judicial sentence of the imperial court. The judgment is given by Campe, pp. 84, 85. The jurists called such a parliament a "convention" to distinguish it from a diet regularly summoned.

In the Mark, finally, to which the Elector had returned
in the spring of 1643, the conviction of common
needs taught both the Diet and the prince the
lesson of forbearance. Frederic William was
affable, moderate, conciliatory. The estates are flippantly
condemned indeed by certain writers because they showed
a will of their own, and discussed measures which it would
appear ought to have been accepted blindly without discussion; but they eventually assumed grave burdens in the
most patriotic spirit. They voted a heavy annual contribution to carry out the Swedish treaty, which in May,
1643, followed the armistice, and another considerable sum
for the support of the soldiery. Their ancient privileges
were then graciously confirmed.

Elector and
Diet in the
Mark.

In this way Frederic William temporarily pacified his
peoples one after another, and acquired at least
the forms of authority in the most remote districts of northern Germany. His vassals dwelt on the
banks of the Vistula and the banks of the Rhine; he
touched the Baltic Sea in the north and the Giant
Mountains in the east; and the Elbe, the Oder, the
Spree, the Havel, and the Memel irrigated the farms of
his peasantry, and facilitated the traffic of his towns. But
these several provinces were far enough from building a
single, united, and homogeneous state. They were separated as widely by differences of character as by intervals
of space, and their relations to the common lord, who was
their only bond of union, ranged over all the systems
which feudalism had bequeathed to Europe. In Cleve
Frederic William was a duke, in Brandenburg a margrave, in Ravenstein a count. He had one suzerain for
the Mark and another for Prussia, while the Netherlands
had a species of protectorate over the Rhineland. He
could scarcely pass from one part of his dominions to
another — from Königsberg to Berlin, or from Berlin to
Cleve — without crossing the territory of some jealous

The general
outlook.

neighbor, who by making his hospitality dear multiplied the difficulties of government. And in each of the several provinces local diets and ancient franchises crossed the young Elector at every step. In such a state of things one will unquestionably fail to see the highest type of a political commonwealth. The system, if it may be called such, was one which an ambitious and energetic prince would be sure to regard with impatience, and to reform, in the measure of his powers, according to the examples which at that time were so abundant in Europe.

Frederic William called this "restoring the sovereignty," and thus supplied his future apologists with a fair and serviceable phrase. It doubtless described to the Elector's satisfaction the policy which he had resolved to pursue; but it was inexact if not dishonest, and deserves the severest stigma that history can affix. On this point two observations require to be made.

Schemes of aggression.

It is a circumstance which led to a most unfortunate confusion of thought, that the idea of sovereignty appeared in political speculation at the epoch when monarchy, as a political system, began to reappear in Europe. The two things were therefore associated as inseparable steps in a beneficent progress. Even the facts of etymology were defied by loyal grammarians of the sixteenth and seventeenth centuries, who taught that to reign was to be sovereign, and conversely; whence the further proposition, that a sovereign state must have an absolute prince, was easily reached. That this sophism was of much positive influence at the time, that it lulled the scruples of any reluctant monarch, or disarmed the resistance of cautious subjects, may indeed be doubted. Revolutions are seldom made or prevented by speculative subtleties. But it might be easily shown that the error was the basis of an important school of political philosophers, and is in part responsible for a radically false interpretation, which is even yet current, of

Sovereignty and sophistry.

the great movement that created absolute monarchy on the continent of Europe.[1]   In this age the publicists draw sharper distinctions.   No one will now dispute that sovereign and monarch are not equivalent terms, that sovereignty describes the quality of a state, not a form of government, and that the supreme public authority may be exercised by one man or a number of men, and in short is possible under the most different political systems.   The elements of sovereignty are concisely if not exhaustively stated by Mohl.[2]   A sovereign state has the right to its own political existence, the right to choose its own form of government, the right to the undisturbed use of its own forces, the right to maintain relations with other states, the right to honor and respect, and the right of self-aggrandizement.[3]   A state which is permanently obstructed in the enjoyment of any of these rights is not a sovereign state, whether the obstructions be moral or material.   In this sense the territories inherited by Frederic William were certainly not sovereign.   They were in a state of legal or political dependence so long as the ties of feudalism bound them to the Emperor of Germany and the King of Poland; and even if these had been dissolved at

[1] The French Revolution was a movement in the opposite direction, and it gave us the no less vicious phrase "souveraineté du peuple."

[2] *Encyclopädie der Staatswissenschaften* (Tübingen, 1859), p. 420. Compare also Grotius, *De Jure Belli ac Pacis*, lib. i. cap. 3, VII.

[3] It cannot be considered necessary to cite authorities in support of what is to-day an axiom in political philosophy.   The reader will find this axiom stated by German publicists of the most pronounced reactionist school; for instance by Stahl, *Philosophie des Rechts*, ii. part II. pp. 162–165.   It is, therefore, the more surprising that a liberal jurist like Dr. von Roenne should describe the King of Prussia as its "sovereign."   See *Pr. Staatsrecht*, i. 106.   I am of course not complaining of the common use of "sovereign" for prince or king, but only of its misuse in scientific discussion, where precision is indispensable.   But even common usage can give us a lesson, for when we speak of a "sovereign prince" we mean the head of a sovereign or independent state.

any time before the Peace of Westphalia they would not have had the physical means of defending themselves. But it must be remembered, on the other hand, that this feudal tie was itself an incident in the form of government, which had long been maintained by the common consent of prince and people. The Prussians regarded it as a constitutional right to invoke the protection of Poland against a legitimate but aggressive ruler. The estates of Brandenburg were as untrammelled as those of Austria. And even when the feudal connection became a burden, and the spirit of the age required that it be severed or ignored, the change did not imply any redistribution of power in the domestic system of Prussia, or of Brandenburg, or of Cleve. The Elector was perhaps justified in asking that the government of his several possessions, in which he himself was only one factor, should be independent in law and in fact of all other powers. But he practically interpreted this in the sense of his own freedom from domestic restraint. Between these two propositions lies all the difference which separates Locke from Filmer, the government of a William from that of a Louis, the history of England from that of Spain, or France, or Austria.

It was also bold sophistry for the Elector to pretend that he was only wresting the prerogative, as his ancestors had enjoyed it, from the hands of its enemies.[1] The general answer to this pretension will be found in the preceding chapter. If the development of political relations is there correctly sketched, the tendency for a hundred years or more had been simply to refine and improve the me-

---

[1] Here is a specimen of the Elector's way of treating the subject: Und weiss man wohl dass sie (i. e. the Prussian estates) sich Dinge gegen meine Vorfahren angemasst und vorgenommen, welche in ihren Freiheiten nicht begriffen sein, etc., etc. Letter to Schwerin, 1662, quoted by Ranke, i. 53. The signs of the appearance of new political conceptions are visible in the assumption that the rights of the estates were conceded by the prince out of the fulness of his power.

chanical action of the estates when they acted, not to enlarge their functions at the cost of the crown; while the
powers of the prince during the same period had grown
more extensive and more precise, had become more personal in theory and better organized for service.[1] The
estates resisted some of the plans of John Sigismond and
George William, but this was the exercise of a discretion
which even if impolitic was not illegal. It was a fair difference of opinion, and the view of the Diet was generally
expressed in the highly constitutional form of refusing
taxes and subsidies. The censure with which historians
have visited this "obstinacy" rests, therefore, on false
conceptions. To condemn a parliamentary system, which
in its very nature was a check upon the will and purpose
of the executive, because in fulfilling that function it now
and then made mistakes, which have been revealed to an
enlightened and critical posterity, is a proceeding no less
mischievous than it is illogical and absurd. But in this
special case it is not certain that the complaint was even
correct in substance. Who was to blame for the condition in which the Great Elector found his inheritance?
Not the estates, at least, for they had steadily resisted the
policy which in spite of them, and with such disastrous results, George William persisted in trying. The evil genius
of Schwarzenberg was an obstacle to Frederic William's
plans, but it was invoked by his own father and armed
with its powers of mischief in contempt of the known feelings of the land. Even the temper of the estates in
Preussen and Cleve had been embittered by early aggressions on the part of the House of Brandenburg.[2] And to

[1] Comp. Lancizolle, *Rechtsquellen*, p. xviii

[2] Droysen says, Die Politik Schwarzenberg's riss die Interessen
der Marken, Preussen, der Rheinlande völlig aus einander. . . . Und
die Stände in den Rheinlanden, die Regimentsräthe in Preussen,
thaten nur ihre Schuldigkeit, wenn sie sich gegen ihren Landesherrn
und seine märkische Politik so argwöhnisch und abwehrend als möglich verhielten. *Gesch. der pr. Politik*, III. i. 146.

cite a single, more general example, is it not clear, in view of the part conceded to the Diet in the Reformation, and long afterwards in all religious affairs, that John Sigismond, who changed his own creed and forced Calvinism upon public recognition in the teeth of the most bitter opposition; that George William, who was a prince without firmness or force of character, and yet could make the obnoxious faith one of the bases of the electoral household, — is it not clear from such illustrations that these margraves were anything but the helpless victims of their estates?[1] A close examination will show that the alleged weakness of the electors was but another name for the weakness of the state itself in war and diplomacy. The authority of the crown over its own vassals and subjects was as great as ever.

Frederic William aimed then at sovereignty, but also at absolutism, and his method was that of revolution.[2] To this end he devoted all his efforts; and it is impossible to deny that he chose his means with unrivalled sagacity, and employed them with a skill and boldness not less great.

During this decade of reconstruction and preparation the Elector held the balance between Emperor and Swede with unfailing dexterity.[3] Even his weakness was a security which with shame he was obliged

The finances.

[1] The delegates of the estates gave Frederic William, on his accession, a formidable list of the arbitrary practices which had characterized the previous regime. Arbitrary power had made no little progress when it could venture to interfere with the administration of justice, but the estates accused George William of "reforming judgments of the Chamber by simple decrees and without previous investigation."

[2] "Auch Friedrich Wilhelm hat mehr als einmal den Ausdruck gebraucht, dass er sich absolut machen wollte." Droysen, III. ii. 505.

[3] How severely this tried his patience and tact is shown in his own letters. "Auf der einen Seite," he writes, in a memorandum quoted by Ranke, i. 41, "habe ich die Krone Schweden, auf der andern den Kaiser; ich sitze zwischen ihnen und erwarte was sie mit mir anfangen."

to accept.   His first military reform seemed to reduce the
real while it only reduced the nominal strength of his
army, substituting a compact, disciplined, and efficient
force for the irregular levies which had before harassed
the Mark; and thus he escaped the notice of his powerful
rivals until he suddenly appeared in the congress of 1645
in the character of a prince whose alliance was to be
prized and courted.   But the increase of the army required the grant of fresh taxes, which law and custom still
left to the bounty of the estates.   Some increase of revenue from the domains naturally followed the return of
prosperity after peace had been concluded, and the ravages of a war, which afflicted the Elector like every other
landholder, had been repaired.   In Preussen where the
demesne lands were rich and extensive [1] this ought to have
been peculiarly the case.   The revival of traffic multiplied
likewise the tolls of road and river, the product of the
mines, the profits of the coinage and of the other royalties.
And even more important than all these in the Mark was
perhaps the beer tax, which after being granted originally
in the fifteenth century from year to year, then for terms
of years, had finally become a settled excise over which
the Diet had lost all control.   But under George William even this had depreciated, both as one of the incidents of the general desolation, and also in consequence
of careless and corrupt management.[2]   The thrift, the
energy, the good sense of Frederic William soon reopened these various sources of revenue, and taught them
to flow with an unprecedented vigor.   But this reform

[1] They comprised in 1647, according to an official report, no fewer
than 50,000 manors. But the contributions of the manors were partly
in kind.

[2] I shall return to this subject in another place, and treat it in
greater detail. See in regard to the beer excise, Mylius, vi. I.
No. 58, and iv. IV. No. 2. The terms of the grant were that the tax
should be levied during the lives of Joachim I. and the heirs of his
body.

itself operated as an increase of the public burdens. The peasants, the knights, and the towns in all the provinces had been so corrupted by years of easy, indolent administration, that they were impatient even under the revival of duties from which they had never been formally released, and which they were still constitutionally bound to perform. Were they not, therefore, much less likely to accept the new burdens that the Elector undertook to impose?

The estates of the Mark became early alarmed about Frederic William's plans, and in 1646 exacted of him a renewed pledge to respect their rights and privileges. During the previous years they had asserted their position with courage and not without success. They had occasionally voted the sums demanded by the Elector, had often insisted first on serious reductions, and sometimes had ventured on absolute refusal; examples of which may be found in the proceedings of 1643, when the Diet ratified the Swedish treaty and voted the means of paying the indemnity; in 1641, when the Elector demanded the support of sixteen companies and the estates, changing their mind, authorized only twelve; and in 1642, when the first treaty with Sweden was unconditionally rejected.[1] The resistance of the estates was the more vexatious because it often had to be overcome at two successive points. It frequently happened during this decade that after the Elector had succeeded in procuring a subsidy from the assembled Diet, the towns refused to accept and furnish their two thirds, which former usage based on their own consent had established as their proportion. They declared in 1641 that the landed gentry had succeeded in escaping nearly all public charges; that they managed to throw their share of the burdens upon their own tenants

Affairs in the Diet.

---

[1] The protests of the estates were often not without a dry irony, as in 1645, when they hoped the Elector would fix "des Landes Lasten mehr nach dem Landesvermögen, als etwa nach der Necessität."

and those of the domains; that for example the nobles in
Teltow and Havelland with their villages did not contribute so much in a year as the wretched town of Mittenwalde, whose citizens had been reduced from three hundred in number to twenty-two, contributed in a month.
I see no reason to doubt the general justice of these complaints. They agree fully with all that experience teaches
in regard to the character of the nobles and their relations
to the other orders; and history leaves no doubt about
the lamentable disasters which had overtaken municipal
life in the course of the Thirty Years' War.[1] It is possible, therefore, that the demand of the towns for a new apportionment of the extraordinary taxes was as just in substance as in law. The objection of the nobles was no less
natural from their point of view. Thus dead-locks frequently arose, as they do under any constitutional system;
but at that time the machinery of state provided no means
of solution, and the Elector could bring the cities to terms
only after long and difficult negotiations.[2]

If the estates in their conduct and policy were fully
The general within their constitutional rights, it seems no less
excise.   clear that they were not inspired by any original
hostility to the Elector. They would not have granted
the excise to a prince whom they were determined to crip-
ple. The specification that the proceeds of this excise
were for the support of the troops shows also that the land
was not opposed in principle to the military reforms of the

---

[1] To the ravages of the war had been added those of the plague.
Droysen gives some official figures, which show that while the combined cities Berlin-Cölln had 1,236 houses before the war, the number had fallen to 1,000 in 1645; and in 1653 was only 1,042.

[2] In 1643 the proportion of the towns was fixed by agreement at
59 per cent. Coelln, *Hist. Archiv* (Berlin, 1819-20), i. 72, says erroneously two thirds, and again, iii. 72, he gives the apportionment correctly, but assigns it to the year 1743 instead of 1643. His useful
work is full of typographical errors, and contains some for which the
printer is probably not responsible.

Elector.[1] It was only when the number of the regular soldiers became ominously large, and made it clear that extra subsidies would be annually required, that the Diets began to examine, to discuss, to amend, and even to reject the propositions of their prince. And soon after the peace of 1648 the policy of Frederic William in the other provinces began to alarm even the most docile vassals in the Mark.

The Elector had introduced Brandenburg troops into Preussen and into Cleve in violation of usage and of right; and in both these provinces the estates made an earnest resistance. Their resources for such a struggle though unlike were not unequal. Cleve had the advantage of distance, of the Emperor's patronage, and of Holland's protection; while the free union of the orders permitted her Diet to dispense in a measure with the usual summons from the Elector. Preussen had an equivalent privilege in her right of appeal to Poland. But in neither of these provinces did the people themselves succeed after 1650 in absolutely defeating the Elector's main purpose, although they obstructed and mutilated special measures. It was of no avail that the Rhenish estates threatened in 1649, if their grievances were not redressed, "to employ those means which issue from the rights of man and the laws of God, and are guarantied in the privileges of the land;" that in 1651 they formally authorized the refusal of the taxes exacted by the Elector; that they menaced with punishment every official who should levy such unlawful contributions.[2] Frederic William kept the "foreign" soldiers in the province, and sup-

Progress of usurpation.

[1] The Act is in Mylius, vi. I. No. 106. The excise was granted " zur besseren Erreichung des von unserer Soldatesca bedürfenden Unterhalt," etc.

[2] I use the word in its technical sense. It had come to be partially equivalent to " tribute," as designating a special revenue, raised in emergencies of war by measures which to-day hardly bear examination. See Campe, p. 55, Note X.

ported them from this arbitrary revenue, as long as they were essential to his purpose. In Preussen the resistance was nearly as fruitless. The landraths refused indeed to meet in the informal council to which the Elector invited them, and in 1651 the influence of Poland caused a regular Diet to be convoked. But before and after the Diet taxes were assessed and collected at the Elector's discretion.[1] Brandenburg troops were quartered on the people, and Calvinist officers shocked the taste of the native Lutherans. It was only during the Swedish and Polish complications that Frederic William's hold on the province was seriously threatened, but even then the danger was from abroad.

Thus the estates of the Mark, instead of making a factious opposition to the Elector's plans, had, by their generous endowment of the army, really aided to subvert the rights and liberties of their brothers in other parts. They were even too easy and obliging, and the consequences were soon felt by themselves. It was not perhaps a just retribution, but it was at least a penalty for their imprudence, that the Elector next turned his attention to the Mark, and after three years dismissed the General Diet, which had been so long a formidable power in the state, forever into history.

This discussion has, however, somewhat anticipated the course of events. Before Frederic William could complete the work of usurpation his attention was claimed by a project of marriage, by petty disputes in the Rhine territories, and by the negotiations for a general peace.

It had been originally intended that the prince should espouse Christine, the daughter of Gustavus Adolphus. This had been the great King's desire; and after Frederic William became elector the alliance seemed still to commend itself by a variety of political considerations, not the least of which was that

Marriage of
Frederic
William.

---

[1] See the history of these years in Orlich, i. passim.

it offered an easy solution of the Pomeranian dispute. But it might also bring the Kingdom of Sweden under the sceptre of Brandenburg, and to Sweden the King of Poland laid claims, which the Elector could not openly resist. The estates of Sweden, too, seemed averse to the transaction; and it is ungallantly alleged that the destined bride had herself developed qualities which cooled the original ardor of her suitor. The project was therefore reluctantly abandoned. Frederic William next turned toward Holland, where in his boyhood he had known and admired the Princess Louise, daughter of Frederic Henry of Orange. With the frankness permitted to maidens of her rank she met the Elector's overtures with a ready acquiescence. Her father approved the plan, the estates ratified it, and voted the bride an annual support of twenty thousand guldens. The marriage day was fixed; and the groom entered the Hague with a retinue which may not have dazzled the opulent Dutchmen, but which severely strained the resources of the privy purse, and excited not a few invidious comments from the outspoken people of Brandenburg.[1] The ceremony was performed on the 27th of November, 1646, although owing to her father's illness it was some time before the bride took up her permanent residence in Berlin. Tradition describes Louise as being amiable, pious, and attractive; as entering warmly into all, even the illegal, schemes of her husband; and as abounding in those benevolent works which are the peculiar privilege of her sex.

In respect to the quarrel which broke out with Pfalz-Neuburg in 1646, opinions may differ as to whether the Elector was a wanton aggressor, or an unselfish champion of religious freedom. His apologists take, of course, the latter view, and represent the Count Palatine as guilty of oppressing the Protestants

Relations with Pfalz-Neuburg.

---

[1] So the common account, though Droysen makes the display less imposing.

11

in the districts which he acquired by the partition; of making unconstitutional exactions; and of systematically violating the treaty of 1614. But not the slightest evidence is offered for these charges, while it is certain that Frederic William's summary proceedings aroused the suspicions of Holland, and, if they had not been seasonably arrested, would have invited the intervention of the other powers. In any event it was an attempt to redress one wrong by another. To bring Brandenburg troops into Cleve was illegal, to quarter them on the province and support them by arbitrary requisitions was a gross outrage; and it does not follow that the estates, which refused their assent to such measures, were less indifferent than the Elector to the interests of their Protestant brethren. They used only their lawful parliamentary discretion. But this discretion had already become hateful to Frederic William; and although foreign pressure obliged him to give up his enterprise against the Count Palatine, after effecting nothing beyond the restoration of the *status quo*, and the estates refused any discussion of their constitutional rights, he resumed the work in calmer times, and with better success.

While the Elector was thus threatening a new war the powers were laboring at Münster and Osnabrück to put an end to the old one.

Since the conclusion of the armistice between Brandenburg and Sweden, the general struggle had passed through many vicissitudes, but had been on the whole unfavorable to the House of Austria. No great imperialist general had arisen after the death of Tilly and of Wallenstein. But the resources of the Swedes in men, in military talent, and in money, seemed inexhaustible. When Gustavus fell Banner came forward; when Banner died a successor was found in the infirm yet energetic and audacious Torstenson, who twice encamped under the very walls of Vienna. France, too, on the accession of Louis XIV., and under the influence of Mazarin,

End of the Thirty Years' War.

had begun a more active participation, and given a more decided turn to hostilities. The Emperor had long been anxious for peace, and the only question was how to accomplish that end with the least sacrifice on his own part.

A conference of the imperial estates at Frankfort-on-the-Main was, therefore, planned and carried out. Frankfort Conference. The great dignitaries of the realm, both secular and ecclesiastical, were all present, either in person or by proxy. Brandenburg, too, accepted the invitation; though with significant reserves, which became more accentuated as the deliberations proceeded, and placed the Elector finally at the head of the opposition to the Emperor. The policy of Ferdinand was early revealed. He proposed to have the war treated as purely a German affair; but under this specious phrase was concealed a plan to have the Empire act as a whole in the coming congress, and to bind the separate princes by votes of the Frankfort Diet, in which the Catholic interest had, of course, an overwhelming majority. It was in effect an invitation to the Protestant princes to tie their hands in advance, and was naturally declined. In the end, too, some of the Catholic electors began to see that Ferdinand was less concerned about the welfare of the Empire, or even about the cause of their religion, than about the aggrandizement of his own house, and their weight was thrown into the scale with Brandenburg against him. The result was, therefore, that the princes were left free to send their own representatives to the congress, and to defend their own interests, if necessary even against the Emperor himself.

Two congresses were made necessary by the complicated nature of the struggle. The Emperor was at war Congress of Westphalia. with France and with Sweden; France was at war with the Emperor and with Spain; Holland was at war with Spain alone; Spain was at war with France and Holland, but not with the Swedes; the Swedes were at war only with the Emperor; and the minor states of Germany were divided, some being allies of the Emperor, some of Sweden, and some neutral. Such confusion had never been known in the politics of Europe. That the negotiations for peace should have been reduced to any form or system is marvellous; but after much diplomatic fencing the multitude of subjects was finally brought within the scope of two congresses. The Emperor negotiated at Münster with France, at Osnabrück with Sweden.

No sooner were the congresses formally opened, April, 1645, than all the potentates of Germany, great and small, Catholic and Protestant, rushed thither like hungry vultures; while the two foreign powers, which from opposite sides of the Empire had been fighting the cause of the Reformation, demanded, not with equal justice but with equal emphasis, indemnification for their outlays and their efforts. In this unseemly scramble the humane interests of peace, and the sincere labors of a few upright men, were almost obscured.

Among all the claimants no one showed itself more eager and forward than the power which had been most backward in meeting the dangers and responsibilities of the war. Even the callous diplomatists of Austria and Sweden were shocked at Brandenburg's unblushing greed. Here was a state which had never lifted a hand honestly and bravely for the Protestants; which had served the Emperor only with phrases and protestations; which had sought the alliance and protection now of the Swedes, now of the Austrians, according to the fortunes of the war; which had speculated on its very weakness and timidity; and which now came forward with the demand that the two belligerents should admit its claim to a province, for which both of them had sacrificed thousands of lives and millions of treasure. Many things are indeed called fair in politics which are unfair and iniquitous in morals. But I cannot wholly indorse the usual strictures upon Austria and Sweden for their alleged union against Brandenburg, since it seems to me that the slender feudal claim which the electors once acquired to Pomerania had been long since forfeited by repeated acts of treachery to both.

The general argument of the Elector was clear and straightforward. His right of succession in Pomerania dated back to the Middle Ages, and had been often confirmed by imperial decrees or by treaties, of which that of Prague in 1635 was the latest. On this treaty, too, the Elector founded his special claim as against the House of Austria. To Sweden he denied any counter-right, even that of conquest. But the Swedes were actually in possession; and since Brandenburg had lent no sufficient aid in driving them thence by force, the Emperor felt himself to be under no great obligation to take the part in the congress of a worthless ally against an honorable and manly foe. In the first project of a treaty the Elector's pretensions were, therefore, calmly ignored. Pomerania was assigned to Sweden, and the Elector was only offered a slight compensation in the secularized bishoprics of Minden, Halberstadt, and eventually Magdeburg. The plan was rejected with an energy unusual in the politics of Brandenburg. It is true that if it had been adopted without his assent he would have been unable to resist it at the time by force; but with the logic of a consummate statesman he reasoned that Sweden to secure the possession would have to maintain a large army, that while a Swedish army remained in northern Germany the Emperor could not disarm, and that, even though a temporary peace should be agreed on, war would sooner or later be resumed.[1] Sweden's demands were indeed somewhat exorbitant, and throw grave suspicions upon the motives with which she had latterly supported the war. It is also true that she had long been drawing

[1] Report of the Abbé St. Martin, quoted by Droysen, III. i. 221.

liberal subsidies both from some of the German states
and from France, while her own outlays had become inconsiderable. But on the other hand she insisted no less
stubbornly on the great cause of religious freedom. It
was owing to her powerful advocacy in the congress, as
well as to her victories in the field, that the religious
peace of Augsburg was reaffirmed, that the Calvinists
were placed on the same footing as the Lutherans, and
that the Protestants were secured a representation in the
tribunals of the Empire.

For three years the discussions dragged wearily along.
More than once the disruption of the congress seemed
imminent and inevitable; the combatants seized their
arms; Wrangel and the Swedes were again in Bohemia.
But in the course of time there appeared a rivalry between
France and Sweden, and in this Frederic William found
his opportunity. The encouragement and support of the
French delegates gave him an advantage, which
in the end so far prevailed over the Swedes that
they waived their claim to Pomerania as a whole, and
consented to share it with Brandenburg. The Elector
with equal prudence, though unwillingly, accepted the
plan. The details were then easily adjusted.

*The com-
promise.*

The great act was finally consummated and proclaimed
to the world, by the voice of cannon, on the 24th
of October, 1648. Although many parts of the
treaty concern Brandenburg only remotely, its
great importance seems to require that all at least of its
leading features be given in this place. I shall adopt the
arrangement of Heeren [1] by dividing the subjects taken
up and regulated by the congress into three classes : first,
the territorial and the other indemnities to various powers,
German and foreign ; second, the provisions in regard to
religious equality; third, the political reorganization of
the Empire.

*The final
peace.
1648.*

[1] *Handbuch,* 3d ed. p. 173.

1. France received the Austrian Alsace; the recognition of its sovereignty over Metz, Toul, Verdun, and Pignerol; Sweden, Fore-Pomerania and adjacent islands, Wismar, Bremen, and Verden, with representation in the German Diet and five million thalers indemnity; the Elector of Brandenburg, Rear-Pomerania and the ecclesiastical fiefs of Magdeburg, Camin, Minden, and Halberstadt;[1] Mecklenburg, the cities of Schwerin and Ratzeburg; Hesse, Hirschfeld, and some minor accessions; Brunswick, the expectancy to Osnabrück; Electoral Saxony, the Lausitz as provided in the treaty of 1635; Bavaria, the larger part of the Palatinate on the basis of the spoliation of 1622. In nearly all the transfers of territory, except the last, some degree of respect was shown for vested rights and law. Pomerania in particular was a vacant fief, the last duke having died in 1637; and the church domains were without lords whose titles could be successfully maintained.

Territorial readjustments.

2. The great merit of the treaty, so far as principles are concerned, is to be sought in the guaranties which it contained of religious freedom. These were with one important exception liberal, just, and all that Protestantism could at the time expect. Thus it was provided that in all secular affairs Catholics and Protestants should be placed on the same footing; that the Calvinists should enjoy all the rights accorded by law or treaty to Lutherans; that religious relations should be restored to the basis of 1624; that the Imperial High Court should thenceforth consist of an equal number of judges from each of the two great branches of the Christian church; and that every prince should have the right to make his own religion that of the land, with the condition, however, that such of his subjects as refused to conform might have three years in which to emigrate. The last provision is of course the obnoxious one. But none of

The religious articles.

[1] Magdeburg as a duchy, the others as principalities.

the rulers of Prussia have ever exercised the power which
it granted.

3. The most sweeping changes which the treaty worked
in the constitution of the Empire affected, by
largely increasing, the rights of the particular
states. Their discretion in the conduct of their
domestic affairs was more clearly defined, and the princes
acquired the power of negotiating treaties and forming
alliances with foreign states, though not against the Empire. Holland and Switzerland were excluded from the
confederation; and a new electorship, the eighth, was
created for the Count Palatine in place of the one which
had been transferred from him to Bavaria. Some of
these articles of course merely recognized existing facts.
The republic of Switzerland had long since practically
ceased to belong to the Empire, and the territorial princes
had already learned the habit of making treaties with foreign states. But it was desirable to have such facts and
usages formally embodied in the public law of the Empire..

*Constitution-
al changes in
the Empire.*

If we now consider the bearings of the Treaty of Westphalia upon Brandenburg in particular, it will
appear that the Elector reaped immense advantages with comparatively trifling outlays. The
Lutheran belief of his subjects in the Mark and in
Preussen, the Calvinist belief of himself, his family, and
his people in Cleve, were not only secured against actual oppression, but were recognized in the public law of
Germany as entitled to all the rights and privileges of
Catholicism. His civil and political authority in his own
dominions was protected against the vexatious interference of the Emperor. He acquired a position as an
European prince, free to send and receive ambassadors,
to form lawful engagements, and in short to exercise one
large class of the rights of sovereignty. And he received
a valuable addition to the hereditary possessions of his
family.

*Political
gains of
Branden-
burg.*

The full importance of the territorial acquisitions will appear even from the few data which are accessible or trustworthy.

Rear-Pomerania, or Hinter-Pommern, comprised, loosely speaking, the portion which lies east of the river Oder. It contained about eight thousand Eng- *Material gains.* lish square miles, and was peculiarly important because it joined both the New Mark and the Ucker Mark, opened a nearer route to Preussen, and afforded additional ports on the Baltic. The territories of Magdeburg, Halberstadt, and Minden included some three thousand square miles. But the characters and conditions of these several acquisitions touched the extremes of pastoral squalor and cultivated opulence, Pomerania being divided between a brutal and ignorant nobility and a race of spiritless agricultural serfs, while the southwestern districts brought in a population of skilful artisans and traders, with wealth, intelligence, and refinement. Of the number of inhabitants in each I can find no authentic details.

CHAPTER V.

FROM THE PEACE OF WESTPHALIA TO THE DEATH OF THE GREAT ELECTOR.

THE congress solved many of the problems over which
Results of the Peace. war had raged for a generation throughout the
Empire, but even the solution raised new issues
full of embarrassment for the statesmen. It need scarcely
be said, too, that these chiefly concerned the territorial
changes. Since the war had lost, in its later years, the
character of a strife between the principle of religious
freedom and the principle of ecclesiastical absolutism;
since its objects, at least on one side, had become secular,
political, selfish, and sordid; since, too, the Emperor had
learned that he could not crush Protestantism with the
sword, nor destroy the independence of the princes, nor
convert the Empire into a close personal monarchy; — the
guaranties in behalf of the reformed faith, the relaxation of feudal ties, the decentralization of the imperial
system were reforms for which public opinion in general,
and the temper of the negotiating parties in particular,
were so well prepared that they were readily adopted by
the congress. But the issues which were developed later
in the war came up, on the other hand, fresh, active, and
determined. How territory could be won or saved, how
dynastic prestige could be enhanced, how the factors of
political influence in Europe could be adjusted to the
greater advantage of this or that state, — such were really
the burning questions at Münster and Osnabrück. But
the settlement could in most cases give a power only the

opportunity of self-aggrandizement. To utilize the opportunity after the congress was the work of statesmanship; and of all the princes who returned with booty from Westphalia not one understood this better than Frederic William of Brandenburg.

The treaty gave him the title to important districts in northern Germany, but only the title. He was left to acquire possession of them for himself, *Attitude of Sweden.* without the suggestion of any plan by the Congress, or the promise of any aid from its members; and the Swedes, who still held them with their armies, proved to be unreasonably obstinate, or justly prudent, about facilitating the transfer. They were entitled under the treaty to an indemnity of five million thalers, to be raised by assessments upon the several circles, or administrative divisions of the Empire. The right was not and could not be impeached. But the thrifty creditors asserted a species of lien upon the occupied places, and refused to evacuate them until their debt was paid. They were inexorable, and the Emperor was helpless or indifferent. Unable to move the Swedes, abandoned by all his neighbors, without an army of his own, the Elector could only meet the emergency, in so far as it concerned him, with courage, patience, and ingenuity.

The Elector's share of the Swedish indemnity, or rather of the first instalment, was about one hundred and fifty thousand thalers. This was raised by the arts in which he was such a precocious master, tendered to the enemy, and accepted. Frederic William then demanded the prompt surrender of his lands. The Swedes so far complied as to evacuate Minden and Halberstadt; but in regard to Pomerania they interposed various *The Pomeranian question.* pleas for delay, such as the necessity of settling the exact boundaries, the dispute about the banks of the Oder, the extent of territory belonging to Stettin, Wismar, Verden, the partition of the Pomeranian debt,

the guaranties for the remaining payments,—pleas of which
it is not essential here to determine the validity. It is
enough that the Swedes remained, and that the interval
between the adjournment of the Congress and their final
departure, in 1653, was filled up with a course of intricate,
obscure, and perplexing negotiations.

In home affairs the Elector was not less active, and far
more successful. The peace had left him with
The Elector's
home   an army of about eight thousand men ; and this
policy.   force he was resolved both to enlarge and to improve. But the Diet insisted rather that it should be reduced. Other princes, said a parliamentary address,
" had pursued that policy. In Magdeburg the war contributions had ceased; likewise in Mecklenburg, which
had its own troubles with the Swedes; in Saxony, in
Lüneburg, throughout the whole Empire, the larger part
of the troops had been dismissed. Brandenburg was the
only state in which after the conclusion of the peace fresh
burdens had been put upon the people. The Elector was
not beneath other princes in power, intelligence, and wisdom ;— why should he not strive to equal them also in
those kindly virtues, which make rulers akin to the gods ? "
The Diet offered only eight companies, or sixteen hundred men, to be supported by a monthly outlay of five
thousand thalers ; and it cherished " the most loyal hope
that his highness would not impose upon the people, ex
absoluta potestate, burdens not authorized by the collective estates." This appeal was disregarded, as were also
the more decided protests which followed. He was willing and ready, the Elector said, to relieve the land as fast
as the public welfare would permit ; he had already
waived many of his rights in view of the bonum publicum ;
he had quite ignored his private interests, and thought
only of the peace and prosperity of his people ; but now
the estates themselves must admit that Pomerania and
the Mark had one and the same liege lord, were " membra

unius capitis." The last figure he also applied to Cleve,
Preussen, and all his territories; but the special object of
his efforts at this juncture was to compel the Swedes to
surrender Rear-Pomerania, and any hour might lay bare
the necessity of enforcing the claim by the sword.

Two years later, in 1652, he was ready to go a step
farther. The Diet had granted a considerable
subsidy for a term of six years, and doubled the
grist tax for the same period. But this liberality only
whetted the Elector's appetite. He proposed to "lighten
the burdens of taxation by equalizing them thoroughly
and justly, since this would contribute to the improvement
of the land, to confidence, and to unity," [1] — which harmless language really concealed a scheme for making the
direct taxes, or the "contribution," permanent
like the regals. The estates were now thoroughly alarmed. The nobles declared with quaint emphasis that such a scheme would "throw them out of the
constitution." Colonel Burgsdorff, whose fidelity to the
Elector had been approved in a grave crisis, now refused
to join in the work of usurpation,[2] and insisted that the
freedom of the estates was in danger. The Diet, he
said, would become superfluous if the Elector were no
longer obliged to ask it for money; the door would be
opened to despotism if there were no restraint upon the
will, the fancies, the caprice of the Elector, and a standing army blindly obeyed all his orders. This spirited
protest was not without its effect upon the Diet. The
monstrous proposition was rejected; and the estates, taking the offensive, even drew up a sweeping bill of grievances which they laid before the Elector. But Frederic
William knew the antagonists with whom he had to deal.
He saw in this brief display of courage the last flickering

---

[1] The transactions are in Mylius, vi. Th. I. Nos. 115 and 116.

[2] He had in fact resigned his commission as soon as he became
aware of the plot against the liberties of the land.

of a fire which was about to go out in eternal darkness; and he already felt sure of the future. The Diet was adjourned with only a vague promise that it should soon be reconvened, and its complaints considered.

The organic act of 1653[1] is in large part only a repetition or reaffirmation of the one adopted the year before. Like that it roams freely among a multitude of subjects; and though keeping close to positive and concrete relations defines them with the comprehensiveness of a permanent constitution.[2] It is strictly a written charter. It announces general principles for the administration of justice, for the partition of pecuniary burdens, for the conduct of state institutions, for the freedom of religious belief and worship, for the mutual relations of the several social orders; and even those articles which seem to provide for special cases really but half conceal universal rules of law. The instrument has an impressive look of antiquity. Its source had to be sought far back in the Middle Ages; and as it moved down through the centuries it had accumulated new articles, and assimilated them into a common system. It had grown with the growth of social interests. Its scope had been repeatedly enlarged in order that it might embrace all the cares of the citizen, and all the functions of the state. But this flexibility, far from being a practical defect, was a useful and even necessary virtue. It does not lessen but rather enhances our right to treat the instrument as the reënactment of the fundamental national charter, in which the amendments alone were new. It had

Constitution of 1653.

---

[1] Mylius, vi. I. No. 118.

[2] In the usage of that time, however, the word "constitution" designated not the organic public law as embodied in a "Recess," but rather a civil code or codification, including judicial procedure. Such an one was drawn up by Distelmeier (Mylius, vi. III. Nos. 2 and 3), but never adopted, and the estates seem to have demanded one in vain from the Great Elector. Ibid. vi. I. No. 146.

conserved the original features that gave it stability, and adopted such new ones as facilitated growth.[1]

This was the last general Diet held in the Mark. An attempt of the estates a few years later to meet without a summons called forth a vehement rebuke from the Elector, and was not repeated. The historic Diet, which for centuries had legislated like a free parliament, now shrivelled into a petty board or commission for revising the lists of the assessor, and auditing the accounts of the exciseman. Frederic William was alone in the government. Suppression of the Diet.

About the time that the Elector was thus carrying out his violent purpose in Brandenburg, the negotiations with Sweden came to a successful close in the Treaty of Stettin. Rear-Pomerania was accordingly evacuated, and the Elector took formal possession of the land. On his northeastern frontiers, however, a new war was gathering. Treaty of Stettin.

We have already seen how Christine, daughter of Gustavus Adolphus, and since 1644 Queen of Sweden, failed to become the wife of Frederic William. As an alternative her cousin, Charles Gustave of Pfalz-Neuburg, became a candidate for her hand, and in the expectation of his success he had been recognized in 1649 as the eventual successor to the throne. But the Queen was capricious in her humors, masculine in her tastes, scandalous in her morals; averse to matrimony, she finally declared her resolution to remain single; and in 1654 she even renounced the crown, which then passed to Charles Gustave. The new king was one of the most successful of the generals who were trained in the hard school of the Thirty Years' War. In his person the audacity, the skill, the ambition of the great Gustavus seemed to be reproduced, and he felt at the outset of his Sweden and Poland.

[1] This view of the Recess does not seem to be greatly different from that of Lancizolle, *Rechtsquellen*, pp. xviii. and xix.

reign the necessity of signalizing his accession by some brilliant military exploit. Fortunately for him a pretext was not wanting. The crown of Poland had never relinquished its claim to the succession in Sweden, — a claim which was indeed sound according to the strict law of dynastic inheritance, but had been invalidated by a vote of the Swedish Diet, and was distasteful to the Polish estates. But John Casimir, the King of Poland, paid no regard to the wishes of Sweden or his own people ; violated even a pledge which he himself had given not to reopen the question ; protested against the acknowledgment of Charles Gustave ; and solemnly announced his own rival claim. The result was a declaration of war on the part of Sweden, and hostilities were begun with the usual vigor of that state.

The necessities of the campaign at once forced Charles

The Swedes in Preussen. Gustave, as thirty years before they had forced Gustavus Adolphus, into the ports and through the territory of Preussen. West or Polish Preussen was well fortified along the coast, and especially at Dantzic ; and it was considered easier to disregard the neutrality of the Elector and reach Poland by way of his dominions.

1655. That discreet prince threw no serious obstacle in the path. It is true that he proclaimed neutrality as his father had proclaimed it at many critical epochs of the Thirty Years' War. He drew a few thousand troops from Brandenburg into the province. He wrote minatory letters, issued protests, manned the frontiers on the north and the west. But his resistance ended in mere demonstrations ; and when finally yielding to necessity he gave the Swedes the right of passage through Preussen, they promptly expanded the concession over Brandenburg as well, and led an army from Pomerania into the very heart of Poland. The campaign of 1655 was short, and ended in the complete overthrow of the Poles. John Casimir fled to Cracow ; his armies dissolved; and Charles Gustave to finish his victory returned to West Preussen and besieged Dantzic.

It was natural that these events should be watched with grave anxiety by Frederic William. He had declined the Polish alliance, which was offered to him on liberal conditions, as he had declined the alliance of Sweden, and probably for the same reasons. By both parties, he conceived, he and his father had been wronged; and miscalculating the relative strength of the belligerents and the probabilities of the war, he had reasoned that, as he could hope for justice from neither of them, his true policy was to let them wear each other out in a fruitless struggle, while he should reserve his intervention for the moment when it would be decisive. But a single campaign had crushed Poland; and the Swedes, now at the gates of Dantzic, might next sweep East Preussen into their grasp.

Position of Frederic William.

In this crisis he committed a serious error, — the more serious and surprising as it ignored wholly the lessons of the campaign. He opened communications with the Poles for an alliance and a renewal of the struggle. His participation was to be somewhat limited in respect both to the number of troops which he should furnish, and to the services in which they might be employed; but the step was nevertheless unfriendly, or even distinctly hostile to Sweden. News of these proceedings reached Charles Gustave, who anticipated the danger, such as it was, with characteristic promptness. In the dead of winter he broke camp in West Preussen, marched directly upon Königsberg, and summoned the Elector to do homage to him as a suzerain, who by the defeat of the Poles had entered into possession of all the Polish claims against the Duchy. That the pretension was well founded in feudal law, as understood at the time, is by no means certain; but the Swedish King declined to discuss technicalities. There was no

Overtures to Poland.

1656. Action of Charles Gustave.

11

alternative for Frederic William. By the Treaty of
Königsberg, January 17, 1656, he became a vassal and an
ally of Sweden. He granted to the King the use of his
ports, the right of passage for his armies, and the power
to call upon him for an eventual contingent of Prussian
troops, too small, however, to be of much weight in a
great war.

In Poland, meanwhile, a species of popular uprising took
place. The nobles roused themselves from their apathy,
and at banquets copiously pledged mutual support in a
determined effort to save the country. An apparition of
the Virgin at Czenstochow reproached the timid populace for their indifference under the misfortunes of their
country, and itinerant priests harangued the faithful with
all the ardor of crusaders. The Polish deserters in the
service of Sweden returned to their original allegiance.
Even John Casimir himself was finally carried away by
the widespread enthusiasm ; made the most liberal pledges
to the peasantry ; and soon reappeared in the field with
an army vastly superior in numbers to that of his adversary. Charles Gustave was undismayed. He again invaded Poland, and won some trifling victories, but the enterprise was on the whole unsuccessful, and he was forced
to retire into West Preussen.

Frederic William was now placed in a more favorable
position. Both the belligerents were suitors for his friendship ; but Poland, presuming too much on her temporary
good fortune, adopted an unwise tone of command, which
provoked or rather frightened him into the arms of Sweden. A new treaty, that of Marienburg, June 25,
1656, was the result. It was in effect a treaty
of alliance, both offensive and defensive, against the
Poles and their gentle allies, the Tartars. Its political
provisions were unimportant. Sweden surrendered to the
Elector some territory conquered in Polish Prussia, and
modified in some respects the terms of the feudal relation ;

Treaty of
Marienburg.

but the essential articles were those which defined the future military coöperation of the two powers.

Charles Gustave at once resumed hostilities. The Elector hesitated. He hoped that the mere report of the alliance would bring John Casimir to terms; and in order to facilitate his conversion he sent a French diplomatist, who was busy in those parts, as a mediator. But all overtures were rejected by the King and his confident advisers.[1] Frederic William then gave his army reluctant orders to march, and on the 27th of July the allies reached the outskirts of Warsaw.

The allies invade Poland.

Prussian historians give the invaders a total force of from eight to sixteen thousand men, and place the strength of the garrison at forty thousand. A Polish pen would probably reverse these figures. The exact truth can never be known, but if the disproportion was not very great either way, it is doubtless safe to assume that it was at least not in favor of the allies. The amazing confidence of the Poles must have rested on superiority of numbers, for they had learned the folly of trying to cope with the Swedes on equal terms, and their contempt for the Brandenburg contingent, though less absurd, was not warranted by actual experience. The allied lines closed rapidly about the city. On the 28th the Polish outposts were driven in, and the works approached; but the confidence of the Poles rose with the imminence of the danger. The city had put on holiday attire. A scaffolding had been erected along the bridge over the Vistula, and on this favored place the beautiful ladies of the nobility gathered to admire the valor of their kinsmen, and to witness the annihilation of the enemy. The housetops were covered with spectators, the windows glistened with patriotic eyes. All was pride, enthusiasm, exultation; and

Battle of Warsaw.

[1] The Swedes, the King pleasantly observed, he had presented to the Tartars for their breakfast, and the Brandenburgers he intended "to bury so deep that neither sun nor air will reach them."

by every class of society, by peasant, burgher, priest, and noble, the dawn of such an auspicious day for the fortunes of Poland was hailed with pious and vociferous gratitude.

The Poles seem to have fought at first with courage and ardor, though without the method which secures success, or the endurance which mitigates defeat. On the 29th the Brandenburgers carried an important strategical point, from whence they could bombard the works. The Poles then perceived their peril. Over and over again they charged the hill with the flower of their army, while around the flanks and rear of the enemy the Tartar horsemen essayed the most audacious but ill-calculated and futile movements. The Elector held the position, and his troops bivouacked on the field which they had won. The next day, the 30th, the allies resumed the offensive. The height of Praga was the key to the situation, alike for the Poles and the allies; and when after a desperate struggle this had been carried by the Brandenburgers under Sparr, and the Swedes under the King himself, the field was already won, and the city lay prostrate at the mercy of the foe. No further serious resistance was made. A panic seized the Polish army, which dispersed in confusion over the country; John Casimir fled; the allies entered Warsaw, and the city was plundered in the most ferocious style.

At this point, however, the harmony of the allies came to an end. Charles Gustave urged, as was natural, that the Poles should be pursued, and the conquest of the country be made complete. But the Elector refused. He had kept his word, he said; the Brandenburgers had done their duty; the Tartars were in Preussen; he must return to his own people, and attend to his own affairs. He returned, accordingly, to Königsberg, where his presence and the presence of his soldiers was indeed urgently required. A horde of Lithuanians

Defection of the Elector.

and Tartars had invaded the Duchy, and in a short time had destroyed hundreds of villages, massacred the helpless people, and carried off the sound and vigorous into slavery. Avoiding open engagements, they scoured the country in small but active bands, which were finally driven off only after a long time, and with the greatest difficulty. About Charles Gustave troubles even graver were swiftly gathering. Forced by the defection of his ally to abandon Poland, he had barely returned to West Preussen, and begun anew the siege of Dantzic, when the Poles swarmed about Warsaw again, more numerous and more defiant than ever. The Grand Duke of Moscow declared war. The Danes attacked him by land and by sea. From this list of enemies the King first selected his Scandinavian brethren, and set off for Denmark, abandoning, Dantzic, which John Casimir occupied in triumph.

The Elector's situation was now extremely perilous. From Sweden he could of course exact any terms; and in the Treaty of Labiau, November 20, he obtained the formal dissolution of the feudal tie, and the recognition of his independence in Preussen. *Treaty of Labiau. 1656.* But what was this concession worth against the Poles? The Republic had never recognized the transactions between Charles Gustave and the Elector; and in its view the union of Preussen with Sweden and its dissolution were equally invalid. And John Casimir was again in the field, leading an overwhelming force, and eager to chastise the Brandenburgers for their share in the battle of Warsaw; while in all parts of the Elector's dominions, in the New Mark and Pomerania, bands of Tartars were laying waste the fields and slaughtering the people. But at this crisis the mediation of the Emperor came as a welcome relief. The Poles thought it prudent not to refuse; and another treaty, that of Wehlau, September 19, the last but one in the long succession of compacts, established peace and an alliance be- *Treaty of Wehlau. 1657.*

tween Frederic William and John Casimir. Poland recognized, as Sweden had already done, the independence of Preussen, ceded to the Elector some territory which had been taken from the Swedes in Fore-Pomerania, and agreed to bear the expenses of the coming campaign; while Frederic William restored the Polish districts, which were still in his hands, and engaged to coöperate against Charles Gustave.[1]

With this convention the Elector's practical interest in the struggle may be said to end. In no other

The Elector's diplomacy.

part of his career was his duplicity used with such admirable artistic skill; in no other did it produce such brilliant and substantial results. So long as it was necessary to teach Poland a wholesome lesson of his power, the Elector was a firm ally of the Swedes. As soon as a reconciliation with the Poles offered better hopes of profit than further coöperation with Sweden, he passed promptly over to the other side. No sense of honor, no scruples of conscience seem to have governed his elastic purpose; he consulted only his interest, and in the end carried off nearly all the spoils of the contest. Even the stately Pufendorf is moved by this affair to something like enthusiasm. His pen throbs under a new impulse; his narrative becomes almost sprightly; and his terseness nearly betrays him into epigrams. But historians of the modern school are more fastidious. Ranke is grateful for the Treaty of Wehlau, yet prudently evades any discussion of the means by which it was obtained; while others, like Droysen and Stenzel, excuse rather than defend the Elector's supple diplomacy. The strictures of Charles Gustave were of course more severe, within the limits of prudence. But the King of Sweden was an aggrieved party, and the asperity with which he rebuked his unfaithful friend, though not unwarranted on moral grounds, would naturally

[1] Carlyle, *History of Friedrich II.* i. 266, note, confounds this treaty and the one the year before with Sweden.

be dismissed as an outburst of personal chagrin.[1] At present, however, we are concerned with the contents, not the legitimacy of the compact. It is enough that by the surrender of his share of the spoil gained in the campaign of the previous year, the Elector purchased the release of Preussen from all the feudal ties which had hitherto bound the province to Poland. His title as duke was made complete and indefeasible. He and his heirs in Preussen were thenceforth to do homage to no suzerain, to acknowledge no master, to be received as equals into the society of sovereign princes.[2]

Independence of Preussen.

The campaign which followed was distinguished by little except the brilliant tactics and heroic valor of the Swedes. They easily defeated the Danes in the open field ; and when winter set in they crossed on the ice, and sought them out in the most distant recesses of their northern home. Then, after forcing upon them an ignominious peace, they returned to the continent, and to the consternation of the Elector marched directly upon Preussen. But their progress now began to cause general alarm throughout Europe ; and a combination of Austrians, Poles, Brandenburgers, and Dutch was formed against them. Even Charles Gustave then saw the hopelessness of the struggle. Negotiations for peace were opened under the auspices of England and France ; and although the King himself died before a settlement was reached, the Treaty of Oliva, May 3, 1660, put an end to hostilities, and probably averted an European war.[3]

Death of Charles Gustave.

It remained for Frederic William to remodel the domes-

---

[1] See the correspondence between him and the Elector, or a summary of it, in Pufendorf, i. lib. VII. In particular the King's letter of December 6th ought to have had interest for Pufendorf the jurist, as well as for Pufendorf the historian.

[2] Art. V. concludes, . . . cum summa atque absoluta potestate, sibi habebunt, possidebant, regentque, absque omnibus ante hac præstitis oneribus. . . .

[3] All of these treaties are in Dumont, *Corps Univ. Dip.* vol. vi.

tic institutions of Preussen, otherwise his purpose in the
Treaty of Wehlau would be only half accomplished.

But this task presented serious difficulties. The suzerainty of Poland had been surrendered, not absolutely, but with conditions; and in one article
of the treaty it was expressly stipulated that
the Elector should respect and conserve the rights, privileges, and liberties of all classes of people in the Duchy.[1]
If the rest of the instrument was valid could this provision be fairly repudiated? Or if an essential condition in
the treaty could be brushed away by one of the contracting parties, had not the other a right to insist on the entire restoration of the original situation? One cannot say
that this alternative proved of much service to the Prussians. The tendency of the age, the conditions of the
crisis, the relations of their neighbors, — all seemed to
conspire against them. In the first place the attempt to
question the treaty itself led at once into a labyrinth of
legal subtleties, of obscure fictions, in which the more vital
issues, both political and constitutional, were nearly lost.
What was the sense of the treaty of 1466, of 1525?
Was the dominium supremum of the province,
held by Poland as an indisputable right, also
an obligation, which no act of hers could terminate?
This is what the Prussians practically held. They argued
that the province formed an integral part of the Republic
of Poland, that their hereditary prince was only a tenant
of the King, and that the dominium supremum could not
be surrendered without putting an end at the same time
to the Elector's title. They declared especially that the

Preussen and the Treaty of Wehlau.

Protest of the estates.

---

[1] Art. IX. The stipulation extended indeed only to privileges, etc.,
huic conventioni non derogantibus, which, Droysen, III. ii. 519,
paraphrases in the words " so weit sie der Souveränetät nicht entgegen
seien." This is accurate enough if sovereignty be taken in the sense
of the treaty, i. e. independence in respect to foreign states, but for
the Elector the word had a broader signification, as even Droysen
himself shows on page 507 of the same volume.

immediate authority and the ultimate supremacy could not legally be vested in the same person. But these propositions, which would have had no little force two or three hundred years before, in the full bloom of the feudal system, were too weak in the seventeenth century to arrest the march of events. They exercised the ingenuity of lawyers without at all shaking the resolution of Frederic William. There was even a want of dignity, an appearance of weakness, or at least something not quite manly and spirited in this querulous refusal to part with a guardian and protector, who had contemptuously cast them off; and the considerate critic will hasten to draw a veil over this part of the story.

It is therefore the more gratifying to know that after this brief technical contention had spent its force, and the issue between the province and the Elector had assumed the true form of a constitutional struggle, the estates defended their cause with tenacity and courage, and displayed examples of the most splendid civic virtue.

I should like to relate in detail the history of this remarkable struggle. It would be a work of respect and affection to describe the fearless patriotism of Kalkstein and Rhode, — the one a patrician general, the other a plebeian burgher, yet as twin heroes in the battle for liberty, teaching their countrymen that the interests of the province were indivisible. It would inspire the humblest pen to sketch the noble characters, and recount the stirring incidents that adorn the records of an epoch so honorable to the gallant Prussians; the fidelity of the rural landraths whom the Elector and his agents could neither seduce nor frighten from the path of duty ; the firm prudence of the oberraths, who desired to please an exacting prince, and yet feared to offend an aroused people; the indignant, eloquent, and even defiant protests which were hurled in the face of Radziwill and Schwerin; the intrepidity of the Diet, which survived re-

The struggle for liberty.

peated dissolutions, and the harangues of the market-place, where freedom of speech was defended by armed citizens; the pacific and prudent counsels of Frederic William's envoys rejected by Frederic William himself, who despised a willing as he abhorred a reluctant subject; the tardy arrival but prompt action of the Elector; the triumph of military force in the streets of Königsberg; the arrest of patriots by a breach of faith on the part of the first politician of the age; and in the end the overthrow of the constitution and the subjection of Preussen to an absolute prince. The facilities of a complete narrative would enable me to show that the estates were not irreconcilably hostile to the Elector, that they recognized the validity of his title, and asked for no other guaranties than those fixed by law and prescription; that they only contended for the right to enjoy their hereditary freedom under the constitutional sway of a prince, for whose better qualities they had both respect and admiration. I should enlarge on such topics with genuine interest if the limits of this work did not forbid.

In the distribution of the parts of this drama the Elector suffered the lesser players to occupy the stage *Men and offices.* during the earlier scenes, and reserved his own appearance for the showy and decisive climax. His favorite minister, Schwerin, a man of moderate views and cautious methods, was sent to the province in an informal diplomatic capacity; but he had no authority which the estates recognized, and could hold officially no communication with them. The office of statthalter or viceroy was also unknown to the constitution, although Radziwill in command of the troops saved it at least from contempt. The legal executive power was confided to the oberraths, or crown commissioners, as they may be called. They belonged, as a rule, to the local nobility, and being for that reason naturally in sympathy with the estates, furnished a crude form of ministerial responsibility. The landraths, or sheriffs, were still farther removed from the Elector, and still more closely identified with the landed gentry. In the cities, finally, there was the magistracy, with the burgomaster at its head, the schöppen, with the schöppenmeister as their foreman, the guilds and corporations, and all the other elements of a high spirited, patriotic, and undaunted population.[1]

The estates were convoked in the spring of 1661, for the first time since the Treaty of Wehlau. Violent attacks were at once made on the treaty; but these had been foreseen, and Schwerin was neither alarmed nor embarrassed. The leaders soon learned, therefore, that these tactics would be of little avail without the coöperation, or at least the encouragement of Poland; but although signs were not wanting that the Republic already repented of the bargain of 1657, and would cancel it at the first opportunity, she was not in a position to render active assistance.[2] The Diet began, therefore, to shift its position. It reserved still the right to reject the treaty, but laid more stress on the conditions under which it might eventually be accepted. These conditions were that no change should be made in the administration of the province; that every person should be solemnly confirmed in the possession of his land, goods, and public offices, and in the enjoyment of all his civil and political rights; that the soldiers which had been promised to Poland should be raised from the tenants of the domains; and finally, after other specifications less important, that the Elector

Diet of 1661.

---

[1] Compare on this subject Isaacsohn, *Gesch. des pr. Beamtenthums*, ii. 11 et seq. The landraths with the two bishops formed the first estate, the nobles and knights the second, and the burgesses the third.

[2] On the contrary the Elector even procured a reaffirmation of the King's fidelity to the treaty. His ambassador at Warsaw, Hoverbeck, was a sharp-sighted, energetic, and unscrupulous politician, and his reports give suggestive pictures of the state of society at the Polish capital. But that the Elector should insist on fidelity to treaty engagements was certainly a grim stroke of humor.

should ratify the whole with an oath, and agree that the estates should meet every two years with or without a summons.

The Elector anticipated the "considerations" and "gravamina" of the Diet by a scheme of his own, which was sent off to Königsberg before the rival instrument came to hand. But the estates refused to discuss it. The Proroga- oberraths even declined at first to lay it before tions. them, and only yielded to the solicitations of Schwerin after a spirited protest, which recorded their official dissent as ministers and their indignation as patriots. The feelings of the Diet were rapidly communicated to the land; the storm grew more violent and dangerous; and Schwerin saw that for the time nothing could be done. The Diet was therefore prorogued.

In the next session, which began in January of the following year, a practical question of revenue occupied and Session of divided the Diet. It had become necessary to 1662. provide for a subsidy voted some months before, and opinions differed as to the form of tax which should be adopted. The two upper orders, with the natural instinct of land-holders, favored the excise, which fell chiefly upon the towns. The burgesses, no less generous, recommended a head and property tax, from which the nobles were not exempt.[1] But this disagreement was an opportunity that Frederic William hastened to seize; and the questionable expedient of "complanation," a species of arbitration which feudal princes had sometimes claimed the right to exercise when their estates failed to agree,[2] enabled him to form an alliance with the two orders

---

[1] See the report of Schwerin, dated March 28.

[2] "Jus complanandi," out of which had later been made a jus complanandi absolute. See Muelverstedt, p. 135; Raumer, Codex, ii. 201. Curiously enough the American President has a species of jus complanandi in case the two Houses of Congress fail to agree on a day for adjournment. Const. art. II. sect. 3.

against the third. But the towns denied the legality of the measure, refused to pay the excise dues,[1] and at Königsberg nearly precipitated a civil war. The burghers patrolled the streets day and night, unawed by the troops which Radziwill had about him, or by the great guns of the castle above the city; and vigilantly guarded their leader, Rhode, from arrest. It was not until the Elector himself appeared on the scene that the intrepid patriot was surprised and seized. Even then Frederic William hastened to promise that Rhode should have a speedy and fair trial, but kept his word with characteristic fidelity. The captive hero was sent to the fortress of Peiz, where after a confinement of sixteen years, which the captor never ratified by a judicial sentence, and Rhode himself scorned to terminate by submission, he died in 1678.

The Königsberger may justly claim a modest place with the Rienzis, the Marcels, the Hampdens of history. His opportunities were fewer than Rhode. theirs, the stage on which he worked much smaller, the measure of his success far narrower ; while servility and slander, the officious and welcome instruments of his victorious rival, have labored to make his cause and his memory odious. An absurd story became current, and is even accepted by Baczko, that Rhode was a mere paid agent of the Jesuits. The charge has no other basis than the fact that his brother was a Catholic and lived in Warsaw ; but the interest of the Prussians in Poland clearly did not need the aid of religious sympathy, while if Rhode had refused even to solicit a pardon, and preferred a lingering death in prison, on account of a cause of which he was only a hired advocate, he would have to be regarded

---

[1] In one of Radziwill's letters, dated July 31, 1662, he hints the suspicion that the seeming acquiescence of the two upper orders was given because they knew that the resistance of the towns would be kept up, and the Elector's plans be thwarted without any risk on their part.

as a monstrosity alike by the historian and the psychologist. Even the timid subject who is afraid to deny, ought to be ashamed to believe so silly a libel. And yet since in all Prussian histories the adulation of Frederic William and his successors excludes even common justice to Rhode, it is left to foreign pens to call attention to this humble defender of constitutional freedom.

The treacherous arrest of Rhode aroused once more the knights, who discovered that while selfishly fondling and dandling their own class interests, they had imperilled others which were common to them and the towns. The resistance was therefore taken up and renewed. Although Königsberg was prostrate, the country squires were still free; if Rhode was a prisoner the Kalksteins were active and resolute, and their influence at Warsaw was undiminished. It is, therefore, not strange that the Elector, weary of the vexatious strife, and convinced that his vigor in Königsberg had crushed the spirit of armed revolt, found it prudent to invite a compromise.

His first "assecuration," [1] or charter of rights, was not, however, acceptable to the estates. It protested too much for an honest instrument; its pledges were fortified by too great a profusion of oaths; its scope, emphasis, and elaboration were all suspicious; and it wanted those prosaic details which, more than sounding phrases, determine the value of a political contract. It was accordingly replaced early the next year by another, more practical and more satisfactory.[2] Since this second assecuration was acceptable to the Diet, which in return acknowledged Frederic William as the lawful and only prince, we shall be justified in regarding it, and the accompanying act of the Diet, as the instruments by which the public law of the province was brought into harmony with the new order of things. The assecuration was a bill of rights, to which the Diet gave the concrete

Overtures of the Elector.

---

[1] Nauwerk, p. 127.   [2] Ibid. pp. 130–137.

form and the practical sanctions of a legislative enactment. The one contained the general bases of a treaty of
peace; the other was the treaty itself. What rights, then,
were defined, and what guaranties enacted?

In seeking an answer to these questions, one first meets
the unexpected admission, in the style of an ex- Charter of
cuse or apology, that the estates ought to have 1663.
been invited to the negotiations at Wehlau; and in order
that the article might have more than a historical value it
was added that the omission should not be made a precedent for the future, but that thenceforth the Diet should
always be consulted in such important affairs.[1] This last
provision is next taken up alone, and expanded into a
more diffuse and elaborate paragraph, of which the sense
is that the powers of the Elector under the new system
shall be no greater than the sum of the powers before
held by himself and the King of Poland. The impartial
administration of justice is assured; the rights of the Lutheran and the Roman Catholic religions are confirmed;
no new taxes are to be imposed, and no war begun without the consent of the estates; and the local officials are
declared to be secure in their places during good behavior.
But the most important provision of the instrument was
probably the last. It is there solemnly agreed by the
Elector that even without any special emergency, and on
the simple demand of the estates or the petty council, a
Diet shall be summoned every six years for the redress
of grievances and for general legislation. The estates
in other words accepted a formal promise of periodical
Diets in place of that guaranty which they had enjoyed
before the era of indirect taxes in the power of the purse.

---

[1] . . . und bei andern solchen wichtigen Tractaten und Handlun-
gen, so dies Herzogthum Preussen betreffen, in Kriegs- und Friedens-
zeiten, allemahl unserer getreuer Stände, Rath Gutachten und belieben
gefordert, und ausser diesem hinfuro Kein Schluss noch Verenderung
gemacht werden solle. . . .

They cannot have supposed, however, that the one was equal to the other.

The legislative act first disposes of the disputed sub-
The final act. sidy by the method of complanation, but without prejudice for the future; makes various provisions for the administration of the public archives and the domains; and afterwards enumerates at some length the power of the oberraths. The attributes of these officials had been one of the most hotly contested points of the struggle; and it is possible that in the reorganization both extreme views were discarded. The prince acquired greater personal initiative when in the Duchy, and granted the council a wider discretion during his absence. Finally the measure established a board of thirteen members, armed with authority to examine and pronounce upon any grievances of the estates that might fail to receive redress from the government or the legislature; but whether this board had power to correct the omission, or could only make fresh representations, does not clearly appear in the article.

On a hasty glance it might seem that the advantages of this settlement were fairly divided between the two parties, but the antecedents of the problem ought to be considered as well as the literary form of its solution. The language of the instrument makes no difference between the recognition of an existing right and the concession of a new privilege. In this way the bounty of the Elector is unfairly magnified, for it is evidently a false assumption that the conflict was merely between two parallel sets of historical rights and powers. A collision in such a case would have been impossible; and a compromise, if the thought itself be not absurd, would simply have been drawn along the old line of division. A juster statement, therefore, would fix the issue between the ancient rights of the Diet and the innovations attempted by the Elector.[1]

[1] Comp. Lancizolle, *Königthum und Landstände*, p. 9.

How many of their privileges ought the estates to surrender, was one question ; how many of its aspirations could prerogative realize, was another ; and both are answered in the assecuration and the recess.   But these answers were not so much the work of legal or historical interpretation as of patience and endurance, of political strategy, of moral and even physical power.   The discretion reserved to the Diet was all that it saved from its former rights.   The functions gained by the crown were so much added to its previous attributes.   Thus in effect a repartition of the public powers had taken place, and through this process the centre of political gravity was shifted visibly in the direction of the crown.   By an equal distance of course it receded from the estates ; hence their profits from the transaction were purely fictitious.   It left them standing, not upon a broad level foundation, where they could rally their forces and fortify themselves against fresh attacks, but upon the side of an inclined plane, down which their own weight and the Elector's efforts would slowly drag and push them to destruction.[1]

The fate of Colonel von Kalkstein, who was the head of the refractory nobles, presents circumstances even more aggravating than those in Rhode's case.   Rhode suffered from a breach of faith and a denial of justice ; but the outrage, however gross, was at least a local and domestic one.   Kalkstein was seized by a violation of international law on the part of an ambassador, who, himself enjoying its protection, ought to have been the more scrupulous to uphold its obligations.   It is true, Kalkstein had himself broken what may be called his parole.   Arrested in 1669 for an alleged treasonable correspondence with Poland, — the same being an appeal to

Kalkstein.

---

[1] Lancizolle, *K. und L.* p. 10, describes this process as " die Ertheilung der Assecuration an die Stände im Jahre 1663, und die unmittelbar darauf, ohne neue Zeitumstände beginnende nicht-Beobachtung derselben."

7

the Diet of Warsaw to enforce the treaty of Wehlau, which the Elector by his aggressions in Preussen had grossly violated, — he had been sentenced to life imprisonment, but after the lapse of one year released on condition that he retire to his estates, remain there, and abstain from further seditious intrigues. Not long subsequently, however, he had escaped to Warsaw, arguing that a pledge extorted by force was not binding. The Elector demanded his rendition, which the King of Poland properly refused. Much angry correspondence passed, and the case became a critical one, when Brandt, the electoral envoy at Warsaw, succeeded in arresting the exile secretly, and spiriting him away into Preussen. Naturally Poland protested against this outrage, which made no little stir in Europe; and Brandt received a nominal reprimand from his master. But there is no doubt that the abduction was ordered by Frederic William himself, and that he had committed a most flagrant breach of international law and comity. Kalkstein was beheaded at Memel in 1672.

To complete the story of Frederic William's war upon local autonomy and parliamentary rights it is necessary now to return to Cleve, and to those lesser principalities which were acquired during his career.

In Brandenburg after 1653 the Elector had only to ignore his parliament and allow it to die from neglect and destitution; in Preussen he pursued a mixed policy of force, intrigue, and persuasion, which led in the end to the same result; but in Cleve his triumph was that of brute violence. What he had done to one man at Königsberg he threatened to do to the whole Diet at Duisburg. He was not inclined, he wrote to the governor, to permit any delay; if the estates would not listen to reason he knew other means of carrying through his purpose. The opening speech of Maurice [1] was no less emphatic, and much more explicit. He declared that the

Aggression in Cleve.

[1] October 28, 1660.

two charters of 1649 and 1653 weighed like chains of
slavery upon the Elector's independent spirit. They required the governor himself, as well as all lesser officials,
to be confirmed by the Diet; they forbade the levy or
introduction of regular soldiers in the province; they permitted voluntary parliaments, which was contrary to universal law; and they put a variety of other most vexatious
fetters upon the discretion of a benevolent prince. The
Elector could no longer endure this. He was coming to
Cleve, added the governor significantly, with an ample military force, and all evil-disposed persons would do well to
reflect what a responsibility would rest upon them if they
should persist in their obstinacy.

These were arguments which it was difficult to resist.
The estates had no serviceable troops at their command,
and the Elector was leading thither the veterans who had
stormed the heights of Praga, and had taught even the
invincible Swedes a lesson of discipline and valor. Armed
resistance was therefore out of the question; and the more
timid or less refractory leaders of the Diet made overtures
to the governor, which led to negotiation and at length,
November 3, to the formal acceptance of the modified
recess.

Since Frederic William had long systematically defied
the earlier charters, — had appointed his own stattholder
and other officers, had raised and maintained troops, had
levied taxes, and in short had conducted the government
in utter contempt of all the limitations of law and usage,
his desire to have those limitations removed, and his own
absolutism confirmed by the Diet, will appear unnecessarily
and unreasonably strong. It is probable that here as in
Preussen he was thinking of his successors. All the quarrels which he left unsettled would be inherited by his son;
and both the character of the next elector and the circumstances of his reign might be less favorable to victory.
If he could therefore convert the forced submission of the

various diets into voluntary acquiescence, and thus give a title in law as well as in fact to his usurpations, he would be able to leave his successor a nation of loyal and obedient subjects. It would only be necessary after becoming an absolute ruler to make his absolutism tolerable by broad and enlightened measures. A good example of integrity in the public finances would encourage the spirit of thrift and industry ; and under the influence of sweeping reforms, skilfully fitted to the tastes of the several classes, the country would in time forget the anarchical freedom which it had once enjoyed, and become reconciled to order, discipline, and authority.

It deserves mention, too, that in September, 1666, another treaty of partition in respect to these lands was concluded. The Elector received Cleve, Mark, and Ravensberg, about one third of the whole territory ; the rest was retained by the House of Neuburg. Guaranties were exchanged in regard to religious freedom, the division of the Rhine tolls, and mutual aid in case of hostile invasion ; and if one of the contracting houses should become extinct the other was to receive its share, and reunite the territories. This convention was approved by the Emperor.

New treaty with Pfalz-Neuburg.

The next year brought the Elector a cruel affliction in the death of his consort, Louise of Orange. They had been married, as we have already seen, in 1647, and two years afterwards a son had been born, who died, however, in early childhood ; and when after the lapse of several years no second heir appeared, the patriotic princess offered to accept a divorce, and leave the Elector free to choose a wife more likely to gratify the just desires of himself and people. The offer was of course declined by Frederic William, with what seems at the time to have passed for a heroic exercise of virtue. But it was not without its material rewards. In 1655 Louise finally presented him with a second son, Charles

Death of the Electress.

Emile, and subsequently with two others, Frederic and
Louis, of whom Frederic alone reached manhood.[1] Charles
Emile died in 1674, Louis in 1687. But both of them
survived their excellent mother, who after a short illness,
which was not effectually checked by a journey to the
Hague, died at Berlin on the 8th of June, 1667.

After the death of Louise the Elector's dynastic solicitude suddenly grew more acute. She had left
him three sons, so that the chances of the direct
succession were reasonably sure; yet he hastened
to repair her loss, and enlarge his household, by espousing,
less than one year later, the widowed Duchess Dorothea
of Brunswick. Of the fruitfulness of the second Electress, not even Luther could have complained. She bore
him no fewer than seven children, of whom six survived
their father; but the historians who dare to speak disre-
spectfully of so warlike a person record the fact, or the
opinion, that the characteristic traits of the stepmother
were brilliantly realized in Dorothea.

The Elector's second marriage.

About the time that the Elector introduced this active
belligerent into his family, the peace of Aix-la-
Chapelle had for a time put an end to the war
which was raging on the broader field of European politics. Louis XIV. had retreated before the Triple Alliance,
and the Spanish Netherlands were relieved of his armies.
But that the King regarded the interval as a mere truce,
and would hasten by diplomatic means to prepare for a
renewal of the struggle on a more favorable basis, was
perceived from the first by every power except Holland,
which under De Witt appeared to be the victim of a singular optimism. It was not until Louis actually reopened
the war, in 1672, that the Republic awoke from its delu-

Louis XIV.

---

[1] He was born at Königsberg, and the happy circumstance moved
a local poet to the following prophecy: —

Königs Berg sieht Friedrichs Geburt. Was deutet dieses Zeichen?
Musen! Ihr weissagt mir: König wird Friedrich sein.

sion, and learned that both its allies, England and Sweden, had deserted it. De Witt's life was the penalty for his imprudence, and William III., Prince of Orange, came to the front.

Louis had not only broken the Triple Alliance, but he had even brought England and Sweden into his own camp. In Germany his agents were not less active and scarcely less successful. The Emperor played an ambiguous part, in alliance now with, now against France, and when possible nominally neutral; but on the whole he made no effective opposition to Louis' plans. The minor princes were easily won by French threats or French gold. Frederic William alone showed discernment and resolution. He was attached by personal and political ties to the House of Orange; and little suspecting probably the nature of Sweden's engagements to France, he rejected all the offers of Louis, and took the field with an army in support of Holland.

Branden-
burg and
France.

Nothing was accomplished in this first campaign. The combined Brandenburgers and Austrians marched to the Rhine; manœuvred fruitlessly in the region of Treves, Mayence, and Coblentz; and returned to Westphalia without having struck a blow. The Elector then entered into negotiations with Louis; and, in spite of the protests of the Dutch, concluded a treaty of peace on the 6th of June, 1673. A little later, in December, he actually formed an alliance, offensive and defensive, with Sweden, whose hostility he dreaded even more than that of the French.

The peace with France lasted just one year; the alliance with Sweden never existed except on paper. In July, 1674, a new triple alliance was formed against Louis, this time between the Empire, Spain, and Holland; and the facile Elector at once joined it. He agreed to furnish a contingent of 16,000 troops, and was promised the command in chief of the operations on the upper Rhine. Unfortunately the comedy of the

New alli-
ance against
France.

previous campaign was merely repeated, for although the allies this time crossed the Rhine, and defeated Turenne, they failed to follow up the victory, and practically nothing was gained.

While at Strasburg, Frederic William received alarming news. A Swedish corps, 12,000 strong, had invaded Brandenburg; and the province, stripped of all its soldiers, was at the mercy of the foe. *The Swedes invade Brandenburg.*

It was necessary, therefore, to give up the French campaign, which promised indeed no decisive results, and return at once to Brandenburg. But a variety of reasons imposed the greatest circumspection upon the Elector. The Swedes had not declared war, and proposed rather the most friendly intentions; but the Elector, they said, was waging war against their ally Louis, and treaty obligations forbade them to desert him. If the Elector would recall his army from the Rhine they would retire from the Mark. In fact they conducted themselves in the country with moderation and good order. Frederic William took account of these circumstances, and feeling the need of securing allies before attacking the invaders, he proceeded to the Hague, where Holland and Denmark pledged their active coöperation. England was to remain neutral. His army then took up its march from Franconia, where it had passed the winter, toward the Elbe, and, conducted by the Elector in person, arrived there on the 11th of June, 1675. The strictest secrecy had been enjoined, and the Swedes were taken wholly by surprise. *Counter movements of the Elector.*

The enemy lay along the line of the Havel, their two main bodies being at Brandenburg and at Havelberg. Policy required that the junction of these two forces should if possible be prevented. To this end the Elector determined to send a flying force of cavalry and artillery across the country to the town of Rathenow, which was one of the keys to the whole Havel region, and *1675.*

was manned only by a few companies of Swedes. The
enterprise was wholly successful. The guards were surprised by a squadron of dragoons, and driven in, while a
boat load of pioneers forced the south gate, and a third
column seized in the same way the mill gate. The city
was then carried by storm.

The hardest work yet remained. Rathenow was a valuable strategical point; but the Swedish armies were yet
intact, and the Elector's infantry had been left in Magdeburg. It had since indeed continued its march northward, but was still many miles distant, when Frederic
William learned that the two Swedish corps, breaking
camp respectively at Brandenburg and Havelberg, were
hastening to effect a junction at Fehrbellin, the most important pass through the swamps and morasses of the
Havelland. This had to be prevented at all hazards, but
what could be done without an army?

The Elector succeeded in collecting about six thousand
men, chiefly cavalry, with thirteen guns, and on
the 16th of June set out for Fehrbellin in order
to intercept the column of Swedes retreating from Brandenburg. Their rear was struck the next day, and on the
18th the whole army was forced, by the persistent attacks
of the Brandenburg dragoons, to make a stand. This was
at the village of Hakenberg, about four miles from Fehrbellin. The Swedish force is liberally put at from ten to
twelve thousand, with thirty-eight cannon. The odds
were certainly great; and the more prudent officers in the
Elector's army counselled delay, or at least flank movements, rather than an open engagement. Another party,
more impetuous, was for action; to it the Elector promptly
yielded. The veteran Derfflinger, who had advised delay,
showed himself, nevertheless, a hero in action; and by a
brilliant charge carried a height, planted artillery upon
it, and poured a fatal fire into the ranks of the enemy.
Gradually the bulk of the Elector's force was collected on

Battle of
Fehrbellin.

or about this hill; the Swedes must recapture it or lose the day. Three times they made the attempt; and though they were each time repulsed the situation was growing critical for the defenders, when after the third attack Frederic William ordered a counter charge, and, falling upon the Swedes before they had recovered, changed their temporary retreat into a final rout, and hurled them in wild disorder through the pass of Fehrbellin. The victory was complete. Prisoners and booty were taken; and the flying Swedes were pursued to the frontiers of Mecklenburg.

The day of Fehrbellin is still regarded, notwithstanding all the triumphs of Frederic and William, as one of the proudest in Prussian history. It was the first time since Gustavus landed in Germany that the Swedes had been beaten in the open field except by superior numbers; and the lesson was the more bitter as being administered by a prince whose skill had hitherto been shown chiefly in choosing allies, and avoiding danger. The world was amazed. A new power had arisen in the north, and all political calculations were rudely overthrown. What shall be done next? was the anxious inquiry of diplomatists.

For Sweden the immediate problem was, however, military rather than diplomatic. Not only would the prestige of her arms be lost unless she could retrieve her fortunes, but even her possessions in Germany, dearly as they had been bought, and her authority in the councils of Europe, so gratifying to her pride and so necessary to her independence, were seriously imperilled. For the Elector followed up his victory with promptness and vigor. He had an army flushed with triumph, full of confidence and enthusiasm. His generals had seen their leader manœuvre with the art of Turenne, and fight like a soldier of the ranks. Even the people were this time not averse to war, for hatred of the Swedes had become a patriotic passion,

shared by every class.   Denmark had given Frederic
William an alliance, which interest, more powerful than
good faith, required him to maintain, and which proved
to be of the greatest practical value. Of the alliance with
the Emperor both the opportuneness and the value may be
questioned.

Early in September operations were resumed by the
combined forces of the Elector and of Denmark,
and were easily successful. The Swedes were
practically expelled from Germany, retaining through the
winter only the fortified towns of Stettin, Stralsund, and
Greifswald ; while Frederic William had reconquered
the rest of Pomerania, including Wolgast and Wollin,
both important places on the Baltic.   The year 1676
brought also no decision, and no very important engagements.   The Swedes made an effort to recover Wolgast
but failed; the allies were forced by severe weather to
give up the siege of Stettin, and go into winter quarters.
Little was therefore gained except at sea, where the
Swedes were of course no match for the combined Dutch
and Danish fleets.

In the spring of 1677 the siege of Stettin was resumed,
and by the 1st of August the investment was
complete.   The city was popularly held to be
impregnable.   The " virgin city " it was proudly
called by the burghers, because its streets had never been
defiled by the tread of a hostile army.   The advantages
of its position were favorable to defence ; stout hearts beat
within the breasts of its citizens.   Three thousand Swedish troops were within the walls, and the commander,
Colonel Noht, was an officer of reputation, alike for skill
and for courage.   But neither relief from outside nor a
successful sortie was among the contingencies on which
the garrison could count ; and nothing was possible except
to make the best resistance which their honor demanded
and their means permitted.   For four months the bom-

*Further op-
erations.*

*Siege and
capture of
Stettin.*

bardment continued. Hundreds of thousands of shots were fired against the works ; by day and by night shells burst in the streets ; flames destroyed one after another the public buildings, and even the private houses of the citizens ; Noht himself was killed ; provisions and munitions were nearly gone ; and yet the besieged fought undismayed. The allies began to doubt. Voices were heard in favor of giving up a hopeless enterprise, and seeking easier triumphs elsewhere. The Elector saw, therefore, that it would be difficult much longer to hold his army together ; and it was resolved to make a last desperate effort to carry the exhausted but still defiant place by storm. Notice was sent the town to remove the women and children ; the assault was fixed for the 13th of December. On the 12th the city surrendered. "The virgin," said the note of the Swedish officer, ^{1677.} "throws herself into the arms of her illustrious suitor." So much time was required to clear away the débris from the streets that it was a month later when the Elector and his wife made their triumphant entry into the city.

The capture of Stettin was a highly creditable achievement in a military sense, but it rather injured than improved the Elector's political prospects. It roused the Swedes themselves and their allies, the French, to fresh exertions, and awakened the jealousy of Austria and of Holland, both of which powers hastened to conclude separate treaties of peace with Louis. The Elector, that stern moralist, protested against such perfidy, but in vain. Only Denmark remained true ; but Denmark was not a great military power, and the French were threatening Cleve. Frederic William himself then proposed peace, and negotiations were begun ; which were, however, frustrated by the refusal of France to accept anything less than the restoration to the Swedes of all the territory which they had lost. The Elector refused, and the war was resumed. Stralsund was the first object of attack, the same Stral-

sund which fifty years before had so successfully resisted
Campaign of the great Wallenstein. It is true that in the first
1678.　　siege the town kept its water communications
open, and was even supported by friendly fleets, while the
sea was in this case controlled by allies of the besieger;
but the seizure of the commanding island of Rügen was
nevertheless an audacious enterprise, and the surrender of
the town after a brief bombardment was doubtless due to
military necessity. Stralsund capitulated on the 17th of
October, 1678, and Greifswald, the only Pomeranian fortress remaining in the hands of Sweden, on the 17th of
November.

The scene of hostilities was now transferred to the
Hostilities in province of Preussen. A considerable Swedish
Preussen.　　army marched in from the north, and meeting
no resistance from the local militia hastened on towards
Königsberg, the capital, intending to capture the city
before any part of the Elector's troops could arrive from
Pomerania. It happened, however, that the movement
had been anticipated, and several thousand cavalry thrown
into the city. Königsberg was saved; and General
Görtzke even took the offensive as soon as the Swedes
began their retreat. The Elector with the main army
arrived too late for the actual fighting; but his march
in the dead of winter, in intense cold, and part of the way
even in sledges, across the ice of the Frisches Haff, was
a trying task nobly performed.

Thus the Swedes lost another campaign, another army;
and negotiations for peace were once more tried. Still
the Elector could obtain no more favorable terms. France
insisted as before that everything should be restored to
Sweden, and that the Elector's arduous efforts and costly
victories should count for nothing in the settlement.
From the Swedes he was, indeed, for the time relieved.
To heal the wounds and repair the losses of these disastrous years, to raise new armies and plan new invasions,

and to find fresh allies among the neighbors of Brandenburg, were occupations which would fully employ their
leisure for many months to come. But with the decline
of Sweden rose the activity of France, and Louis threatened to march straight upon Berlin. The Danes began to
waver, the King of Poland inclined toward the enemy.
And the Emperor's doubtful friendship was likely at any
time to pass into open hostility, and to change with it
the attitude of other princes in the Empire.

There was evidently no alternative for the Elector. On
the 29th of June, 1679, at St. Germain en Laye, Treaty of peace.
a treaty of peace was concluded between France
and Sweden on the one side and Brandenburg on the
other; and on the 2d of July, with an anguish which will
easily be conceived, Frederic William signed it at Berlin.[1]
By its terms all of Swedish Pomerania, except a small
strip along the right bank of the Oder, was restored.
France evacuated Cleve, and agreed to pay an indemnity
of 300,000 crowns. These conditions were certainly hard
for the Elector, and the feelings of rancor which they left
are not difficult to understand. But the reader has sufficient acquaintance with Frederic William's treatment of
France, Holland, and Sweden, of his own weak sense of
good faith, justice, and honor, to answer the question
whether he had a moral or a political right to expect any
special forbearance from the European powers.

His resentment was first shown at the cost of the Emperor. In 1681 Louis XIV. seized the city of Strasburg,
in circumstances which it is not necessary here either to
describe or to judge, but which were of course extremely

---

[1] It is said that the Elector in affixing his reluctant signature repeated the line: —

Exoriare aliquis nostris ex ossibus ultor.—Æneid, iv. 625.

The story is pretty enough to be true, and probably is not false;
though it may not be improper to remind Lieut. Col. von Cosel (Geschichte des pr. Staats. i. 282) that the line expresses not a prophecy
but a wish.

humiliating to Austria. The Elector looked on with sin-
ister satisfaction. Two years later the great alliance
Elector and against Louis was formed, and the Emperor ur-
Emperor. gently appealed to Brandenburg to join it. Frederic William refused, and even opened friendly negotiations with France. But when the Turks appeared before
Vienna, and threatened after capturing that ancient and
beautiful city to spread over all Germany, the Elector so
far relented as to promise military aid against them, the
equivalent being certain concessions in Silesia. An army
was actually formed for the enterprise, and General von
Schoening intrusted with the command. But it never
crossed the frontier. With or without reason the Emperor
became suspicious of the Elector's ultimate intentions, declined his aid, and gave King John Sobieski of Poland
the privilege and honor of saving the imperial city. In
1686, however, a small detachment of Brandenburg troops
was more welcome. Under Schoening they fought bravely
against the Turks, and as compensation the district of
Schwiebus was ceded to the Elector, though not without
reserves which confirmed his belief in Austrian duplicity.

Frederic William was now drawing toward his end.
For several years he had been a great sufferer from the
gout, and to this complaint was added in the spring of
1688 the dropsy, but even in the very presence of death he
relaxed in no degree his interest in the affairs of
Illness and
death of the state. On the 27th of April he was carried in
Elector. an arm-chair to the great hall of the Rathhaus,
where he took leave of the ministers, the magistrates, and
other officials, and held a discourse to his son Frederic on
the true duty of a ruler and the correct maxims of government. A copy in writing, much enlarged, was handed
to the future elector at the same time. Two days later,
April 29, 1688, the Great Elector died.

For obvious reasons I shall not attempt to give a detailed estimate of Frederic William's character. He

must be judged chiefly by his acts; and if these seem to give a higher opinion of his talents than of his morals, of his achievements than of his measures, it is the fault of inflexible history not of the impartial historian. And in some fields of action, as foreign politics, not even his talents were always skilfully employed, not even his achievements were unmixed and indisputable blessings. Probably the release of Preussen from the Polish bond was the most striking of his triumphs, although even this was long only a precarious theoretical gain, and cost him years of trouble and labor before it came to be fully realized. But in the midst of vacillation, of tentative schemes, of failure and disappointment, he kept the one great object of his life, the vindication of his own will as the supreme authority in the state, immovably before his eyes; and in this he was brilliantly but deplorably successful.

CHAPTER VI.

STATE OF THE COUNTRY UNDER THE GREAT ELECTOR.

THE preceding chapter described in the order of their occurrence the leading events of the war between Frederic William and his various diets, the only war in which the Elector was gratified both by victory and the fruits of victory. But it omitted, as out of place in a mere narration, an extended discussion of the real significance of the struggle; of the revolutionary spirit which prompted and the revolutionary triumph which ended it; and of the decisive influence which the result would necessarily have on the future destinies of Prussia. That omission must now be supplied.

The war on the constitution.

Although the issue was practically between two mutually exclusive forms or theories of government, it does not appear that it ever presented itself to the Elector in any such comprehensive shape, or that his immediate purpose had been thought out as part of a systematic scheme. What he desired was relief from a vexatious personal restraint. He had ends to pursue, which either were not those of the estates, or were not attainable through the means that the estates were willing to sanction. It is true that his impatience under their opposition to this or that measure gradually led to the denial of their right of opposition in any case; that their refusal of particular subsidies cost them in the end all power of control over the taxes, the revenues, and the purse of the state; and that the distribution of political authority was thus radically changed. But in his earlier years the Elector was apparently satisfied if he could only carry through the project of the hour. Speculative theories of absolutism were not in favor. Having no great wars on hand, even his views of the military establishment were modest; and the Mark, impoverished as it was, made sacrifices, both of opinion and of treasure, which deserved gratitude, not rebuke and subsequent treachery, from Frederic William. But his forbearance ended with the situation which for a time made it expedient. As soon as treaties with foreign powers gave him the pretext, and an obedient army the means, he came openly forward in the character of a prince determined to destroy local freedom in all the provinces which events had brought under his sway.

This was his policy with Prussia, the Mark, and Cleve; it was likewise his policy in all the other territories, in Minden, Halberstadt, Magdeburg, and Pomerania. But their own condition, history, experiences, — all that contributes to form the political character of a people, — made the subjugation of the younger and lesser dependencies more than usually simple. They had

Policy in the newer territories.

had their spirits crushed by the severity of military rule. Their resources had disappeared before the exactions of rival armies, succeeding one another in the work of plunder. Wherever a petty prince had ruled the doctrine of absolutism needed no fresh introduction. And to all new subjects not Catholics the head of Protestant Germany was a deliverer, whom it would be ungracious to catechise about the source of authority, or the operation in politics of the natural law perceptive. For his part the Elector did not formally dissolve the estates in any of these new dominions. He simply set up a more vigorous executive force over against them. They survived without much change for many years, and even continued to meet for the exercise of such corporate functions as the Elector had left them; but since in doing homage they had renounced, formally or tacitly, all and any of their ancient rights which were incompatible with the new position secured by

14

treaty to Frederic William, they had in effect put their
honor and their fortunes into his hands.   In every conflict of interpretation two questions had to be answered :
What were the ancient rights of the estates ?   What was
the character, and what were the boundaries of the authority acquired by the Elector ?   Thus in place of one tech-
nicality, in place of one problem, two arose ; but Frederic
William was a stern logician, and when his syllogisms
failed promptly drew the sword.

That the Elector thus continued to respect the outward
form and corporate character of the estates in these dominions, while in the Mark itself, as we have seen, he dis-
In the Elec-   persed the Diet into a score of impotent councils,
torate.   may be ascribed to a distinction which though
somewhat subtle was not inconsistent with his general
policy.   The Kurmark, it must not be forgotten, was that
one of his territories from which Frederic William derived
his chief title and dignity.   As elector of Brandenburg
he was not only a favored peer of the great German commonwealth, whose emperor he helped to choose, but he
had also a character in Europe, corresponded familiarly
with all its princes, and fought battles or made treaties
with the Grand Monarque himself.   The Mark formed,
therefore, a complete state, and gave its lord a political
character.[1]   It is evident accordingly that the united
estates of the Mark, which when convoked as a diet exercised independently one class of functions in a recognized
state, and thus shared with the prince the authority of the
central government, were somewhat different from the
estates of those outlying dependencies which from time to
time had fallen to the House of Hohenzollern, which were
provinces almost from their very nature, and were liable

[1] This was not less true after Prussia ceased to be a vassal state.
Even in the Treaty of Wehlau itself Frederic William is first described as " Marchio Brandenburgensis," while " Dux Prussiæ, Cli-
viæ," and the others follow as subsidiary titles.

at any hour to be set aside as appanages for needy heirs of the family. These diets were easily regarded as local and provincial, and therefore as needing no further dismemberment; while that of Brandenburg was a political, and, in a certain sense, a national representative body. In Brandenburg it was therefore expedient, and the composition of the state made it easy, to resolve the Diet into its original members; instead of united to recognize only separate estates; instead of a general parliament of the Kurmark to maintain only local parliaments of the New Mark, the Old Mark, and the other lesser divisions; and thus to rob the ancient assembly at once of its prescriptive rights and its historic dignity. When this had been done Frederic William, as an elector of the Empire, remained the sole representative of the political unity of the Kurmark.

In this way Brandenburg was reduced to the level of provincial subjection, and henceforth has only a local interest as one of the members of a rapidly consolidating state. Its history fairly illustrates the general course of decline. The Diet of Prussia continued indeed for a time obstinately and spitefully to defend its right of control over the local budget; but in the other provinces the estates slowly lost their unity of action, discarded entirely the habit of legislation, and accepted the humble part of irresponsible advisers. This reduced itself in most cases to the mere right of choice between the two wings of a cruel alternative.

An incident out of the later years of Frederic William's reign will show the form in which questions were still submitted to the estates, and the extent to which their coöperation was still permitted. Allusion has already been made to the fiscal experiments which the rivalry of the orders caused to be tried in the Mark.[1] At first when the form of taxation was in question

Changed spirit of the estates.

[1] The pedants of the age also took up the question and hotly dis-

the towns agreed to the excise, which was finally adopted
for a term of years. But as the tax did not prove productive enough to suit the Elector, the method of direct
contributions was substituted, and in its turn gave rise to
disputes over the apportionment,[1] making it extremely difficult for Frederic William to arrange the final subsidy of
1653. This grant again expired in 1660, and the whole
subject was once more thrown open. For the next few
years the records are meagre. It does not formally appear by what method or by what authority the Elector
continued to procure money for the support of the troops,
but the inference is not too violent that the contribution
was simply prolonged, and that the Elector's command was
a sufficient warrant for every tax-gatherer. Be that as it
may, the altered spirit of the estates is clearly shown by
the proceedings of 1667. In that year there was a conference between the Elector or his ministers and the deputies
of the towns and the nobles ; but these deputies do not appear to have called their prince to account for the illegal
levying of taxes during a period of years, nor to have demanded a general Diet as the constitution ordained, nor
even to have claimed for themselves the right to determine
the amount of revenue to be raised. They were modestly
satisfied with the honor of being consulted about its proper
source or system. The cities again championed the excise;
the knights still clung to the direct tribute ; but neither
class of delegates presumed to reopen the question of
budget right.[2] The Elector finally, in the exercise of his

cussed it in countless pamphlets, most of which are now lost. Comp.
Roscher, *Geschichte der National-Œconomie in Deutschland* (Munich,
1874), pp. 319 et seq., from which it appears that the balance of opinion was in favor of indirect as against direct taxes.

[1] Isaacsohn, ii. 118 et seq. ; Ranke, i. 58–66.

[2] In 1683 the estates complain that the land is on the point of
breaking down under its heavy burdens, especially in view of the
erlittene Miswachs, der hin und wieder getroffene Hagel-schaden,
der nicht geringe Mäusefrass, etc. Evidently the blow which the **Mark**

prerogative, gave each order the privilege of raising its quota in its own way.[1]

Other examples would only confirm the melancholy tale. The people everywhere yielded, sullenly indeed yet far too readily, to physical force ; and thus permitted the steady progress of an usurpation, which they must have felt would never retrace its steps. But the helpless protests which they occasionally made show that their legal scruples were less easily overcome, that a sense of the constitutional outrage inflicted upon them long survived their practical acquiescence in the new order of things, and that many years would have to elapse before prescription would come in to ratify injustice.

Even to this day, it may safely be said, nobody has attempted to defend in law the conduct of the Great Elector. Widely as publicists or schools of publicists may differ in regard to the attri- The plea for the Great Elector. butes respectively of the lord paramount and his estates in Brandenburg-Prussia, and therefore about the line of division or coöperation between them, they unite in support of the two fundamental propositions, that the estates had certain rights which ought to have been inviolable, and that Frederic William did nevertheless wantonly violate them. The one proposition involves a statement of law, the other of fact ; but they are equally clear and equally strong. In place, therefore, of a merely technical argument for the validity of a rule which nobody seriously disputes, and of a review of facts which are already given in the foregoing pages, it will be better to pass at once to the only practical excuse that has ever been put forward in behalf of the Elector. It is admitted that his course was contrary both to written and to unwritten law, but it is added that as a

suffered in the overthrow of its constitution was not too keenly felt by people who could thus class it with the ravages of the hail and the field mouse !

[1] Ranke, i. 64 ; A. F. Riedel, *Der Brand.-Pr. Staatshaushalt*, p. 31.

wise statesman he had to obey, however unwillingly, the imperative voice of expediency.

Whether expediency ought ever to set aside the clear prescriptions of law is a question which was keenly debated by the casuists of the seventeenth century. It is a barren controversy in any case since it involves the prior definition of at least one term which will not reduce itself to scientific precision; to ascertain the expedient is nearly the same as to accept it. Hence in nearly all states the suspension of the laws in grave crises is an admitted practice, but forms and guaranties are provided, and the arbitrary is made as harmless as possible. Such was the case, for instance, with the dictatorship at Rome, of which the modern analogue is the proclamation of martial law. But this illustration was of little service to the Elector's apologists, because it described an interruption of law which the law itself expressly contemplated; or, in other words, it was an expedient by which the constitution was temporarily set aside in order that it might the better be preserved. But the measures of Frederic William were wholly different from this, and cannot be tried by the same tests of criticism. He did not suspend the constitution for a brief time in order that he might afterwards restore it reformed and strengthened; he deliberately overthrew it, and put another in its place. And the steady march, the imperious mien, the bluff frankness of this usurpation, shuts out the theory that the estates, as the guardians of the ancient liberties, were deceived or duped. They were simply cowed, and except at Königsberg seem hardly to have inquired whether forcible resistance had not become a right and a duty.

This question might again have been resolved into two, which seem to cover the case: Was the relation between margrave and people of the nature of a compact or political engagement, mutually binding upon the parties? and

Examination of this plea.

had the people, or the estates, a right to insist, by force
if necessary, on the fulfilment of the engagement? On
both of these issues the estates might with confi- Views of
dence have appealed to the philosophy of the age. contemporary publi-
They would have found Grotius and Pufendorf cists.
expressly teaching the doctrine of the social contract, and
Hobbes leaving it to be deduced from his leading dogma ;
while some of these, and other publicists no less famous,
granted the power of enforcing the contract, that is if one
pleases, the right of revolution, in the broadest terms.[1]
I shall offer a few observations on the first, and only on
the first branch of the subject.

The theory which makes civil government the result of
a convention between men in a state of nature is
practically false, but its popularity in the seven- Theory of
the social
teenth century shows that there was even then a contract.
spontaneous tendency on the part of thinkers to regard
reciprocity in rights and duties as the chief basis of the
state. It was not a tendency which they had acquired
from the study of the influences about them. The remnants and traditions of feudal society, the course of history since the age of Charlemagne, the Germanic principles diffused so copiously over Europe, — these were not
the sources from which Bodin and Suarez, Grotius and Pufendorf drew the lesson of social or political reciprocity ;
for the original institutions had no learned literature, and
were not invariably represented by their best features.
The political philosophy of the seventeenth century was
therefore almost by necessity classical, drawing its abstract
theories from Aristotle, its examples from Greece and
Rome ; and the conclusions which it reached, no matter

---

[1] Si rex partem habeat summi imperii, partem alteram populus
aut senatus, regi in partem non suam involanti vis justa opponi po-
terit, quia eatenus imperium non habet, etc. Grotius, *De Jure Belli
ac Pacis*, lib. i. cap. 4, XIII. See also Pufendorf, *De Officiis Hom.
et Civ.*, lib. ii. cap. X.

how correct in style and comely in shape, were nevertheless like a mere accumulation of statues, valuable only in
art.   The breath of life being denied to them, it was impossible for them to elbow their way among the energetic
practical ideas which were then dominant in Europe.   Even
the influence from which they did derive a certain mechanical or automatic vitality, the revived Latin jurisprudence,
was itself an alien intruder, without sympathy for the
original native institutions into which it had forced its
way, and still provoking friction at a multitude of points.

But it is a great mistake to suppose that one must return to the speculations of Aristotle, and the
practice of the antique world, for the principle
of checks and balances in the state.   A century
later Montesquieu found it in the English constitution,
uncorrupted by foreign alloy, modified only by the natural
conditions of its own growth, erect, vigorous, active ; and
he correctly traced it back to the primeval woods of Germany.[1]   The inequality of classes in the Teutonic system
was the germ of mixed government, or limited monarchy.
It is now generally recognized that " a perfect democracy
is the most perfect despotism."   It is fully admitted in
practice, even by republics where the will of universal suffrage is the supreme law, that the expression of that will
must be tempered by mild formalities, and its execution
made subject to prudent delays, without which an individual or a minority would have no defence against oppression, and impetuous councils no opportunity of revision.
These are purely formal restraints, but they may be ascribed even in the most artificial system to a necessity as
old as political government.   They are indispensable to
any state which lays claim to stability.   In feudal Ger

Merits of the Germanic system.

---

[1] M. Guizot, *Histoire des origines du gouvernement représentatif en
Europe* (ed. Paris, 1851), i. 85, meets Montesquieu's observation,
" ce beau système est sorti des bois," with some painfully literal criticisms.   But M. Guizot was defective in the quality of imagination.

manic society, on the other hand, the equilibrium of powers in operation, and their equitable development during a long period, were favored by natural, and could dispense with mechanical aids. If a natural force is better than a mere arbitrary contrivance, if a vital principle in institutions is of more value than an inanimate rule, if an organic distribution of functions according to the original conditions of its being is more favorable to the vigor and growth of a political system than the petty cords and pulleys of human art, the Germanic state, with or by reason of its inequalities, was superior to those modern democracies which by levelling all distinctions have made a dumb instrument out of a living body. It was not indeed superior for many of the practical purposes of government. Under it police, justice, legislation, and many other formal charges of the state, were of course less efficiently organized than they had been in the complex system of Rome, or are in the Romanized Prussia of to-day. A modern state protects one citizen admirably against another; but in the mediæval state were all citizens less independent of the central power? It seems to me, notwithstanding the many sombre incidents of feudal history, — the hardships of the peasantry, the lawlessness of an occasional prince, the cruelty of private warfare, the frequent insecurity of person and goods, — that civil and even political rights in the Middle Ages were not the less clearly understood, the less highly prized, or the less bravely defended, because they were the rights of classes and not of persons; that on the contrary the very restlessness and disorder of mediæval society, the constant obligation of self-defence, gave to privileges, which were already hallowed as the legacy of innumerable years, the additional value, almost from hour to hour, of a recent and painful conquest.

By the term privileges, again, I do not mean to designate alone the recorded concessions made by the suzerain to his vassals, or the powers usurped, Progress through strife.

and often abused, by the one party or the other. These had indeed, or in time gained, a validity which no legal assaults could shake; but there were others which claimed a natural or original legitimacy, which were lodged with the several orders as part of their definition and their life, and which instead of destroying really preserved the balance of the state by the fierce persistence of their warfare. The danger was only in the cessation of the strife; health, vigor, energy, progress were in its maintenance. For under the sanguinary terms that in rhetoric describe this conflict will be found that perennial play and counterplay of forces, that eternal oscillation of rival energies, which in the state, as in nature, and in all the relations of life, is an indispensable condition of power and achievement. Nor does this view shut out the readjustments and redistributions which the fortunes of the struggle may effect or assist. It does not ascertain a fixed law of division between the elements of public activity, and then condemn them to a dull routine of advance and retreat, of attack and defence, in which there is no vital contact, and therefore neither progress nor production, but rather encourages genuine organic changes because they prove the soundness of the natural functions, and are the inseparable signs of growth. And the greater this facility of adoption and development the less easy will it be for the play of the forces to fall into a lifeless mechanical action. A permanent truce between the elements with stagnation, and a complete victory of one element with the destruction of the other, are equally fatal to a political system in which power is shared between rival classes or orders, and in which rights are balanced by corresponding duties.

The fiction of a compact or convention is peculiarly *Principle of reciprocity.* useful in any discussion of feudal monarchy because that system gave to the principle of reciprocity — the first quality of a contract — so commanding a position. It was indeed not the convention of Hobbes or Rousseau. It was not an arrangement under which the people surrendered all their rights to a single prince, or one upon which the individual man had absolutely impressed his own tastes and views. Nay, it may perhaps be denied that a breach of this contract by one member released the other or others from their obligations, since this would be equivalent to a dissolution of society, and is not seriously to be considered. But the absence of penalties for the violation of an engagement does not render the engagement less sacred in the eye of the moralist. Ethics are stronger than constitutional fictions; and though the law may call a king irresponsible he has really a higher responsibility than any minister or any subject, otherwise limited monarchy would be impossible. The engagements of civil society under the eternal compact of nature are twofold. There is the duty imposed on each member to perform his specific, prescribed part; and there is the general obligation to respect the sum, the distribution, and the coördination of the parts. Concretely this truth finds expression in every constitutional system. The duties of the citizen are defined and his rights guaranteed, but he is also pledged or bound to support the form of institutions thus established, as one which cannot be changed except by common consent, or otherwise according to the method prescribed by the laws themselves. In states which have no written charter this truth is not the less important. Exact provisions of law not being at hand, formal changes ought to be preceded by the collation of historical rules, by the test of indispensable necessity, and by the proof that their manner and substance are in harmony with the essential spirit of the government.

An institution or a custom is not to be condemned, then, because it is old, not always even when its age and familiarity are its chief claims to favor, The state a vital organism.

provided no grave interest suffers permanently by its re-
tention. But the case is especially strong when the venerable member enters into a great system as an organic and
integral part. A fixture, an artificial limb, a mechanical
appliance can be removed without much danger to the
life or character of a state; but vital organs, however
much time may seem to have impaired their energy and
usefulness, are so intimately bound up with the whole in
physiological union, that the prudent statesman will propose an amputation only as a rigorous and awful necessity.[1]

If these conclusions be now applied to the case of
Prussia, it will appear that in the enterprise
which the Elector undertook, the burden of
proof fell upon him, not upon the estates; that even
waiving the question of casuistry, whether success can ever
justify wrong, the test of success or expediency must be
incomplete because the opposite policy of adhering to the
old system was not tried; that the publicists of the age
either expressly recognized the wisdom of restrictions
upon the power of the prince, or taught a theory of the
social compact from which such restrictions can be logically deduced; that in Germanic and feudal society these
restrictions had at once the antiquity of an original creation and the sanctions of an implied contract, so that any
essential change ought either to have had the character of
an organic process, or, if an artificial measure, to have con-
formed to the traditions and genius of the system; that of
the several sources from which the public law of a state is
derived, not one furnishes any excuse for the usurpations
of Frederic William; and that his pretended reform was
therefore nothing but a revolutionary attack upon the historical institutions of his country, — an attack which involved both a violation of written and acknowledged obli-

*The Elec-
tor's crime.*

[1] On this subject modern conservatism can add but little to what
Aristotle has so admirably said in the *Politics*, lib. ii. cap. 5.

gations, and in a larger sense a betrayal of the chief rule
of social conservation, fidelity to the spirit and genius of
a state.

The censure so justly due to this Elector's treatment of
the estates may also be applied in a measure to
the changes which he made or attempted in the The administrative service.
administrative system, since local self-govern-
ment, or the participation of the estates in purely executive affairs, was a principle as old and as valid, although
not quite as self-asserting, as that of the public control of
the purse. But after the independence of the diets had
been crushed, and thereby a new constitution created, it
was the more reasonable that the other institutions of the
state should be brought into harmony with it; and from
this point of view the further measures of Frederic William might seem to be excusable if not meritorious. In
this part of his task he was, nevertheless, far from successful. He fixed the seat of authority according to his own
views, and reduced his various dominions to a common
rank, but he still wanted the power to assimilate them all
in a real system of provincial administration; it was long
indeed before his mind even grasped the idea of such a
reform. Local institutions were still too strong, and local
patriotism still burned too fiercely. Concentration rather
than diffusion was, therefore, Frederic William's policy;
and this process necessarily revolved about himself as the
sole embodiment of the central authority. He as their
common lord was all that bound the principalities together either in law or in feeling. The administration
was centralized only so fast as he took it into his own
hands, distributing decrees, ordinances, laws, through immediate retainers, who formed as it were a body cabinet
about his own person; and so long as political unity
was wanting, this necessarily continued to be the case.
The mission of the Elector was therefore to correct this
preliminary evil, and prepare the way for the reforms

of his successors. They safely restored the administrative fractions because he had first created the political whole.

The distinction may, I think, be observed, and it is not without value in the present discussion, that throughout the Elector's dominions the system of government offered the greatest uniformity at the lowest and the highest points of the scale, while the intermediate stages showed the most diversity. And this fact has an easy historical explanation. The lower instances, whether of police, or of justice, or of fiscal control, being the farthest removed from the central administration, were more independent of the central authority, and longest conserved, in the privileged autonomy of the towns and the manors, one of the most characteristic institutions of the Middle Ages. The prince himself, on the other hand, and the immediate representatives of his supremacy, preserve the same outward type through all the vicissitudes of their actual careers. A municipality in Cleve was not much different from one in Brandenburg; a duke of Prussia and a duke of Pomerania were clad in about the same garb. But between these two extremes lie the intermediate arrangements by which the lord of the land established his connection with all classes of his people; and here prevails a perplexing variety, illustrating the fluctuating fortunes of the long struggle between local self-assertion and the rising spirit of absolutism. On the one hand may be seen the knight of the manor, the bailiff on the domains, the magistrate in the towns, who preserve order, interpret the laws, and collect the dues; on the other, a prince who is now a feudal superior, now a feudal owner, now a feudal patron, but always a personal ruler in whose name justice is administered and the revenues are applied. The uncertain element everywhere was the channel or channels by which the dispositions of the prince were conveyed to the people, and the participation of the people

Obstacles to administrative unity.

made itself felt by the prince. It was very easy for the authorities of a city to collect the excise, or for a knight of the shire to arbitrate between his tenants; and this is as true of Cleve as of Prussia or the Mark. It was not difficult for Frederic William to spend the revenues which he received, or to pronounce judgment on ultimate appeal, whether it concerned one territory or another. But the rules of procedure and the administrative steps which bridged the space between the common lord paramount and his remoter vassals were as diverse as the soils, the landscapes, the annals, and the characters of the provinces themselves.

The previous margraves had been content as a rule merely to assert their right of proprietorship over these later acquisitions, without presuming to meddle much with local laws and customs. But even their proprietorship was long an empty form, barren and unsubstantial. The powerful councils or boards of government in Prussia and Cleve seldom contested *Centralization and local self-government.* indeed the faultless title of the Hohenzollerns, and gave it at least the seal of negative assent; but they also refused to reduce their own pretensions, and in the guise of executive agents acted the part of political regents. If now that class of officials who were next under and nearest the person of the elector, through whom alone his decrees could reach the lower orders, and whom, therefore, he would naturally strive first to discipline for an uniform service, were able, even down to the time of Frederic William, to preserve their peculiar local types; if one reflects, too, on the new elements of variety and confusion brought in by the conquests of this prince himself; it becomes clear not only that a mediæval chaos still reigned in the administration of this complex state, but also that the common ruler wanted many of the attributes associated by modern thought with political authority. Two great reforms had therefore to be effected, and Frederic William

224 HISTORY OF PRUSSIA.

accepted necessarily the first. He hardly attempted to introduce uniformity of system and practice in the affairs of his several dominions ; but he successfully imposed the principle of his own supremacy upon every official, and made it felt as a positive force throughout the whole frame of local polity.[1]

In Prussia the four chief dignities, that of the ober-hofmeister, of the chancellor, of the oberburg-graf, and of the obermarschall, who together formed the college known as the oberrathstube, were hereditary. When vacancies occurred, however, the electors had sometimes procured the introduction of their own candidates, on rare occasions even of aliens. The system in Cleve and the Rhine territories had passed through great vicissitudes, but at the time they fell to Frederic William the crown had recovered the right to appoint the three higher officials, the landhofmeister, who had charge of the finances; the marshal, public safety; and the chancellor, justice and internal administration. These executive officers had seats again in the Privy Council, which was a deliberative body. It appears that when the change of dynasty aroused the fears of the estates they reclaimed some of their former influence over the administration, and even Frederic William yielded to them in a measure. In Pomerania the interregnum and the Swedish occupation had maintained an exceptional state of affairs for several years before it was actually acquired by Frederic William ; and during that period the estates were more than usually powerful. By the constitution of 1654 adopted by the Elector and the Diet the government was to consist of a president, a kanzler, a hofgerichtserwalter, a schlosshauptmann, and two temporary members. The existing functionaries were to be retained, and in filling vacancies the Elector was restricted in his choice not only by the positive participation of the estates, but

The various local systems.

---

[1] Comp. Isaacsohn, ii. 93 et seq.

also by a variety of prescriptions about the character and qualifications of the nominees themselves. The temporal government of Minden was in the hands of a kanzlei, and after the annexation this body continued in function, though under the presidency of the statthalter. The estates had a considerable share in fiscal affairs. In Magdeburg the Elector at first left the landraths, or sheriffs, who were in close sympathy with the estates, in the enjoyment of their vast influence in the central administration. The executive organ proper was the council, of which only natives were members.

It might please the antiquarian taste of a few readers, but for others would be an intolerable digression, if I should attempt to explain more in detail the organization and action of the public service in all the different territories, especially since under Frederic William I. the work of the Great Elector was taken up again, and to political unity was added administrative uniformity. The learned or curious are, therefore, referred to the works of Isaacsohn, whom I have chiefly followed, of Raumer, Cosmar and Klaproth, Nauwerk and others, as well as the general histories of the state, and the monographs, which are abundant, on the different provinces.

The personal representative of the Elector in each of the territories was the statthalter or vicegerent. During the first half of the century the office had been, as I have shown by one or two examples, chiefly ceremonial; and the incumbents rarely succeeded, even by physical force, in breaking down the barriers of provincial jealousy. But their impotence was not necessarily due to any defect in their titles, in their personal qualities, or in their official methods. They were simply held in check by the local boards of government, and the proper flow of hierarchical discipline was therefore made conditional on a radical reform in the spirit and the constitution of those sincere and resolute defenders of home independence.

The provincial governors.

This is one of the first reforms in which the Elector's prerogative may be seen in practical operation. After long negotiations, and sometimes not until the last means had been employed, he succeeded in substituting for that odious rule which kept the councils in active harmony with the estates everywhere except in the Mark, the right for himself either of absolute appointment or of nomination with the consent of the estates. These latter fought their case with great energy and persistence. When driven out of one position they fell back to another; when they lost the control of the higher officials they still required the Elector to appoint only resident natives of their own land.[1] But by patient and gradual approaches Frederic William carried even this stronghold. Where he had not power or influence enough openly to force his own favorites upon the local councils he insinuated them, by one pretext or another, into advantageous places, which they could utilize at least as spies and informers; and there were not wanting renegades among the territorial nobility, who were of course rewarded with positions of trust and profit, and who like all renegades showed more zeal and fewer scruples than the older believers. Nothing could be said formally against the employment of such men. They were indigenous not exotic growths; and therefore fully within the terms of the constitutional rule. But the spirit of that rule was not the less violated in their appointment.

Local boards of government.

The course of political centralization, accompanied as it was by the rapid growth of personal government, naturally worked no little change in the Geheimer Rath, or Privy Council. We have already spoken of its formal organization by Joachim Frederic, and of its reorganization in a Calvinistic sense by John Sigismond; it is now necessary to trace its fortunes under Frederic William. The modifications which he introduced affected both its form and its spirit.

The Privy Council.

[1] Comp. Isaacsohn, ii. 140, 141.

Under the two previous electors the Diet, an independent body, was alienated from the crown by religious differences, while the council, being composed of confidential and sympathetic advisers, rose to a position of singular influence and authority. It could not indeed legislate. It could not introduce a new tax, or pass a new law, or change in any essential respect the constitution of the land. But the prerogative of the prince was practically intrusted to it; and prerogative was daily widening its scope with the increase of the public territory, and the multiplication of political interests. The sentiments of the land were expressed by the Diet, but the will of the Elector was first shaped and then executed by the council. All this was changed by Frederic William.[1] He permitted the council still to advise, but not to dictate; nay, to advise even in respect to matters on which it had formerly been necessary to consult the Diet, but the final decision was reserved, both in theory and in practice, by the Elector. It continued to be composed of two classes of members, — the statesmen who held the great offices of state, such as the governors, the chancellor, the treasurer, and so forth; and the councillors proper, who administered no special trust, and had chiefly deliberative voices when the sessions were held. But since the complaint had always been, under the earlier electors, that the first class showed too little deference for the second, — the authority of the few leading officials being so great that they easily imposed their will upon their colleagues and made their opinion that of the council, — the Elector tried to introduce a stricter equality of functions and powers. He aimed to make the council a real board of revision upon the acts and policies of the ministers, and to elevate it above any control except his own. But human nature

Its reform by the Elector.

---

[1] The reform ordinance of 1651 is published by Isaacsohn and by Cosmar and Klaproth.

was too strong even for him, and the favorite servants whose abilities commanded his respect were not easily checked by an artificial device. The council was, however, indebted to the Elector for a real increase of dignity. By giving seats in it to the governors of the different territories, and by creating departments out of the affairs of those territories, he lifted it above the character of a purely Brandenburg institution; out of a local governing he made a national advisory board. But in the scale of rising importance the great officials easily held their own.[1]

This was peculiarly true of the general commissioner for war,[2] the president of the exchequer,[3] and the chancellor, in whom it is easy to detect the germs respectively of the minister of war, the minister of finance, and the minister of justice in modern Prussia, although the process of evolution is rather more distinct in the last two than in the first. All three were, however, created or remodelled by the Great Elector in the style and the spirit of a soldier.

Leading ministers.

The duties of the general commissioner for war were originally of a mixed character, partly civil and partly military. He was the chief of staff, as that term is now understood; and was charged with the details of military organization and supply, being aided at headquarters by the army chancelry, and in the interior by the " land commissioners," or county constables. Over these latter the estates had a form of con-

General war commissioner.

---

[1] The distinction, so appalling to the modern bureaucratic mind, between " wirklich," or real, and titular privy councillor first appears in 1682. It also became customary, not long afterwards, to give to the former the further predicate of " Excellency." Comp. Cosmar, and Klaproth, p. 219.

[2] General-Kriegs-Commissarius, not to be confounded with the marshal, an officer who also flourished for a time as commander of the forces.

[3] Hofkammer president.

trol or revision through the land and city deputations, independent boards, and not a little obnoxious to the Elector. The first step, therefore, was to emancipate the commissioners from this awkward restraint. But Frederic William did not stop even there, for, while he enlarged the functions of those officials in many ways, and even gave them in a measure the civil police in their respective districts,[1] he also inserted other agents of his own between the tax-payers and the deputations of the estates, and gave them the novel and dangerous power of supervising the assessment and collection of the contribution.[2] He thus not only asserted what he called his own rights, but he also usurped an indisputable right of the land.

The contribution being a military tribute, these tax commissioners were regarded as belonging to the military establishment, and had seats with the constables in the provincial commissions, at the head of which was the territorial or provincial commissioner.[3] These boards reported, of course, to the general commissioner at Berlin. In 1675, finally, the administration of the military funds was completely detached from the other revenues, and put into the hands of this official, a change which shows perhaps more vividly than any other the true character and aims of the Elector's policy.

The *The military revenues.*

The military income having thus parted company from the ordinary or hereditary revenues, the care of the latter fell to the president of the exchequer. His was a difficult and unenviable task.

---

[1] Isaacsohn, ii. 160.

[2] Steuer-Commissare they were called. Their appearance on the scene is recorded by Mylius. *Corp. Const. March.* iv., Abth. III. cap. 2, No. 9. See also Isaacsohn, ii. 189–191. This encroachment caused much ill-feeling in the cities, as is shown by the frequent complaints of the magistrates. See, for instance, Orlich, i. 453, 454.

[3] Ober-Kriegs-Commissar. Following the analogy of other branches of the public service, the "General-Commissariat" for the entire state and the "Provinzial-Commissariat" for the Kurmark were perhaps identical bodies.

The useful work of Dr. Riedel shows us in the predecessors of Frederic William a series of princes whose finances were without system, and whose purses were always empty. The private revenues of Joachim Frederic amounted only to 40,000 thalers yearly; the records of the public income which flowed into the hofrenthei are lost. John Sigismond had about the same receipts for the kammer or " chatulle," and from other sources, such as the domains and the regals, something over 200,000 thalers annually during the years of which the accounts were preserved. Both of these electors derived their incomes exclusively from Brandenburg, including, of course, both the Kurmark and the New Mark ; while in Cleve and Prussia, even after they were annexed, the costs of administration and other expenses easily consumed the revenues. It was not until the time of George William that the latter yielded a small surplus for the general treasury. But it would be rash to assume that that prince enjoyed for that reason any exceptional prosperity. The revenues rather declined under his administration, both relatively and absolutely ; for while he is credited in 1622 with nearly 300,000 thalers from all sources, he had in 1638 less than 40,000.[1] He thus fell below, at the end of his reign, not only his own higher figures, but also those of his immediate predecessors. That his outlays far exceeded his means would seem to follow from the frequent use and large issues which he made of " schatzanweisungen," or treasury bills, secured by the future profits of the domains ; but in spite of this temporary relief he was still unable to maintain an army.

The first object of Frederic William, when he came to power, was, as we have seen, to secure the necessary means for his military reforms, and this was accomplished by the aid of contributions, or subsidies. The civil service and the household expenses had, there-

Civil revenues.

Schemes of reform.

[1] Riedel, *Staatshaushalt*, pp. 9, 10; Isaacsohn, ii. 97.

fore, to be met by the remaining revenues, which were wholly inadequate. But although the Elector realized this fact from the first, and was clear as to he necessity of prompt relief, he was apparently not quite so clear in regard to the best method of relief. A series of experiments followed. In the reorganization of the Privy Council a special board of four members was appointed for the general supervision of all the finances,[1] but the plan failed to give satisfaction. There was probably jealousy among the members of the board; they had too many other duties; they wanted unity of purpose and action. Centralization having failed, the opposite policy was tried. The lines of distinction between different revenues and different outlays were more sharply drawn; the treasury was divided into two sections, one for the civil service and one for the household accounts;[2] the war minister arose on the one hand, the finance minister on the other; while the administration of the privy or personal purse was kept by the Elector in his own hands.

But if the general conduct of the treasury suffered for a time from this instability of purpose, *The domains.* one would hardly look for order in the lesser charges, which, both in a fiscal and a hierarchical sense, led up to the treasury. The most important of these was, of course, the demesne lands; and we have already alluded to the early attention which they received from Frederic William, as well as to the improved fruitfulness which under his care they began to show. But their development was still slow and unsteady. It was interrupted not by dis-

---

[1] Geh.-Raths-Ordnung, December 4, 1651.

[2] The latter was the "Hofstaatsrenthei." Its mission was to meet the expenses of the palace officials, and to it were assigned certain revenues, taken either from the privy purse or from the public treasury. Such were, for instance, the profits of the mint at Königsberg, a share of the Rhine tolls, and the returns from certain domains. See Riedel, p. 15, and, for details, the tables in the appendix of his work.

putes of fact, for the successive visitations had only confirmed the Elector's suspicions that the domains were not
doing their duty, but by divisions of opinion among the
councillors themselves when they were called upon for
positive remedies. After a time, however, the Elector
was persuaded to try a modified lease system, which did
not much differ from an ordinary farming of the revenues,
as appraised by the visitors, to the local tax officials.[1]
This system, again, followed the fortunes of ministers. It
disappeared when Gladebeck became chief of the exchequer; but after the old method had had a brief trial it
reappeared under Knyphausen. He was an enlightened
and sagacious statesman, full of resources, and read or
trained in the best experience of the age;[2] and the system of leasing the domains for terms of years at a fixed
rent remains to this day the policy of the Prussian crown.[3]

The royalties, being under the same administration as
the domains, naturally rose with their prosperity
and fell with their decline. In particular the
grain tax, which was levied as an export duty on the
home article, and as a transit duty on that coming from
abroad and passing through, was one of the most productive, in spite of the attempt of the landed gentry to resist

The
royalties.

---

[1] So at least Huellmann, *Geschichte der Domainen-Benützung*, p. 45,
whom I follow in preference to Riedel, because his version better explains the subsequent measures that were taken. Riedel himself
says, indeed, that the system of Admodiation, " oder Verpachtung,"
was introduced (p. 16), and on the next page he describes the minister Gladebeck as overthrowing this reform because he was an enemy
of the lease system. But a lease system proper had not yet been attempted.

[2] Knyphausen's reform scheme is summarized by Isaacsohn, ii.
258, 259.

[3] Huellmann, p. 82, 83, who has some statistics of the improvement
of the domains in the next reign. Riedel, p. 17. From 1701 to
1710 experiments were indeed made with the system of hereditary
leases, which proved, however, a great failure, and carried its authors
down with its own ruin. See infra, chap. viii.

its imposition.[1] The salt monopoly yielded somewhat more. The post, too, brought in a very considerable annual surplus, which was laid aside or paid out as an extraordinary fund.[2] With the mint the Elector made sorry work. He had, indeed, the example of many of his neighbors for debasing the coinage, and is, perhaps, not to blame in that age for ignorance of the truth that public dishonesty is a public calamity, above all the dishonesty of a prince who robs his own subjects. But it is difficult to believe that an enlightened statesman like Schwerin advised such a policy.[3]

Toward the end of his reign, and in consequence of his restless efforts, the Elector's pecuniary fortunes *Increase of* began sensibly to improve. The accounts of his *revenue.* chatulle are known for thirty-six years; they show an annual average of 122,000 thalers. The hofstaatsrenthei was not founded until 1673; and since its funds were derived from sources which the other charges had first to surrender, since it also drew in some cases directly upon these for relief, no little care is necessary, in footing up the total aggregate, to avoid double entries of some of the items. This frequent transfer of money from one set of funds to another makes it, in fact, extremely difficult to reach accuracy in a computation like the present. The hofstaatsrenthei was a diversion, not a creation, of reve-

---

[1] They claimed an exemption from it as one of their privileges, and tried even to find a confirmation of their claim in the recess of 1653. Frederic William contested this, and seems to have had the best of the argument. In any event the resistance probably went no farther than protests after the Elector had commanded them "gnädigst und zugleich ernstlich" to pay the tax.

[2] Riedel, *Staatshaushalt*, p. 24.

[3] Riedel rather assumes than affirms the fact. All that is known is that Schwerin and Tornau, or Tornow, were at that time (1651) the Elector's councillors in mint and currency matters. See Geh.-Raths-Ordnung, art. 18. The various edicts on the subject are in Mylius, iv. I. cap. 5, No. 35, and the following numbers.

nue ; and yet it nowhere appears that the other funds decreased in the ratio of its increase. The Great Elector was surrounded by luxury and pomp. Of simple personal tastes, he reasoned that a certain outward state was due to the dignity of his position, so that the expenses of the official household rose with startling rapidity. In 1674 the receipts of the hofstaatsrenthei were some 115,000 thalers. In 1681, after it had been reorganized, they amounted to 231,000. In 1688, finally, they grew to 367,000, — the expenses of the Elector's illness and burial requiring a special assignment of 143,000 thalers. The annual income of the hofrenthei, the ordinary civil service fund, is estimated by Dr. Riedel at 156,000 thalers ; that of the marine — a special charge — at 50,000 ; the post surplus at 80,000. These five separate funds comprise together the total rental of the domains and permanent revenues from all the territories.[1] It encourages Riedel to assign Frederic William during the later years of his life an annual income from these sources, and other irregular ones, of which the yield can only be conjectured, of 800,000 or 850,000 thalers, out of which were defrayed all the costs of civil administration except the diplomatic service, which was supported from the military fund. This fund, or the contribution, to which in 1682 a stamp tax had been added, produced annually some 1,600,000 thalers. Civil, military, and personal income amounted, therefore, to two and one half million a year.

Besides this the Elector received between the years Loans and 1674 and 1688 nearly three millions in the form subsidies. of subsidies or war indemnities from abroad, and nearly one million in loans.[2] The tables of accounts given by Riedel in his appendix are full of irregularities

---

[1] The sums credited in the accounts to the other provinces represent, of course, only the surpluses which they contributed above the cost of local administration.

[2] Riedel, p. 34.

and inconsistencies. The entries are sometimes topical, showing the character of the revenues; sometimes geographical, showing only the province, kreis, or manor, from which they were derived; and the fiscal odds and ends recorded in the public ledgers prove but too clearly that the exemptions, the privileges, the dispensations, accorded or recognized by previous electors, still survived even down to the end of the seventeenth century. In 1663 Frederic William introduced a system of voluntary scutage, or pecuniary compensation in the place of knight's service, but no record of it appears in the treasury accounts.

Yet this prosperity seems unreal and deceptive when contrasted with the facts that the public officials were wretchedly paid, that the crown was always in debt, and that the Elector was perennially in want of money. Official salaries. The treatment of the civil servants, even up to the highest ministers of state, was at once shabby and dishonest. Their promised salaries were wretchedly low, and in many cases took no other form than promises — the only species of capital with which the Elector was always well supplied. Thus some members of the Privy Council received barely three hundred thalers yearly. Schwerin, when filling the very highest offices, and wielding a power second only to that of Frederic William himself, was put off with the slender pittance of twelve hundred thalers, and was fortunate if he received even that in ready cash. The widow of Gladebeck, a narrow-minded but deserving official, is seen three years after her husband's death trying in vain to recover the arrears of his pay in something better than treasury bills, which nobody would accept. In 1651 Frederic William suddenly and arbitrarily reduced all public salaries by one half;[1] and

---

[1] See in Cosmar and Klaproth, p. 216, the letter to Count Sparr, notifying him that his pay would thenceforth be 600 thalers instead of 1,200.

the only compensation that the victims enjoyed was that of assignment now and then to local offices in the counties, the profits of which, mostly in kind, they were permitted to draw without any serious additions to their labors.

The judicial reforms of this elector were not important.

Justice.

There was some shifting of jurisdictions here and there; plans and counter plans were proposed and considered, sometimes tried, but oftener dismissed untried;[1] and so far as method or system can be discovered at all, it had no higher aim than to assert more clearly the unity of justice throughout the realms by tracing it back to a common personal source. Thus in Preussen, Frederic William hastened to extend the newly acquired "sovereignty" to the judicial institutions. The provincial law was there codified, and in a more advanced condition than in the other territories; the route and order of appeal were well defined; but in the last instance the active interference if not the formal judgments of the Warsaw jurists reminded the Duke of Preussen that he was still a vassal. But after the treaty of Wehlau had established the political independence of the Elector in the Duchy, a superior court of appeal was set up as the symbol and agent of his judicial independence. The scale of justice was thus completed. There were municipal, communal, and manorial courts of first instance for the peasants and burghers; a privy court, with a civil and a criminal division, as a tribunal of second instance, for the same two classes, and of original jurisdiction for the nobles and those otherwise privileged; and finally, the superior court of appeal as the last forum for civil causes.[2] Penal judg-

---

[1] This was the fate of an elaborate project which was drawn up by the vice-chancellor, Andreas Kohl, but, being submitted to the estates in 1643, was quietly smothered by them. The constitution of 1653 contains some thirty articles about the course of justice, the attributes of the courts, and so forth, but they are chiefly repetitions of existing rules.

[2] The members of the Ober-Appellations-Gericht seem to have been named absolutely by the Elector.

ments in the ultimate resort were reserved by the Elector for his personal examination. This reformed scheme was finally ratified by the Diet in 1663.

In Cleve-Mark the course of events was not essentially different. The three important dates are 1651, 1661, and 1669; and to these correspond respectively the separation of administrative from purely judicial procedure ; the organization of a mixed commission as a tribunal of appeals in the third instance ; and the declaration of the rule that the legal principles announced by the courts should not be published, or have the force of law, without the consent of the estates. This reservation which the Elector was obliged to concede to the Diet, implying as it did a want of local confidence in the courts, also seems to suggest the inference that these latter were largely under the influence of the government.

The judicial functions of the Privy Council oscillated to and fro with the unsteady purpose of the Elector. Some form and degree of revision over the judgments of the chamber, and even, in certain *Judicial functions of the council.* cases, of interference at earlier stages, had long been exercised by that body; and various attempts had been made to regulate and systematize the practice. With Frederic William a new era of experiments began. A long procession of orders, decrees, proclamations, reaching from 1641 to 1670, may be found in Mylius and are summarized by Klaproth. Each measure generally undid the work of its predecessor; so that the Privy Council had now a voice in specified cases, now a species of appellate jurisdiction, now a form of arbitration between the higher courts ; but the final result was that it practically lost its judicial character, and retained only a general administrative supervision over the course of justice.[1] The service of the Great Elector was not too well supplied with efficient jurists, nor were the law and its administration among his chief solicitudes.

[1] Compare Cosmar and Klaproth, pp. 195–197.

In the mean time Roman law having settled itself firmly into its usurped position, Roman forms of thought and methods of state were likewise pushing themselves farther and deeper into the habits of political life. Nothing shows more clearly the march of this invasion than the growing use of Latin in official papers, since the language itself was but the frail covering for new conceptions. In this respect the seventeenth century differed vastly from the thirteenth or the fourteenth. The mediæval Latin was not a foreign but a privileged tongue, which to the learned and elegant world was as natural as German to the peasant or the burgess. The mass, which was celebrated in Latin, was indeed the mass of the Latin church, and had never been fully divorced from the example and influence of Rome; the canon law was tinctured with the spirit of the language in which it was preserved; but in earlier times the various papers which record the acts of government were simply written in a species of Latin that had been long domiciled, and had acquired partial rights of citizenship in Germany. Yet it gradually passed out of use, as the language of the people became also that of the courtiers and scholars, and when after a long absence it reappeared with the Roman jurisprudence the conditions of its employment were radically different. It was no longer the improved vehicle of German law and justice. It was no longer a mere convenience in practical use, content loyally to serve the ancient rights and institutions of all classes of people. It came back in the sixteenth century as the bearer of strange ideas. It came to subvert, not to maintain, to overthrow, not to consolidate. It was the indispensable medium of all those new principles and maxims to which the national speech stubbornly refused to shape itself.

Out of the state papers of the age of the Great Elector one may construct the grammar and the vocabulary of absolutism. The frequent terms " reso-

Roman law.

The dialect of despotism.

lution," "constitution," "modi generales contribuendi," "confirmation," "complanation," "beneficium supplicationis," and a multitude of others that might be cited, suggest claims or powers which are distinctly and characteristically Roman, and mark the triumph of imperial ideas over the more clumsy but less servile conceptions of Teutonic and feudal society.   For Frederic William these terms had a strong but natural fascination.   Although a man of action, the Elector was a tireless letter-writer; and the long epistles in which he set forth his views of prerogative and passive obedience were not the less cogent because they were seasoned with learned foreign words, and thus flattered the early pedantic sense of the people to whom they were addressed.   In Molière's play the illiterate plebeian was promptly won by the word " mamamouchi." - Is it not also possible that many honest Prussians were more easily reconciled to political encroachments which wore the purple and had the splendid carriage of imperial Rome?

But the powers even of a Frederic William and the opportunities even of his long reign were not adequate to the full realization of the autocratic schemes which strode in this borrowed finery.   The Elector died as he was born, a vassal of the Emperor.   He failed to centralize the administration in a single province, much more to bind all the province together in a single system.   He was unable, or he neglected, to codify the laws of the Electorate, and thus to hand his name down to posterity with that of other autocrats, who have half excused their successful usurpations by the wisdom of their practical reforms.   It cannot even be said that his financial measures were enlightened, comprehensive, or liberal ; or that they had anything further in view than the immediate interests of the privy purse.   But if Frederic William produced neither a code, nor an uniform civil service, nor a permanent system of law-making, he at least asserted the principle of his own

supremacy in justice, in the executive, in legislation. As
an actual ruler he lived from hand to mouth, and hardly
founded a settled existence. But he levied the means of
subsistence when and where it pleased himself, and this
was the essential thing at that time ; since he not only
supplied his own daily wants, but also cleared the way for
his successors, who imposed this involuntary purveyance
as a final system upon the people.

As an organizer the Elector's most intelligent and most
successful labor was given to the army. It was practically
created by him.

At the time of his accession the defence of the Mark
The military depended wholly on the irregular feudal levies ;
system. while in the other territories not even these were
at the service of the Elector. There was little discipline
and little real military spirit. The commanders were dissolute young nobles. The weapons were poor ; munitions
and supplies of war were scarce ; there was no adequate
system of fortifications. Slowly and laboriously, as we
have seen, Frederic William improved this state of things,
and when he died left his successor a well-equipped, well-
drilled, and experienced army of twenty-five thousand
men. Fortresses protected the frontiers of all his provinces. The arsenals were stocked with weapons and am-
munition. At Colberg a school was founded for the training of young officers. And the treasury had a reserve
fund, wrung by enormous taxes from the people, and prudently saved for any emergency which might require a
sudden campaign or an unusual increase of the army.

In one respect, indeed, this army was inferior to those
which issued from the feudal system in its better days.
The knights who marched under Albert the Bear against
the heathen of Pomerania, the burghers who gathered in
the market-place and rushed to defend the walls on the
sound of the alarm bell, were at least full of the spirit of
the cause which they served. With them zeal supplied

the defects of discipline, and patriotism lent vigor to the pike or the halberd. But the armies of the seventeenth century had been built up in the course of devastating wars, waged without cause or principle; and that of Brandenburg, like the others, gradually lost its national character and its national feeling. The soldiery formed a class, and a class separated by sharp lines from the mass of the people. Useful in war, it was a burden in peace; for although the Elector drew up a stringent manual of discipline, and affected to make the officers responsible for all excesses of their men, the means of control were not always adequate, and in the vicinity of a regiment the rights of property were ill understood.

Some excellent general officers grew up with this system. The oldest and the highest in rank was Otho von Sparr, a renegade from the Austrian service, of whom Lumbres, a French critic, wrote that he was "not an officer of genius, but experienced, firm, and trustworthy; better fitted to execute than to plan; adapted rather for a small than for a large army, for defensive than for offensive operations."[1] His administrative talents were, however, of a high order. Derfflinger had received his training with the Swedes, and he never rose much above the rank of an empiric, although a skilful and successful one. To the energy and audacity of the cavalry general, Prince Frederic of Hesse, the Elector owed, if not the victory of Fehrbellin, at least its opportunity. Luedke was another officer who distinguished himself in the same engagement. All of these were faithful servants of their master; and from him it was possible to learn useful lessons both of strategy in a campaign and of demeanor on a battle-field.

In the same way there arose in the civil service a school of men thoroughly familiar with the Elector's plans, and fitted to carry them out with intelligence and discretion.

General officers.

---

[1] Quoted by Droysen, III. ii. 174.

16

Schwerin, Blumenthal, Kleist, Götze, Dohna, Wesenbeck, these were men differently endowed by nature, and not always tolerant one of another; but they agreed in devotion to the Elector, and in them may be found the germ of the Prussian bureaucracy. Some of them have been referred to in other places, and their special characteristics will therefore be already known to the reader.

For the higher offices, both civil and military, the Elector continued to prefer the nobility, or when a meritorious plebeian was favored he usually received a title with his commission. This partiality admits of no defence, and it calls for no special censure. It is the rule in Prussia even to-day; and a prejudice which can withstand the levelling tendencies of the nineteenth century must have been far more difficult to eradicate from a society which had just issued out of feudalism.

But Frederic William's fondness for the aristocracy showed itself, unfortunately, in more serious matters and in more vicious forms. In Preussen he dissolved the league between nobles and towns, and broke the spirit of the Diet by introducing the excise, and lifting the burdens of the landed proprietors. In the Mark the recess of 1653 confirmed the fiscal exemptions of the nobles, and in the same ratio increased the hardships of the burghers. Between the fortunes of the two classes, as modified by the Elector's reforms, there was accordingly a vast difference. The nobles exchanged one class of privileges for another, — that of commanding their own levies in the field and of wielding authority through the Diets, for that of the highest positions under the Elector, with the renewal, in a more stringent and odious form, of all their power over their tenants and retainers. The Elector's ordinances reduced the peasantry to a state of practical servitude.[1] The cities were robbed of their franchises and crushed by taxation, until citi-

Class legislation.

---

[1] See the series of ordinances from 1678 to 1683.

zenship in a municipality became a burden instead of a privilege. But noble birth was an assurance of the Elector's favor, and if accompanied even by mediocre talents led to office and influence. The privileges, rights, and duties of these different classes were defined with no little precision. In the towns particularly, where the compactness of the population made possible a more minute supervision over habits and morals, the Elector's regulations were extended to the most trivial and ludicrous details. First of all there was the division of the inhabitants into three categories, with the assignment to each of its own degree of honor and estimation. In the upper or first class were included the municipal officers, the clergy and teachers, and the aristocratic or patrician families; in the second the more considerable traders; and in the third the artisans and generally the proletariat. Each class had its own distinguishing costume, its own social privileges, its own rigid schedule of duties reaching even into the sacred penetralia óf domestic life. Luxury was under the ban; the bills of a wedding feast were scrutinized by the public censors. It was not even above the dignity of the victor of Fehrbellin to require each burgher to lay out a garden, and plant shade trees about his house.

The effect of this sumptuary legislation was doubtless beneficial as regards the character of the people. Frederic William's aim was, however, more specially a fiscal one; hence he did not rest at mere negative measures of restraint upon extravagance, but tried, by a policy of public encouragement, not judicious in all its details,[1] by schemes of internal improvement, by efforts at colonization, by the endowment of commercial and manufacturing enterprises, actually to increase the productive resources of the state. The influ- Encourage-
ment of
industry.

---

[1] One of the most injudicious schemes was that of a gold colony on the African coast.

ence of Colbert was spreading rapidly throughout Europe, and the fallacies of the mercantile system affected the economical policy of every state.

The Rhine provinces needed no subsidies, for their industries had survived all the perils of the century, and their cloths and metallic products were among the best in Germany. Prussia had its cereals, its fisheries, its traffic in amber. But the Mark, originally less favored by nature, and wasted by the repeated invasions, showed neither the power nor the disposition to restore its industries, until the Elector infused fresh blood from abroad into its sluggish veins. Dutch colonies had been founded at an early day by the Princess Louise. The repeal of the edict Foreign of Nantes and the expulsion of the Huguenots colonists. opened the way for French exiles, who came in large numbers, were liberally treated, and gave a powerful impulse to industry, above all in the finer mechanical arts. The more important effects of this immigration were not felt, however, until the next reign.

It is beyond doubt that the morals of the Elector's people, especially those in the Mark, had sunk, in State of morals. the course of the Thirty Years' War, to a point deplorably low. Without that active share in the struggle which would have fostered at least the sterner military virtues, and yet reduced to that squalid misery which too often generates the baser animal vices, they seemed lost to the original instincts of decency, and even to those prudential considerations on which social morality so largely depends. Drunkenness was an universal evil, and robbed the peasant of the little which he could save from the troopers of Wrangel and Wallenstein. The frail tenure by which the tradesman held his wares, the uncertain profits of the mechanic's labor, even the cheapness of life itself, fomented a species of cynical indifference to the future, and a profligate tendency to make the most of the present ; out of which naturally grew improvidence, idleness, extravagance, and waste. The marriage tie was loosely worn. The nameless vices which destroy domestic happiness and pervert the relations of the sexes seem to have been appallingly familiar and general. That theft, robbery, and murder were almost legitimate professions, or rather were so common among at least the lower classes that law-breakers, as such, could hardly be called a distinct sect, appears but too clearly from all the accounts.[1]

Against this national demoralization the church, as such, effected little. The clergy, even when not touched themselves by the universal taint,[2] were paralyzed by their own internal dissensions. Lutheran and Calvinist were still arrayed against each other. That the Swiss confession was on the whole steadily gaining ground, that the countenance of the court gave it a certain social prestige, that it had fought and triumphed in the Thirty Years' War, — these were so many reasons not for less but for more resentment and hatred on the part of the rival establishment. Frederic William himself professed doctrines of toleration which were akin to indifference. It was no concern of his, he said, in which church his subjects chose to save their souls ; and if closely pressed he would perhaps have added, or even if they neglected to save their souls at all.[3] For although, like most men of that age, he could correctly repeat the prayers of

Church and clergy.

[1] The evidence for this view is so abundant that it need not be given. It is found in contemporary annalists, in sermons, in the accounts of travellers, and in a great variety of public papers. In respect to these latter it may be said that while the existence of general laws against crime do not prove that it is specially prevalent, a long series of special enactments and urgent executive proclamations, in the tone at once of command and exhortation, do warrant the conclusion that society is in a diseased state.

[2] The Elector found it necessary to forbid the employment of drunken chaplains in the army. Keller, *Pr. Staat*, v. 622.

[3] An edict of 1654 forbade the publication of controversial pamphlets ; another of 1659 forbade the rival sects to libel and slander each other.

the liturgy, and, as became his station, attended church
and took the sacrament with pious regularity, he showed
little solicitude for the vital interests of religion, and suffered its ministers to languish in poverty. Such an example was not likely to increase the influence of the clergy
among the people.

For the intellectual wants of the population a little
though not much more was attempted. Some
Education. timely aid to the university at Frankfort on the
Oder saved that institution from immediate though not
from eventual death. A similar school was founded at
Duisburg for the Rhine territories, and the university of
Königsberg, which Duke Albert had established in 1543,
worthily guarded the interests of learning in the northeast. At Berlin and Königsberg state libraries were endowed and generously thrown open to the public. But for
the common schools, and for the education of the masses,
I cannot discover that any systematic measures were taken
or even proposed.[1] The sums which the Elector squandered on alchemy would have equipped and maintained a
brigade ; and the exaggerations of the wildest humor are
almost surpassed by a plan submitted by an adventurer
named Skytte, and soberly accepted by Frederic William,
for a "universal university" at Tangermünde, on the
Elbe. The statutes of this novel institution were actually
published, but the scholars and wits of the whole world
did not hasten to seize its advantages, and the beneficent
scheme was dropped.

A literature hardly existed. The hymns of Paul Gerhard may still indeed be heard in German
Literature. churches ; and they prove that, without being a
poet of the first class, or even a creative writer in any
sense, he understood the laws of metrical form, had a certain homely gift of language, and felt especially the deep

---

[1] This is practically admitted, but of course excused, by Horn, *Leben Fr. Wilh. des Grossen*, p. 103.

pathos of Christianity, which he sang in simple yet musical verse to the delight of millions. But in the pulpit of St. Nicholas, at Berlin, Gerhard was the most intolerant of Lutherans. In spite of repeated remonstrances, of warnings, even of the Elector's edict against polemical preaching, the ardent poet persisted in attacking the Calvinists with the most savage violence, made even an affair of conscience out of his conduct, and was finally banished from the Mark, — a martyr not to his religious zeal, but to his religious bigotry. With Gerhard poetry disappeared from Berlin. The capital of Preussen, Königsberg, was more ambitious, and has preserved the names of three poets of this age, Dach, Robertin, and Albert, to whom is ascribed the character of a school. And the so-called Silesian poets, among whom Opitz was the pioneer, were widely read, and had no little literary influence in Brandenburg, as in every other part of Germany. The birth of philosophy was reserved for the generation after Frederic William, while of the historians whom he patronized two, Rocolles and Leti, were foreigners; Händreich, a German, is forgotten; and Pufendorf accomplished little until the next reign. Theological works alone were abundant; but their tone and style argue as little for the charity of the writers as for the taste of the readers, if indeed they had any readers outside the clergy and the censors. Even the Elector himself, though he had an undoubted vigor of expression, is not revealed in his correspondence as a person of much taste, culture, or refinement, or as a ruler from whom liberal and discriminating literary patronage could be expected.

The Elector has been described as a believer in alchemy, and it should be added, as a proof of the low intelligence which prevailed, or of the intense bigotry of the age, or of both, that the belief in witches, which seems to be a necessary stage in the enlightenment of all Protestant peoples, reached the highest

Witchcraft.

point of fanaticism during this reign. The phenomena of
the delusion were not specially different, except, perhaps,
in the degree of their brutality, from those which have
been elsewhere observed. On account of the general degradation of morals, any superstition would be likely to
take a peculiarly gross and odious form. Whether or not
the Elector himself was a victim of the popular fallacy is
not clear; but it does not appear that his officials made
any serious effort to arrest it or to prevent its excesses, —
a failure indeed for which there were illustrious examples.

It is common among German writers to ascribe the decay of the public taste and morals in this age to the influence of France, or rather to the fashionable habit
of copying the French in all matters of dress,
speech, decorum, etiquette, diet, and dissipation. The fact
of the habit cannot be denied, and the general inference
drawn from it is correct. But the limits of the inference
ought to be strictly observed. The model was not wholly
a bad one to imitate, and the French themselves deserve
no reproach for furnishing it. If they possessed, as they
undoubtedly did, the highest standard of taste, the most
elegant manners, the most refined and polished language,
the greatest proficiency in all the arts and graces of life,
they were natural objects of envy, but not of enmity, on
the part of their neighbors, nor, it must be said, of judicial historians in the nineteeenth century. They may not
merit gratitude, but they certainly do not deserve censure,
for the progress which their culture made through its inherent excellence, through its own subtle and mysterious
force.

The propriety of adopting a foreign people's speech, or
tastes, or habits, is, however, a question which is often
quite independent of their actual superiority. The essential thing is the spirit which prompts or the judgment
which guides the imitation; and these are perhaps as
often vicious as virtuous. With the Germans of the sev-

French influence.

enteenth century this was certainly the case. The motives of the imitation were false, and accordingly the worst instead of the best traits of the French were selected for copying. The French drama, French literature, French wit, were admirable; but the strictest adherence to the unities would not make a Racine out of a playwright of Leipsic or Vienna, and a dull German pedant might spend his life in the study of French without creating a single epigram for the world's delight. An imitative elector of the Empire could build up a second Versailles only by taxing his people to the point of ruin. It was even worse in the domain of morals and manners, for the Germans, wanting both the means and the gift for elegant licentiousness, could only produce the evil without its polish; so that what was at Paris a privileged, decorous, and discreet luxury became in Germany a coarse debauchery, a dissolute fashion, sparing no class of the people. Even the attempt to ape the rich toilets and courtly manners of the French was first absurd, and then pernicious. The rude Pomeranian squire, with his wig and gold lace, and his awkward spouse, panting under the torture of her stays, were harmless, except to themselves, so long as their appearance only amused the school-boys on the street. But when the passion became a general one it impoverished many families, and worked widespread demoralization. In respect to the example and influence of the Prussian court, the evil did not indeed reach its climax until the next reign; but even Frederic William liked to import his dancing-masters from Paris, and to employ, though in sadly reduced proportions, the ceremonial of the French king.[1]

The population at the time of the Elector's death cannot be ascertained with even approximate accuracy. No

---

[1] A couplet of contemporary doggerel describes not inaccurately the nature of the Gallic usurpation: —

> Frankreich hat es weit gebracht; Frankreich kann es schaffen,
> Das so manches Land und Volk wird zu seinem Affen.

formal census was taken until 1816, and if its results are
trustworthy, as they doubtless are, they still
furnish no basis of comparison with the seventeenth century. Nothing remains, therefore, but
conjecture, more or less supported by scattered data.
The Elector himself declared on his death-bed that he had
increased the extent and population of his country by at
least one third ; from which it would follow that, if the
number of the latter at George William's death is correctly given at nine hundred thousand, it ought to have
been twelve hundred thousand in 1688.   But the figures
usually given are some three hundred thousand more than
this, or about one and one half millions.   The territorial
accretions can of course be measured more accurately.
George William left, in round numbers, thirty-five thousand square miles ; Frederic William, forty-eight thousand,
— an increase, therefore, under the latter, of thirteen
thousand.

*Population
and
territory.*

CHAPTER VII.

FROM THE ACCESSION OF FREDERIC III. TO THE ACQUISITION OF THE CROWN.

THE period that immediately followed the Great Elector affords an instance of a species of historical sequence which, though not invariable, is at least frequent and often striking. What the age of Louis XV. was to that of Louis XIV., what the age of Charles II. was to that of Cromwell and the Puritans, such was the age of Frederic III. at Berlin to that of his predecessor, — an age or era of relaxation, ease, indolence, and luxury, coming after one of action, achievement, and severe tension. It was as though a strong hand had suddenly lost its hold on the affairs of state. The characteristic of the previous reign had been mere force, by which a superior will asserted itself in defiance of law and justice ; and although Frederic inherited an established situation, with many of the agents to which it owed its establishment, the dynamic element, if the term may be used, was handed down to him only in a form or degree vastly reduced. His task, though not unimportant, was, therefore, as compared with his father's, modest and even humble. It would not be incorrect, or perhaps paradoxical, to say that it was best performed when he simply enjoyed, since to enjoy was also to preserve, the fruits of another's triumph ; but it was a task imposed on him by the highest reason of state, and to that extent gives his reign a claim to recognition and respect.

The new Elector was apparently not full of admiration

for either the character or the policy of his father. With more political sense than filial affection, he declared that The general policy. he wished to escape the reproach of similar instability and untrustworthiness in alliances ; that he was determined to avoid rude acts of violence, like those practised upon Rhode and Kalkstein, as well as, in general, all severe and arbitrary measures. He was anxious to have, above all things, "a lovable government."[1] Always favorably inclined toward Austria, he had, as crown prince, rejoiced in the treaty of 1686 as the return to a sound policy, and when he acquired the power that line of conduct became a settled rule of state. The public service, too, as left by Frederic William, was not at first materially changed. Even the younger and later officials of the father were retained by the son, so great was already the force of inertia in the government; and when men remain systems are seldom at once overthrown. The Elector's desire to soften the asperities of political rule was, therefore, a limited one, and affected rather temper and methods than forms or machinery. The machinery was too useful to be discarded, and Frederic soon learned to treat the general acquiescence in his own conduct as an approval of the system itself.

Nor was this view wholly a delusion. If the historical portraits do not deceive, the Great Elector had the unhappy gift of making measures already offensive in themselves even more offensive by his manner and temper. The policy of despotism was aggravated by the arrogance of a despot. He usurped power, and he usurped it with brutal and unnecessary violence ; and his policy, being a progressive one, never rested on what it had acquired, never suffered the people to reconcile themselves to their losses, but prepared for them daily surprises in the scheme of aggression, until no citizen felt safe in the possession of

[1] Frederic's own words to the Saxon envoy. Quoted by Droysen, IV. i. 18.

any sort of civil or political rights.[1] He tried experiments in government as lightly as an artist experiments with colors on his palette. His subjects were not permitted even to learn the duties of one form of slavery before it was replaced by another, probably not less severe, and certainly not more familiar. This policy of unrest and agition was only arrested by Frederic William's death, but it was fortunately arrested for many years. His successor seemed wisely content to accept things as he found them. He long delayed any general reorganization of the army or its affiliated charge, the finances, his ambition being apparently satisfied by the not inglorious conduct of Brandenburg troops on many European battlefields, and his solicitude for an efficient civil service not including the idea of improvement. His tastes were showy but amiable. His wants were extravagant but not oppressive; and though he wrung vast sums of money from the people, he was not avaricious, nor even thrifty, but spent his revenues in a generous, splendid, and not impolitic hospitality. The unqualified contempt with which this prince is commonly treated in history seems, therefore, somewhat unjust. His achievements in war and foreign politics were not only respectable in themselves, but they were also of a character, like many of his home measures and his personal habits, to strike and gratify the spectacular sense of his people, and thus lighten the task of the tax-gatherer. Hence no serious resistance is recorded to the amount or the manner of the tributes exacted by him. It would be too much to say that he popularized the system of raising taxes without the consent of the Diet, but he at least made it more and more familiar, until the idea that the old

---

[1] "A man can accommodate himself to any settled state of things, even to one opposed to his convictions, because under it there are no fears for the future ; but he cannot accustom himself to a state of things varying from day to day, because each day gives birth to fresh fears." Talleyrand to Louis XVIII., June, 1815.

method could ever be restored gradually faded out of the
public mind.

Frederic was the second son of the Great Elector by
his first wife, Louise of Orange; born in 1657,
Frederic's youth and education. he was thirty-one years old, and in the prime of
manhood, when the government fell to him. In
his education two stages may be distinguished. Up to
1674 he enjoyed the training and suffered the comparative neglect of a younger son; the death of his older
brother made him heir-apparent, and, it is probable, gave
a somewhat different turn to the course of his studies
and instruction. His teachers or governors were men of
high character and unusual acquirements. Until his fifth
year he was, like his younger brother, under the general
charge of Otho von Schwerin, who has already been often
and honorably mentioned, — a statesman, a liberal scholar,
and a devout Christian. Schwerin was followed by Eberhard von Dankelmann as special tutor and guardian of
Frederic. Dankelmann was a young man of rare promise;
and though the severity of his discipline called forth frequent protests from Frederic's mother, and after her death
from his grandmother, it does not appear that the tutor
was shaken in his pedagogic methods, or that the young
prince suffered any exceptional hardships. The rigor of
Dankelmann's policy may have the better prepared Frederic for the ordeal to which his stepmother afterwards subjected him. And by a natural reaction the ill-treatment
which he received from this accidental parent led the prince
to cling only the more closely to Dankelmann ; out of the
tutor to make a companion, friend, and confidant ; to give
him unreservedly the charge of his personal affairs; and
to raise him, after his accession, to the highest posts of dignity and power in the state.

As a youth Frederic was generous, and, with fits of
Early char- irritation, amiable; but his earliest and most
acteristics. striking characteristic was his intense personal

vanity. His constitution was weak, his body deformed, his nature sentimental and effeminate. He was indifferent to the perils and the glories of the battlefield; but his love for show, pomp, and ceremony began when he was a child in the nursery, and grew upon him during the whole term of his reign. It is therefore easy to understand why his burly father showed so marked a preference for the more manly older son, and why, even after Frederic became the heir and hope of the house, he continued to treat him with undisguised contempt. Happily Frederic's second wife, the Princess Sophie Charlotte of Hanover, whom he had espoused in 1684, supplied a partial corrective to the weakness of her husband.

The first care of the Elector after his accession was to set aside, or at least to neutralize, the effects of the paternal will left for his guidance. The will was simply one more addition to that long series of territorial partitions, by which so many electors had sought to satisfy the claims of paternal affection at the sacrifice of important dynastic interests. Under its provisions Frederic was to retain the Electorate with the electoral dignity, but some of the lesser provinces were assigned to his step-brothers as appanages. The influence of Frederic William's second wife was apparent in this arrangement. She had a natural interest in the fortunes of her sons, while the Elector had little confidence in the future of the son of Louise; and the consequence was the testament of 1686, which was intrusted to the Emperor Leopold as executor.[1]

Testament of the Great Elector.

The overthrow of this will was, as a domestic measure, simple enough. Frederic held a meeting of the Privy Council, submitted the instrument to the opinion of the members, and then, by an act of state, formally declared it

[1] The instrument is given in the appendix to vol. i. of Ranke's *Pr. Gesch.* (ed. Leipsic, 1874), and in Droysen, IV. iv. 195–202; comp. also IV. i. 14, iv. 161, 162.

invalid.   It was contrary, he said, to the fundamental law
of the house as proclaimed by Albert Achilles,[1] and this
was evidently true, but urgent and not less obvious reasons of state were doubtless more potent in the matter
than merely technical considerations.   In any event, this
summary proceeding was far from closing the case.
Other parties were interested in the will, and some of
them, among whom fortunately the brothers themselves
were not included, seemed disposed to make no little
trouble.   The brothers accepted an early and easy accommodation, but the Emperor refused to surrender the unlucky paper, and even insisted on the strict execution
of its provisions.   It soon appeared, however, that his
stubbornness was intended to compass ends of his own,
quite foreign to the testament.

In the year 1537 Joachim II. of Brandenburg and the
Duke of Liegnitz formed a sort of hereditary
pact,[2] by which the two houses were made mutually heirs, each of the other.   If the House of
Brandenburg should become extinct, the fiefs which it
held of the Bohemian crown were to pass to the Duke of
Liegnitz, while the extinction of the Duke's family was to
put the Hohenzollerns in possession of Liegnitz, Wohlau,
and Brieg, valuable territories in Silesia.   Ferdinand of
Austria, as King of Bohemia, denounced this transaction.
A vacant fief reverted to its lord; and Ferdinand reasoned that Joachim could not lawfully cede the right of
reversion to lands which he held of the crown of Bohemia.
Against the Duke of Liegnitz Ferdinand's case was
scarcely less clear; and where the law failed he applied
force.   He easily coerced the Duke into cancelling the
treaty, and the estates of Liegnitz into doing renewed

*Branden-
burg and
Silesia.*

[1] Droysen, IV. iv. 164, 172.
[2] Erbverbrüderung, an untranslatable term, in spite of Mr. Carlyle's Heritage-Fraternity.   Heritage is not Erb, but Erbschaft, and
Fraternity is not Verbrüderung, but Brüderschaft.

homage to Bohemia. Brandenburg protested, refused to surrender its copy of the compact, and there for a time the matter rested. It was not supposed that either of the contingencies named in the treaty, that is, the extinction of either of the contracting houses, was likely soon to arise; and there seemed no urgent necessity for immediate action. But in 1675 the young Duke George William of Liegnitz died without heirs, and the question was unexpectedly reopened. The Emperor promptly occupied the territory as a vacant fief of the Bohemian crown; the Elector Frederic William, deeply involved in the Pomeranian campaign, was in no position to assert his claim; and it was not until after the Treaty of Nimeguen that he demanded the surrender of Liegnitz, Wohlau, and Brieg, under the compact of 1537. The Emperor refused, in the first place from a natural greed of territory; in the second place, from a not less natural reluctance to see a Protestant power admitted in such close neighborhood to his hereditary possessions. But two circumstances made the Emperor eventually incline to a compromise. The one was that the Elector had begun negotiations with France looking toward an alliance against Leopold; the other was that the troops of Brandenburg were needed in the war against the Turks. Frederic William, too, soon saw the folly of enlisting Louis XIV. in an enterprise which had so distinct a Protestant character as the extension of his power into Silesia, and he was also ready to modify his pretensions. In this mood the two monarchs resumed the discussion, and the result was the treaty of 1686. Austria surrendered the Silesian kreis or county of Schwiebus; the Elector renounced all claim to the disputed territories of Liegnitz.[1]

Ranke justly inquires how the Elector could sign, how a statesman like Paul von Fuchs could advise him to sign, so unequal a compact. But it soon *Affair of Schwiebus.*

[1] March 22. Droysen, IV. iv. 157.

transpired that the Emperor was not in earnest even in
the slight concession which he seemed to admit into the
treaty. His envoy, a Baron Fridag, really conducted at
the same time two separate negotiations, one official with
the Elector and his ministers, one unofficial and secret
with the crown prince Frederic; and the work of the first
was practically undone by the result of the second. Con-
flicting versions are given in respect to the method of the
transaction — the form or degree of pressure put upon
Frederic, the extent to which he was duped, his real preference in the matter. The Prussian view is that the cession of Schwiebus was represented to Frederic as the result of a French intrigue, aiming to embroil Austria with
Brandenburg, and, therefore, if persisted in, dangerous to
peace.[1] The opposite view is that Frederic himself took
the initiative, in order that he might be able to claim the
good offices of Leopold in the matter of his father's testament.[2] But whatever the Prince's motives may have been,
the pledge was given. While Frederic William was signing a treaty which so far admitted his claim as to give
him Schwiebus, his son privately signed another engagement, by which he agreed to restore the kreis immediately after his accession.[3] The death of his father, two
years later, gave Frederic an opportunity to execute the
compact.

It is true that he showed at first reluctance and hesitation. He alleged his previous ignorance of the controversy, his right to reconsider a pledge thus extorted from
his inexperience; and he made various pleas for some
modification of the odious engagement.[4] But nothing ex-

[1] Ibid. IV. iv. 187, 188, Frederic's own version, September 19,
1689; and pp. 311, 312, a somewhat piquant statement to the same
effect, though of a later date, by the minister Ilgen.

[2] See the various pro-Austrian statements, ibid. IV. iv. 183–187.

[3] Droysen, III. iii. 818, has the treaty, or the revers, as it is called.
The date is February 28, 1686.

[4] See the letter of Frederic written from Bonn in 1689 in Ranke,

cept time was gained. The Emperor insisted on the strict fulfilment of the promise, and he had in the will a valuable agent of coercion. The Electress, too, had family reasons for urging the restitution. Her father was ambitious of the electoral honor; and since for this the Emperor's favor was indispensable, she easily discovered reasons for surrendering Schwiebus and receiving in exchange the surrender of the will. On this basis the matter was finally adjusted. Schwiebus was restored to Austria.[1] The compromise with Frederic's stepbrothers received the imperial sanction; the testament of the Great Elector was practically cancelled; and the Duke of Hanover, though head only of the younger branch of the House of Brunswick, was made elector.

1694.

During these years other and more serious affairs were not however neglected. Frederic was full of both personal and dynastic ambition, but he was also devoted in a less selfish spirit to the cause of Protestantism, and this devotion largely influenced his foreign policy. The continent was rent by the great duel between the House of Austria and the House of Bourbon; and though these were both Catholic, the former was in some respects the less offensively, or rather the less dangerously Catholic, and Frederic had, therefore, religious as well as political reasons for taking the side of Leopold. But in England he had a chance to support William of Orange in an enterprise which was distinctly and avowedly Protestant.

European politics.

The scheme to dethrone James had been known to the Great Elector, and had been by him communicated just before his death to Frederic and to Dankelmann.[2] It

Pr. Gesch. (ed. Leipsic, 1874), i. 365, note; Droysen, IV. iv. 188–191.

[1] January 10, 1695; date of the treaty of retrocession, December 20, 1694. The Elector was promised in return the expectancy to East Frisland. See Droysen, IV. i. 99, and the notes.

[2] Ibid. III. iii. 806 et seq.

was heartily approved by both.   There was, indeed, at the

The Elector and the English Revolution. Prussian court, as there has always been, a French party, and many of its members were in the pay of Louis ; but though they could betray the secrets they could not dictate the policy of the Elector. Bentinck, William's envoy, coming to Berlin to sound Frederic soon after his accession, found him already convinced.   The formal negotiations between Bentinck and Fuchs, the Elector's commissioner,[1] were even followed, on the 30th of June, by a secret interview between Frederic and William, at which a defensive alliance was concluded.   The Elector promised six thousand men who during the absence of William should aid to cover the Dutch frontier against the French.[2]   Even the Emperor was won for a sympathetic neutrality, though by arguments hardly reconcilable with those addressed to the Protestant princes, and not wholly creditable to William's character for candor and sincerity.

Whether Brandenburg troops actually accompanied William on the enterprise itself is a question which has been much debated by the historical scholars of Prussia. Pufendorf, who lived at the time, plainly assumes that such was the case ;[3] and until recent years it may be said that their country's supposed share in the glorious enterprise was one of the things of which patriotic Prussians were not least proud.   But the cold scientific spirit of

[1] See Frederic's instructions to Fuchs, the latter's report, and other documents in the appendix to Ranke's *Eng. Gesch.* (ed. 1874), vol. viii.; *Theatrum Europæum*, xiii. 414, 415; Droysen, IV. iv. 213–217.

[2] The terms of the engagement made them little less than mercenaries.   They were to be paid and maintained by Holland, were to obey its orders, and could be recalled by the Elector only in case his own territories should be attacked.   Droysen, IV. i. 21, note.

[3] His words, referring to the Battle of the Boyne, are, primus impetus in exterius cingulum fiebat a Brandenburgica legione.   Ranke "believes Pufendorf," in the first edition of his *Pr. Gesch.*, but omits the belief in the last.

modern inquiry has overthrown this generous tradition. The Prussian general staff has examined the question on every side, in the light of all the knowledge which the archives afford ; and has reached the conclusion that none of the Elector's troops took part in the Irish campaign, or even crossed the channel with William.[1] So far as can be learned Frederic was represented only by one active warrior. Marshal Schomberg, a soldier of fortune but a brave and skilful one, fell at the Battle of the Boyne ; and with him disappeared that whole " Brandenburg regiment " which Macaulay in his fancy saw landing with the foreign auxiliaries of William.

The prudence of the Prince of Orange in securing his rear by timely alliances was amply justified by events. Even before he embarked Louis began a movement which, though nominally aimed at the Empire, and intended to reassert his authority in German politics, also menaced the Netherlands, and created just the emergency for which William had gained the aid of Brandenburg. The immediate occasion was an archiepiscopal election at Cologne. For this purely German See the French King favored a protégé of his own, the Cardinal Fürstenberg, Bishop of Strasburg, while the German powers supported the rival candidacy of the Prince Clement, brother of the Elector of Bavaria. A double election was the result ; but the Pope, who was then on ill terms with Louis, confirmed Clement. Louis correctly saw in this result a certain humiliation for him, and at once invaded the Empire.

Hostile attitude of France.

He had counted on the support, or the neutrality, or at least the hesitation, of the German princes, and, as it appeared, not wholly without reason. First of all, the Emperor himself began to waver. To resist Louis was one thing, for Louis and he worshipped the same gods ; but to resist Louis in behalf of the Prince of

Hesitation in Germany.

[1] See Droysen, IV. i. 274, note 20.

Orange and to facilitate the overthrow of a Catholic king in England, was another and a widely different thing, calling for caution and reflection. The Elector of Mayence promptly opened the gates of that important fortress, and with them the Palatinate itself, to the French troops. Even Saxony was agitated by doubts and divided councils, and but for the earnest labors of Frederic might have fallen entirely away from the common cause. It was Frederic alone, according to his biographers, who held the German Protestants together, and even stiffened the resolution of Leopold himself; and if we are compelled to reject the theory that his subjects actively participated in the English Revolution, it is no little satisfaction to be able to record the fact that his firmness on the Rhine set William free, and made the revolution possible.[1]

The initial year of Frederic's reign thus saw the outbreak of another of the many wars provoked by the ambition of Louis XIV. It is no part of my purpose or my duty to write the general history of this struggle, or even in much detail the history of the events in which Prussia was more directly engaged. Frederic's share in the war, though respectable, was not prominent or glorious; and the political bearings of the struggle upon the fortunes of Prussia are more important than the story of sieges on the Rhine, or campaigns in the green valley of the Neckar. The main thread of the military events must nevertheless be followed.

At the outset Louis acted with promptness, if not, as Bishop Burnet thinks, with precipitation. Frederic's measures were energetic, though precautionary rather than aggressive; the Emperor and the Diet shrank from open war; and William of Or-

Louis invades Germany.

---

[1] "And this," says Burnet, — that is, the treaty between William and Frederic, — "gave the Prince of Orange great quiet in prosecuting his design upon England." *History of His Own Times* (London, 1833), iii. 298.

ange sailed undisturbed across the channel. To attack
the Empire instead of Holland was an undoubted error on
the part of Louis. The devastation of the Palatinate was,
to say the least, another error ; for it does not appear that
the invasion alone caused any overpowering outburst of
indignation, calling imperatively for instant and determined action. The Diet at Regensburg showed little
spirit. It met and adjourned ; debated and doubted ;
feared to convert discussion into preparation, and preparation into measures. From such a spectacle Louis took
fresh confidence, and even while abandoning, after laying
waste the Palatinate, felt little alarm lest vengeance in
the form of an aroused and united Germany should over-
take and punish him. He had seized the passes of the
Black Forest ; had occupied without resistance Mayence,
Spires, Kaiserslautern, Worms, and Heilbronn ; had successfully besieged Phillipsburg and Heidelberg ; and had
laid in ruins such of these places as he could not or would
not retain. To resist him little had been done beyond the
occupation of Cologne by the troops of Frederic.

Everything depended on the fate of William's enterprise, and although there was an unpardonable ignorance
on the continent of the real state of public feeling in
England, German princes could not be expected to know
— what James's own countrymen did not know — that he
would fly without firing a shot. This suspense was finally
relieved by the news of the easy triumph of the revolution, and the French ambassador was dismissed from Regensburg. But even then the Emperor was not ready for
active measures. It was not until April, 1689, that he
formally issued a declaration of war ; it was a The grand
month later before he concluded with Holland alliance.
the treaty which, after the accession of England, Savoy,
and Spain, united nearly all Europe in a definite league
against France.

In the mean time the combined forces of Frederic and

the Dutch had succeeded by a series of brisk and not unskilful movements in clearing the lower Rhine of the
French as far up as Bonn, where, however, they held
strongly fortified positions on both sides of the stream.
An attempt by the Cologne garrison to surprise and
storm the works on the right bank failed. A second more
systematic attack was therefore planned, but in the midst
of the preparations the Emperor's declaration of war was
made known to Europe, and at once imparted a new character to the struggle.

Frederic, who had been in attendance at the Diet dur-
Siege of   ing the weary councils, at once joined the army,
Bonn.   and took command of the forces gathered before
Bonn. He had at his disposal something over thirty
thousand men, including his own troops and those of the
allies, well equipped with siege artillery, and led by veteran generals like Schöning and Barfuss. The French
garrison, under Colonel Asfeld, numbered barely eight
thousand. But the tactics of Asfeld and the heroism of
his men were aided by divided councils among the besiegers, by quarrels between the Prussian generals, and by
bad management of the imperialist cause, so that it was
not until the 12th of October that the place surrendered.
The garrison had become reduced to fifteen hundred efficient men.

Mayence having also fallen, the allies thus regained
possession of the last German fortress on the Rhine. The
troops then went into winter quarters, and the princes returned to their respective capitals, Frederic through Minden, where he received homage, to Berlin, where he was
welcomed as a mighty conqueror.

The next campaign opened late in the season, and dis-
Campaign   astrously for the allies. Louis, adopting a plan
of 1690.   of action which a year earlier might have kept
William of Orange at home, and for a time at least have
saved the Stuarts, transferred his operations from the

Rhine to the frontier of Holland, and won some signal victories. At Fleurus the Duke of Luxemburg administered a crushing defeat to the Prince of Waldeck. The districts of Liege and Aix-la-Chapelle were occupied and plundered; and the French advance in this direction even pushed across the lower Rhine. Nor were their victories confined to this quarter. In Italy the Duke of Savoy was defeated; and even on the sea, the peculiar element of the English and Dutch, their fleet was destroyed by the French Admiral Tourville. James was in Ireland, whither William had gone to meet him, and the affairs of the grand alliance were in sad disorder. The Emperor, more interested in fighting the Turks on the Danube than the French on the Rhine, lent only a feeble coöperation in the west. The Hessians quarrelled about the season when they should enter the field, and ended by remaining in camp. Disputes about subsidies, disputes about quotas, disputes about rank, command, and precedence, thus consumed the summer, and the campaign left the French, though not the exiled Stuart, in a high state of enthusiasm.

The pacification of the Scots, and the final defeat of James at the battle of the Boyne, enabled William and England to give more direct attention to the war on the continent; and in 1691 the king came in person to Holland. But his name seemed to have lost its charm. William was not a great general, perhaps not even a popular leader, but in previous campaigns he had shown a coolness, a dogged persistence, a fortitude under trials, which made him a formidable soldier, respected by his own armies, and feared by Louis. Now, however, he not only lost the fortress of Mons, but was easily outgeneralled everywhere by Luxemburg.

William himself threw the blame, and not wholly without reason, on the allies. They had no settled plan; no unity of purpose; no experienced generals; no real conception of the needs of the crisis; no sincere and generous enthusiasm for the common cause. There had been quite too many princes in the German army, men who knew nothing of war, and never seriously meant to fight; but who dearly loved the pomp, pride and circumstance of military life. Frederic himself early learned wisdom, and after 1692 left the war to his soldiers. It was finally agreed to intrust the general command of the imperial armies to the Margrave Louis of Baden, an officer of fair ability; and he made it an emphatic condition of acceptance that no elector should appear in his camp. But he had only moderate success. Although he checked an invasion of Franconia, he effected little west of the Rhine, and until 1695 the French generals easily held their ground.

The burdens of the war were keenly felt. Without any well-defined object on the one side or the other, Trials of and conducted, at least by the Empire, with little the allies. vigor and no success, it exacted nevertheless heavy and uninterrupted sacrifices both of life and of treasure. Even in France the strain began to be felt; " the country," wrote Fénelon to Louis, " is a vast hospital." Even England flinched under William's reverses, and the tories went into open opposition. If these two opulent states, which no invasion had afflicted, and which were the real parties in the war, became weary and at times discouraged, is it strange that the German powers, little interested in the motives of the struggle, exposed to attack at many points, lamed by internal discord, reduced almost to bankruptcy, and withal engaged in a hardly less desperate contest with the Turks, should bear with extreme impatience the obligations of the grand alliance? Of these powers Prussia had been the first to take up arms. Both the zeal and the fidelity of Frederic had withstood severe tests, and the resources of his state were sorely tried. He had kept his contingent up to the full strength of twenty thousand men, who were represented on every great battlefield. For their conduct at the successful battle of Namur they won the thanks of William himself. In Hungary they were also employed against the Turks; but although they and their master were duly complimented by Leopold, their services were forgotten when the emergency had passed. The other princes of the Empire were treated with equal ingratitude, and hoarded up a common fund of resentment.

The Elector's treasury suffered acutely. He had, of course, forfeited the French subsidies on declaring war against the French king; the promised subsidies of Holland were irregularly paid; those of the Emperor were far in arrears. Frequent drafts upon the fund accumulated and left by the Great Elector, —which amounted to a million thalers,[1]—became therefore inevitable, and greatly reduced the legacy of that thrifty prince. The large deficiencies which remained were supplied by the usual expedient of taxes, either reimposed or wholly new. The officials were assessed as in the days of the Great Elector. The Jews were taxed according to a scale which rose with the prolongation of the war. Head-money was levied in 1691, and again two years later; and stamp duties were a source of revenue to which recourse was frequently taken.

Financial difficulties at Berlin.

Frederic's father, or Frederic's son, would have met these drafts upon the military budget by severe retrenchment in other fields. But Frederic himself knew no such word as economy. He was prodigal by nature, and he was also, if the belief may be reaffirmed, prodigal from policy; for while in a general sense the prestige of his state was not a little enhanced by displays of wealth and splendor, many of his particular schemes, though ruinous to the exchequer, were otherwise conceived in a wise, liberal, and beneficent spirit.

Frederic's extravagance.

[1] Droysen, IV. i. 5.

The Elector may have failed to distinguish very clearly between the two classes of extravagance, between outlays which merely gratified his own love of display and outlays which stimulated the higher tastes of the people; between the purchase of gold buttons for a lackey's coat and the endowment of a school of letters or an academy of arts. But a certain equilibrium not unfavorable to him may nevertheless be found. Literature and art thrived with the court establishment. The university of Halle atones in a measure for the sums squandered on French dancing-masters, on schools of etiquette and text-books of heraldry.

The intellectual revival at Berlin was borne along, as it were, on the waves of an ecclesiastical revolt.

Berlin an intellectual centre.

Two schools, hostile to the prevailing tone of thought in the Protestant church, and in a certain measure to the accepted body of doctrine, arose about the same time, and by a happy coincidence both found refuge at Berlin. Spener was the leader of the popular or pietistic revolt. The other faction had a cosmopolitan and rationalistic basis, and included several men of remarkable talent, Leibnitz being its most eminent though not its most zealous member.

Spener held liberal views both of church doctrine and of church government; and at Frankfort-on-the-

Spener and the pietists.

Main, where he first won his reputation, he was often called on to resolve the doubts and remove the scruples of illustrious persons. Believing strongly in the value of private association among Christians, he founded in 1670 several so-called " collegia pietatis." These were voluntary gatherings of believers whose piety partook largely of the emotional nature, and craved opportunities for more intimate and less formal expression than was furnished by the institution of public worship;[1] but they

---

[1] They were somewhat similar, probably, to the "prophesyings" in England under Elizabeth.

were objects of suspicion to the clerical authorities, and in an earlier age would have been rudely suppressed. Spener vindicated the "colleges" in a series of pamphlets directed against the narrow and exclusive spirit of the sects, especially the Lutherans. The Lutherans replied, and the fierce tones of the controversy were heard in the most remote parts of the Empire. Driven out of Frankfort by the clamor of the orthodox, or attracted to Saxony by professional ambition, Spener next appeared, in 1686, at Dresden as court chaplain. But he met there a more bitter opposition than at Frankfort. The professors at Leipsic and Wittenberg assailed him with volleys of angry brochures. Leipsic was a trading city, and its theology had the respectable moderate tone of an opulent and somewhat worldly population ; but it was still orthodox and conservative. Wittenberg was more positive and dogmatic, as became a school which lived on the traditions of Luther. Eventually, therefore, Spener was driven also from Dresden, and he next repaired to Berlin. Here he was warmly received, and soon drew about him a band of gifted and ardent disciples.

Christian Thomasius, a young jurist who had studied Grotius and Pufendorf, was a reformer of a different stamp. Radical and restless, though a Thomasius. professor at Leipsic, fond of advancing paradoxes and defending fallacies, he was a genuine sophist both in intellectual acuteness and in intellectual temerity. He excused polygamy, and followed his master Pufendorf in drawing the principles of natural law from reason, and not from the letter of Holy Writ. He was a pioneer in the use of the German tongue, which he employed both in the class-room and for philosophical discussion ; founded and conducted the first scientific periodical in the national language ; preferred the old German to the imported Roman law ; and in successive publications attacked with rare courage and prophetic anticipation some of the reigning delusions of the age, such as the right to punish heresy, the belief in witchcraft, the lawfulness of torture. His literary and controversial fertility seemed inexhaustible. He even wrote novels, now forgotten, but which at the time were effective weapons of assault upon pedants, bigots, and hypocrites. The fate of such a rebel was therefore inevitable. If the orthodox censors had been shocked by Spener's homely, unconventional piety, they were roused to fury by the keen and audacious satire of Thomasius. He was expelled from the faculty and fled to Berlin. But exile only stimulated his intellectual activity.

Samuel Pufendorf was the senior, and in political philosophy the master, of Thomasius ; but although a German by birth, the years of his manhood were passed in Sweden, and it was only late in life that he became identified with the court of Berlin.   Professor Bluntschli thinks that Pufendorf has been unduly neglected in recent times ; that he is erroneously treated as a mere pedant, laboriously reproducing the ideas of others, while he was in reality one of the most satirical, witty, and original of writers.[1]   It is certain that he was frequently involved in quarrels, now with his professional rivals, now with his university colleagues, now with his patrons.   It may be that the cause of these quarrels was his liberal and independent spirit.   He wrote at least one book, a satire on the political system of the German Empire, marked by subtle humor, penetrating views, and wise suggestions.[2]   But in his philosophical works there is little trace of originality, though a tone of cautious and moder-

Pufendorf.

---

[1] _Geschichte der Staatswissenschaft_ (3d ed. Munich, 1881), p. 138. But Leibnitz, a contemporary, said of him that he was " parum jurisconsultus, minime philosophus."

[2] _De Statu Imperii Germanici_, by " Severinus de Monzambano," first published at Geneva in 1667.   Bluntschli, ubi supra, pp. 138, 139, quotes, but questions, the statement of J. J. Moser that the work had a circulation in Germany alone of more than 300,000 copies.

ate liberalism characterizes them all.[1] His histories, that of Gustavus Adolphus, that of the Great Elector, and the one, which his death in 1694 left unfinished, of Frederic himself, show that the official historiographer was granted, as became his office, complete freedom of the archives; but otherwise they reveal little disposition to independent criticism, and little capacity for picturesque narration. His merits are perhaps best stated by Ranke. He says that Pufendorf "first released the law of nature from the fetters of theological systems, and without denying revelation vindicated the claims of reason." [2] This, if true, was an important service; and it cannot be doubted that Pufendorf, in spite of the restraints of his official position, exercised at Berlin a healthy intellectual influence. But he wrote in Latin, and hardly belongs to German literature.

Of Leibnitz, finally, a greater man than any of these, and one of the foremost spirits of that or any age, it must be said that, while he was active in the culture of the German language and literature, he was not exclusively identified with the court of Frederic. There were as many capitals in Europe which afforded him hospitality as there were subjects which employed his pen. He makes discoveries or writes essays in connection with mathematics, physics, law, theology, philosophy, philology, morals; he is now at Leipsic, now at Paris, now at Berlin, now at Rome, — a comprehensive and cosmopolitan genius. But a good part of his later years were passed in Berlin, where the vanity of Frederic, and the more intelligent support of the Electress, enabled him to carry out some of his favorite schemes.

Besides these German scholars there was also at Berlin

Leibnitz.

---

[1] The most important are *De jure naturæ et gentium libri octo*, and *De officiis hominis et civis*, published first respectively in 1672 and 1678.

[2] *Pr. Gesch.* ed. 1874, i. 454.

a large number of French Protestant refugees, who were
already distinguished in letters and science.
French
scholars. Such were James Lenfant, who was a fierce
enemy of the Jesuits and wrote histories of the church
councils ; Isaac Beausobre, who is still known by his
learned work on the Manicheans ; Vigolles, who prepared
a chronology of the Old Testament ; and Lacroze, who
made researches into the Coptic and other obscure tongues.
These were all men of fervent piety, and their Gallic wit
and taste and eloquence agreeably seasoned the intellectual diet of Berlin society. To the list of foreign scholars
ought perhaps to be added the Catholic Vota, a Jesuit
from Warsaw, who was a frequent and, on account of his
intellectual gifts, a welcome guest at Frederic's court, and
the English, or rather Irish, deist, Toland, who was in
Prussia in the early part of the next century, and wrote a
description of what he saw.[1]

At length the time came when it seemed desirable to
find for the Frondeurs thus assembled at Berlin,
University
of Halle. or astray throughout Germany, some organ of
expression more dignified than vituperative tracts and
pamphlets ; and Frederic, encouraged by Spener and Dankelmann, gave ready encouragement to the scheme of
a university at Halle. Thomasius was already there,
teaching his peculiar doctrines and methods in a private
school.[2] Others, friends and rivals of Thomasius, soon
followed ; and the first faculty included Stryk, a famous
jurist, Breithaupt in theology, Franke and Stahl, with
Seckendorf as chancellor. At the formal dedication in
1694 Fuchs, one of Frederic's ministers, delivered a long
discourse, which naturally did not want the usual panegyric of an illustrious patron, and in which by a some-

[1] John Toland, *An Account of the Courts of Prussia and Hanover*
(London, 1706).

[2] See in Isaacsohn, ii. 279, n. 1, the curious patent by which Frederic gave his sanction to this school.

what daring flight of fancy the orator declared that Minerva ought to be the symbol of the Prussian state, because that state was at the head of the arts both of war and peace, — this in the age of Condé and Turenne, of Locke, Newton, Bossuet and Fénelon! But even the exaggeration of the phrase has value as historical evidence, for it was due to a healthy spirit of intellectual enthusiasm, and describes the hopes if not the achievements of the time.

It is creditable, too, to the young school that being thus firmly established it did not at once lapse into a narrow and unfruitful conservatism. The irrepressible Thomasius was at war half the time with his own colleagues. Franke audaciously reviewed Luther's translation of the Bible, and treated the great master with such freedom that even Spener uttered a mild though ineffectual protest. Contempt for authority, for prescription, for all the idols so laboriously set up by the doctors of Lutheranism, seemed almost to be a canon of the university. Such an intellectual ferment had not been seen in Germany since the Reformation. But the ferment was a sign of vigorous life, and Halle soon rose to be the first Protestant school in the Empire.

Wit and learning and taste enjoyed at Berlin the graceful and discriminating favor of the Electress Sophie Charlotte, a woman of excellent personal charms, of intellectual gifts, and of no little originality of mind. She was fond of philosophical and theological discussions, to which with true liberality she invited men of the most opposite schools of thought. The Calvinist, the Lutheran, and the Jesuit were equally welcome when they brought instruction or entertainment; but her highness, having an adventurous mind, also studied Bayle, and coquetted with the rising scepticism of the age. Leibnitz was her friend, and her influence procured for him the charter and endowment of the Academy.[1] She was an

[1] He once observed to her : " Es ist nicht möglich Sie zufrieden zu

18

appreciative patron of art; and the finest monumental
structures which now adorn the capital, — the arsenal, the
equestrian statue of the Great Elector, and the enlarged
castle on the Spree, — are the work of Schlueter, and date
from the reign of Frederic. For poetical gifts she had a
quick eye and prompt recognition. One Canitz, a jurist
by education and a diplomatist by trade, wrote vers de
société, as well as light comedies which were produced at
court to the delight of the Electress and the horror of the
clergy. Besser, the master of ceremonies, was also a poet,
but he impaired his literary fame by a loyal epic of one
thousand lines. Sophie Charlotte was fond of music, and
played the harp; had travelled in many countries; spoke
many tongues; and to a light heart which cheered and
charmed her friends she joined grace of person and manner, fine womanly tact, an open disposition, and perfect
sincerity. Eulogy has not exaggerated the merits of this
admirable woman. It is no disparagement of her husband to say that her name ought to be inseparably associated with the birth of art and letters in Prussia, and
with the movement which transferred the intellectual supremacy in Germany from the Catholic south to the Protestant north.[1]

It will, however, be inferred from this brief reference to

Her inde-
pendence.
Sophie Charlotte's character and tastes that she
would probably be a poor subject for court discipline, an impatient victim under the pompous formality
which then reigned at Berlin as at all the capitals of Germany. Her whole nature revolted against such absurd
restraints. She could not or would not keep her place in

stellen; Sie wollen das Warum vom Warum wissen," or rather, in
French, le pourquoi du pourquoi.

[1] Comp. Julian Schmidt, *Geschichte des geistigen Lebens in Deutschland* (Leipsic, 1862), pp. 223 et seq. Erman's *Mémoires pour servir à
l'histoire de Sophie Charlotte* (Berlin, 1801), ought to be, but is not the
standard work.

the elaborate ceremonies planned by the Elector, but was continually falling out of the ranks, or committing some breach of etiquette which filled the courtiers and palace marshals with despair. She was at war with nearly every class of her husband's servants. She laughed in the faces of the old generals who bowed their bald heads before her and essayed their melancholy gallantries, while the chamberlains, whose power was out of proportion to their usefulness, were treated with even greater contempt. The more stately and formal the occasion, the more solemn the order of proceedings, the more awful the dignity of prince and minister, of page and lackey, the more likely was the Electress, by some ill-timed revolt, to throw everything into wild disorder. She was, in effect, a permanent cause of disturbance at court, and seized every pretext for escaping to her favorite retreat at Charlottenburg, where in a chosen circle of friends she could set Vota and Spener by the ears over a theological question, or quiz Leibnitz about the causes of things, or perhaps sing with rare pathos, and to the accompaniment of her own harp, some quaint sweet melody which she herself had composed.

Another bitter foe of the court establishment was the minister who had to provide the funds for its support. Eberhard von Dankelmann was still the favorite of Frederic, and the first official in the state. His end was indeed cruel, and was meant to be disgraceful; but during these years he stands forth a true statesman of the antique type, — a Pericles while Athens was yet mistress of Greece, a Cato before any Cæsar had crossed the Rubicon, — a grave, austere, incorruptible man.[1] Like Sophie Charlotte he shunned the revelry of the palace, not, however, because it was tiresome, but be-

Dankel-mann.

---

[1] See the Elector's own flattering testimony in an official report given by Foerster, *Friedrich Wilhelm I. König von Preussen* (Potsdam, 1834), vol. i. Appendix, p. 12; Droysen, IV. i. 116, where Dankelmann is called a Cato, but a " langweiliger " Cato.

cause it was frivolous. It is said that he was never known
to laugh. Frank almost to rudeness, he always retained
in his intercourse with Frederic something perhaps of the
air of the schoolmaster, but of a schoolmaster whose heart
was in the right place, and who scorned to season his advice with flattery, however innocent and politic. He refused gifts openly made, and gifts disguised as sinecures;
and hence, preferring the power of an office to its profits,
he valued even power only because he could make it useful to the state. At the height of his career he held all
the most important public charges accumulated in his
hands, so that the whole conduct of the state, internal and
external, seemed to obey the will of one favored and fortunate man.

The cry of nepotism was raised because six of Dankelmann's brothers were installed in places of profit, dignity,
and influence. But it has been urged in his defence that
nearly the whole force of public officials was leagued
against him; that the brothers were men of character and
efficiency; and that a minister on whom, against his wish,
such vast responsibility was laid ought to have the right
of choosing a few assistants whom he could unreservedly
trust.[1]

No one felt more strongly than Dankelmann the ruinous costs of the war, or had more reason to rejoice when in 1695 the cruel stream of misfortune began to turn. Up to that time Louis had marched
on uninterruptedly from triumph to triumph. Nothing
seemed able to arrest his progress; and so long as no reverses in the field, the rudest and plainest of all lessons

Progress of
the war.

[1] A satire by Besser has this couplet: —

> Das ganze Griechenland hat ehemals sieben Weisen,
> In seinen Söhnen hat sie Dankelmann allein!

From which it may be inferred that the paternal Dankelmann was
still alive to rejoice in the prosperity of his sons. But Droysen, IV.
i. 117, thinks the lines were eulogistic, not satirical.

for such a prince, opened his eyes to the real meaning and possibilities of the struggle, the more obscure and humble means of enlightenment — neglected fields, orphaned families, wasted and ruined towns — were naturally not considered. But fortune could sometimes frown even on the Grand Monarque. Luxemburg was dead ; and Luxemburg, though neither a Condé nor a Turenne, had studied in the school of those illustrious masters, and when aroused by danger had shown the qualities of a great commander. With the death of this formidable adversary William regained, therefore, not his courage, for that he had never lost, but his confidence, which had been often and bitterly tried. The siege of Namur was undertaken with buoyant hopes, which the end justified. On the 26th of July, 1695, the town surrendered. The garrison held out a month longer, when also fell, for the second time in four years, the citadel itself, — that citadel which popular and professional belief had once pronounced impregnable to any foe, and which in this war had seen twice employed, first in the siege, and then in the repair of the works, the greatest living master of military engineering. The genius of Vauban had hastened its fall in 1692, but could not avert its fall in 1695.

The allies thus gained one great victory, and Louis' faith in his own invincibility was shaken. But the direct and indirect results of the fall of Na- _{Dawn of peace.} mur would have been less decisive if another circumstance had not made the desire for peace equally strong with all the powers. Charles II. of Spain was drawing near his end, and the well-known designs of Louis upon the succession could neither be matured by him, nor properly met by the allies, without an interval of repose from active operations in the field. Soon after the capture of Namur the coalition had indeed been formally renewed, but to little purpose. The following campaign led to nothing decisive. The Duke of Savoy had already deserted the alliance, and when in 1696 Louis began to sound the rest of his enemies on the subject of peace he found them all willing to treat. Negotiations opened at Ryswick on the 9th of May, 1697, were protracted, in part by the inevitable questions of rank and etiquette,[1] until the 20th of October, when the last of the several treaties, that between France and the Empire, was signed and proclaimed.

By the treaty or treaties of Ryswick, which were nomi-

Treaty of Ryswick.

nally based on those of Westphalia and Nimeguen, Louis was forced to surrender some of his lesser acquisitions, but secured in return a formal confirmation of his title to Strasburg and Alsace. He recognized William as King of England. The claims of his sister-in-law, the Duchess of Orleans, to the Palatinate were practically abandoned. But by means of one elastic article, or rather clause of an article, apparently designed to protect the Catholics in the restored German territories,[2] the King acquired a most dangerous power which, as has been well said, enabled him to set up Catholicism as a privileged religion in every parish where his military chaplains had said mass. The Protestant princes opposed this provision with energy. But it was accepted by the Emperor and ratified by the Diet; and nothing was left for Saxony and Brandenburg except sullenly to protest against the iniquity.

Frederic carried away at the peace no material trophies, but he won some not insignificant moral advan-

Frederic and the peace.

tages. His conduct throughout the war had been in its main outlines correct and creditable.

---

[1] Thus Frederic himself fought obstinately for the right to be treated as a belligerent, instead of merging the identity of his state in that of the Empire. He maintained that he had waged war in his own name. Comp. Droysen, IV. i. 112.

[2] . . . religione tamen Catholica Romana in locis sic restitutis in statu quo nunc est remanente. . . . Comp. Garden, *Hist. des Traités de Paix,* ii. 173.

He had asserted against the Emperor, and with no little vigor, though not with complete success, his own place in the family of European monarchs, and his fidelity to Protestantism as an issue in the struggle had been constant and effective. And if he had sometimes pleaded for subsidies in a style strangely unsuited to a high-spirited prince; if he had insisted with absurd pathos on titles and predicates, on empty forms and barren ceremonies; if he had been at times mean, punctilious, vain, peevish, and stubborn; his participation had not the less been of real service to the common cause; had won him a right to the gratitude of all who feared the restless ambition of Louis; and had visibly raised Brandenburg in the esteem of all its neighbors.

This is the view which seems to have been held by Dankelmann, and which in more courtly language he strove to impress on the Elector. But it was not the view of the giddy and superficial prince, whom for nine years Dankelmann had wisely and faithfully served. Frederic was keenly disappointed at the contents of the treaty. No account had been taken, he said, of his services; Holland and Spain had not kept their promises to him; serious inroads had been made upon his military fund; in the peace every other power — England, Spain, even Savoy — had been remembered, he himself not, although he had given the death-blow in the English Revolution, and had declared war in his own name against France. Yet he had gained neither reputation nor profit; and all this would teach him not to be too ready in the future to offer his services. The next time he would wait until he had clear and positive guaranties.[1]

The irritation of the Elector was artfully utilized by

The Elector's dissatisfaction.

[1] The Elector's own language on the 20th of August, 1697, as reported by Stepney, the English envoy at Berlin. Droysen, IV. i. 114.

Dankelmann's enemies, and even made the occasion for reviving other and older complaints. Nothing which the ingenuity of malice could invent was omitted. They charged the minister with fraud, usurpation, and treachery; with mismanagement of affairs at home and abroad; with sacrificing the interests of his master in the congress of Ryswick, and with insidious attacks upon the authority of his master at Berlin.[1] Even his virtues were cited against him. That he was no hypocrite, and told Frederic invariably the truth, became now the evidence of disrespect and disloyalty. That he had long, though with little success, struggled for frugality at court, and in the public service, was ascribed to a systematic purpose of crippling the electoral purse, and making the electoral dignity itself poor, mean, and contemptible. And that the usual elements of a court intrigue might all be present, there appeared a base adventurer, who rose swiftly in Frederic's favor, and took his natural place as head of the coalition against Dankelmann.

Intrigues against Dankelmann.

This personage was Kolb von Wartenberg, a native of the Palatinate, who had found his way to Berlin, and had been often employed in irregular services. He possessed a fine figure; had wit and address; was a singularly adroit courtier; but had neither judgment nor capacity, neither honor nor shame, and pushed his own fortunes with unscrupulous energy. Frederic was tired of Dankelmann's austere manner and inflexible virtue. He longed for a minister who would also be a congenial friend; who would share, not reprove, his frivolous pleasures; who would provide him with the means for fashionable debauchery, not lecture him with the stern authority of a schoolmaster. Such a man he found in Wartenberg. A close friendship soon grew up between the plastic prince and the scheming servant, and the union was cemented by the ruin of Dankelmann.

Wartenberg.

[1] See the charges, and Dankelmann's reply, in Isaacsohn, ii. 282 et seq.; Droysen, IV. i. 116, 117.

Of all the charges made against Dankelmann, that which proved most effective, because it touched the most sensitive side of Frederic's nature, was based on his alleged assumption of powers belonging to the elector. The charge was indeed not wholly groundless. Partly from a certain arbitrary habit of mind, partly from contempt for Frederic's low capacities, partly from the survival of some of the spirit of their former relation as tutor and pupil, Dankelmann had perhaps interpreted his powers somewhat too freely, had taken important measures on his own responsibility, and had nearly made an instrument out of the man who by law was the master. In all this there was, however, nothing criminal. It was not a scheme of aggression but a policy of true ministerial responsibility, which Frederic long endured and even encouraged. But as soon as designing knaves convinced him that instead of wisely giving up details to a competent and faithful servant he was really being made the dupe of an ambitious usurper, his aroused vanity burst forth in a furious passion. " Dankelmann wishes to play the elector?" shouted he. "Very well, I can show him that I am the master." It was natural that candid persons should report this utterance to Dankelmann, and that Dankelmann should at once resign. The Elector made some soothing observations, and readily granted the desired dismissal.

The fall of Dankelmann.

But the simple fall of Dankelmann did not satisfy the rancor of his enemies. They were determined that he should be disgraced as well as overthrown ; and to this further persecution Frederic, without perhaps seeing through its iniquity, lent all the resources of the state. A few weeks later, therefore, by order of the Elector, Dankelmann was arrested and thrown into the fortress of Spandau. His estates were summarily sequestrated. But although a nominal charge was formulated against him, and proceedings for his punishment

His arrest and disgrace.

were begun in the courts, the trial was delayed on one pretext or another, — really because there was no evidence, and the jurists showed an honorable independence; [1] until after ten years the case was abandoned, and the victim discharged. The method of his release was scarcely less cruel and unjust than his arrest. But Dankelmann was broken in health and spirits, and was forced to accept a small annual allowance as his only satisfaction. He was required to reside in the city of Cottbus.

The fall of Dankelmann left Wartenberg in the undivided enjoyment of his master's favor. Such an opportunity he would, of course, not neglect. He crowded the public departments with his creatures, men as rapacious and unprincipled as himself. He accumulated in his own hands offices of trust which yielded him an annual return of over one hundred thousand thalers.[2] He procured for himself the permanent grant of vast estates throughout the country, and in order to obtain security for the future he even obtained from Frederic a written discharge, amounting nearly to a promise, that he should never be called to account for his official acts.[3] Safety being thus assured, the plundering went merrily on.

Plunder was indeed with Wartenberg the primary, and power only the secondary object. He wisely avoided the field of general politics, for which he was by nature and training unfit, and which was pecuniarily less inviting than even humbler departments nearer the palace and the privy purse. The autocratic system of Dankelmann was therefore not revived; and a number of meritorious officials, who had long chafed under the hardships of that system, who had rejoiced at and even contrib-

*Warten-
berg's
power.*

*Other
officials.*

---

[1] See the long report of the crown advocate, Durham, in Foerster, *Fr. Wm. I.* vol. i. Appendix; Droysen, IV. i. 123, note 218.

[2] Foerster, i. 29.

[3] It is given by Foerster, i. 30.

uted to the fall of its author, now received their long delayed recognition, and were taken into the direct confidence
of Frederic. The most gifted of these was Paul von Fuchs.
He had been a professor in the university which the Great
Elector founded at Duisburg for the Rhine territories, but
in 1684 was called to Berlin, and given a seat in the Privy
Council with special charge of ecclesiastical and educational interests. But in that age the division of labor was
not strictly regarded. Fuchs was often consulted by
Frederic William, and by Frederic himself, on questions
of general policy; and the removal of his powerful rival
was followed, of course, by a great increase of his own influence. A scholar himself, his sympathies were freely
given to all educational, literary, and æsthetic movements.
Rudiger von Ilgen was another man who had been trained
in the service of the Great Elector, and yet was an active
official under the Great Elector's grandson during more
than half of his reign. His specialty was diplomacy and
foreign affairs. Other names which can only be mentioned are those of Kamecke, Luben, Kraut, Knyphausen,
and especially two Dankelmanns, whose continued employment was a singular answer to the charge of nepotism
brought against their brother Eberhard. Bartholomew
Dankelmann was for many years the skilful and trusted
ambassador of Frederic at Vienna. Daniel Ludolph succeeded the accomplished Grumbkow as minister of war,
and was the author of many wise reforms in military administration.

A charge which had begun to offer many perplexing
problems, and to call for the service of a pecul- The prince
iar kind of talent, was that of the prince elec- electoral.
toral, Frederic William.

He was born in August, 1688, two years after the death
of an earlier child. All the constellations were favorable
at his birth; and the Duchess Sophie of Hanover, his
grandmother, was struck with his "warlike appearance"

284 HISTORY OF PRUSSIA.

as he was brought out for her critical inspection. He was
early put into the hands of French nurses, French gov-
ernesses, French tutors; survived the perils of childhood,
such as swallowing buckles, climbing out of windows, and
fighting with the crown prince of Hanover; and in his
sixth or seventh year was intrusted to a governor. The
person selected was Alexander von Dohna, a soldier and
an upright man, though somewhat stern and unpopular
in his manner. Dohna was accorded a liberal discretion,
which he seems never to have abused; but Frederic himself was not oblivious to the existence of his son, or for-
getful of his own duties as a parent. Foerster quotes a
scheme of studies drawn up by the Elector, which, though
not free from the pedantry of the age, or the author's own
idiosyncrasies, is on the whole just, liberal, and discriminating.[1]

The intervention of the Electress was naturally, however, more direct, and, as might be inferred from her character, more effective for good. The conversations which
she held with the prince, the lessons which she taught him
to draw from his readings, the maxims of private and
public duty which she impressed upon him, show both the
affectionate interest of a mother and the elevated views
of a scholarly, gifted, and noble-minded woman. And the
penetrating eye of Sophie Charlotte early discovered in
her son the germs of that avarice, which in later life became so gross and brutal a passion.[2]

During these years Frederic organized two institutions
which were destined to have in the future no little influence on the progress of art and science. Even in these
enterprises he was perhaps governed as much by vanity as
by any real sympathy with their objects; but they worthily
continued the policy inaugurated with the university of
Halle. They were the academy of arts and the academy
of sciences.

[1] *Fr. Wm. I.* i. 77.   [2] Ibid. i. 103, 105.

The first of these was established in 1696; but although it numbered some promising men, especially ar- Academy of arts. chitects, among its members, it was feebly en- dowed, and worked its way slowly into influence and usefulness.

The other society was more fortunate in having the advantage of Leibnitz's great name and authority. Academy of sciences. Leibnitz's original scheme was of the most comprehensive description, though it appears that its proportions were much reduced in the course of their practical adoption. He urged that the academy ought to take in the whole field of science; that it ought to conduct experiments in the interest of agriculture and the industrial arts; and that it ought to be intrusted with the censorship, which, however, was refused. There were many delays between the inception and the realization of this plan, and it was not until 1700 that the charter was issued. It declared especially that the "société," as it was then termed, should be charged with the purification and improvement of the German language, "in order that the venerable tongue might be preserved in its original independence, and not fall into senseless confusion,"—a result which Frederic and the court, by their neglect of the venerable tongue, were doing their best to hasten; and which the learned body promptly averted by adopting French as its official language, and continuing for many years to use that language in all its proceedings. The academy was also required to interest itself in history, both secular and ecclesiastical, but its products in this field are not of enduring value. The institution was instrumental in bringing about a reform of the Calendar, which was effected in 1701, by calling the 18th of February the 1st of March. In return for this service it acquired the monopoly of the almanac trade. The honor seems trivial, and the business beneath the dignity of science, but the earlier revenues of the academy — and they were only four hundred thalers a year — were derived chiefly from this source. The first volume of the transactions of the society appeared in 1710.[1]

A circumstance which will strike the attention of any person who looks over the roll of the early members of the academy is the large number of French names. It was a number, too, wholly out of proportion to the total strength of the French immigration. Exact data are of course not available. The refugees were dispersed throughout the Elector's dominions, and the movement itself continued for many years, but on any reasonable estimate the ratio of scholars among the exiles must excite amazement. It proves that Protestantism in France, at least as represented by Protestants who fled from France to Prussia, was not a low delusion of the ignorant populace, or, on the other hand, a mere fancy of shallow and sceptical nobles, but an intelligent conviction on the part of some of the most erudite men of the age; men who joined learning to piety; and who, when banished from their country, carried the zeal of scholars as well as the faith of Christians among the people who gave them asylums.

The Huguenots in Prussia.

Some among the refugees, such especially as Lenfant and Beausobre, were pulpit orators, widely known for the fervor and eloquence of their sermons. The civil service and the army found employment for others. And even the artisans, who naturally formed the greater number in every French colony, were not only among the best whom their own country had produced, but were also vastly superior in sobriety, in intelligence, in skill, in the range of their talents, to the workmen of Prussia. It is said that over forty new branches of industrial art were introduced

---

[1] The papers pertaining to the foundation of the academy may be found in the *Histoire de l'Académie Royale des Sciences et Belles-Lettres* (Berlin, 1752). Leibnitz's memorial is in collected editions of his works.

by them. This relieved Prussia in a measure from one form of dependence on foreign lands; it increased the secondary resources of the state; and it stimulated the native artisans themselves to more active and intelligent exertions. The wisdom of permitting the Huguenot immigration was therefore obvious.

But neither Frederic William nor Frederic himself was satisfied merely to offer the refugees a shelter against the storms of religious persecution. They were more than simply tolerated. They were actively welcomed; were assisted from the privy purse, when assistance was needed; were located in advantageous regions; were favored in their industrial enterprises; were encouraged to preserve their own social customs; were permitted to build their own churches, to hold their own worship, to organize their own ecclesiastical system, to have their own schools, even sometimes to administer their own justice in their own courts. French colonies had their own "statutes," or charters, which were often surprisingly liberal. The colony at Berlin was nearly self-governing in respect to many details of social polity, acquired many privileges, enjoyed many exemptions. Others in the measure of their size and importance were favored in the same way; and in fact wherever they were collected in sufficient numbers the French formed a distinct class, recognized as such by the state and by the laws. This discrimination aroused not unnaturally the envy of the native Prussians. They were jealous of the industrial superiority of the strangers, jealous of their exceptional privileges; and while in one sense it was politic to hold out inducements to the exiles to make their home in Prussia, it was perhaps impolitic to surround them with barriers against the desirable process of assimilation with their German neighbors. In spite of this, however, the work of assimilation was done, though slowly. It is remarked by observers that the type of character in towns which received the

Treatment of the exiles.

French colonies is different, and in many respects favorably different, from the pure German type.

It has been shown that the final rupture between Frederic and Dankelmann was, if not caused, at least hastened, by the failure of the latter to obtain at Ryswick any territorial compensation for Brandenburg. But it nevertheless happened that the Elector made in that year, though unexpectedly, some not inconsiderable acquisitions. The Elector August II. of Saxony had been chosen, in 1697, king of Poland, and the honor had cost him, besides the sacrifice of his Protestant religion, great outlays for bribery and other questionable uses. Further extravagance after he mounted the throne added to his difficulties. He applied, therefore, to Frederic for aid, and in return for 350,000 thalers transferred to him the territories of Nordhausen, Petersberg, and Quedlinburg, in the northwestern part of his dominions. Some feeling was shown by the authorities of the ceded districts, but they were held in check by troops.[1]

Territorial purchases. 1697.

About this time, and in part under the influence of this event, Frederic took up seriously a favorite scheme of personal and political ambition, the scheme to acquire for himself the title of king, and for his state the character of a kingdom.

Question of the crown.

The scheme was not a new one. The assumption of the royal dignity is believed, though on obscure evidence,[2] to be a measure which the Great Elector had often earnestly considered; and certain authorities even assert that Louis XIV. once promised moral, if not material support, in case it should be under-

Fails to attract the Great Elector.

---

[1] The transaction was full of legal complications which have no interest for present readers. See Droysen, IV. i. 132, and note 227; Fix, *Territorialgeschichte*, p. 101, etc. The questions connected with Quedlinburg were not finally settled until 1803.

[2] An intimation by Ilgen many years afterwards. Droysen, IV. i. 287, note 162, IV. iv. 312.

taken. But either from prudence or indifference Frederic William gave up the project, so far as he was concerned, and left it to be carried out, if at all, by a successor better favored by circumstances, and more susceptible to its peculiar attractions. These conditions were admirably fulfilled in the character of his own son, and of the times in which he lived.

Indifference toward the scheme Frederic could neither feel nor affect; and even the prudence, which Taken up by Frederic. had taught him during a number of years heroically to suppress his desire,[1] was at length overcome by a series of dynastic promotions among his neighbors and rivals in Europe. He had seen the stadtholder of the United Provinces become king of England. He had seen, in 1694, the House of Hanover raised by the Emperor's act, and with his own assent, to the electoral dignity. And now in 1697 August of Saxony, a prince inferior to himself in resources and influence, mounted the throne of Poland, was addressed by the title of majesty, and was represented by ambassadors who could stand uncovered in the awful presence of Cæsar. This inequality was onerous and hateful to a prince so vain and jealous as Frederic.

The condition of European politics at the end of the century was favorable to the plan. One war The European situation. was preparing along the Baltic, another along the Rhine; and both conflicts seemed likely to offer facilities for the gratification of Frederic's desire.

In the north the parties were Sweden on the one side, and Denmark, Poland, and Russia on the other, Relations of the northern powers. or, more correctly, the respective rulers of those countries: Charles XII., Frederic IV., August II., and Peter. All parties were suitors for Frederic's alliance, and it was expedient to refuse all. But it was possible by adroit management to make even the refusal

[1] Droysen, IV. i. 94 et seq., first finds positive traces of the scheme in connection with the Schwiebus negotiations.

serve the Elector's purpose; to obtain a price even for neutrality; and thus to utilize a conflict which at any other time might have proved inconvenient and dangerous to Prussia. In this light the northern complications were seen by Frederic and his ministers, and they were justified by the attitude of some of the members of the coalition. August of Poland had reasons of gratitude and reasons of policy for the announcement officially made that if Frederic assumed the royal title he would recognize it.[1] The fiery and restless Patkul, who out of personal and patriotic resentment took the lead in organizing the coalition against Sweden, advised the same policy in a report to Peter the Tsar.[2] If Poland and Russia were thus engaged, Denmark, the third member of the league, was not likely to offer any obstacles; while Sweden could not afford, by underbidding her enemies, to convert Frederic's neutrality into open hostility. The northern powers seemed thus pledged to a formal or tacit acquiescence in the Elector's project. These expectations were not all immediately realized, but they describe the reasonable outlook at the turning of the century.

In the southwest, however, a mere policy of neutrality was insufficient. The question of the Spanish succession was growing daily more acute; and although various schemes of partition and various combinations of the powers postponed from time to time the actual outbreak, the rival pretensions of Louis XIV. and the Emperor remained apparently irreconcilable. But down to the death of Charles II. of Spain Louis had effectually deceived England and Holland, and isolated the Emperor. Two successive treaties between the western powers were rejected by Leopold. The second treaty, that of 1700, even recognized an Austrian archduke as principal heir, but it provided for a division of the inher-

Austria and the western powers.

---

[1] January 26, 1700. Droysen, IV. i. 140.
[2] Quoted by Ranke, *Pr. Gesch.* i., ii. 441 (ed. 1874).

itance, and the Emperor stubbornly refused to accept less than the whole. .It looked, therefore, as if all Europe would combine to force the settlement by arms upon Leopold. This was the situation which Frederic prepared to utilize. He could probably have had the recognition of the western powers at the price of mere neutrality, for their preponderance, according to the treaty of 1700, was already sufficiently great. But Frederic was attached by tradition and sympathy to Austria, and as an elector felt that respect was due to the constitutional head of the Empire. He determined, therefore, to procure first of all the Emperor's assent to his plan.

The negotiations were long and their history is obscure. It appears that the ministers whom Frederic consulted were not unamimous in the choice of the Emperor as an ally, or even in approving the enterprise itself. Fuchs advised an alliance with England and Holland, to the neglect of Austria. Ilgen drew attention to the jealousy which the step was sure to arouse, to the awkwardness of the situation if the powers should refuse to recognize the proposed title, and to the advantage of being rather the greatest elector than the weakest king in Europe. Bartholdi, the ambassador at Vienna, dwelt on the difficulties which would be raised by the imperial court, and on the price which would be exacted for its favor.[1] But none of these councillors openly opposed Frederic, and his purpose was not shaken by their observations.[2]

Views of Frederic's advisers.

[1] Ranke, *Pr. Gesch.* i., ii. 442. I may here explain that in the collected edition of Ranke's works (Leipsic, 1874) two volumes are apparently bound in one, although in some of them the paging is consecutive. Before that edition was issued I had noted references to his *Neun Bücher Pr. Gesch.* (Berlin, 1847). This was afterwards expanded into *Zwölf Bücher.*

[2] See his reply to Fuchs' remonstrances in Droysen, IV. i. 139, 140. Noteworthy is this reference to the European situation. . . . weil meine Lande dergestalt belegen, dass fast alle Potentaten Europa's meine Freundschaft nöthig haben, so werde ich noch dieses

The Emperor's scruples were both political and relig-

Catholic
scruples. ious. The House of Hohenzollern was already
powerful; would it not become more powerful
and even dangerous if the head of the house were to
call himself a king and wear a crown? The Hohenzollerns were also Protestants, and the idea of another Protestant kingdom in Europe was abhorrent to every good
Catholic. Even some Poles, otherwise favorable, hesitated on this point. Vota, the Polish Jesuit, and friend
of Sophie Charlotte, was early enlisted in Frederic's
cause; but he seems seriously to have broached a plan to
make the Elector's success easier by first making him a
Catholic. It was argued that only the Pope could make
kings, and that Frederic should humbly apply to him.[1]
Another proposal was that the Emperor should be conciliated by calling the Elector king of the Wends, or king
of the Vandals, or something which would to that extent
dissociate the dignity from the German Empire.[2] But
these devices were all rejected by Frederic, or more probably were abandoned without being formally presented.
Although the Emperor was stubborn and grasping, he
needed help, and Bartholdi, the ambassador, was inexorable. But the favorable decision was probably hastened —
if specific charges, general belief, and intrinsic reason-
ableness establish a probability — by the judicious use of
money, which Frederic's purse furnished, and Father Wolf,

The Em-   an intriguing Jesuit, and other favorites of the
peror yields.
1700.   Emperor, received.[3] At a conference of the im-

grosse Werk mit Gottes Hülfe desto eher mit ihnen durchtreiben.
. . . Rather more characteristic of Frederic is, however, the theory
there expressed that he, being the third elector of the name, ought
to take up the project because omne trinum perfectum !

[1] Stenzel, iii. 89. Droysen, IV. iv. 221–233, gives the text of Vota's
memorial.

[2] Vota proposed "Rex Borussiorum et Vandalorum."

[3] Droysen, IV. i. 144, names especially the minister Kaunitz, and
100,000 thalers as the sum which he received.

perial ministers on the 24th of July it was decided in
principle to grant the Elector's request.

The terms of the transaction were yet to be settled,
and over them the two noble potentates wrangled
for another half year. But finally an agreement
was reached and the treaty was signed. *The crown treaty.* The Emperor on
his part, and " out of the fulness of his power," consented
to recognize Frederic as king in Prussia, with all the
honors and privileges which the title conveyed ; and promised to use his influence to secure the assent of the other
powers. Frederic was thus not to be king in *Brandenburg*, for Brandenburg was a part of the Empire, and
the traditions of the Empire permitted, or were said to
permit, only one crown, that of Bohemia. He was not to
be king *of* Prussia, though the reasons for this distinction
are somewhat too subtle for modern comprehension. He
became king *in* Preussen, a land of which, or in which he
was already sovereign.[1] The saving clause in behalf of
Poland's rights was perhaps called for by historical technicalities, but was of no practical importance ; the Elector
had already indeed given assurances on that point to the
court of Warsaw.[2] The essential stipulations exacted of
Frederic were these: To renew the treaty of 1686 made
by his father ; to furnish eight thousand men in case of
war, and maintain them at his own cost; to contribute
men to the garrisons of Kehl, and Philippsburg ; to relin-
quish the subsidies still due from the Emperor; to support the House of Hapsburg in elections for emperor ;
and to suffer the new dignity to make no change in Brandenburg's relations to the Empire.

This treaty was signed on the 16th of November, and

---

[1] The distinction seems to have been observed only in German. In
French treaties Frederic is always "Roi de Prusse ; " in Latin,
" Rex Borussiæ."

[2] See Dumont, Supplement, v. 536; Lamberty, *Mémoires pour servir
à l'histoire du 18ième Siècle* (Amsterdam, 1735), i. 95.

on the same day the news reached Vienna of the death of
the Spanish king. No event could have been
more favorable to the Elector's plans. So long
as the naval powers, England and Holland, were
in alliance with France, they looked with distrust on Frederic's negotiations at Vienna, and gave him slight encouragement to hope for their support.[1] But Louis was disposed to observe the treaties of partition only until the
emergency which they were intended to meet should arrive. On the death of Charles II. he boldly tore them
up, placed his grandson on the throne of Spain, and thus
threw a challenge in the face of all Europe. The naval
powers then became as solicitious as the Emperor himself
to secure the friendship of Frederic. That friendship was
not dear; and the Prussian crown was early recognized by
Holland, England, and other powers, but not by France
and Spain. The Pope, too, refused to welcome the new
king, and issued a violent manifesto against the whole
transaction. Finally the surviving remnant of the Teutonic knights made about their last public demonstration in a protest against the introduction of a king into
the land, which the order had conquered, converted, and
civilized.

The persistence with which Frederic himself pushed
this scheme, the reluctance displayed and the price finally
exacted by the Emperor, and the vehement opposition of
the Pope, show clearly enough the importance which Europe gave to the proposed change. But to modern criticism the zeal of Frederic and the zeal of his enemies
may seem equally absurd. The promotion was only one
of form, only the exchange of one title for another. It
added not a thaler to Frederic's revenue, not a soldier
to his army, not an acre to his dominions. It might
even seem from one point of view to weaken rather than

The powers and the new crown.

---

[1] See William's letter to Heinsius in *Letters of William III. and
Louis XIV.*, by Paul Grimblot (London, 1848), ii. 437.

strengthen his position, by provoking, as it did, the anger of the Pope and the church; by arousing jealousy and hatred, as it did, among some of the princes of the Empire; and generally by planting the seed of future embarrassments. And not the least of the apparent evils of the step was that it threatened, with such a prince as Frederic, to entail upon the land a vastly increased outlay for a royal establishment. The frantic pursuit of a costly and worthless title has, therefore, been usually treated as the leading illustration of Frederic's frivolity of character.

The vain personal interest of the Elector in the crown argues, of course, no little weakness. But does it follow from this that the prize was unworthy the ambition and the efforts of a practical prince, *Importance of the change.* that it was not a genuine measure of political conquest, and therefore not a triumph of statesmanship? To answer such a question in the affirmative is not, perhaps, to ignore, but certainly to underrate, the part which forms and ceremonies, ranks and titles have played in the councils of Europe in every age of the past, and will continue to play until human nature shall be radically changed. The fact is perhaps not creditable to the race, but there is also nothing discreditable in recognizing it, and even in yielding to it its actual importance. An inequality of mental worth is of course more disgraceful than a mere inequality of rank. But all forms of inequality are irksome; and when inequality of rank can be redressed without any sacrifice of moral principle, the task is perfectly legitimate and even praiseworthy. In this view of the case Frederic was a real statesman, and a real benefactor of his people. To change his title from elector to king was not actually to increase the physical resources at his command; but it gave him greater weight, moral and political, in Europe; and if the citizen is gratified by the dignity and influence of his state, the Elector must be credited with a patriotic and meritorious service. To this consideration, drawn from the relations of Brandenburg in the family of nations, must be added two others of a more local and restricted character. The acquisition of a new and higher title would have a probable tendency to unite and consolidate, first in sympathy and then in institutions, the several territories which made up the Elector's dominions. The royal dignity was furthermore, and finally, a natural step in the course of progress, which, beginning with the first elector of his house, had continued almost without interruption down to the time of Frederic himself.

There was one class of allies whose support was given It is favored by the court. to Frederic in this enterprise without any scruples of conscience, or any interruptions of zeal. Statesmen might weigh the political dangers of the crown. The people might count its cost. To Fuchs and Ilgen in the cabinet, to the peasant or the artisan at his labor, the disappearance of the elector of Brandenburg in the king of Prussia was a process which, however striking to the imagination, and however welcome to patriotism, had to be considered in every light, and accepted, if at all, not because it was without disadvantages, but because the balance of advantages was in its favor. But to the courtiers and favorites, to the officials of the castle from chamberlain to scullion, to all who served the vanity and robbed the purse of Frederic, the scheme was commended by every consideration of power and profit. The servant shines in the reflected glory of his master. It is nobler, or the sentiment of courts makes it nobler, to be the cup-bearer of a king than the cup-bearer of an elector. It is probable, too, that under the king there will be more servants; that the cup-bearer will wear more gold on his coat ; that lawful earnings will rise with the scale of magnificence, and unlawful gains with the march of prodigality ; that in short, that large group of officials who form the establishment and minister to the luxury of a court will become socially more important, and pecuniarily more prosperous.

Under any prince not wholly free from one of the most amiable, though one of the most mischievous vices of his class, this result would be nearly certain to follow. But with a prince like Frederic it was inevitable. It is true that when the greater cost of a royal establishment was cautiously suggested by one of the ministers, the Elector had replied that his household was already organized and conducted in the style of a king; and the statement could have been verified by the accounts of the privy purse. During the reign of the Great Elector the average receipts of the chatulle were 122,000 thalers. For the fiscal year 1687–88 they were only 50,000. The records of Frederic's outlays are not quite so well preserved; in 1697 they were estimated at not less than 270,000 thalers, and by 1713, the year of his death, they had risen to nearly 500,000.[1] This increase was in part effected, too, by the device of diverting into the chatulle the revenues of other funds, and at the cost, therefore, of the efficiency of other departments of the service. The inference is, then, not only that the personal extravagance of Frederic was much greater than that of his father, but also that it steadily increased from year to year during his own reign. As compared with other princes of the same rank the Elector undoubtedly maintained a royal establishment.

The contemporary evidence in regard to the organization and personnel, the manners and morals, of the palace household throws a lurid light upon the figures of the official accountants. It is known approximately what were the annual disbursements of the chatulle; in 1697, as above stated, they amounted to 270,000 thalers. But what were the items

Expenses of Frederic's court.

Prodigality and corruption.

[1] Riedel, *Staatshaushalt,* p. 37, and Beilage X., note.

of this enormous expense ?　This question is answered in part by the stewards' books, and in part, though more loosely, by surviving descriptions of the life which was led at Frederic's court.　After Wartenberg, who was chief administrator of the chatulle, had laid aside his share, the rest was employed to meet the costs of a miniature Versailles, yet a Versailles much more out of proportion than that of Louis XIV. to the actual population and resources of the state.　The personal needs of Frederic and his family were not inconsiderable.　His official mistress, the Countess Wartenberg, would have neglected her opportunities if she had not enriched herself.　Some forty chamber musicians drew on the purse of King Frederic in 1706,[1] and it is fair to assume that Elector Frederic was also not indifferent to harmony, or exempt from its costs. Two thousand thalers annually were allotted to comedians.　A French laundryman, imported at the expense of the state, received a salary greater than some of the ambassadors ; a dancing-master was about on the pecuniary level of a general ; and although the perquisites of a faithful minister in Frederic's service cannot now be learned, it is no little advantage to know that on Saturday, the sixth day of February, 1697, the butler, Peschke, drew three and one half bottles of champagne from his master's cellar.　Other domestics were treated with the same liberality.　The simple roll of palace employees, with their generous pay, and still more generous allowances, is itself conclusive proof of the ordinary extravagance at the Berlin palace.　And the extraordinary though frequent festivities of every kind, — baptisms and weddings ; concerts, receptions, balls ; hunting parties, and garden parties, and dancing parties ; the entertainment of princely guests, the celebration of victories, the commemoration of anniversaries, — these, celebrated with the great-

[1] See the curious transcript from the treasury books in Foerster, *Fr. Wm. I.* i. 62.

est splendor and at ruinous expense, all justify the singular boast of Frederic that his establishment had already attained royal proportions.

But the boast, though a confession of folly in the past, was not a pledge of wisdom for the future. This was clear to the Bessers, and Wartenbergs, and Logiaments; and, together with the presumption which they drew from Frederic's character, explains their solicitude for the success of the royal project. Their foresight was confirmed by the very act which completed the transaction.

It was natural for Frederic to hold, and there was, perhaps, technical soundness in the view, that the crown could not be formally assumed without the ceremony of coronation. The promise so laboriously extorted from the Emperor was indeed a promise to recognize the title of king, and the mere title could have been assumed by a proclamation, or an announcement in any form to the other powers ; but the actual imposition of the crown would undoubtedly lend a certain visible significance, not to be underrated, to the change. Such a ceremony could also reasonably have been made elaborate, solemn, and imposing. The imagination of a loyal public is touched by magnificence which is in harmony with the occasion, and does not violate the laws of good taste on the one hand or of a decent frugality on the other. But magnificence may easily pass into ostentation; ostentation is coarse, obtrusive, odious ; and even those who fail to perceive its vulgarity may easily be provoked to count its cost. These were dangers which it was almost impossible for Frederic to escape. His coronation, though proper enough in itself, and not without some dignity in its details, went, as a whole, so much beyond what was fittting for the occasion or warranted by the state of the public purse, was so overladen with tawdry and offensive splendor, that it is always described, alike by the critic and the historian, with unqualified contempt.

The ceremony was appointed for the month of January, 1701, and at Königsberg, the capital of Preussen. Frederic himself was the chief architect of the festivities, aided by Besser as master of ceremonies.[1]
On the 17th of December, 1700, Frederic and court set out from Berlin, and so extensive was the cortege that it had to move in three sections, and required not less than thirty thousand horses in successive relays. To-day the railway takes the traveller from Berlin to Königsberg in twelve hours. But in 1700 there was not even a good post-road, the country was full of bogs and swamps, and the season was unfavorable, so that it was not until the 29th of December that the noble train drew up at the gates of the old Prussian city. This was the town which had so long denied the right of Frederic William, a stern, fearless, and indomitable man; to be even sovereign duke in Preussen. It was now prepared to accept and perhaps to welcome his weak and frivolous son as sovereign king. Thus far had history moved since the Treaty of Wehlau!

Journey to Königsberg.

On the 15th of January the heralds made formal proclamation, amid the ringing of bells, the roar of cannon, and the cheers of the populace, that the Duchy of Preussen was raised to a kingdom, and that Frederic III., the elector, was Frederic I., the king.[2] The order of the black eagle, still the highest decoration which the Prus-

[1] Besser subsequently published a description of the festivities under the title *Preussiche Krönungs-Geschichte*, 1702. This and the *Mémoires* of Count Dohna, another eye-witness, are the chief authorities on the subject. An elaborate account of the coronation, and of the ceremonial of the Berlin court, is in Dumont, *Corps Univ. Dip.* Supp. vol. v.

[2] Puisque la Providence avait voulu que le Duché de Prusse fût érigé en Royaume, etc., — such, according to Lamberty, i. 380, was the language of the proclamation. It is interesting to learn that the Elector had been assured of the coöperation of other than mere worldly potentates.

sian crown confers, was founded on the 17th.[1] The coronation itself was fixed for the 18th.

Early in the morning of that auspicious day the King's attendants waited upon him in his chamber, and robed him in the prescribed garments of his new rank. The company then repaired to the audience room of the castle. Up to this point the usual etiquette of such occasions had been followed; but now a bold and startling innovation was made. The King of England was crowned by the Archbishop of Canterbury. The Emperor's ambition was to have the Pope place the sacred symbol on his head. The participation of the church, Protestant or Catholic, and through its highest available dignitary, was in short a custom which had the precedents of centuries in its behalf, and seemed to be a fundamental condition of royalty itself. But Frederic showed a spirit of independence, and a spirit of dignity, which nothing in his character led the observers to expect, by seizing the crown and placing it with his own hands on his head. This act atones for much that was absurd in the chase for the crown, and in the coronation itself. The Queen next received her diadem at the hands of her husband; and the pair, seated on the throne, then accepted the homage and congratulations of the company. The final act was a solemn procession to the chapel, where the sacred ointment was applied by two members of the clergy, made bishops especially for the occasion. Festivities were kept up many days at Königsberg, and were resumed later at Berlin. But these, though profoundly interesting to Frederic and the court, are not of engrossing public importance.[2]

One incident from the audience room at Königsberg

The coronation.

---

[1] Lamberty, i. 381, says that this was the execution of a plan which he himself had suggested the year before to Frederic.

[2] An account of these festivities, as well as of the coronation, may be found in K. von Ledebur, *König Friedrich I. von Preussen* (Leipsic, 1878), pp. 281–313.

was, however, so characteristic of the chief actor that it
must not be neglected. Sophie Charlotte was an
industrious snuff-taker. In honor of her proficiency in that art, or out of compliment to her
personal charms, Peter the Great of Russia had once,
while visiting Berlin, given her a gold snuff-box. Now,
as she afterwards wrote to Leibnitz, the tawdry ceremonies at the castle wearied her; she dozed and yawned;
and once, at the most critical and solemn point, when the
gravity of a sphinx was not greater than Frederic's, Sophie Charlotte calmly took a pinch of snuff. Unluckily
the King saw the act, and an aid-de-camp was sent to reprimand the offender.

Sophie Charlotte at the ceremony.

And Sophie Charlotte was probably not alone in her
insubordination. A youth of thirteen heard the rustle of
silk and saw the glitter of diamonds; sat through the
weary audiences, and tramped about in the interminable
processions; until he perhaps began to think of the time
when, as Frederic William I., he would sweep all such
folly and finery away.

CHAPTER VIII.

EARLY YEARS OF THE NEW KINGDOM.

THE adoption of the royal title was not one of those changes which require others, political or constitutional, to follow as a necessary consequence. Frederic was already independent as a duke in Preussen; he could not be more independent as a king. As elector of the Empire he had rights to enforce and duties to perform; and both rights and duties were the same after as before 1701. His relations to his subjects, to the great social classes and corporations, to the administrative service, to the several provinces, were not modified in law by the ceremony at Königsberg, nor was there any imperative reason of policy for attempting to modify them in fact, by a sudden and comprehensive scheme of reform. The adoption of a higher title by the Elector did, however, tend to exalt his prerogative in the popular imagination, and to facilitate the acceptance of new doctrines and new measures. *The new kingdom.*

But for the moment Frederic was not so much occupied with plans for reaping the fruits of his new honor, as with the duty of fulfilling the conditions on which the honor had been granted. A war over the succession in Spain was early seen to be inevitable. Louis XIV., having the choice between the treaties of partition, which divided the possessions of Spain, and the will of Charles II., which left those possessions undivided to the son of the dauphin, affected hesitation, and finally chose to recognize the will. This in itself was suf- *The Bourbons in Spain.*

ficient provocation to all the powers which had signed the treaties, as well as to the Empire. But William III., toward whom all eyes were turned, was held in check by a tory parliament which had greatly reduced the army, and by a nation which was obstinately hostile to war. Under pressure from his ministers he had even in 1701 recognized the Duke of Anjou as king of Spain. The arrogance of Louis, on the other hand, seemed to rise as the spirit of his rivals declined. On the pretext that the Spanish garrisons in the Netherlands were insufficient to preserve order, he boldly introduced French troops. But this was one of the things which neither the English whig nor the English tory was willing to permit, and which Holland had a vital interest in preventing. Parliament at once sanctioned William's demand for the withdrawal of the intruders. The Emperor had likewise his embarrassments, though they were diplomatic and military rather than parliamentary and domestic. The Elector of Bavaria, one of the most powerful of the German princes, recognized the Duke of Anjou, and declared for Louis. His brother, the Archbishop of Cologne, followed this example.[1] And some of the other potentates, still offended by the erection of Hanover to an electorate, listened to French promises, and seized so good an occasion for gratifying their revenge. The King of Prussia was safe for the contingent which he had promised, but not even his course was free from difficulties. He was suspicious of Sweden, whose enterprise in Poland menaced his frontiers, and of the elder branch of the house of Brunswick — Hanover, which had early equipped an army for the support of Louis. In Italy the Emperor acted promptly; but on the Rhine negotiation had to precede action.

Louis had haughtily refused to withdraw his troops from

---

[1] A general war against France, it will be recollected, had been necessary to install this prelate in his See.

the Spanish Netherlands. William hastened, therefore, to the Hague, where he was met by ambassadors from the Emperor; and in September, 1701, *Folly of Louis.* a secret alliance was formed by these two monarchs and Holland for the expulsion of the French from their menacing positions in Italy and the Netherlands.[1] The scope of action thus contemplated was too narrow for the Emperor and for William, though it was as far as the English Parliament was at that time willing to go. . But William counted, and not in vain, on the folly of his adversary. It was a rule of English policy, more resolute even than the determination to exclude the French from the Netherlands, that the crown should not again be acquired by the Stuarts, or by a Catholic of any house ; and Parliament was just giving renewed emphasis to the national purpose by the act of settlement, which, passing over several Catholic claimants, vested the title to the throne, after Anne, in the Electress Sophie of Hanover and her Protestant heirs. Yet when James II. the exiled Stuart died, just after the close of negotiations at the Hague, Louis hastened, in defiance of the Treaty of Ryswick, to acknowledge his son as king of England. This was an affront which not even the tories could endure. Troops and supplies were promptly voted; the issue assumed new dimensions; and although William himself, the great author of the coalition, died before active hostilities began, his spirit gave an impetus which carried England through many years of war.

Frederic was not satisfied with the mere fulfillment of the pledge which he had given to the Emperor. Ambition to show himself a king in fact as well *Action of Frederic.* as in name, hatred of Louis, and the promise of subsidies,[2]

[1] Dumont, *Corps Dip.* viii. 89 ; Garden, *Hist. des Traités de Paix,* ii. 240. The English declaration of war was made May 4, 1702 ; the Emperor's, May 15.
[2] This is more liberal than the version of the King's grandson,

led him to give in his separate and independent adhesion
to the alliance, and as a contracting party to furnish additional contingents. The dispersion of the threatening
Brunswick levies early in 1702 relieved him from one
source of anxiety.

But the attitude of Sweden forbade him to strip his
land of all its defensive forces, and certain military reforms were, therefore, undertaken. In
1701 the situation had seemed to demand an increase of
the army, and it was accordingly raised from thirty to
forty thousand men. But the dispatch of troops to the
Rhine left the available reserves at about the original
figure, though the requirement of military drill from the
peasants on the public domains, which was the beginning
of a species of militia, and was enforced with singular
rigor, created if not an army, at least a stock of material
on which the army could at any time draw.[1] The system of voluntary enlistment was still in force. Bounties
were paid to recruits and premiums to recruiting officers.
The competition among these latter was, therefore, keen ;
and the arts which they practised upon ignorant or waver-
ing candidates for his majesty's service were often not less
cruel, and far less honorable, than rules of forced conscription. Frequent complaints of abuses led to frequent
edicts against the abuses, but as the demand for soldiers
to fill the gaps caused by the bloody battles of the war
grew more urgent and more difficult to satisfy, stringent measures became necessary ; and the ground was
prepared for a regular system of conscription. Desertions
were numerous, although the punishment of deserters was
sharpened by successive decrees, until it reached the last
extreme of severity. A captured deserter could have ear

Military reforms.

Frederic the Great, who says (*Mémoires de Brandbg.* part III.), il
était lié par des subsides, par son inclination, et par ses espérances,
etc. The treaty with the two naval powers is in Dumont, viii. 96.

[1] Comp. Droysen, IV. i. 168, and note 296.

and nose slit, be branded in presence of his regiment, and
be condemned to life imprisonment with hard labor in
a fortress. But if the health of a soldier was permanently injured in the infliction of these penalties his officer was held responsible.[1] It was apparently deemed a
loss to the state if the ear or the nose of an offender was
amputated in so unskilful a manner that the rest of the
punishment, work on the fortifications, could not be carried out.

The civil administration of the army was at this time,
and until 1709, in the hands of Daniel Ludolph D. L. Dan-
Dankelmann, a younger brother of Eberhard. kelmann.
He, too, began his official career under the Great Elector.
Trained in subordinate though responsible positions by
Joachim von Grumbkow, he succeeded that first great
Prussian minister of war in 1691, and worthily continued
the course of reforms inaugurated by him. Improved
systems of recruiting, quartering, and provisioning the
troops were introduced by him; the facility with which
from year to year during the war Frederic met his military obligations was largely due to Dankelmann; and it
was another Grumbkow, Frederic William, who not long
after his death took up the work, and especially in the
next reign carried it so rapidly forward.[2]

The great difficulty was, of course, that of means, and
the minister of war administered the funds of Finance and
the army, as well as the army itself. The expe- revenue.
dients which Frederic had learned in the first war with
France were not neglected in the second. Head-money
was levied from time to time. The contributions of the
rural subjects and the excise duties of the towns were
raised. Loans were contracted in times of great pressure,
and the next king inherited them as debts to be discharged. But the difficulties would have been much
greater, and the measures of the government more oppres-

---

[1] Stenzel, iii. 215.   [2] Comp. Isaacsohn, ii. 263 et seq.

sive, if the subsidies paid by foreign powers had not been liberal and fairly regular. The total receipts from this source during the twenty-five years of Frederic's reign are estimated at fourteen million thalers.[1]

The question of subsidies was not, however, the only one on which Frederic insisted in the negotiations at the Hague. His full recognition as king, with the ceremonial to which the title gave him a right, was delayed by the English court; and it required all of Marlborough's tact and persuasion to make him accept for the time a promise that the matter should be settled to his satisfaction. Another difficulty arose over the choice of a generalissimo for the combined troops of the allies. Frederic did not scruple to claim this office for himself; and although he was perhaps not worse fitted than some of the other candidates, the selection of Marlborough, which William on his death-bed had advised, seems almost a providential escape from a serious blunder.

The campaign of 1702 was preliminary to those which were to follow. The rival commanders were manœuvring for the advantage of position, all apparently in no haste to bring on a general engagement; while Marlborough in particular, thwarted at every step by dissensions in his own camp, had to conciliate a thousand petty jealousies before he could begin systematic operations. But the fortress of Kaiserswerth, which had been turned over to the French by the Archbishop of Cologne, was captured after a vigorous siege, in which Prussian troops took an efficient part. Marlborough's efforts resulted in the fall of Venloo, Ruremond, and Stevenswaert. The imperial army on the upper Rhine carried the important fortress of Landau.

The relations of Frederic and Holland began in this year to suffer a serious friction. The King was, or claimed to be, through his mother and under

Campaign of 1702.

The Orange inheritance.

---

[1] Riedel, *Staatshaushalt*, p. 47.

the provisions of the will of his grandfather, Frederic Henry of Orange, lawful heir to a considerable part of the family possessions of the House of Orange; and an alleged promise of William III. had, in a measure, recognized the claim.[1] But when William's papers were opened after his death, it was found that by a will executed in 1695 he had made the young prince, William Friso of Nassau, his sole heir. It was not in the nature of a Hohenzollern to neglect an opportunity for adding to the landed possessions of the house; and Frederic took prompt measures of force and of negotiation for vindicating his rights. But the delay of the States-General, the complex legal relations of the property itself, and the preoccupations of the parties with the more urgent and critical issues of the war, made a satisfactory settlement difficult, and left the dispute as a source of discord and danger for several years.[2]

In 1703 the disturbed relations between Prussia and Sweden were put on a better footing. Charles XII. had joined the alliance of the Hague, to which Frederic was also a party; but the latter was also on friendly terms with August of Saxony, and had inherited treaty obligations to support Poland against certain forms of danger. Up to this time he had not interfered in the war which Sweden was carrying on against the Republic. It was not certain that he would interfere; but if at any time his interests should seem to be threatened, the treaties of Wehlau and Bromberg would give an additional pretext for action. Suspicion and jealousy marked,

Treaty with Sweden.

[1] That is in 1688, at the time when William needed the aid of Frederic in his English expedition. See Droysen, IV. iv. 216, 217, for Fuch's report of an interview with Bentinck, where the latter's assurances on behalf of William seem to sustain the Prussian contention.

[2] The space which this affair has in the contemporary chroniclers, especially Lamberty, is evidence of the interest which it had at the time, but fortunately long since lost.

therefore, the relation of the courts of Berlin and Stockholm. The naval powers finally undertook to mediate,
and brought about in July, 1703, a treaty between Sweden
and Prussia, by which the former recognized Frederic as
king, and the latter undertook to give no aid to Charles's
enemies.[1] The solicitude of Frederic about the feelings
of his new ally rose at once to the highest point of
warmth. It is said that the bronze group, which, at the
base of the equestrian statue of the Great Elector, represents that prince in the act of knocking off the shackles
of a slave, was removed for a time, on the complaint of
the Swedish ambassador that it might be taken to refer,
as it undoubtedly did, though with not a little artistic
license, to the battle of Fehrbellin.[2] This treaty gave
great offence to the Czar and the King of Poland, but it
was explained as referring only to the recognition of the
royal title.

The year 1703 opened favorably and closed disastrously
for the allies. Rheinberg surrendered to the
Prussians, and Bonn to an investing force commanded by Marlborough, and containing a Prussian contingent under General Natzmer. But Antwerp and Ostend were successfully defended by the French; and on
the Danube the imperial army was out-generalled and defeated by Villars. Five Prussian regiments shared this
misfortune, though the heroism of the young Prince Leopold of Anhalt-Dessau, the first of a family illustrious in
the military annals of Prussia, was in flattering contrast
to the misconduct of higher officers, and saved the retreat
from being a complete disgrace.

The year 1704 seemed, therefore, to promise little encouragement for the affairs of the allies. They
were many; and Louis was nearly alone; but it
was Louis of France, and he had the unity of purpose

1703.

1704.

---

[1] The treaty is given by Martens, *Traités de Paix*, viii. 26.
[2] Stenzel, iii. 123.

that comes from undivided councils, while his enemies were embarrassed by hesitations, jealousies, and disputes of every sort. Marlborough suffered severely from the false position in which he was placed, and had left the winter quarters of the army, at the close of the campaign in 1703, with the avowed intention of throwing up his command and retiring to private life.[1] Wiser councils finally prevailed. The duke returned to the continent in 1704, not satisfied with the position of affairs, perhaps not hopeful of the results of the coming efforts, but determined to try a radical change of policy. The defence of the Dutch frontiers he decided to leave to the Dutch. The post of danger was really on the upper Danube, where the Austrians were vigorously pressed by the Bavarians and French, while the discontented Hungarians were creating fresh troubles in their rear. It was in this crisis that Marlborough, as agreed with Prince Eugene of Savoy, undertook his bold and brilliant march from the Rhine to the Danube. The result was the battle of Blenheim.

In the division of troops between the two commanders the Prussians fell to Eugene. They formed, indeed, the larger part of his infantry, — eleven out of eighteen battalions,[2] — and held, under command of Leopold of Dessau, the extreme right of the allied forces. With cavalry Eugene was better supplied. He is credited with seventy-four squadrons, of which a few were Prussians, and all were Germans. But the cavalry failed to stand the enemy's charges; and Eugene himself testified that the day was more than once saved by the unflinching tenacity of the Prussians, and the energy, the daring, the coolness, the quick eye, and the firm hand of their young commander.[3]

After this victory the two generals led the army back to

---

[1] Coxe, *Memoirs of Marlborough* (London, 1820), i. 292.

[2] Ibid. i. 391, note.

[3] See his letter to Frederic, in Lamberty, iii. 105.

the Rhine and the Moselle, where after the capture of
Treves and other important places it went into winter
quarters.

In the mean time the situation in Italy was causing the
imperial court much anxiety. The Duke of Savoy, having gone over to the allies, was sorely
pressed by the French, and loud appeals for help were
made to all the powers, and to Marlborough. More
troops were urgently needed. They could be obtained
only of Frederic, and Frederic could be moved only by
Marlborough. It was proposed, therefore, that the duke
should go to Berlin on this mission; and at great sacrifice of time and comfort he undertook the journey, setting
out early in November, and arriving on the 22d of that
month. The accounts of the visit are unfortunately meagre. No greater contrast could be presented than that
between the handsome, graceful, manly, persuasive Marlborough, and the weak, deformed, pedantic, foppish, and
ostentatious Frederic; and a full description of their intercourse would be amusing, perhaps useful. But Marlborough's letters, the best source of information on the
subject, are brief and hurried, and chiefly occupied with
the actual business which brought him there. He alludes,
however, to the warmth and splendor of his reception.
"It is not to be expressed," he writes, "the civilities and
honors they have done me here, the ministers assuring me
that no other body could have prevailed with the King." [1]
The duke had in fact carried his point in less than a
week. He had to pacify Frederic in regard to the Orange inheritance, which was again causing trouble, to give
assurance about the Swedes, of whom Frederic was again
apprehensive, and to baffle the intrigues of Russia and
Poland; yet he met in one way or another all of these difficulties, and in return for the promise of an English subsidy, obtained eight thousand Prussians for service in
Italy.

Marlborough in Berlin.

[1] Letter of November 27, in Coxe, ii. 62.

It had been intended that the crown prince, Frederic William, should accompany Marlborough to England. Foreign travel, with a residence especially in Holland, was regarded by the Queen as a possible cure for the vices which were every day becoming more prominent in his character. A youth who in a fit of passion could throw an attendant down-stairs, who had learned to gloat like a miser over his ducats, and whose noblest pastime was to drill a squad of cadets, was evidently in need of some diversion which might turn his tastes into better channels. Sophie Charlotte urged, therefore, a visit to the Hague and to London, and the King finally gave his consent. But the English half of the scheme was thwarted by a fatal calamity. The prince spent some time in Holland, and was actually on the point of embarking with Marlborough for England, when he received news of the death of the Queen, his mother, and immediately returned to Berlin.

The crown prince in Holland.

Sophie Charlotte died on the 1st of February, 1705, at Hanover, after a sudden and brief illness. She retained her faculties to the last. To an officious clergyman, who had offered to administer the last consolations of religion, she sent word that it was not necessary; she knew what in the circumstances he would say; she had already said it all to herself; would continue to say it; and believed that in that respect she stood well with her God. Even in the presence of death her stoical and resolute spirit asserted itself. The ladies of her court stood about her bedside, overcome with grief and weeping bitterly. "Do not grieve over me," said the philosophical woman, " for I shall soon satisfy my curiosity about the causes of things, which Leibnitz could never explain, and give the King an opportunity for a funeral pageant, in which he can gratify all his love of display."

Death of Sophie Charlotte.

The latter part of the prophecy was amply fulfilled.

All the ingenuity of Frederic himself, of Besser, and of the lesser architects of ceremony, conspired to organize a demonstration of which nearly every feature was condemned by the laws of good taste and by the known preferences of the deceased; and in the midst of all this vulgar pomp Sophie Charlotte was escorted to her grave. A higher tribute was paid to her by Leibnitz. "My imagination," wrote Leibnitz to a friend, "keeps this woman with her incomparable qualities continually in my thoughts, and reminds me that she is lost to us forever."

The events of the war in 1705 were decisive for neither party, yet full of discouragement for the allies. 1705. Marlborough was thwarted in his plans by innumerable obstacles, among which the French themselves were, perhaps, the least; and the patience with which he struggled against them day after day is scarcely less remarkable than the skill which he displayed on the battlefield. If he proposed an attack he had first to hold long debates with civilian deputies from the Hague, to harmonize the pretensions of rival generals, to reconcile discordant plans, to adjust painfully the parts of the various contingents in his army; and during such delays the opportunity for action commonly passed away. On the upper Rhine the Margrave of Baden, who commanded the imperial armies, was jealous, insincere, and untrustworthy. Eugene in Italy made no progress; and the Duke of Savoy was again appealing for more troops and more money. The Emperor Leopold had died, and Joseph I., his successor, was not yet master of the many difficulties of his new position. But the gravest troubles were caused by the disaffection of Frederic of Prussia. Frederic complained that the new emperor treated him with too little consideration; that the subsidies were in arrears; that the settlement of the Orange succession was delayed by Holland; in short, that his dignity and his purse were alike suffering from the relations in which he had involved himself.

He threatened to recall his troops from Italy, and did recall three regiments from the upper Rhine. With all of
these elements of discord about him, Marlborough was expected to defeat the active generals and superior armies
of France. He undertook, therefore, another tour of the
German courts, and in November again reached Berlin.

He had already doubtless been apprised of a danger
in this quarter more serious than any question   Marlbor-
about etiquette or subsidies.   The continued   ough's second visit to
participation of Denmark and Prussia in the   Berlin.
war against France depended on the maintenance of
peace between them and Sweden ; and peace was daily
threatened by some new enterprise of Charles XII., by
the busy intrigues of his enemies, and by tempting chances
of profitable intervention.   Toward the end of 1705 the
diplomacy of Patkul had brought Denmark back into the
Russo-Polish alliance.   The wisdom of a similar adhesion
on the part of Prussia was warmly urged by some of
Frederic's advisers, but was opposed by Ilgen, and seems
never seriously to have been considered by Frederic himself.   By such a war, if successful, Frederic would have
conquered from Sweden the rest of Pomerania, and might
have obtained, as compensation from Poland, the rest of
Preussen.   But this could not be done without the aid of
the troops which were engaged in the service of Holland
and the Empire.

The danger was serious, and no person less adroit as a
diplomatist, and less popular as a courtier, than
His success.
Marlborough could avert it. His second mission was quite as successful as the first. He knew Frederic as he was known only to his own family and his own
ministers ; and he omitted no service which could touch
the King's absurd vanity and further the attainment of
his own ends. The story that he once sprang from the
table to hand his majesty a napkin is often and properly
told of the duke's tact and presence of mind. It is not

less illustrative of Frederic's own peculiar weakness. But
Marlborough succeeded in pacifying the King, and in in-
ducing him to abandon for a time his announced, or at
least his suspected intention to secede from the grand alliance. He left Berlin, gratified with his political success,
and, it is probable, scarcely less pleased with the costly
presents that he received.[1]

The next year brought some improvement to the affairs
of the allies. In May Marlborough won the
great battle of Ramillies, and then reduced suc-
cessively Brussels, Ghent, Antwerp, Ostend, and all the
chief fortresses of Brabant. In September Eugene reported the arduous and bloody, but successful battle of
Turin. The Prussians fought on both these fields; at
Turin under Leopold of Dessau, at Ramillies under General Lottum, and in both cases won the praise of their
commanders for valor and discipline.

Campaign
of 1706.

It is, however, beyond doubt that the court of Berlin
took less interest in these great events than in
the extravagant ceremonies by which the year
1706 was made memorable. The first of these was the
bi-centennial anniversary of the university of Frankfort-
on-the-Oder. The occasion was worthy of commemoration, and if observed in the right spirit and with proper
dignity might have gratified all true friends of letters and
science. But while the institution was actually dying
from embarrassments which could have been relieved by a
small part of the money which Frederic annually squandered on court expenses, it was made ridiculous by the
sumptuous grandeur of the anniversary festivities; and it
was weak enough also to elect as rector magnificentissimus

Life at
Berlin.

[1] *Letters and Dispatches of Marlborough* (London, 1845), ii. 333–337.
The treaty for the further lease of the Italian contingent, together
with a secret article guaranteeing the Prussian territories against mo-
lestation by the northern belligerents, is also printed in the same
volume.

the crown prince himself, a youth who could hardly write a grammatical sentence in Latin, in French, or even in German. For this species of folly it had, however, an illustrious example; the university of Oxford had just given Frederic William an honorary doctorate.[1]

But the splendor of this academic feast pales before those which followed a little later. Immediately after the death of Sophie Charlotte the King saw the expediency of making an early marriage for his son; and with this view selected the Princess Sophie Dorothea, daughter of the Elector George Lewis of Hanover, afterwards George I. of England, the cousin, therefore, of the crown prince, as his bride. The prince himself was, of course, not consulted. But he was indifferent toward the other sex, and obediently accepted, apparently without much effort, his father's choice. The betrothal was celebrated at Hanover in June; the marriage rites were performed in November. Notwithstanding the war the bride procured her trousseau in France; and it excited surprise and admiration even there. It is considered worthy of mention that it was submitted to the inspection of Louis XIV. himself, and that he expressed the hope that there were many princesses in Germany rich enough to support such a toilette, since the Parisian shop-keepers would not be likely to suffer,[2] — of which remark the unconcealed satire seems to have escaped the notice of the Prussian writer to whom I owe the fact. In the presence of the wedding festivities themselves the pen of the historian is paralyzed. They lasted three weeks; consisted of balls, ballets, plays, hunting parties, pageants of every sort; the scene oscillated betwen Berlin, Oranienburg, Charlottenburg, Wusterhausen, and other royal resorts; the patience of the bridal pair and the ingenuity of the palace officials were taxed to the last degree.

The resources of the country were not less severely

Marriage of the crown prince.

---

[1] Foerster, i. 115, 116. [2] Ibid. i. 117.

strained. The peasantry were called upon to furnish
horses and vehicles, fat swine and young chickens; and
that part of the population which could not show their
loyalty by tributes in kind were cheerfully permitted to
open their purses to the tax-gatherer.

The turbulent career of Charles XII. of Sweden culmi-
Charles XII. nated toward the end of this year in a move-
in Saxony. ment more audacious and more brilliant than
any which he had as yet attempted. He had driven August out of Poland, and set up a rival king of his own,
Stanislaus Lesczinski, whom many of the powers recognized. But August still clung to his title, and in Saxony contined to plot for his restoration. Charles formed,
therefore, the bold resolution to ignore for the time his
other enemies, Russia and Denmark; to invade Saxony;
and to chastise his hated adversary in his own house. The
King of the Swedes never suffered delay between the
adoption and the execution of a military scheme. He
swept down upon his prey with the swiftness of an eagle;
and before August could arrange either to fight or flee
he found himself helpless in the victor's grasp. In the
treaty of Altranstädt he was forced to renounce the Polish
crown and the Russian alliance; to recognize the title of
the rival King of Poland; and to give the Swedish army
winter quarters in Saxony.

By this achievement Charles suddenly became a power
in European politics. He lay in the heart of
Charles's re- Germany with 20,000 veteran and victorious
lation to the
powers.   troops; one of his most bitter enemies was
prostrate at his feet; Denmark had hastened to make
peace; and the Czar was too remote to be immediately
dangerous. It was nearly in the King's power to make
himself the arbiter of Europe. Tempting offers were
made to him by both the French and the imperialists, and
his camp was the resort of diplomatists from all the leading courts. He addressed a peremptory remonstrance to

the Emperor in behalf of the Silesian Protestants, and at
the sword's point extorted a promise that they should
have better treatment in the future.   Frederic of Prussia
was forced to accept a defensive alliance.[1]   Marlborough
favored this treaty as an expedient for calming the scruples and apprehensions of Frederic ; and it was believed
to be largely due to his efforts that Charles was diverted
from a scheme, which he seems for a time to have entertained, of breaking up the grand alliance, and forming a
league exclusively of the Protestant powers.[2]   The cabi-
nets were relieved from a grave burden of suspense when
Charles's decision was at length announced.   His implacable hatred of the Czar overcame the temptation to make
a career in the west; and in September, 1707, he broke
camp in Saxony, and led his heroic army into the barren
plains and pathless wilds of Russia.

In consequence of Eugene's victory at Turin the French
were compelled to evacuate Lombardy ; and
after the capture of Naples by the imperialists, Further vic-
and an unsuccessful attempt to capture Toulon, tories of
both belligerents suspended their efforts in the south.
Louis applied all his energies to the recovery of the Netherlands.   Eugene joined Marlborough with part of his
army, including the Prussian contingent; and at Oude-
narde and Malplaquet Leopold of Dessau was seen, as
usual, in the thickest of the fight.

At Malplaquet the crown prince of Prussia was an un-
moved witness of the awful slaughter.   He had
joined the army of the allies in the spring of The crown
1709, remaining until November, and his journal prince in
Flanders.

[1] It is in Martens, viii. 73.

[2] On Marlborough's visit to the Swedish camp, and his negotiations
with Charles XII., see Coxe, iii. chaps. 54 and 55.   The statement,
ibid. p. 155, that Frederic was brought over to the plan of a Protestant alliance, wants confirmation, and Droysen, IV. i., note to p. 198,
doubts the reported influence of Marlborough upon Charles's course.

shows the attention which he received from the higher officers, as well as the intelligent interest which he took in all the military movements. The King, in the instructions issued to the prince on his departure, justly felicitated him on the opportunity to learn the art of war under such masters as Marlborough and Eugene.[1]

The prince was also in a measure charged with a political mission, namely, to secure due recognition of his father's dignity and his father's claims in the peace negotiations which were in progress at the Hague. These negotiations proved indeed abortive, and hostilities were resumed. But Frederic was indignant, first, because he was not admitted to them, and, secondly, because the terms proposed by Holland were not, in respect to himself, sufficiently favorable. He therefore enjoined Frederic William to look sharply after Prussia's interests; and the journal shows that the prince endeavored, though without much success, to obey the injunction. In fact, the stipulations which were made in behalf of Prussia in the Treaty of Utrecht were not essentially different from those which Holland had proposed in 1709,[2] and against which Frederic had so vehemently protested. Frederic William, who ascended the throne before the signature of the final treaty, was perhaps aware from his experience in 1709 how hopeless would be the effort to obtain anything further.

Peace negotiations of 1709.

The King's life was scarcely less embittered at this time by other incidents of a domestic and local character. In 1708 alarm began to be felt, or at least to be feigned, about the succession, since a son born the year before to Frederic William had soon afterwards died, and it was not known that the crown

Frederic's third marriage.

[1] See these instructions and the journal in Foerster, i. 130 et seq.

[2] Art. XXI. in the Dutch project, Garden, ii. 274. Comp. Mailáth, *Gesch. des östreichischen Kaiserstaates*, vol. iv. (Hamburg, 1848), p. 443.

princess was again pregnant. The courtiers, especially those inimical to the crown prince, urged the King himself to remarry. He was then fifty-one years old, but the scheme appealed to his patriotism or his vanity ; and, after looking through the list of available candidates for the honor, he decided to espouse the Princess Sophie Louise of Mecklenburg-Grabow. The betrothal was celebrated, and soon afterwards the wedding itself. But the King failed to enter into the solemnities with his usual enthusiasm, for he had learned in the mean time that the crown princess was pregnant, and that the hopes of an heir did not depend on the sacrifice to which he had rashly pledged himself. The marriage was, therefore, a trial which subdued even his usually buoyant spirits. And the character of the bride herself, who proved to be a religious monomaniac, and a Lutheran besides ; who thwarted a plan of Frederic's for uniting the two Protestant sects, and set the rival pulpits to fighting more bitterly than before ; and who often burst into the apartments of the King in fits of religious ecstasy, and frightened him by wild and incoherent harangues, did not tend to increase the happiness of an already unhappy bridegroom. The fanaticism of the Queen finally passed into madness, and she became an object of deadly terror to the King.

In 1709 the plague, which for some time had been hovering on the frontiers of Preussen, burst through all the barriers erected against it, and swept The plague. over the province with destructive fury. The accounts of its ravages are heart-rending. Parents fled from their infected children, and children from their infected parents ; whole villages were depopulated ; in Königsberg seven thousand persons died in five months ; and the total number of deaths in the province up to the extinction of the disease in 1711 is computed at nearly two hundred and fifty thousand. It spread into Polish Preussen, where in the city of Dantzic alone it is said to have counted thirty-

two thousand victims.[1] Pomerania did not wholly escape,
and even at Berlin the most vigilant quarantine was necessary. The gross and widespread social evils which naturally followed this visitation may be left to the reader's
imagination.

The third of the local afflictions which at this time
vexed the soul of Frederic was a ministerial crisis, ending in the fall of Wartenberg.

Ministerial crisis.

That vulgar favorite had succeeded down to 1709 in
baffling all the hostile schemes of his enemies, of whom
the crown prince was one, and enjoyed Frederic's absolute
confidence. Allied with him in this distinction was the
Count Wittgenstein, a man as unprincipled as himself.
The highest offices of state were given to them in name,
though the real intelligence and labor were generally furnished by ill-paid and unrecognized subordinates, while
they themselves had the honor and drew the emoluments.

Both alike were hateful to their colleagues and to the
people, yet it is characteristic of the state of affairs at
Berlin that the fall of the powerful pair was if not
brought about at least facilitated by a quarrel of women
over a question of precedence. The arrogance of the
Countess Wartenberg was out of proportion even to her
husband's position and authority. She had fortified herself in her views of her social prerogatives by concession after concession obtained from the King, until her
demands became intolerable to all the other ladies of the
court. With the wife of the Dutch ambassador she once
had, before the whole court, a hand to hand struggle for
the leading place in a procession, and the dexterous Besser found no little difficulty in separating the angry combatants. The quarrel was made an affair of state. The
ambassador complained to his government; and Frederic responded by a threat to recall his troops from the

[1] See, for these statistics, Stenzel, iii. 187, 188, and the authorities
cited by him.

Netherlands unless an ample apology was offered to the Countess Wartenberg. But finally even the King became weary, not of Wartenberg, but of Wartenberg's wife, and the circumstance was promptly utilized by the better elements of the official household. These were represented especially by Kamecke, Printzen, the Dohnas, Blaspiel, F. W. Grumbkow, and Ilgen, able and popular officials, who had long chafed under the oppression of the favorites.

Wittgenstein was the first to fall, being basely deserted even by Wartenberg himself. Charges of official peculation and official cruelty were brought against him; and on the report of a committee of jurists, to whom they were referred, he was arrested by a file of soldiers and thrown into the prison of Spandau. The hisses of the populace greeted him as he was escorted through the streets of Berlin. He was eventually compelled to pay a fine of twenty-four thousand thalers, and to leave the Prussian territories.

Fall of Wittgenstein.

Wartenberg, the other leader of the camarilla, did not long survive his comrade, although his fate was less cruel and ignominious. He was summoned to give up his seals of office, and ordered to retire to his estates in the vicinity of Berlin, whence he was soon afterwards sent to Frankfort-on-the-Main, with a liberal pension. The King parted from him with the greatest reluctance. At the final audience both wept; and their relations, even after the favorite's departure, remained so cordial that the mere mention of Wartenberg's name was enough to throw the ministers into a panic. It is said that Frederic once offered to take him back if he would come without his wife, a condition which Wartenberg, to his honor, rejected. He died, however, in 1712.

Of Wartenberg.

In the redistribution of places which followed these removals Printzen became grand marshal of the court, while Ilgen and Blaspiel acquired charge respectively of foreign affairs and of army ad-

The reconstructed ministry.

ministration.[1] These were all deserving officials; they
were entitled to promotion on their own merits. Yet as
Dankelmann had been overthrown by an intrigue which
brought Wartenberg and his friends to the front, so these
had in their turn fallen before a coalition of which Ilgen,
Printzen, and Blaspiel were the beneficiaries ; and it was
only a happy accident that the new men were more deserving than their predecessors.

Such was the vicious uncertainty of Frederic's system!
It is doubtful if he really had a good judgment
Statesmen
and   of character, and it is certain that merit was not
courtiers. the test applied in the selection of officers, certain indeed that the method of selection could not often,
even by chance, produce satisfactory results. The King's
ideal minister was Wartenberg. Adroit, supple, cunning ;
a master of flattery ; yielding outwardly to all of Frederic's humors ; seeming to dissolve his own personality
wholly into that of his master ; yet really bending and
twisting him easily about ; a selfish, scheming, unscrupulous adventurer, Wartenberg was exactly fitted to serve so
weak, vain, punctilious, and conceited a king. It is true
that the qualities of the courtier are sometimes associated
with political talent and personal integrity. A man justly
ambitious, anxious to serve the state, and full of self-respect, may observe reasonable forms of deference toward
his prince, may smooth the sharp edges of intercourse by
tact and persuasion, may to a certain extent pardon honest
frailties and humor innocent whims. In an absolute monarchy this spirit of forbearance is indispensable to a minister. But it is also true that the perfect courtier, that is
the one who can succeed with a bad as well as with a good
prince, is rarely possessed of these higher qualities, either
of mind or of character, which give the statesman his title
to respect. Frederic was a bad prince, not so much because of his positive vices, as because of his want of posi-

[1] See Isaacsohn, ii. 306 ; Ledebur, *König Fr. I.* p. 465.

tive, manly virtues. He was probably incapable of sympathy with open and visible dishonesty. But he was also incapable of sympathy with the higher kind of honesty, that honesty which is outspoken, which is courageous, which scorns to flatter, which holds dissimulation to be a crime, which sees no moral difference between concealment and falsehood, between the suppression of facts and the perversion of facts. Dankelmann was an honest statesman, and Dankelmann's fate will be fresh in the reader's mind. Wartenberg was a perfect courtier, and to him Frederic clung with the most passionate tenacity ; stood as a stubborn barrier between him and the combined efforts of the best men in the state; refused up to the last moment to take credit in the man's iniquities ; and when finally forced to dismiss him contrived to make the dismissal almost a compliment.

The path to Frederic's favor was not, then, direct or honorable. There were good men in his service, honest, faithful men ; but they were generally in *Favoritism.* subordinate places, where their influence was felt rather than seen. Some of them held offices requiring technical knowledge, and were for that reason indispensable. A few, perhaps, had rendered services or shown abilities which even Frederic could find no decent pretext for ignoring. But as a rule favoritism, and a capricious favoritism, ruled in all branches of the service ; and intrigues, cabals, conspiracies made up the daily life at the court of Berlin.

This being the case, it was natural that there should be little stability in either the principles or the methods of administration. The larger constitu- *State of the constitution.* tional features were indeed, as has already been stated, left essentially unmodified, as well by the change of dynasty in 1688 as by the change of title in 1701. In theory the estates had still some voice in legislation, — though there was no effective organ by which that voice could make itself heard; and some control over the public purse, — though the control was exercised only in ratifying the demands of the crown. In theory the landed gentry had much power in county administration, and the burgesses in municipal affairs; though this power was perennially in conflict with the rival attributes of the central government. In theory the independence of the courts and the forms of law afforded security for the citizen against arbitrary seizure of his person or his goods; yet it has been shown that Dankelmann was long imprisoned without any trial, and that Wittgenstein, though a civil official, was arrested by soldiers and confined in a fortress. During this reign the government seems to have been, in short, in a transition stage. It was not wholly a despotism in law, or wholly a despotism in fact; but it was rather a bridge over which absolutism, starting under the Great Elector, passed to its complete triumph under Frederic William I. There was a gradual improvement in the use of arbitrary methods, but no systematic attempt to give those methods greater regularity and authority.

In the lesser details of administration there was, however, no fixed policy even of conservation. Changes were introduced according to the influence of favorites or the necessities of the hour; and while in some branches of the service the general tendency, rather by accident than by intention, was toward improvement, in others experiments followed one another without any order of organic or logical progression.

The latter description holds good especially of fiscal legislation. Some of the expedients, which the costly wars and the court extravagance led the government to adopt, have already been mentioned in their proper connection, but some other measures and incidents are interesting, both for their own characteristics and for the light which they throw upon the irresolution and recklessness that prevailed in the official councils.

Fiscal experiments.

One of the most important sources of revenue continued
to be the crown domains. It was in fact rather
as a land-owner than as a land-ruler that the *Domains.*
King enjoyed a permanent income, and had means for de-
fraying the expenses of the palace and the civil administration. The luxury of the one and the efficiency of the
other depended, therefore, in the first instance, on the pro-
ductiveness of the domains. But this again was dependent
on a variety of conditions, some of which the government
could not, and some of which it could control. It could
not at all control the soil or the weather. It could only
in a measure control the methods of husbandry, the intelligence of the tenants, the fidelity of the stewards. But it
could absolutely control the general administration, both
as to persons and as to systems.

Very early, therefore, in his reign, Frederic seems
to have given his attention to the domains, and to the pecuniary wisdom of some change in their management.
The general conduct of these immense properties was in
the hands of the president of the exchequer. In 1689 he
was reinforced in the discharge of this part of his duties
by a special board of five councillors;[1] and the good results of their undivided attention to the charge became
gradually visible.[2] But Frederic was not yet satisfied.
Ten years later he constituted a new administrative body,
the general directory of domains,[3] at the head of which
was placed the fortunate Wittgenstein.

During all these changes of organization the system of
fixed leases, as reintroduced in 1681,[4] was not *Hereditary*
disturbed. But the new directors, daily prod- *leases.*
ded by Frederic, and eager for official success, showed a
fatal readiness to listen to schemes and projects, no matter

---

[1] Geheime-Hofkammer.
[2] Riedel, *Staatshaushalt*, p. 39.
[3] General-Ober-Domainen-Directorium.
[4] Comp. supra, c. vi. p. 232.

how revolutionary in character, if only fresh and outwardly attractive. An enterprising official of the treasury,
Luben, proposed to substitute a system of hereditary for
that of time leases.[1] The plan was promptly adopted by
Wartenberg and his party, then by Frederic, and in 1701
its trial in some of the provinces was ordered. There was
unquestionably a sound principle underneath this scheme ;
if carefully matured, made flexible enough to suit the different local conditions, and then gradually introduced, it
would eventually have led to a species of copyhold tenure.
But the work, being rashly begun and badly managed,
could end only in failure. It aroused much local opposition, and it had a strong group of enemies at court, the
crown prince himself being a member ; and when, after
some years, the experiment failed to yield the results
promised by the exuberant Luben, the King himself was
ready to abandon it. The system fell, therefore, in 1710
with Wartenberg and Wittgenstein, and even the general
directory was abolished.[2]

Among the various fiscal expedients tried from time to
time, several are worthy of mention, if only for
their absurdity. One of these was the wig tax,
and another the carriage tax, both first imposed in 1698
for Berlin alone, — the latter " in order to defray the cost
of paving the streets," — and both afterwards extended
over the whole kingdom. As taxes upon luxuries they
were correct in principle, but not well conceived in respect

Other fiscal
experiments.

----

[1] " Erbpacht " for " Zeitpacht." Comp. Isaacsohn, 294 et seq.

[2] There is a copious literature on this incident, though Stenzel, iii.
177, note, complained that there was no complete and trustworthy history of it. Ranke's account (*Pr. Gesch.* i., ii. 462 et seq.) is brief, but
contains a lucid discussion of the principles involved. Comp. also
Riedel, *Staatshaushalt*, pp. 39, 40. All of these authors approve the
general purpose of the reform, which it is evident would, if not prematurely checked, have revolutionized the agrarian relations of the
state. Riedel makes the total revenue from the domains at the time
of Frederic's death 1,500,000 thalers.

to form and details. An attempt was made to enrich the treasury by a monopoly of the brush traffic; and to further this object a score of edicts in regard to the treatment of swine, the seasons at which they should be plucked, the disposition of the bristles, were issued by a prince whose dignity could be satisfied with nothing less than the title of majesty. The King even took up with a base swindler, calling himself an Italian count, who pretended to have the secret of making gold. He was fitted out with a laboratory, paid a handsome salary, petted and honored in every way; and although his public experiments regularly failed, Frederic's credulity long survived all trials. When at length he was undeceived his vengeance proved to be only the more cruel for its delay. The alchemist was hanged at Cüstrin in 1709.

The judicial reforms were neither many nor important. In 1702 the privilege de non appellando, as it was called, or the denial of the right of appeal to the imperial courts, in this case in respect to suits involving less than twenty-five hundred guldens, already possessed by the Electorate, was extended by an arrangement with the Emperor to the other German territories; *Privilegium de non appellando.* and as a preparation for this measure a general court of appeals had been established the year before.[1] Out of this grew in time the Prussian supreme tribunal.

In regard to criminal jurisprudence the most striking circumstance was perhaps the severity of the penalties. Theft from the palace was a capital *Criminal law.* offence; the offender, if a man, being hanged; if a woman, being beheaded, or drowned in a sack.[2] A soldier who committed a burglary must, according to an edict of 1699, be hanged; and in 1700 this penalty was

---

[1] Ober-Appellations-Gericht. But cases were to be decided according to the local law of the province from which they came.

[2] Gesackt. Pardon was declared inadmissible, though it is difficult to see how the crown could thus alienate one of its inherent rights.

extended to all burglars, with the provision that the execution should take place before the house where the offence
was committed. Suspected poachers could be subjected
to the ordeal by oath, or to torture. But many of these
regulations applied only to Berlin, which seems to have
been infested for several years with organized bands of
robbers, the evil reaching such a point that in 1705, at
the funeral of Sophie Charlotte, the citizens were organized into a special guard to protect the houses from burglars. It does not appear, however, that the certainty of
punishment, on which its efficacy most depended, was equal
to its theoretical severity.

The most characteristic feature of Frederic's legislation
was, however, its capriciousness, its want of
method, its unfortunate instability. Frederic
was far from being a great constructive, organizing genius; and too many of his officials found their advantage, not in impressing upon him systematic schemes
of reform, but in basely humoring all of his crude and
reckless fancies.[1] The result was that an important work
of consolidation and unification in nearly every branch of
the public service was left for his successor.

*Vaccillation
in internal
measures.*

It is therefore remarkable that of all the public interests which this government conducted its diplomatic policy seems to have been the most outspoken,
straight-forward, consistent, and honest. There
was, during Frederic's reign, none of that cynical statecraft,
that calculated duplicity, that facile and shameless perfidy,
which had characterized the reign of his father. There
was little of that vacillation of policy which in his own

Diplomacy.

---

[1] "Revolutions happen daily in the councils of our little court, for
what is advised one day and agreed on by one party of councillors,
is obstructed and altered the next day by another party; each being
willing to insinuate themselves (sic) with their master, and to make
him believe they seek nothing but his grandeur." Dispatch of the
English envoy, Lord Raby, quoted by Stanhope, *History of England*
(London, 1872), p. 143.

time marked the conduct of many departments of internal administration. Even the changes of person were less frequent than in other branches of the service, and did not exceed the number which natural causes and the inevitable vicissitudes of twenty-five years would make necessary.

The temptations to adopt an adventurous foreign policy were at all times abundant, and were such as the Great Elector would have eagerly obeyed. The enterprise of William of Orange, the ambition of Louis XIV., the rivalry of France and the Empire, the question of the Spanish crown, the conflicts between the northern powers, the embarrassments of Poland, — all of these offered facilities for an unscrupulous prince, and some of them facilities for a prince not destitute of scruples. But Frederic held a straight and uniform course through all the shifting phases of the diplomatic situation. He adopted at the time of his accession the policy of a close alliance with the emperor, and he adhered to that policy, at no little cost to his purse and to his self-respect, down to the day of his death. He was originally ill-disposed toward Louis XIV., and the flattering offers of friendship made to him by that monarch proved invariably futile. It was his early and fixed resolution not to be drawn into the disputes of the northern powers; this, too, was a difficult task successfully performed. And that Protestant interest which was specially represented by the union of the naval powers, England and Holland, had his sympathy from the outset, and continued to keep it, in spite of provocations peculiarly great to a prince constituted like himself.

It has already been shown that Frederic was keenly disappointed at his treatment in the congress of Ryswick. A still greater indignity was, in his judgment, preparing for him in the negotiations for closing the pending war, though fortunately he did not live to see it embodied in the Treaty of Utrecht.

The preliminaries of 1709, which aroused at the time

Frederic's suspicions, and were by him called to the atten-
Progress of tion of the crown prince, ended in nothing. The
the war. allies insisted on the surrender of the Spanish
monarchy to Austria, and Louis could not undertake to
aid in deposing his own grandson.[1] The war was then
resumed and Malplaquet was fought. But Louis was still
unconquered. Alone against all Europe — for Bavaria
was crushed, and Spain was rather a source of weakness
than of strength — his veteran armies on the Rhine and
on the Moselle, his accomplished generals, Villars, Bouf-
flers, Villeroy, Vendome, fought desperately over every
foot of ground in Germany and in the Netherlands; and
when driven out of these drew a cordon about the frontiers
of France, which all the efforts of the allies never succeeded effectually in piercing. Peace must therefore
come, if at all, from other causes than the defeat of the
French.

These causes proved to be two, which arrived almost
Defection of simultaneously. The one was the overthrow of
England. the whigs in England, and the appointment of a
tory cabinet. The other was the death of the Emperor
Joseph without lineal heirs, and the accession of his
brother Charles VI., the candidate of the allies for the
Spanish throne. The English tories were bent on humiliating Marlborough and ending the war; the claims of
Charles became much less cogent to the allies when their
success meant the reunion of the crowns of Spain and
Austria. The English tories took advantage, therefore,
of the new situation to make secret and separate overtures
to Louis. No more infamous transaction is recorded in
the annals of European diplomacy.

This defection of England proved fatal to many of the
Congress of schemes with which the other allies came to the
Utrecht. congress of Utrecht. It had been supposed that
the alliance would treat as a whole with France, and would

[1] As actually proposed in the preliminaries. Garden, ii. 275.

be able to bring the combined weight to the support of separate interests. Each power furnished its plenipotentiaries, therefore, with a clearly formulated list of demands.[1]

But this hope of joint action was dissipated at an early day. France insisted, of course with the support of England, that she should negotiate separately with each member of the alliance, and this arrangement was therefore adopted. The French representatives then presented a statement of the bases which they were willing to adopt. In regard to Prussia they offered only to recognize the title of king.[2]

The other powers then made their counter-demands, Prussia among the rest.[3] Frederic demanded to be recognized as king of Prussia ; to be guaranteed by France as sovereign and legitimate prince in Neufchâtel and Valengin, in which quality, as heir of the House of Orange, the allies and the authorities of the two counties had already acknowledged him ; to be put in possession of the principality of Orange, which was within French territory ; to receive lands in the Franche Comté as indemnity from France, and the district of Guelders in the Spanish Netherlands as indemnity from Spain ; to obtain certain concessions in behalf of the French Protestants who had taken refuge in his dominions ; and finally to have article IV. of the Treaty of Ryswick revoked.[4]

Demands of Prussia.

[1] The plenipotentiaries of Prussia were Doehnhof, Metternich, and Bieberstein.

[2] Garden, ii. 290.

[3] These may be found in various publications; for instance in Lamberty, viii. 44 et seq.

[4] In this century the singular fact has been brought to light that in 1712, while the Emperor Charles was denouncing at Utrecht the betrayal of the alliance by England, he was himself secretly instigating the Pope to urge Louis to make no concessions to the Protestants. See Garden, ii. 336 ; also the appendix. Comp. supra, c. vii. p. 278.

The claims of the other allies were not less sweeping, and were in many respects as hostile to one another as to the propositions of France.

The result was a compromise between France, Prussia, and Holland in the form of a treaty between the first two. The title of king of Prussia was recognized, as well as that of prince of Orange. Guelders was ceded as Frederic had demanded. The right of sovereignty in Neufchâtel and Valengin was admitted. But Prussia was obliged to renounce its claim to the principality of Orange; [1] and the Treaty of Ryswick was not modified.

The result.

The northern complications also vexed the patience and tried the fidelity of Frederic down to the last moment. In 1707 Charles XII., having for the time secured his rear by his bold invasion of Saxony, and his defensive treaty with Frederic, had set off for his arduous campaign in Russia. But at Pultawa, in 1709, a crushing defeat arrested his brilliant career; his army was broken up, and he himself became a fugitive in Turkey.

Defeat of Charles XII. at Pultawa.

The enemies who had been left behind at once hastened, with the instinct of vultures, to rend and divide the carcass of the dead lion. August reinstated himself in Poland. Denmark prepared to invade Pomerania. The Czar, victorious at Pultawa, returned to join in the work of plunder on the Baltic. The dismemberment of the Swedish empire was the order of the day, and Frederic was invited, as he had often before been invited, to join the league and take his share of the spoils.

Resumption of the war on the Baltic.

The situation was, however, more trying than at any earlier epoch. The Swedes being now on the defensive, their enemies would, of course, seek to carry the war into Pomerania, and this Frederic was bound by treaties and

[1] Guelders was treated as a substitute for the principality. Droysen, IV. ii. 32.

by self-interest to prevent. Yet he could offer no resistance without calling back the troops engaged against France ; and this, too, was forbidden by his honor and his inclinations. The intervention of the naval powers and the Emperor was therefore solicited and obtained. In 1710 was adopted the so-called concert of the Hague, which proclaimed the neutrality of Pomerania. A little later the threatening attitude of Denmark and Poland led to a second " concert," by which the allies took the neutrality of Pomerania under their own protection, and agreed to enforce it if necessary by arms. But not long afterwards the grand alliance itself began to dissolve, and lost accordingly its hold upon the northern situation. The Emperor was left to fight alone against France ; and the Danish and Saxon mercenaries being more than ever indispensable to him, he was obliged to purchase their further coöperation by leaving Pomerania to its fate.[1] The Russians, Danes, Poles, and Saxons then broke into the province on all sides, laid siege to the chief fortresses, robbed and burned and murdered from one frontier to the other, and then sat down to plan a scheme of partition. Frederic negotiated actively for Sweden, but did not draw a sword in her defence. The treaty of 1707 with Charles was thus only negatively observed.

Frederic himself did not live to see the formal adoption of the Treaty of Utrecht. He died on the 25th of February, 1713, and the treaty was not signed until the 13th of April ; but the leading articles were practically agreed on before his death, so that he knew in general how many of his claims could expect to be realized, and how many would have to be waived. He survived

Death of Frederic.

---

[1] Charles XII. had protested from his exile in Turkey against the action of the allied powers, and his enemies hastened to seize so good a pretext for treating it as not binding upon themselves. The protest is in Dumont, viii. 258 ; the two " concerts," ibid. viii. 249 and 254.

also long enough to see a new and dangerous turn given to the northern troubles, but died before they were finally settled.

The political horizon, as the King looked out upon it toward the end of his career, was thus not wholly cloudless. But he was gratified just before his death by an auspicious family event, which consoled him for many a disappointment in war and diplomacy. A third son was born to the crown prince on the 24th of January, 1712. Two others born earlier had died in the cradle; the first, as is supposed, from a nervous shock caused by the heavy guns with which the King thought it necessary to welcome the arrival of a grandson; the other from the burden of a golden crown, which, also by order of the scrupulous Frederic, was placed on his head at the ceremony of baptism. But the third prince survived alike the roar of the artillery and the weight of the crown; and by a peculiar felicity the King's last public appearance was on the first anniversary of the birth of the young Frederic. This second Frederic was afterwards to be known to the world as Frederic the Great.

Conclusion.

CHAPTER IX.

FOREIGN POLICY OF FREDERIC WILLIAM THE FIRST.

FREDERIC WILLIAM I. was twenty-five years old when
the death of his father left the government in The second king.
his hands. He took up the charge with the
promptness and the vigor, the bold intelligence and the
unsparing realism, which the courtiers had long observed
and deplored in his character; and even before the burial
of his predecessor he had the machine of state well under
control. And it was a control vastly different from that
of the previous twenty-five years.

It had been the desire of Frederic to have an amiable
government, — a government which, without giv-
ing up any of the powers acquired for it by the Frederic's principles of government.
Great Elector, should use those powers with gen-
tleness and equity; should consult wisely the feelings of
the whole people; should reconcile rival sects, rival classes,
rival interests; and should make the various public elements, the army by its sword, the universities by their
science, the diplomatists by their treaties, the artists by
their monuments, the laborers by their prosperity, all
contribute to the grandeur and glory of the common
fatherland. It is true that this ideal stopped far short of
realization. There were many inexcusable abuses, many
unnecessary hardships, and therefore much reasonable discontent in every year of Frederic's reign. The lives of
his soldiers were sacrificed in Flanders and in Italy, on
the Danube and on the Meuse, in wars provoked by the
ambition of kings at London and Paris and Vienna. He
squandered the tributes of the people in the gratification

22

of his own personal luxury. His palace and court set an
example of frivolous pleasures, of profligate manners,
which spread demoralization through all ranks of society. It is also true that the personal character of Frederic was largely responsible for these evils, and for the
failure of his own ideal. And yet the ideal was in the
circumstances a noble one; and if the King's own character was inadequate to its realization, it is not the less
proper to admit that his instincts and aspirations were
correct.[1]

Now the new king's maxims of state were far more
simple, practical, and thorough than these. They
were such as the meanest understanding could
grasp. To make the government strong in treasure and soldiers, to destroy the last remains of parliamentary rights and local independence, to crush remorselessly
the slightest show of insubordination, and to make himself
an absolute despot in form and in substance, — this was
the policy which, with all its consequences, was proclaimed
by Frederic William I. Montesquieu had not yet taught
that the principle of despotism was fear. But this young
Prussian king, to whom philosophy was a sealed and
odious book, had been an apt pupil in the experience of
twenty-five years; had learned that in an absolute monarchy the weakness of the prince is the weakness of the
state; that a people robbed of their liberties cannot be forever appeased by the mild face and sweet words of the
robber; and that in the end despotism to be stable and
respected must be terrible. It was not enough, according
to this view, for such a state merely to assert the doctrine
of passive obedience. It was a waste of time to attempt,

Policy and aims of Frederic William I.

---

[1] " The precept . . . for the construction of poems is equally
true as to states, non satis est pulchra esse, dulcia sunto. Edmund
Burke, *Reflections on the Revolution in France.* Droysen, IV. ii. 4,
calls it the doubtful (zweideutig) glory of Frederic to have been one
of the most popular of Prussian rulers.

like the Great Elector, to justify usurpation and absolutism by metaphysical theories or frail historical inductions, when power was in the end the only test. But in any event the syllogisms of the grandfather, and the forbearance of the father, if ever useful, had served their purpose; and it was both possible and politic for the son to adopt bolder maxims and sterner measures. He was resolved not only to expect but to command absolute submission; and not only to command, but to command with such an imperial voice, with such an awful mien of authority, and with such a visible and unhesitating purpose of coercion, that reflection would be appalled at the thought of its own temerity, and doubts would vanish before they had even been formulated.

This was a cruel, brutal, savage theory of government; but it was intelligible and practical. And Frederic William was the man to carry it out to its last consequences.

He wanted, indeed, many of the personal qualities which make a despot dignified, noble, picturesque, and impressive. He had not the tastes or the capacity to become an Augustus or a Louis XIV. The grand air, the stately carriage, the imperial magnificence, the love of glory, the passion for great affairs, the contempt for details, all the forms and show, the sweep and splendor of power, were unfitted to his genius and hateful to his mind.[1] His manner wanted dignity and self-control. His temper was violent. His language was coarse, insolent, and brutal. He was incapable of doing a kind act gracefully, and he made even just severity seem like heartless persecution. His vices were low, mean, sor-

Leading traits of character.

---

[1] The two types of character are well contrasted in the "L'état, c'est Moi" of Louis XIV. and the "Ich habe kein Geld" of Frederic William. Both phrases suggest the absolute ruler; but while the former calls up all the resplendent glories of the French monarchy, the latter pictures only a crowned miser, rattling in his strong box the money extorted from the people.

did, and vulgar. And even his virtues sprang more often
from a cold indifference than from a moral enthusiasm;
were calculated, selfish, and unsocial; chilled rather than
warmed the atmosphere in which he lived. Yet this swag-
gering, ignorant, savage ruffian proved to be one of the
keenest politicians and greatest legislators of his age.

His task consisted of a negative part and a positive
part. That he would attempt, and probably perform, the first of these duties had long been foreseen by the officials of the household, and the death of
Frederic was, therefore, an event the thought of which
had always filled them with dismay. If, again, a reform
were necessary, as it unquestionably was, promptness and
even severity in its execution would have a wholesome effect. This, too, the victims might in candor have admitted. But the time and manner of the blow characterize
the unfeeling tyrant quite as much as the wise reformer;
and make one almost sympathize with men who otherwise
deserve no sympathy. As soon as Frederic had closed his
eyes in death, the afflicted son strode through the mob of
attendant officials, ordered Printzen, grand marshal of the
court, to bring the list of palace employés, and with one
stroke of the pen swept them all out of existence. "Herewith," said he, "I relieve you all of your charges; but
you will not retire until after the burial ceremonies." To
Printzen, was therefore left the agreeable duty of com-
municating this measure to his comrades in affliction; and
the effect which the announcement produced needs no description to make it clear. The old band of retainers met
for the last time at the funeral of their lamented master,
which the piety of the king, rather than his preference,
made as gorgeous and magnificent as possible. That
ceremony finished, the work of retrenchment was taken
up in detail. The master of ceremonies and court poet,
Besser, received an instant dismissal; the King cared only
for military pageants, and never read poetry. The office

(marginal note: Preliminary reforms.)

of herald at arms, which had charge of escutcheons and
titles and pedigrees, was abolished. Printzen's own emoluments were reduced from forty to twelve thousand
thalers, though he had the ironical satisfaction of telling
the King that he was really richer after than before the
reduction, because, since his profits were formerly derived
only from estates assigned to him by the crown, and really
brought him in nothing but debts, a smaller salary in real
money was an actual improvement.[1] The rest of the court
establishment was carefully revised, and reduced in numbers and pay to the lowest point of efficiency. A noble
contingent of cooks, stewards, butlers, pages, footmen,
ushers, musicians, players, and dancers found less profitable but more useful service in the army.

The civil and military list was next put through the
same process. Sinecures were swept away, offices
abolished, salaries and pensions cut down ; every
person and function in the long catalogue was
scrutinized with microscopic precision. No useless official
was retained, though exalted rank, long services, gray
hairs, feebleness, and poverty might plead for him. The
cost of the general staff and the higher officers, including
pensions, was alone reduced from 276,000 to 55,000 thalers ; and the rate of savings was probably not lower in all
the other reforms throughout the service.

The administration of the finances was reorganized with
a view at once to a smaller outlay and a larger
income. First of all, and characteristically, the
chatulle, that fund which in the previous reign had met
the private expenses of the king, which had had its own
corps of officials, and which year by year had been drawing more rapaciously upon the revenues, was wholly abolished as a distinct institution, and its receipts were turned
back into the civil treasury. A fixed sum was then assigned to the King himself and to the Queen, as pocket-

The civil
and military
list.

The finances.

[1] Foerster, i. 175.

money.[1] All the several boards, directories, colleges, and the like, which had previously divided the administration of the civil revenues, and of course greatly increased its cost, were then consolidated into the general finance directory.[2] At its head was placed the privy councillor von Kamecke. Subordinates were likewise appointed to direct, under Kamecke, each of the several divisions or bureaus. Every one of these changes was toward simplicity, economy, efficiency, and centralization. And the reform was for the time completed by an edict, in 1718, entailing the public domains forever to the crown.

The domains thus entered upon a third stage, and a new conception, in respect to the right of ownership in them. According to the original theory, they were the property of the state;[3] and could be sold, or even pledged for loans, only with the consent of the Diet. When the diets were abolished they became practically the private property of the prince, with relations like any other private property. Finally the edict of Frederic William changed their title from fee simple to fee tail; and it was put apparently out of the power of any prodigal successor to sacrifice them. An opinion of the Halle jurists was even obtained to the effect that the hereditary lease of a domain was a " species alienationis," and, therefore, unlawful. This, of course, gave the final blow to so much as still remained of Luben's scheme.[4]

The King's interest in these estates continued keen and close throughout his whole reign; he preferred them to any other source of income. And this was not for any constitutional reasons, such as gave the English demesne

The domains.

[1] Handgeld; the King's allowance was 52,000 thalers. Riedel, *Staatshaushalt*, p. 54.

[2] General-Finanz-Directorium, March 27, 1713.

[3] This was expressed in the legal maxim, Kammergut ist Staatsgut. Roenne, *Staatsrecht*, ii. 796.

[4] Six years was the usual term for which thenceforth the leases were granted.

lands so peculiar an importance to the crown. It was not because they were beyond the reach of parliament, for there was no parliament; and the King's control over other revenues, the excise or the "contribution," was scarcely less complete and absolute. His interest in the domains was purely an economical one. He held them to be the most stable and most fruitful source of revenue, and on them, too, his own peculiar gifts for administration found their favorite and most successful exercise. Hence it was his policy not only to maintain intact such crown lands as he found on his accession, but also by new purchases continually to add to them. His agents were instructed to keep a sharp lookout for opportunities to buy real estate. He was the great land speculator of his time.

The military revenues, — that is, chiefly, the contribution, or direct tax on the rural population, and the excise in the towns,— were simplified by being made uniform for the whole kingdom, and their administration was also made more direct, more economical, and more efficient. The head of this department, Frederic William von Grumbkow, was extremely ambitious, and not without talent for administration. But he owed his original appointment in no small degree to his singular capacity, not always scrupulously used, for intrigue, to his diplomatic adroitness, and his perfect mastery of Frederic William's character, or characteristics.

The military revenues.

The head of foreign affairs finally was Ilgen,[1] one of the few high officials of Frederic's service who was retained by Frederic William. Ilgen was a cool, astute, experienced diplomatist; with as much honesty as the ethics of the age required of his profession; intelligently devoted to the interests of Prussia; unobtrusive in his official methods; respected by his colleagues at

The foreign office.

[1] Nominally assisted by Printzen, and Count Christopher Dohna. Droysen, IV. ii. 23.

Berlin, and by his rivals at other courts; a thoroughly sagacious, prudent, safe politician.[1] He enjoyed a much higher degree of independence than any other minister. Yet this was not wholly, perhaps not at all, owing to the King's appreciation of his superior attainments. The King himself knew many things better than his ministers, but of foreign politics he knew little, and of the diplomatic art nothing. He could command his own subjects in a loud voice and bad grammar, and they obeyed; but to reason and to persuade; to conceal, evade, and prevaricate; to carry a point by address and insinuation; to await contingencies; to parry attacks; to appease resentments; to compose notes in Latin or French; to dance with the wife of an ambassador; to remember titles and observe etiquette, — all this was beyond his power, and he hated it from the bottom of his heart. If he meddled in diplomatic negotiations he was nearly sure, at the most delicate crisis, to ruin everything by his strident tones and frantic gestures, by his swagger and bombast and arrogance. Of this defect he seems, moreover, to have had some suspicion. He was not in general willing to discuss his own limitations, or to admit that he had any, but in foreign affairs he practically though not formally acquiesced in Ilgen's leadership. "Tell the Prince of Anhalt," wrote he, "that I am the field marshal and the finance minister of Prussia."[2] But he did not add that he was the minister of foreign affairs.

It happened, nevertheless, that foreign affairs of the most urgent nature engaged his attention from the very outset of his reign. In the Treaty of Utrecht the King had indeed only to ratify an accomplished fact. Frederic had given orders but a few days before his death to sign the treaty; and his name, not that of his son, appears in the instrument as the con-

Prussia and the peace of Utrecht.

---

[1] Comp. Droysen, IV. i. 202, 203.
[2] The King to Grumbkow, March, 1713.

tracting party. But difficulties and delays arose about the proposed cession of Guelders to Prussia. The Emperor made claims to the Spanish Netherlands which were, in fact, eventually admitted ; and although he refused to accept the Treaty of Utrecht, it was desirable for Prussia to obtain from him, as a safeguard for the future, a renunciation in respect to Guelders. This was not obtained until fourteen days after the accession of Frederic William, and Ilgen, who had conducted the case with singular skill, had then the pleasure of announcing its final success. The personal pride of Frederic William had not been engaged, like his father's, in the scheme to get the whole of the Orange inheritance. To get even part of it, as Meurs, Lingen, and Neufchâtel, was in his view a considerable triumph ; and Guelders, on which his only claim was that of conquest, had both fiscal and strategical importance.

The northern problem was, however, more complicated and serious. But its solution was in part facilitated by the peace of Utrecht, which set free a considerable force of Prussian troops, and enabled the King to speak with emphasis and decision.

The situation in 1713 shows on the one side Russia, Poland, and Denmark; on the other, Sweden, aided in a measure by the Duchy of Holstein- The north. Gothorp, and authorized by the treaty of 1707 to call also on Prussia for aid, to the extent of 7,000 men. The King of Sweden was absent in Turkey; the guaranty for the neutrality of Swedish Pomerania, denounced by both sets of belligerents, was practically given up; and the confederates were rapidly clearing Germany of the Swedes. The last and final aim of their campaign was to seize the fortified cities on the Baltic. Of these Stettin, at the mouth of the Oder, was the most important to all the belligerents; while Frederic William, who saw with impatience its possession by Sweden, was even more reluctant to see it fall into the hands of Sweden's enemies. An

agreement was, therefore, concluded with the Duke of
Holstein, heir-presumptive to the Swedish throne, for the
evacuation of the city by the Swedes, and its occupation
by troops of Holstein and Prussia.[1] But, to the surprise
of all parties, the Swedish commander stoutly refused to
act his part in the play, refused to surrender the town
without an express order from Charles. Frederic William was thus for the moment completely baffled, and the
allies hastened to seize the opportunity. A Russian force
invested Stettin and, after a short siege, captured it.[2] But
the Czar, having hopes yet of drawing Prussia into the
coalition, simulated forbearance in the hour of victory,
and consulted the King in regard to the disposition to be
made of the conquered city. The result was the so-called
sequestration treaty, October 6, 1713, between

Sequestra-
tion of
Stettin.

Russia and Poland on the one side and Prussia
on the other. The substance of the arrange-
ment was that the allies agreed to intrust Stettin to Frederic William for safe-keeping, and he agreed to pay them
the costs of the siege, and not to surrender the town until
after the conclusion of peace.[3] The allies undertook in
the mean time not to continue the war in Pomerania, and
Prussia guaranteed that the province should not be made
the base of hostile operations on the part of Sweden. The
next day Stettin was occupied by a mixed garrison of
Holstein and Prussian troops.

But this was not the end of the matter. Charles XII.,

Return of
Charles XII.

who had approved the apparent contumacy of his
lieutenant in refusing to give up the city, now demanded its surrender by Frederic William, after he had

---

[1] *Theatrum Europæum*, XX. p. 611; Droysen, IV. ii. 47, 48, etc.
The treaty was ratified June 30, 1713.

[2] September 29, 1713.

[3] Dumont, viii. 409. The sum to be paid was 400,000 thalers,
one half by Prussia to Russia, and the other half by Holstein to
Poland. But Prussia was also to advance the latter sum temporarily.
Comp. Droysen, IV. ii. 58, 59.

redeemed it with his own money from its captors.   This
was obviously impossible; for Frederic William, to whom
400,000 thalers was a large sum of money, insisted on the
repayment of the ransom, while Charles as stubbornly refused to believe that the amount had ever been paid.   He
scented a conspiracy to swindle him out of his fortresses ;
and, worst of all, a nominal ally, pledged by a solemn treaty
to give him aid, was a party to the swindle.[1]   It is not
strange that he reached the conclusion that nothing but the
sword could save him.   No hope remained of engaging the
Porte in another campaign against Russia; and early in
November, 1714, the undaunted hero left his asylum in
Turkey, and riding night and day in disguise across Europe, arrived on the 22d of the month at the gates of
Stralsund.   It was really his last foothold in Germany.
Stettin was in the hands of Prussia; and Bremen and
Verden were held by the Danes, only to be sold a little
later to Hanover.   England, through George I., thus ac-
quired an interest in the struggle; Charles stood absolutely
alone.   Courtesies were exchanged on his arrival with
Frederic William, but they were only courtesies.[2]   It was
early apparent that the Prussian king had no intention of
giving up Stettin.   As soon as Charles conceded one point
Frederic William or his ministers raised another, and
Charles learned in a short time that he was dealing with
a nature not less obstinate than his own.   The theory of
Charles was that since Prussia meditated war, it would be
politic to begin the war at once, without waiting until the
Russians and Poles should again take the field.[3]   The
Prussian pretence was that Charles himself intended war,

[1] Heeren, *Europ. Staatensystem*, p. 379, speaks of the höchst
zweideutige Rolle Preussens, and inquires to what except war it
could lead with such a prince as Charles XII.

[2] See Foerster, ii. 27; Droysen, IV. ii. 105, n.

[3] Stenzel, iii. 264–266, seems to think this theory was justified by
Frederic William's conduct.

and that it would be wise to shut him up in Stralsund before he could reorganize his forces.[1]   Accordingly certain

Prussia joins his enemies, 1715. military movements of Charles in the neighborhood of Stettin, not one of which, however, affected territory included in the sequestration treaty,[2] were eagerly seized by the Prussian war party as an excuse for war.   An offensive alliance was therefore formed in April, with Denmark, Hanover, Saxony, and Poland.[3]

The Prussian troops began at once to concentrate for Preparations for war. active operations, under the immediate command of Leopold of Dessau.   The King proposed also to take the field in person.   On his departure from Berlin, April 28, he left with the ministers a letter of instructions, almost in the nature of a farewell testament, which deserves to be reproduced, not so much because it is intrinsically important, as because it is so highly characteristic of the author and of his system of government. " My wife," he says, " shall be informed of everything, and her opinion asked.   And since I am only a human being, and may be shot dead, I command you all to care for Fritz " — i. e. the crown prince, Frederic — " for God will reward you and I give you all, from my wife downwards, my curse, that God may punish you as well here as hereafter, if you do not bury me at Potsdam, in a vault of the castle church. You shall make no ceremonies, on my life and body no ceremonies or festivities, except to let the regiments fire volleys in the vicinity.   I feel assured that you will obey these instructions with the

---

[1] See Ranke, i., ii. 491, 492; Droysen, IV. ii. 105.

[2] Stenzel, iii, 268.

[3] The Prussian manifesto of May 1 declares, with a great profusion of negatives, that the King has " bei wahrendem diesem Kriege nicht einmal niemalen das Geringste nicht vorgenommen," etc. Foerster, ii. 29–32, has the German text; Lamberty, *Mémoires*, ix. 285 et seq., gives a French version; and there is a good English translation in the *Historical Register* for 1716.

greatest exactitude in the world." Other injunctions of
the same kind had been given by the King during his occasional absences the year before. Thus, "if anything
arises threatening war, or otherwise important, let my
wife be informed and consulted. Otherwise nobody except the privy councillors shall meddle in my affairs, not
a soul." Again, "no money shall be paid out except
what is specified in the budgets; if an extraordinary case
arises, ask my wife; if she approves, let her sign the order." This was certainly a novel system of ministerial
responsibility, yet the King's confidence in his wife is not
a disagreeable trait.

But his dislike of officious meddlers, of gossip and intrigue, sometimes led him into difficulties. During the negotiations with Sweden some important secrets leaked out, to the embarrassment of
the Prussian schemes, whereupon Frederic William issued an order which amounted to a social proscrip-
tion of the whole body of diplomatists at Berlin. The
members of the Privy Council and their families were forbidden to visit the foreign envoys, to have any conversation or private intercourse with them, to correspond with
them, even to meet them in society. Only the minister
of foreign affairs could hold any relations with them. It
was also to be notified to the diplomatists that the King
was offended at the attempts of some of their number to
mix in the domestic affairs of Prussia, to stir up dissensions among the ministers, and to discredit them with
their master.

This is a good illustration of Frederic William's diplomatic tact. Some of the principles announced in the
order are sound and wholesome; but, put in the King's
violent manner, they provoked the indignation of foreign
courts, so that the edict of non-intercourse had to be formally retracted, on the Emperor's demand, so far as it
applied to the imperial envoy, and it was soon tacitly

abandoned as to the rest.[1] To cane the ambassadors of
great kings was a different thing from caning street
urchins and apple-women.

Stralsund was the objective point of the military operations which the allies now began; and by the
middle of July, 1715, they had the place invested
with a force of nearly 50,000 men. Of these 32,000
were Prussians, many of them veterans. They had held
Eugene's right on the day of Blenheim, had looked destruction calmly in the face at Cassano, had stormed over and
over again the deadly trenches of Malplaquet, had indeed
campaigned all over Europe in the service of foreign
states; and now, with refilled regiments, bright new uni-
forms, and improved arms, they prepared to fight in the
cause of their own country, and under the eyes of their
own king. Danes and Saxons made up the rest of the
50,000 besiegers. And to resist them, Charles shut himself up in Stralsund, still defiant, still perhaps hopeful,
with 9,000 Swedes.[2] Besides the city itself, he undertook
to hold the adjacent island of Rügen, which, as the Great
Elector had once proved, was of vital importance in such a
siege. Usedom, below Stettin, was taken on the last day
of July without much difficulty. The works at the mouth
of the river Peene were carried by storm on the 21st of
August, after the Swedish garrison of only 300 men had
borne for seventeen days a bombardment from the heavi-
est Prussian guns. These outlying posts being thus reduced, the allies were enabled to concentrate more troops
about Stralsund, and to push the siege with greater vigor.
But on account of bad weather, it was not until the 19th
of October that the first line of trenches was opened.

This was, however, only a beginning, and the approaches

Siege of Stralsund.

---

[1] Droysen, IV. ii. 95, n.

[2] I do not vouch for any of these figures. The strength of the belligerents is differently given by different writers; my own are a medium between extremes.

still promised to be slow and difficult, when the besiegers were unexpectedly helped forward by a sort of amphibious officer, bred in one of those floating Baltic towns, and now serving in the Prussian army.

Outside the main fortifications the Swedes had a formidable line of earthworks, stretching from the sea on the east to the impassable swamps which formed an equally strong natural defence on the west. These works impeded the construction of parallels, and could not be carried by storm. But a certain Colonel Koeppen was familiar with the neighborhood, and he recollected that at low tide the water receded some distance from the northeastern terminus of the outer defences, or at least that it could easily be waded. Deserters confirmed this statement. Koeppen offered, therefore, to lead a small party around this accessible yet hazardous point, and thus surprise the Swedes in their rear, while they were being attacked also in front. The night of the 4th of November was chosen for the attempt. A feigned attack was made on the extreme left, a serious attack near the right; and to support this latter movement, while taking advantage of the diversion created by the other, Koeppen and his party of volunteers crept up unperceived to the edge of the sea, waded around the marshes, and fell upon the defenders in the rear at the very moment when they were successfully repulsing the assault from the front. The result was a complete victory. Several regiments of Swedes were taken, and nothing except the permanent fortifications stood between the besiegers and the city.

These proved, however, singularly stubborn, and another flank movement was therefore attempted, this time on the island of Rügen. The ease with which this was accomplished shows, perhaps, loose generalship on the part of Charles, but more probably shows the impossibility of defending all points with the

The outer works carried.

Seizure of Rügen.

small force at his disposal. Leopold of Dessau, the
"Dessauer," was intrusted with this enterprise. Twenty
thousand men were assigned to him, a force nearly three
times as large as that which the Swedes mustered in the
whole region. The landing was therefore effected without
much difficulty on the 15th of November; earthworks
were rapidly thrown up, and the next morning the attack
of Charles was calmly awaited. It was not necessary to
wait long. As soon as the King of the Swedes learned
what had been done, he collected a small force — not over
fifteen hundred men — and, taking no account of inequalities in number or position, marched unhesitatingly against
the intruders. But it was impossible to dislodge them
from their intrenchments. Again and again the Swedes
charged up to the very muzzles of the Prussian guns; repeated checks were only so many signals for fresh assaults; the King, exposing himself like a common soldier,
was wounded and disabled; and yet while no impression
was made on the enemy, the ranks of the Swedes grew
thinner and thinner, and each new formation gave fresh
emphasis to the story of slaughter. From a sombre necessity, therefore, Charles called off his battalions, and the
little force sullenly retired to the main land. It was a
new experience for the Dessauer thus to sit calmly behind
breastworks, while a smaller force dashed itself hopelessly
against them. There was not much glory in the victory
for him, nor much shame for Charles in the defeat. But
it sealed the fate of Stralsund.

Troubles rapidly accumulated around the unlucky
Swedes. In November Russia had formally joined the coalition, and resumed operations. England, sharing in a measure Hanover's interest, and alleging Swedish interference with her commerce in the Baltic, took up an attitude hardly to be distinguished from open hostility. The Danish fleet had defeated that of Charles in two engagements, and commanded the mouth

Progress of the siege.

of the harbor.   Meantime, too, the allies vigorously
pressed the siege.   The counterscarp was carried by storm
on the 5th of December.   Breaches began to appear in
the walls as a result of the steady bombardment, and
preparations were made for a general assault.[1]   But humanity forbade the exposure of the population to the fate
which the custom of war at that time inflicted upon a city
carried by storm ; and as Charles himself, who had never
learned the art of capitulation, refused to give the word,
he was persuaded to embark for Sweden, and let others
make terms with the victors.   No little dexterity was
needed to avoid the Danish fleet, but a Swedish frigate
was at length reached, and the baffled hero sailed gloomily
away to the kingdom which he had not seen for   Fall of the
thirteen years.   The next day after his departure,   town.
the 23d of December, the town surrendered.   Wismar, the
only remaining Swedish post in Germany, fell in April,
1716, into the hands of the Russians and Danes ; and the
newly conquered territory, or, generally speaking, that
part of Swedish Pomerania which lies west of the Peene,
was put in charge of the Danes, whose king formally received homage.   The section between the Peene and the
Oder, including Stettin, remained in the firm grasp of
Prussia.[2]

This was Frederic William's first and only war ; henceforth he will interest us chiefly as a legislator and administrator.   But it will be necessary to keep a
hold on the main thread of European politics,   State of Eu-
                                                 ropean rela-
and this will be rendered easier after a brief   tions.

[1] Croissy, a French agent in Stralsund, made a last effort to save
the city, proposed a truce, etc., but he was promptly suppressed by
Ilgen.   See Lamberty, ix. 309 ; Droysen, IV. ii. 143, 144.

[2] The Prussian official "Journal de la campagne en Poméranie de
l'an 1715," given by Droysen, IV. iv. 328–361, is the authority which
I have chiefly followed.   According to Droysen it corresponds sub-
stantially with a similar record kept by the Saxon staff, and still preserved in the Dresden archives.

23

review of the leading situations and issues during this period.

The Emperor having refused to accept the Treaty of Utrecht, the war was nominally continued on his part for another year. But no serious battles were fought; and finally Eugene and Marshal Villars, brushing aside the helpless diplomatists, met like soldiers, knowing the cost of war, to make an effective peace. The result was the Treaty of Rastadt, March 6, 1714. This was confirmed by the Diet, in spite of some chicanery on the part of the Emperor; and ratifications were exchanged at Baden, in Switzerland, on the 7th of September. Austria received the Spanish Netherlands, and was confirmed in the possession of her conquests in Italy, namely, Naples, Sardinia, and Milan. The electors of Bavaria and Cologne were released from the imperial ban, and they in turn recognized the ninth electorate, or that of Hanover. The treaties of Westphalia, Nimeguen, and Ryswick were reaffirmed. But no peace was concluded between the Emperor and the Bourbon King of Spain; and their rival claims were therefore only suspended, those of Philip V. to the Italian territories, those of Charles VI. to the Spanish throne.

In France Louis XIV. died on the 1st of September 1715, and left as heir to the throne his greatgrandson, then an infant. The Duke of Orleans was made regent, in open disregard of the injunctions of the great King. The regent was a man without moral character, and without very strong political qualities; but he had sense enough to know that the Treaty of Utrecht had made England for the time the arbiter of Europe, and he wisely adhered to her and the House of Hanover.

England saw in 1714 two significant changes. The one was the accession of the Elector of Hanover as George I.; and the other, the overthrow of the

tories and the restoration of the whigs to power.   The
schemes of the Stuart pretender made it necessary for the
government to keep up its continental relations ; while the
new system of public loans facilitated the use of subsidies.

The Spanish policy suffered at once from the weakness
of the King, the ascendency of the Queen, and
the ambitious intrigues of Cardinal Alberoni. _{Spain.}
The most reckless enterprises were attempted.   The Austrian possessions in Italy were attacked, and not without
success, in spite of the interference of England.   A plot
was formed to overthrow the Duke of Orleans, and unite
the crowns of Spain and France, in violation of the Treaty
of Utrecht.   Alberoni had combinations at nearly every
court of Europe, and his love of notoriety was amply gratified.

Even Sweden was drawn into his calculations.   Charles
XII. was served, after the fall of Stralsund, by a
minister, Goertz, as reckless and unscrupulous as _{Sweden.}
the cardinal himself ; and the King, who had just been
driven out of Germany, and found resistance even in Nor-
way, did not hesitate to enter into a plan for aiding the
pretender to establish himself in England.   But Charles'
stormy career was ended by his death in the trenches before Friedrichshall, in December, 1718.   His schemes of
revenge fell with himself ; the notables sent Goertz to the
scaffold ; and Sweden sank quietly to the place of a power
of the second order.   Formal treaties of peace, which had
been impossible during Charles' life, were then made with
the members of the hostile coalition one after another.
That with Prussia, February 1, 1720, confirmed Frederic
William in the possession of Stettin and Fore-Pomerania
as far as the river Peene, and including the islands of
Wollin and Usedom ; but Sweden received two million
thalers as compensation, and the rest of her possessions in
Germany were restored.

Russia came out of the long struggle a new and impos-

ing power in Europe. As the price of peace Sweden was
compelled to surrender Livonia and the fairest territory
along the northern Baltic; while the internal reforms of Peter, as well civil as military, gave a
European character and European importance to the state.
It was, therefore, not found surprising that in 1721 he assumed the imperial title.

Russia.

The value of the territory which Frederic William acquired from Sweden was not apparently in proportion to the costs of the war. The debtor side
of the official account shows an aggregate outlay of nearly
four and a half millions,[1] not including the two millions
which were payable under the treaty of 1720 to Sweden;
if this be added, the total cost of the enterprise foots up
over six million thalers. Yet the annexed territory comprised only some two thousand English square miles, and
its revenues would hardly pay the interest on its price.
What then were the benefits of the transaction for the
King? They were several: the acquisition of a flourishing seaport two days distant from Berlin, with all the
commercial and naval advantages which followed from its
possession; the termination of the northern war, which
had been scarcely less destructive to neutrals than to belligerents; the removal of an ambitious neighbor, who
might at any time become an enemy; the rescue at the
same time of Swedish Pomerania from the not less dangerous hands of Russians, Danes, and Saxons; and finally,
the prestige which such a spirited achievement, at the very
beginning of his reign, gave to the young monarch. It
insured him the respect of Europe, but it also created new
responsibilities in the still critical state of continental relations.

Prussia.

---

[1] Foerster, ii. 46, 47. The 400,000 thalers paid to the allies for
Stettin, and 200,000 subsequently exacted by Poland, are included in
the statement. In all, then, Frederic William seems to have paid
600,000 thalers "an dero hohe Alliirte."

It lies beyond the scope of this work to trace out the long and crooked course which European diplomacy pursued during the next twenty years; and the wars which from time to time broke out, though still employing the fine genius of Eugene, were also far removed from the frontiers of Prussia. Frederic William was equally reluctant to sign a treaty and to draw the sword. But it was less easy to avoid the former than the latter, for it was an age of treaties rather than of battles; and the King was occasionally drawn, in spite of himself, into doubtful diplomatic transactions.

Between the years 1713 and 1725 three widely different sets of combinations appear among the leading powers. The earliest was formed between England, France, and the Emperor with the avowed object of maintaining the treaties of Utrecht and Rastadt against the ambitious schemes of Spain. The next epoch was marked by overtures from Spain to the two other western powers, the useless congress of Cambray, and the temporary isolation of the Emperor. In the third scene Spain and the Emperor draw near together, and France and England are in their turn alarmed. This was the stage at which Frederic William became a participant.

It was brought about in this manner: The Emperor Charles VI., having no male heirs, and being reluctant to see his possessions pass to the female heirs of his older brother, Joseph I., had formally modified the disposition made to that effect by his father, the Emperor Leopold, in favor of his own daughter, Maria Theresa. The edict which announced this grave constitutional change was the pragmatic sanction. It had been duly proclaimed in the hereditary states of the Hapsburgs, Austria, Bohemia, and Hungary; but it was desirable also to have it recognized and guaranteed by the other powers, and to obtain this favor the Emperor was willing to pay almost any price.

It so happened that about the same time Philip V. of
Spain was also in search of allies. The new
regent of France, the Duke of Bourbon, had cut
short Philip's attempt at reconciliation, which involved
some marriage projects, by taking as a bride for his ward,
Louis XV., not Philip's sister, to whom he had been betrothed, but a Polish princess, the daughter of Stanislaus
Lesczinski, and the indignity was keenly felt. The King
of Spain sought revenge, and of course threw himself
into the arms of the Emperor, who embraced him with
equal fervor. The result was that these two potentates,
who for twenty years had been implacable enemies, and
who were still nominally at war, formed in 1725 an alliance which went to the last extreme of effusive friendship.
The Emperor renounced his claims to the Spanish throne;
Philip guaranteed the pragmatic sanction; and mutual
assistance was pledged in case of war. There were even
rumors of matrimonial engagements which might result
in the reunion of the Spanish and Austrian monarchies.
England and France represented, of course, the opposite
interest; and the two rival leagues then began to bid for
support at the various minor courts of Europe.

Frederic William was first won by the Anglo-French
party, a success which they owed as well to his
temporary alienation from the Emperor, as to the
fair conditions which they themselves offered. The King
had been for a considerable time on ill terms with Vienna.
Dissensions had arisen on account of Frederic William's
espousal of the cause of the oppressed Protestants of the
Palatinate, on account of various decrees of the imperial
courts of justice, which guarded vested rights against his
wanton aggressions, and perhaps most of all on account of
Charles' evident reluctance to see him acquire Jülich and
Berg on the extinction, which was foreseen, of the Neuburg line. In some of these cases the King was undoubtedly in the wrong, but the consciousness of the fact made

Spain and Austria.

Treaty of Hanover.

his irritation only the keener.[1] The various representatives of the rival party offered him, on the other hand, the most attractive terms: compensation in Courland, territory in Silesia, the assurance of Jülich-Berg, and even, in case of war, the obligation to furnish only five thousand men. The Queen supported the western powers with arguments of a domestic nature, based on a marriage scheme which she then had at heart. Ilgen was kept in ignorance of the negotiations. The result was that in the Treaty of Herrenhausen at Hanover, September 3, 1725, Prussia became the ally of England and France. The treaty contained, among other provisions, this: that none of the contracting parties should, without the knowledge of the others, enter into any kind of an engagment with, or even receive propositions from the rival powers.[2]

In view of this article it will, therefore, seem incredible that within a year Frederic William not only deserted these allies, but even formed a secret alliance with the Emperor. Yet all of this actually occurred.

Ilgen, we have seen, had no knowledge of the treaty until ordered by the King to sign it. Grumbkow supported it, though for reasons not purely political, but rather, as historians darkly hint, in consequence of very cogent pecuniary arguments advanced by George I. The

---

[1] Much light is thrown on these disputes, especially on the King's manner of conducting them, in the correspondence of Eugene, Count Seckendorf, Frederic William himself, and others, in Foerster, appendix to vol. ii.

[2] Ranke, iii., iv. 47–50, has some interesting details of these negotiations. For the causes of Frederic William's discontent with the Emperor, see Stenzel, 291–294, and again 535, 536. The treaty contained some secret articles, the full text of which has only lately been revealed, but the guaranty in respect to Jülich-Berg, which was one of them, was at least suspected, for it is mentioned in the Austrian diplomatic correspondence of October in the same year. See Foerster, ii. appendix, p. 51, letter No. 34 ; Droysen, IV. ii. 380, 381 ; Coxe, *Memoirs of Sir R. Walpole* (London, 1800), i. 428, 429.

Dessauer was not less violently opposed to the transaction; a rupture was the consequence, and the veteran warrior re- tired in a passion to Halle.[1] Grumbkow was left master of the situation. But about this time there appeared at Berlin, casually as it were, a Count von Seckendorf, who had served as a Saxon general before Stralsund, and was now in the diplomatic service of the Emperor. He had also been arguing with Grumbkow, and Grumbkow, that sen- sitive logician, had already repented of his share in the Hanover bargain. Frederic William had always had a partiality for Seckendorf; and it suited his personal pref- erence not less than the Emperor's purpose to have the unexpected visitor located at Berlin as imperial ambassador. The first though somewhat pre- mature fruit of the mission was the so-called Treaty of Wusterhausen, October 17, 1726.

Treaty of
Wuster-
hausen.

In this change of front the King was also aided by his antipathies. Frederic William had never ad- mired his Hanover relations, neither George I., his father-in-law, nor the second George, his brother-in- law, especially the latter, who, according to gossip, carried off the bride that the Prussian prince had selected for himself, and forced him to take up with his rival's sister. With a person of such strong passions the chagrin of the defeated suitor would not unnaturally affect the political conduct of the king. And further irritation was caused by the occasional clash of contrary interests during the Swedish war, and at intervals subsequent to that. In any event Frederic William was never on cordial terms with the contemporary Georges; and was accounted by the European diplomatists an enemy both of the reigning

Causes and
influences.

[1] Or did the rupture take place before the treaty? Authorities differ on this momentous question, but the correspondence quoted in the second volume of Foerster seems to fix it in 1724. The fact that the two men held opposite views of the Hanover business is not, how- ever, disputed.

house and of the policy of England. This feeling was artfully utilized by Seckendorf.

A dispute between the parties to the Treaty of Hanover also came opportunely to the aid of the imperial agent. England and France affected to regard it as an offensive alliance. Frederic William not only held it to be merely defensive, but was early alarmed at the consequences for him and his state if the other view should prevail. If the western powers should attack the Austrian Netherlands, or should even attempt by force to overthrow the Ostend company, a commercial monopoly set up by the Emperor to the great indignation of Holland and England, his own territories would be attacked first by the imperialists, and would become the theatre of war. To secure Prussia against such a contingency he demanded fresh guaranties, and this demand was met by evasions.[1]

Finally Seckendorf labored to appease the King's resentment toward his own master, which, if scarcely less strong, was perhaps less personal, by making some concessions and promising to secure others, by judiciously stroking the back of the bear, and soothing his savage temper. This required prudence, but was not difficult to a skilful hand. Seckendorf had lived much in the King's neighborhood, and had learned how to manage him.[2] In this particular business he had, too, the original sympathy of the Dessauer, the acquired support of Grumbkow, and, as he himself reports, at least the acquiescence of Ilgen.[3]

The treaty, when finally signed, was not wholly according to the King's, nor wholly according to the Emperor's wishes. The pragmatic sanction was Tenor of the treaty.

[1] See Seckendorf's report of a conversation with the King, in Foerster, ii. Urkundenbuch, No. 40.

[2] His methods of treatment are described in his letters to Eugene. Foerster, ii. Urkundenbuch, passim.

[3] Seckendorf's reports in regard to Ilgen are, however, full of contradictions. The minister of foreign affairs seems to have been the only person at Berlin whose depths the envoy never fully sounded.

guaranteed by Prussia; the Prussian rule of inheritance by the Emperor. And the Emperor gave certain loose promises to use his efforts to secure a settlement of the Jülich-Berg controversy in a sense favorable to Frederic William's pretensions. That is essentially all there is of this famous treaty. Yet it created no little excitement in Europe, and indirectly caused the ruin of many an imposing diplomatic programme.

The direct bearing was this: the western powers wished to use the Emperor's anxiety about the pragmatic sanction as a means of forcing him to retract the concession to the Ostend company. They had hoped by the Treaty of Hanover to secure the King of Prussia for their cause. But the King rejected this interpretation of the treaty, professed utter indifference toward the company, said he cared nothing about a lot of " cheesemongers," and by the Treaty of Wusterhausen eventually accepted and guaranteed the pragmatic sanction.

In the mean time the European powers were arranging themselves on one side and the other. Russia had joined the Emperor; Holland, Sweden, and Denmark, the opposite party. The outbreak of war seemed imminent.

Frederic William was in a sore dilemma. He had first protested against the Treaty of Hanover because the other parties gave it too wide an extension. Then he entered into the compact of Wusterhausen, under the singular impression that because it was not openly in conflict, therefore it could not be essentially in conflict with the first engagement.[1] And finally he fell into dispute with the court of Vienna about the sense of this last treaty. A more flagrant case of gross diplomatic imbecility it would be difficult to find. All through the ne-

Fresh per-
plexities.

---

[1] According to Droysen, IV. ii. 425, Prussia gave England a written declaration to the effect that nothing had been concluded, either with Russia or with the Emperor, contrary to the engagements of the Treaty of Hanover.

gotiations, and the subsequent controversies over the meaning of the negotiations, Frederic William appears as a man without clear views or well-defined ends ; as arrogant, selfish, insolent, and yet superficial ; as a prince swayed now by suspicion, now by greed, now by jealousy, now by passion, now by caprice, now by prejudice ; overruling his most capable ministers in the assertion of his own will, and then walking blindly into the traps set by designing strangers. Seckendorf, while humoring completely his temporary whims, always writes of him in terms of the most perfect contempt. That he did not fall into more serious dangers is doubtless owing to the circumstance that sometimes a sense of his own ignorance led him to consult men better informed than himself, and even to be guided by their advice.

The disputes over the interpretation of the Treaty of Wusterhausen — disputes which may be traced out painfully in the official and other records [1] — led the two courts finally to abandon it before it had been ratified, and to begin negotiations for a new and more intelligible compact. These negotiations were prolonged over two years, and ended at length in the secret Treaty of Berlin, December 23, 1728.[2] Six weeks later the ratifications were exchanged. The importance of this treaty, as well because it marked the point of flood-tide in Frederic William's Austrian sympathies, as because of the bitter recriminations to which it afterwards gave rise between the two courts, makes necessary a brief statement of the two leading questions which it was intended to settle, and of the form of settlement which it was supposed at the time to make. It so happened, too, that neither of these questions required for its equitable adjustment any

Treaty of Berlin.

[1] Foerster, Ranke, Droysen, Seckendorf's papers, the works of Eugene, etc., etc.

[2] This treaty is given, though, according to Droysen, with some immaterial errors, by Foerster, ii. Urkundenbuch, p. 314 et seq.

real material sacrifice by one party to the other. The greed of the two courts and the art of diplomatists gave them a wholly factitious importance.

It is evident, for instance, that the pragmatic sanction

The treaty and the pragmatic sanction. abridged in no respect the rights of Prussia. Frederic William made no claims to any of the territory of the House of Hapsburg; and even if the fact had been otherwise, his claims or his rights would have been made neither weaker nor stronger by the succession of Maria Theresa instead of some other heir. He was interested at most only in her choice of a husband, and even in that only so far as it might affect the next imperial election. This appears from the terms themselves of the final agreement. After long and weary excursions over the whole field of imperial politics, after the most patient and profitless diplomatic manœuvring, after the inevitable bickerings over quotas, contingents, equivalents, compensations, the numberless proposals and counter-proposals finally reduced themselves to a simple guaranty of the pragmatic sanction given by Prussia to Austria, and the acceptance by Austria of the condition required by Prussia. The guaranty applied to all the territories held by Austria, and included a pledge to give Prussia's vote to the future husband of Maria Theresa for emperor. The condition was that the archduchess' husband be a prince " sprung from ancient German stock of princely quality." [1]

In the matter of the Jülich-Berg dispute, again, the

The treaty and Jülich-Berg. Emperor, to meet the views of Prussia, was not required to sacrifice any of his own rights, but only to use his influence in behalf of Prussia as against the rival claims of a third power. Since the partition made in 1666 between Brandenburg and Neuburg, events had taken place which gave a new significance to that compact. It had been stipulated that in case of the

[1] . . . aus altem deutschen Reichsfürsten Geblüth. . . .

failure of direct descendants of either of the contracting
lines, the other should inherit its share, and the territories
be reunited. In 1688 the head of the House of Neuburg
had succeeded the Simmern, or older branch of his family,
on its extinction, in the Palatinate and the electorship.
But the reigning Elector, Charles Philip, was now seventy
years old, infirm, and without male descendants ; and
the question arose whether his death would be a casus
fœderis under the arrangement of 1666. This the Prussian jurists answered, of course, in the affirmative. But
Charles Philip was naturally reluctant to have his possessions divided after his death ; and in order to secure the
succession to the whole for the collateral branch of Sulzbach, which would in any event inherit the Palatinate, he
had married his oldest daughter, in 1717, to the oldest
prince of that house. Three daughters were the issue of
that union, and Pfalz-Sulzbach was, according to Charles
Philip, the proper eventual successor in Jülich-Berg. The
case had other complications, which may, however, be
passed over.[1] It is by no means certain that from a legal
point of view the Prussian contention was just, and the
proceedings of Frederic William warrant the suspicion
that he himself was convinced, if not of the weakness of
his cause in the tribunals of the Empire, at least of the
advisability of securing an extra-judicial support, on which
he could lean for aid even against an adverse decision.
He early waived his claim in respect to Jülich, insisting

[1] Thus a sister of Charles Philip had married the Emperor Leopold, and an imperial commission had, after an examination of the
titles, reported pro forma that Charles VI. himself, the son of this
marriage, was the true and only legal heir to Jülich-Berg. But this
opinion was binding on no one. Then the Elector Charles Philip had
two brothers, who, as Roman Catholic ecclesiastics, were, of course,
unable to perpetuate the succession, but who claimed the right to
succeed at least to the administration of the contested province after
the Elector's death, and to enjoy the revenues during their own
lives.

only on Berg, with the seigniory of Ravenstein. He agreed to accept the city of Düsseldorf subject to the military necessities of the emperor in time of war. The demand for an equivalent from Austrian territory in case of failure to obtain Berg was abandoned on the objection of the imperial court.[1] All that the King really obtained was the transfer to him of the rights of the Emperor in Berg — rights which had never been judicially ascertained, and were not admitted even at Berlin — and the promise that the Emperor would undertake to procure the assent of the Elector Palatine to the proposed settlement. If the treaty should be infringed in any of its provisions by either party, then the whole was to become, or might be treated as becoming void.

The King concluded this treaty on his own judgment, and, as it appears, against the advice of his ministers. Ilgen had died, greatly to Seckendorf's relief, during the negotiations; and Borcke and Knyphausen, the remaining Prussian commissioners, insisted on a written order, and a full discharge from all responsibility, before affixing their signatures.[2] Nor is this all. The urgency and persistence, the noisy threats and peevish protestations of the King, contrast strangely with a tone of indifference which in unguarded moments he assumed toward the treaty, both before and after its conclusion. His firmest reliance seems to have been not on a written compact, but on an assumed identity of interests between the two states; not on Austrian good faith, but on Austrian necessities. It was because he believed his friendship and alliance to be indispensable to the success of the Emperor's plans, and not because after long haggling he had obtained in writing the vague promise of contingent

The King's standpoint.

[1] Droysen, IV. iii. 35.

[2] Droysen says that Knyphausen, as a supposed adherent of the English alliance, was obnoxious to Seckendorf, but that Borcke had been introduced as a warm friend of Austria.

favors, that he broke completely away from the western powers, and threw himself unreservedly, with an almost ludicrous warmth of devotion, into the arms of Austria.[1]

This much it is necessary to say in the interest of justice to all parties. But it must also be admitted that there are strong reasons for suspecting not only that the court of Vienna took a different view of Austria's interests and Prussia's value, — this indeed it had a perfect right to do, — but even that it never intended to observe the stipulations in regard to Berg in the sense in which Frederic William, encouraged by Seckendorf, had been led to understand them. One of these reasons is, that Austria took care to have inserted in the treaty various reservations about the powers of the emperor as supreme arbiter between the German princes, and the respect due to the authority of the aulic court of the empire, in which the disputed succession to Jülich-Berg was already judicially pending, — reservations which the King's ministers suspected, but which were too fine and technical for his own comprehension. But a stronger reason is the circumstance that the Emperor had as early as 1726 concluded with the Elector Palatine a treaty, which contained in respect to Jülich-Berg promises exactly the opposite, in substance and tendency, though not in words, to those made the same year, and again in 1728 to Prussia.[2] In 1726 Charles VI. guaranteed Berg to the House of Sulzbach as the price of its accession to the Austro-Spanish alliance. Two years later, this engagement being still in force, he undertook to secure the same territory for Prussia on the condition of its accession to the alliance. This transaction has always been treated by Prussian writers as a characteristic piece of Austrian duplicity, and as practically invalidating the Treaty of Berlin,

Suspicious conduct of Austria.

---

[1] Comp. Droysen, IV. iii. 35, 38, 41.

[2] Treaty of December 29, 1726. Droysen, IV. ii. 452, n., has the Jülich-Berg articles.

including, of course, the guaranty of the pragmatic sanction. Now the Austrian intention to deceive is probably
beyond question. The Sulzbach treaty was a secret one,
like that of Berlin, was not communicated to Frederic
William, and was not, in fact, fully and authentically
known to him until several years afterwards. This being
true, the conduct of the Emperor becomes from any point
of view indefensible. But although one of the two parties
to whom Charles VI. had promised Berg was sure to be
betrayed, it by no means follows that Prussia was the
victim selected. Its treaty was the latest, and might
claim to supersede the other. Besides, although the Austrian intention to deceive is clear, it is not equally clear
that the deception was complete. Rumors of the negotiations between the Emperor and the Elector Palatine
reached Berlin through various channels in the course of
the conferences with Seckendorf. Brand, the Prussian
envoy at Vienna, reported his suspicions as early as the
summer of 1626. Ilgen seems to have suspected them,
and to have endeavored to put the King on his guard.[1]
But his majesty was not then, or pretended not to be, prepared to believe in such treachery, listened to no warning,
placed full confidence in the strength of Prussia's position,
and ordered the treaty to be ratified.

It is furthermore true, and the truth is in some measure
an excuse for Frederic William's blind precipi-
tancy, that the European situation made it difficult for him longer to evade an open and unre-
served decision between the two rival coalitions. He was
forced to choose, and he chose the Emperor rather than
the Emperor's enemies. He accepted the Treaty of Berlin
with a full understanding of the obligations which it imposed on him, with a sincere belief that their punctual
fulfilment would place the Emperor under a debt of gratitude which would long be an advantage to the House of

The treaty
and the Eu-
ropean
crisis.

[1] Droysen, IV. ii. 417, 421, 451.

Prussia, and with the expectation, too, that the casus fœderis would very soon arise.

Fortunately for Frederic William, and for many other potentates, the war-cloud broke away nearly as suddenly as it had gathered. This was owing in great measure to the influence of two minis- *The war-cloud breaks.* ters, each powerful in his own country, and each devoted to a policy of peace: Sir Robert Walpole in England, and Cardinal Fleury in France. And their efforts were aided by the Emperor's solicitude about the pragmatic sanction. In 1728 he agreed to suspend the Ostend company for seven years; in 1731, to abolish it entirely; and the chief grievance being thus removed, the powers generally acknowledged the pragmatic sanction, and war was for the time averted.

The next crisis arose in 1733, when on the death of August II. the Polish throne became vacant. This event had long been anxiously awaited by *Crisis in Poland.* the powers, and each had endeavored by negotiation and intrigue to prepare for its arrival. The leading candidates for the succession were Stanislaus Lesczinski, the same whom Charles XII. had set up as king after the expulsion of August, and whom August had in his turn expelled, and August's own son, the prince electoral of Saxony. Lesczinski, as the father-in-law of Louis XV., had the support of France, and, as a native of Poland, that of the Diet of Warsaw. For the young August his father made, of course, strenuous efforts; but he had alienated the Emperor by refusing to acknowledge the pragmatic sanction, and even setting up claims of his own to the Austrian succession, based on his son's marriage with a daughter of the preceeding emperor, Joseph I.[1]

[1] If females were to be recognized in the succession, August's contention was not a bad one. The Emperor had, in fact, succeeded his brother Joseph I. in Austria by virtue of that very salic law which he now sought to overthrow. For Joseph left daughters, and one of them was the princess electoral of Saxony.

370 HISTORY OF PRUSSIA.

The first measure was a preliminary treaty between Russia, Prussia, and Austria in 1732, by which they agreed to prevent the accession of Lesczinski or any other French candidate to the Polish throne, if necessary, by force ; and to endeavor to secure the election of the brother of the King of Portugal. Prussia was to receive as compensation the eventual support of Russia and Austria to the succession in Courland. August strained every nerve in the mean time to secure Frederic William for his cause. The most flattering offers were made, which the latter, however, professed not to take seriously. Each king felt, and probably with reason, that the other was playing a double part. Frederic William was extremely anxious to penetrate his rival's true purposes ; and as August was fond of the bottle, Grumbkow, who was also a hard drinker, was sent to spend an evening with the King of Poland, and with the aid of wine to draw out his secrets. This heroic contest of endurance ended in an unexpected victory for Grumbkow. The King drank himself beyond the point of volubility into a heavy stupor, from which he recovered only to die on the 1st of February, 1733.[1]

The tripartite treaty of 1732 was left unratified by the

Prussia is isolated. Empress of Russia, and chiefly on account of Courland, for Prussia the essential provision. Frederic William was, therefore, free to choose between the rival candidates. August III. promptly applied to him on his father's death ; but Frederic William, regarding himself as indispensable, indulged in the most extravagant demands. In this he overreached himself. August, turning to Russia and Austria, made satisfactory terms with them,[2] and the King of Prussia was left completely

[1] *Mémoires de Brandebourg*, part IV. p. 47; Stenzel, iii. 649; Foerster, ii. 114 et seq.; Grumbkow's own report to the King, Berlin, January 13, 1733, in Droysen, IV. iv. 408–415.

[2] It is believed that August offered to secure Courland for Prince

isolated. Lesczinski slipped surreptitiously into Warsaw, and was unanimously elected by the Diet; but a
Russian army drove him out, and besieged him in Dantzic, where he had taken refuge. The preference of the
people of Poland in the choice of a king of Poland was, it
will be observed, completely disregarded by all the powers ; and each sought — Prussia as selfishly though not
as wisely as the rest — only its own advantage.

In consequence of these events, France declared war
upon the Emperor, and the Emperor summoned War between
Frederic William to furnish his contingent of France and the
10,000 men, as promised in treaties. The King Empire.
hesitated. He had previously urged the Emperor to leave
the Russians to manage Poland, so that if France should
begin hostilities the Empire would have a clear case. He
now pretended that the cause was not an imperial but
only an Austrian one, and that he was not bound to contribute troops ; but Seckendorf, who sometimes, though
not often, lost his temper, or from his acquaintance with
Frederic William knew when it was politic to show indignation, declared outright at table that the King had
promised the troops, and an honorable man always kept
his word. Frederic William replied with equal passion,
and a violent rupture seemed imminent. Grumbkow saw
the danger and was equal to the emergency. He took
from his pocket a small top, and set it spinning on the
table, to the great destruction of the glasses. The King
inquired what that was. "A toy," said Grumbkow,
"which I bought for the prince Henry." Frederic William was overcome by the comical nature of the proceeding, became mollified, acknowledged his error to Seckendorf, and agreed to furnish the 10,000 men.

Drinking bouts and humming-tops, — such were the

Biron, favorite of the Russian Empress Anne. See Ranke, Pr. Gesch.
iii., iv. 198. For the Emperor he guaranteed the pragmatic sanction.
See Mailáth, Gesch. Östreichs, iv. 605.

methods of diplomacy at the court of Berlin in the year
1733! Since the death of the accomplished

The King's bad diplomacy. Ilgen the nominal conduct of foreign affairs had
been in the hands of Knyphausen, Ilgen's son-in-
law, and an old soldier, General Borcke; but the real
power was Grumbkow, with whom Seckendorf, the Emperor's envoy, continued on admirable terms.

It is evident that the situation was becoming too intricate for Frederic William's simple and straightforward
intelligence. Cool and expert schemers tied him fast in
their diplomatic nets, and listened without fear to his
frantic imprecations. The usual device of men baffled in
argument, or vexed by the superior coolness and ease of
the adversary, is increased violence of tone and manner,
by which, however, they only expose their real weakness.
This was Frederic William's great mistake. So long as
his arrogance and brutality were novel, they may have
caused a certain respect, especially since it was known
that he had an army and a fund; but Seckendorf and
others soon probed this shallow bluster, and unconcernedly
allowed it to flow on.

One of the King's most furious outbursts was caused by
the discovery that he had been deserted by Russia and
Austria, and outwitted by August III. He fairly made
Berlin resound with his curses and threats; he would take
up the cause of the besieged Lesczinski; he would chase
the Russians home, and escort the fugitive king in triumph back to Warsaw. But Seckendorf knew perfectly
well that he would do nothing of the sort. The siege
went on without any disturbance from Prussia, and with
only a single, a heroic yet wholly inadequate, attempt by
the French to raise it. Lesczinski escaped in disguise,
but the city fell into the hands of Russia, and was turned
over to August III. as king of Poland.

Frederic William treated in the same style the quarrel
between the Emperor and France. While full of resent-

ment toward Charles VI., and hourly assailing him in the most violent language, he yielded in the end, gave his vote in the Diet for a declaration of war in the name of the Empire, and sent his 10,000 troops to join the imperial army. The fine appearance and bearing of the Prussians attracted much attention, as they marched to the scene of hostilities. But either their discipline and self-restraint were less perfect, or the King's own folly made them the innocent agents of his cruel vengeance, for they left bitter memories in every country through which they passed. And they did no fighting when they reached their destination. Eugene was nominally generalissimo of the forces, but Eugene's days of action were over; and dissensions among the other officers, as well as between the princes whom they represented, caused the time to be spent in fruitless marching and counter-marching in every direction except toward the enemy. Frederic William himself visited the imperial camp, but it does not appear that the inaction especially vexed his ardent spirit. In Italy the Austrians met nothing but reverses; and the next year, 1735, they concluded a hasty and ignominious peace with France, to which not long afterwards Sardinia and Spain, the allies of France, acceded.[1] The imperial army was then disbanded, and the several contingents returned to their own homes.

Prussia was not invited to the peace negotiations, and the contents of the treaty were only made known to Frederic William after its adoption. Such contemptuous neglect was little likely, of course, to make him more conciliatory. But the indignities were not wholly in the form of the proceedings, for in the compact itself France abandoned Lesczinski, her own protégé, and recognized August as king of Poland; so that the problem was finally settled without Frederic William's

Abrupt end of the war.

Exasperation of the King.

[1] Austria surrendered Naples and Sicily to Don Carlos, a younger son of Philip of Spain. Even Eugene advised the Emperor to yield.

aid, and Seckendorf was master of the situation.[1] The
Emperor even neglected to give the King notice of the
marriage of his daughter, Maria Theresa, with Francis of·
Lorraine.

The old King, now broken down in health, returned
baffled and sullen to Berlin. He had let Cour-
*Disappoint-
ment about
Berg.* land, Polish Preussen, Elbing, slip through his
hands. He had also wantonly sacrificed several
chances to have Jülich and Berg guaranteed to him by
the western powers; but believing that the Emperor was
pledged to him, at least in respect to Berg, by the treaty
of 1728, he had awaited the death of the Count Palatine,
and the extinction of his direct line, with confidence.
The Count Palatine awkwardly persisted, however, in out-
living Frederic William, so that the actual crisis did not
arrive. But the King had the mortification before his
death of learning that the Austrian guaranty of Berg was
worthless; that Charles VI., even while promising to
secure the duchy for Prussia, had also promised to secure
it for the House of Sulzbach; that of the two promises,
that to Sulzbach was supported by both the sympathies
and the antipathies of the Emperor, by his friendship for
a Catholic ally, and his hatred of a Protestant rival ; and
that the intrigues of the imperial court had brought about
a general resolution on the part of the European powers
to exclude Prussia from the succession.[2]

Frederic William's eyes had first been opened in the
course of an interview which he held with the Emperor at
Prague in August, 1732.[3] As his anxiety rose his demands became more moderate. In September he was

[1] Lesczinski received Lorraine, but it was to fall to France after
his death, while the Duke of Lorraine took Tuscany in exchange.
[2] Ranke, iii., iv. 235.
[3] Memoir of the Prussian minister Podewils; Grumbkow to Seckendorf, October 3, 1735; Droysen, IV. iii. 162–167. It was evident, the King wrote, that England, Holland, and the princes of the
Empire were unwilling to see Prussia become stronger on the Rhine.

willing to accept Berg and Ravenstein without Düsseldorf, provided he could obtain possession in a peaceful
manner. Then the Polish complications, and Frederic
William's treatment of them, created a feeling of bitter
resentment in Vienna. Sharp notes were exchanged, Prussia was charged with all the failures of the imperial arms,
and the outlook for Berg seemed dark enough. In 1737
the King offered to pay Pfalz-Neuburg 1,200,000 thalers
for the surrender of its claims to the duchy, but the offer
was promptly refused.

The next year the opposition to Prussia culminated in a
demonstration of a highly theatrical order. The *The great
powers
against
Prussia.*
four powers, Austria, France, England, and Holland, combining, as they said, only to prevent a
breach of the peace, and to secure equitable treatment for
all claimants, presented identical notes through their ambassadors at Berlin to the King of Prussia.[1] The tenor
of the demand was that the King's envoy at the Hague be
authorized to enter into a conference with the representatives of the four " impartial " powers, and a delegate from
the Elector Palatine, upon the question of the Jülich-Berg
succession, and that, pending the decision of the conference, Prussia should undertake not to attempt the forcible
seizure of the duchies. The Elector Palatine, to whom a
similar invitation had been extended, hastened to accept,
on condition that Prussia recognize the provisional occupation of the disputed territory by Sulzbach. But Prussia
replied to her invitation by a pointed though courteous
refusal.

The situation seemed now to afford no escape except
through a French alliance. This involved a
complete change of policy, and a change grossly *Treaty with
France.
1739.*
abhorrent to the King's sense of German patriot-

[1] February 10, 1738 ; for Austria, Baron Dernrath; France, Marquis Chétardie ; Holland, General Ginkel; England, Captain Guy
Dickens.

ism, but he pretended to find no alternative. Overtures were accordingly made to France, and, as the coalition had already begun to fall asunder, were well received. The negotiations were conducted at the Hague, and with the utmost secrecy, by the respective residents there, Marquis Fénelon for France, Luiscius for Prussia, both clear-sighted, sagacious, and active men. By the end of March the treaty was ready. On the 5th of April it was signed.

The provisions of the treaty, so far as they concerned Jülich-Berg, were not essentially different from those which had been accepted by Austria in 1728. France now undertook, as Austria had then undertaken, to secure the assent of Charles Philip to an equitable partition; Prussia to have all of Ravenstein and the greater part of Berg; Sulzbach, the remainder, with one million thalers in money. But in return for the good offices, and, in case the Elector Palatine should die before accepting the settlement, the military assistance of France, the King gave a general promise to regard French and Prussian interests as identical in European politics, the methods of coöperation to be agreed on as emergencies arose.

In the Anglo-Spanish war an emergency soon arose, whereupon France promptly presented its demands. And almost at the same time the King learned that, by a treaty concluded in January, 1739, Austria and France had guaranteed the claims of Sulzbach to the whole of the Jülich-Berg succession.

For these manifold disappointments it was but slight compensation that in 1732 the King had suc-
Orange es-
tates settled. ceeded in effecting a final settlement of the
1732. Orange inheritance. Prussia received, however, but little in addition to the districts which she had previously acquired by force and by temporary conventions. The expectancy to East Frisland, on the other hand, assured to Prussia at the time of the Schwiebus affair, still awaited realization, and was contested by various rival claims and interests.

In reviewing the diplomatic history of this reign, the reader will justly reach the conclusion that Frederic William failed chiefly because his Conclusion. methods lacked steadiness and consistency. A state bent on self-aggrandizement has sometimes the choice between several courses. By a shrewd diplomacy it may take advantage of the needs of other states, and from time to time obtain a good price even for its inaction. It may discard negotiations altogether, and adopt a simple policy of brute force. Or it may even combine diplomacy and force, provided the relations between the two are carefully adjusted, and each used only in its own appropriate way. But Frederic William neither adopted one of these methods exclusively, nor combined them in any way in which their union could be made effective. The use of each was impaired by a vicious admixture of the methods which properly belong to the other; negotiations were conducted in the style of the battlefield, and threatened battles vanished in clouds of diplomacy. The result was that rival states learned to have no confidence either in the King's treaties or the King's battalions. His manner made him hateful without making him terrible.

From another point of view, however, the humanitarian will find great satisfaction in the history of this reign. The evil of war was at least averted. Frederic William taxed his people to the last point of endurance in order to raise and maintain a large army, but he sacrificed little of their blood, and little of their treasure in wars of ambition. That this was owing to any humane scruples does not indeed appear; but the fact itself, whatever its cause, may be gratefully recorded.

CHAPTER X.

FREDERIC WILLIAM'S ADMINISTRATIVE REFORMS.

ALTHOUGH the diplomatic record of this reign was far from brilliant, it would be wrong to ascribe the fact to a decay in the power and prestige of the state itself. The King was a bad diplomatist, and accomplished little. But the very circumstance that he could insult his neighbors and escape chastisement, that in spite of gross provocations his territory was never invaded, proves that Prussia herself was beginning to play on the diplomatic stage a part somewhat higher and stronger than the one which she held in the preceeding reign.

New importance of Prussia.

Frederic I. hired his soldiers out practically as mercenaries to rich but unmilitary allies. Frederic William I. negotiates treaties, and enters alliances as an independent European prince, having a position, a character, a dignity of his own. But if this change cannot be attributed to the difference between the characters of the two kings, what is the explanation? There was, undoubtedly, a vast difference; but it was a difference which, other things being equal, would lead one to expect a greater not a smaller degree of self-assertion from the first king. He had a higher sense of his own personal and official importance than his son; he acted better in many respects the character of a king; but in the stern, practical, unsentimental affairs of European diplomacy he held relatively a far lower rank. The explanation is simply that Frederic I., though a prince of amazing pretensions, had few soldiers and little money, while his successor was well supplied with both. The resources of Frederic William I. were not only adequate to any undertaking which he felt called upon to attempt in his own interest, but they also gave him an influence, unknown to his father, in every great European crisis. This was the result of the reforms which, beginning with his accession, continued through the whole course of his reign. It is necessary, therefore, now to describe these reforms, which for convenience may perhaps be classified as military, fiscal, judicial, and administrative. Each of these classes also involved constitutional changes, either as a preliminary condition or as a practical consequence; and these will attract the interest even of readers who would otherwise be indifferent to mere formal modifications in the system of. government.

It is related by all historians that when Frederic William as crown prince was in the camp of the allies in Flanders he was twitted by the young officers on the military weakness of Prussia. "Your father," said they, "could not maintain fifteen thousand men in the field without our subsidies." *Frederic William makes and fulfils a prophecy.* The sneer was probably unjust, as it certainly was impolite, but, just or unjust, it touched a sensitive side of the prince's nature. If they had said that Prussia had no art, no scholars, no universities, he would have acquiesced; for he knew little of Schlueter, of Leibnitz and Thomasius, of Königsberg and Halle; and his contempt for them was in proportion to his ignorance. But when the military strength of his country was questioned he at once revolted. "I will prove to you," he said, "that Prussia can support thirty thousand men, all with her own money." [1] When Frederic William died he left an army of ninety thousand men, no foreign debt, and a large fund for future use in the treasury!

The quality of the army was raised by successive meas-

[1] A story quoted by all Prussian writers.

ures of general reform; by scrupulous attention to all the
details of organization, equipment, and administration;
and by the unremitting, patient, and laborious efforts of
the drill-sergeants. The first drill-sergeant of the kingdom was the King himself. That he could successfully
command soldiers in the field may be doubted, but few
men in Europe could better prepare them for the field by
the discipline and practice of the drill-room.

Even as a youth Frederic William's delight was in
soldiers. At the hunting-seat of Wusterhausen,
The royal
drill-ser- a few miles southeast of Berlin, the prince se-
geant.   cretly collected a few stalwart rustics — the germ
of a famous regiment of grenadiers — and then seized
every chance to run away from his lessons or games, to
'call out his squad of warriors, and drill them with the
precision and fidelity of a martinet. This fancy he kept
up after he became king, and when he could gratify it on
a larger scale. He was fond of details of every kind,
but for military details his affection rose to the height of
an absorbing and commanding passion, grotesque indeed
and often troublesome, yet not unmanly or unproductive.
Grand parades were, of course, frequent; they were the
chief entertainment which Berlin offered to distinguished
guests. But the King's practical sense taught him that it
was not such showy and costly displays which make an
army efficient, useful though they indeed are in many ways.
A review is not a cause, but an exhibition of results; and
the success even of a review depends on the intelligence,
the regularity, the thoroughness of the preliminary work.
And while most princes of the age were willing to confine
their participation to the spectacular part of military life,
Frederic William plunged daily into affairs of routine,
set a personal example of conscientious attention to par-
ticulars, and enforced by actual supervision the highest
degree of fidelity upon every officer of the army. A captain never called out his company for exercise without a
nervous apprehension that the critical King might at any

moment appear on the scene. The drill-sergeants were in deadly fear of the cane which Frederic William laid over their shoulders on the slightest provocation. An error in evolutions, an unpolished musket, a missing button, exposed the offender to a whipping, and his officer to a reprimand more terrible even than a whipping. Neglect of duty was, however, the unpardonable offence; and as the King was himself the hardest worker in his dominions, he was at least not inconsistent or selfish in permitting no excuse of climate, or season, or weather to interrupt the work of military drill. The whole country was a training school for soldiers. The rattle of muskets, the tramp of armed men was heard summer and winter from the Memel to the Rhine; and neither the ridicule of his neighbors, nor the hardships of his own people, could shake the resolution of the great drill-sergeant.

The army was increased as steadily and surely as it was improved. Frederic I. left nominally about Growth of 30,000 men; but the ranks did not always cor- the army. respond to the rolls, and there was a looseness of organization throughout the whole service. The first duty was, therefore, to simplify and consolidate the existing establishment, and it was happily made easier by the return of troops from the field after the peace of Utrecht. New regiments were also created. Three were made possible by the reductions in the court expenses ; and others were added from time to time as the condition of the funds, and the success of the recruiting officers, permitted. The losses at Stralsund were not great, nor did the operations of the siege much disturb the work of reorganization and augmentation. By 1725 the army had risen to 64,000 men. In 1740, the year of Frederic William's death, it numbered about 89,000, 64,000 being infantry,[1] and the best in Europe.

[1] Foerster, ii. 294, 295. There are, however, various estimates of the strength of the army at the time of the King's death.

At the outset of his reign Frederic William introduced a system of conscription, which, however, had the effect of driving young men out of the country. It was, therefore, suspended in 1714.[1] Enlistments were again by law made voluntary, and stringent edicts were issued against the use of constraint by recruiting sergeants.[2] But it is evident, from the number of complaints on the subject, that abuses were frequent; and there is too much reason for suspecting that the government, without openly encouraging, nay, while affecting openly to discourage it, did secretly connive at the use of fraud, and perhaps even of force. It is evident, for instance, that a decree of March 9, 1714, declaring that the suspension of impressment should not apply to idle and good-for-nothing vagabonds, was dangerously vague and elastic.

How recruits were obtained.

The struggle for recruits between the agents of the different regiments would of itself create a strong disposition to excesses. But it also led to another evil of quite a different sort. Mere boys, children, even infants in the cradle, were not exempt from the visits of the recruiting officers; were enrolled by anticipation, as it were; ticketed as the property of this or that regiment; and then claimed when the military age was reached. The result was that these youthful recruits learned to insist on the privileges of their military character, and defied the jurisdiction of parents and teachers. Foerster tells an amusing and yet instructive story of a venerable schoolmaster, who sought and obtained from a colonel the privilege of wearing a red scarf, in order that by the aid of that thin military disguise he might have an authority over his pupils which as a mere pedagogue he was unable to assert.[3]

Abuses.

---

[1] Stenzel, iii. 347.
[2] For instance, May 9, 1714, May 22 and 26, 1721.
[3] *Friedrich Wilhelm I.* ii. 295.

The nominal repeal of the law of conscription failed, therefore, to restore confidence. The emigration continued, in spite of ferocious edicts against it; fugitives were classed as deserters; and desertion was a crime for which the King's resources hardly afforded an adequate penalty. Nor was any distinction made between deserters who were natives and deserters who were foreigners. A recruit who was obtained in the territory of Mayence having escaped, the general to whose command he had belonged, sent a squad of soldiers across the frontier to drive away all his father's sheep. The venerable shepherd, innocent of his son's crime, appealed to the archbishop. The archbishop remonstrated with the King. But the King fully approved the general's conduct, and ordered him not to release the sheep until the deserter should be restored,[1] in other words, until he should be hanged, — a pleasant dilemma for the father.

If Frederic William was ready to practise such cruelties, and run such risks, for ordinary recruits, what scruples could be expected to check him in *The tall grenadiers.* the work of filling up and keeping up his own personal and favorite regiment, the " tall grenadiers ? " This brings us to one of the most brilliant inconsistencies of his character. In most things coarsely, offensively, even brutally practical, the King had in this passion for big soldiers one of the most singular whims which ever possessed a human being. In comparison with it his father's love of court display seems a venial weakness, if not a laudable virtue. Seckendorf writes about the famous corps in terms which reveal the contempt of the experienced soldier; the King, he observes once, seems to value his soldiers not according to length of service, but according to length of body. One of the first acts of Frederic II. was to disband the giants. Yet no suspicion of the costliness of this luxury, or of its utter uselessness as a military institution, seems ever to

[1] Foerster, ii. 302.

have entered the mind of the King; and down to the day of his death he pursued the chase for big grenadiers with unabated energy.

The nucleus of the grenadiers was, as above stated, the

The traffic in giants.
toy company of Wusterhausen. This was easily expanded into a regiment on the death of Frederic I.; was called the king's own; was fed and caressed and petted and humored, as a child by its fond parent, was supplied with the largest recruits which could be found in the world. A colonel dreaded to parade his command before the King, lest his majesty should snatch the tall men from the ranks, or should chastise him if there were none. Sometimes the theft was made good to the despoiled commander by an order for money, with which he could procure other recruits of the same stature;[1] sometimes even this sort of restitution was omitted. For choice specimens liberal premiums were paid to the recruiting officers, and if a candidate hesitated to enlist voluntarily he was bribed, betrayed, forced into the service, even kidnapped and dragged away to the barracks of the grenadiers at Potsdam. In spite of all the edicts against impressment, a six-footer had no security; he was a predestined soldier. A village brewer, who had the misfortune to be tall, was seized in his bed, and only released on his providing a substitute of the same height, which transaction cost him a thousand thalers. On one occasion a recruiting party entered a church during divine service, and began to pick out the most eligible worshippers, when the congregation, incited from the pulpit, seized and roughly treated the intruders; the King disciplined the clergyman, and took no measures against the soldiers. In Magdeburg

---

[1] See in Foerster, ii. 298, note, the King's letter to General Marwitz, where the general is promised 6,000 thalers for eight men confiscated from his proprietary regiment. He is enjoined to use the money only in supplying the vacant places. Comp. Seckendorf's report in Foerster, ii. Urkundenbuch, p. 38.

an insurrection nearly broke out owing to an infamous attempt to extort money from a rich merchant by the threat of impressment.[1] Not even the universities were safe. In Halle a tall student was kidnapped in broad daylight on the street; and to the petitions of his father the King replied, " let there be no arguing; the man is my subject." [2] The alarm became so great that this university was nearly deserted by Prussian students, who could safely pursue their studies only in foreign schools, such as Jena, Leipsic, and Göttingen; yet Frederic William, when the evil was reported by the rector, endeavored characteristically to correct it, not by removing its cause, but by violent and savage decrees. No subject, he declared in one of the mildest of these orders, should obtain a civil appointment in Prussia who had not studied three years at a Prussian university. Since the press-gangs made it almost impossible for a youth, unless a dwarf, to complete such a course, the outlook for his majesty's civil service was not made brighter by this measure.

The King's weakness was early revealed to his neighbors, and judiciously used to carry points which otherwise might have been unattainable. The most politic scruples, the strongest prejudices, the most stubborn opposition, could be overcome by a timely gift of tall grenadiers. They became a regular factor in diplomacy, as often as Prussia was concerned. When George I. wishes to bring Frederic William into the Hanover treaty, he bribes him with grenadiers; when Seckendorf sets out to break the Hanover treaty, and bring Prussia over to the Emperor, he writes to Vienna for tall recruits; the Czar Peter trades a batch of Muscovites, who had no merit but size, for an invoice of skilled Prussian mechanics. By this paltry device a king, gener-

Diplomacy and grenadiers.

1 Stenzel, iii. 356.

2 " Soll nicht resonniren (sic) ist mein Unterthan." Foerster, ii. Urkundenbuch, p. 71.

ally watchful and suspicious, was made the perfect dupe of
shrewd diplomatists, and led blindly about in the crooked
paths of European politics.

The grenadiers were made up of men of every tongue
and every nationality.[1] The chief duty of the
ill-paid and ill-treated envoys of Prussia at foreign courts was to buy grenadiers at good prices, and send
them on to Berlin, where they were assured a princely reception. The ambassador Borcke in England smuggled
a gigantic Irishman, engaged as lackey, over to Prussia,
and the prize cost 9,000 pounds sterling. Paris furnished
its contingent; and from Italy two fine specimens, one
a priest, the other a monk, were obtained. The King's
agents pried into every corner of Europe with the industry of detectives; were as well known as the Jesuits, and
even more hated. It is stated that in the Austrian duchies
there were at one time three hundred Prussian recruiting
officers. Many states permitted the so-called " friendly
recruiting " in behalf of foreign armies, and so long as
this condition was observed the emissaries of the King
were not guilty of any breach of hospitality.

Foreign acquisitions.

But in the lesser German states they too often tran-
scended these limits. That formal orders were
ever given them to use fraud and force is,
of course, improbable; but, knowing their master's disposition and their own interests, they deceived
where they could not openly hire, and kidnapped where
they failed to deceive. They became, accordingly, the
terror of Germany, and of all the frontier populations.
The Saxon peasant feared to come to town on market day.
The Hessian mother frightened her noisy children with
the threatened visit of a Prussian sergeant. No man who
towered above his fellows felt safe, and tall men went
about, if not with their lives, at least with their liberties

Troubles with foreign states.

---

[1] It is estimated, indeed, that over a third of the entire army were
foreigners. Preuss, *Friedrich der Grosse* (Berlin, 1832), i. 131.

in their hands. And, what is perhaps the strangest thing, Frederic William, who disliked war, and never intended to see his beloved grenadiers exposed to the real dangers of the battlefield, was several times on the point of hostilities with states which objected to the violent abduction of their citizens. The frontier of the Netherlands was not safe until the Dutch hanged two Prussian officers. England might have declared war, in spite of the act of settlement, to secure the release of some Hanoverians, if Seckendorf had not persuaded Frederic William to yield. If a too zealous Prussian "Werber" was apprehended, the King, instead of apologizing for the offence, disavowing him, and leaving him to his fate, would at once make a great outcry, plead the comity of nations, threaten reprisals, if the plaintiff happened to be weak, and in the end would probably retain the recruit and secure the release of his agent. The King's retaliation took strange forms. The Berlin chaplain, Rheinbeck, was offered a rich living in the free city of Hamburg, but Frederic William refused to dismiss him ; Hamburg, he said, had no scruples about asking for his preachers, yet made a great outcry if he laid hands on some rascally recruit. The Dutch ambassador applied in behalf of the university of Leyden for the famous jurist, Heineccius, of Halle, and received a curt refusal. "No tall fellows, no professors," said the King, who put scholars, preachers, and grenadiers all on a level, or the latter, if anything, above the others. Even when some more than usually gross outrage, or a particularly emphatic demand for redress, checked for a moment the King's ardent purpose, and forced him to declare himself, he would only make general promises of forbearance ; would privately commend and reward a detected kidnapper, to whom he had to administer a nominal reproof ; and after the matter had blown over would resume the old methods.[1] Toward the end of his reign the indignation

1 See the various promises and orders in Foerster, iii. 301 et seq.

and threats of Europe, but not a sense of its infamy, led him to forbid the system of man-stealing in foreign states. Giants continued to be lawful prey in the King's own dominions. They continued to be desirable prey even in the dominions of his neighbors; but as those neighbors showed a most uncivil and absurd reluctance to see their subjects stolen by Prussian brigands, it became necessary, when evasion and hypocrisy, insolence and defiance, would no longer suffice, to put at least a formal end to the evil. That such an evil could ever arise in a civilized state is one of the minor wonders of the eighteenth century.

The last point of absurdity was, however, reached in the King's scheme for breeding a special and permanent race of grenadiers. Males he had in the regiment itself. To obtain females, he instituted a further recruiting service, among the massive wives and daughters of the peasantry. The simplest rules of decency and humanity were violated. Women were sent from the most remote provinces, hurried pitilessly over long journeys, and mated with the giants at Potsdam. Even Frederic William himself did not hesitate to seize stalwart wenches, whom he met by the roadside, and send them to Potsdam with notes to the commander of the king's own. The prizes were often assigned to particular grenadiers by the King himself. It follows, of course, that the birth of a child from one of these mariages forcés was a great event of state, in which the King took the most acute interest;[1] but the historians do not report that the results of the system corresponded to the expectations of its author. In fact the King's reign ended before the new generation of giants could come into active service.

Propagation of grenadiers.

It must be said, however, that if a grenadier's bride could overlook the manner of the wooing, and the moral degradation of her position, she might take some pride in her sudden elevation into a higher so-

Treatment of the giants.

[1] Comp. Foerster, ii. 300.

cial sphere. The king's own was a species of select aristocracy. As compared with the soldiers of the line, the grenadiers had the treatment of princes of the blood ; nay, rather better treatment, for princes of the blood were pounded and starved, while the Potsdam favorites lived on delicacies, did no work, and were handled as tenderly as infants. To secure them the blessings of domestic life was one of the least of the King's thoughtful attentions. As they had been bought like rare animals at fabulous prices, it was necessary to relieve them of every inducement to escape, to make their cages roomy and comfortable, to give th m frequent exercise in the open air, and to feed them in a style much above that to which they had been accustomed. All this involved liberal outlays of money, and the cost of the giants rose up into the millions.

In 1733 an edict [1] did away even with the pretence of voluntary recruiting for the army, and the system of conscription was practically restored. This was in one sense a relief to the public. The evils of the past were largely due to the absence of fixed military circumscriptions, since, on account of the strict obligation resting on the colonels to keep their regiments full, every village was the scene of battles between the recruiting officers ; eligible recruits were nearly torn in pieces by the rival claimants ; and, in the fury of this competition, justice and law were little respected. The new system of quartering and distributing the troops assigned to each regiment its own territory, beyond which it could not go in search of recruits, and which could not be invaded by the agents of other corps. With certain exceptions every youth was bound to serve in his own local regiment, and was not even permitted to serve in any other.[2] It was a crude system of universal military ser-

The conscription restored.

[1] Cantonreglement, 15th September. Droysen, IV. ii. 17, says 1732.

[2] Stenzel, iii. 358; Foerster, ii. 309.

vice, with all the hardships which that term implies; but
it was at least an open and honest system, and free from
the gross irregularities of the old method.[1]

Frederic William was effectually aided in practical military work by Leopold of Dessau. The Dessauer was a man fashioned and tempered much
like the King himself; coarse like him, and passionate
like him; equally obstinate, arrogant, despotic, and cruel;
not less contemptuous of letters, art, and refinement, not
less exclusively devoted to physical and material ends.
There were, however, two important points of difference.
Frederic William affected to consult only the interests of
the state, and gratifies the inquirer now and then with
outbursts of an impulsive and brutal yet wholesome
equity; while Leopold was a person of bitter personal
animosities, vindictive by nature, and unscrupulous in his
methods of revenge, — a dangerous enemy, whose moods
everybody dreaded. But, on the other hand, the Dessauer had had more experience of war than his master,
was a better practical soldier, and understood more completely the details of army management. King and general supplemented each other, therefore, in respect to special knowledge, and their similarity of taste and character
enabled them to work harmoniously together. If Leopold
in some sudden fit of passion retired storming and raging to
Anhalt, his keen love of military work soon brought him
back to Berlin. Frederic William was not the less ready
on his part to pardon such insubordination, for he had a
just appreciation of the Dessauer's merits, liked his society, and was probably a little afraid of him. Thus the
two kept up singularly close relations, — too close, indeed,

The Des-
sauer.

[1] See Stenzel, however, iii. 359, on the practical defects of the new
system. The worst of these arose from the failure to specify in the
regulation how many new recruits should be levied each year. Tall
men, too, were excepted even from the exemption accorded to certain
classes. The conscription was expected to furnish half the necessary
number of recruits. Droysen, IV. ii. 17.

for the comfort of other òfficials, who hated the favorite's manner, and dreaded his angry sword.

The most radical measure of Frederic William, and one which, though coming somewhat early in his reign, may nevertheless be treated as the logical conclusion of the military reforms, was the conversion of tenures in chivalry into allodial tenures. The measure was at once military and financial; and it may, therefore, serve as a convenient bridge for the transition from reforms which improved the army to reforms which enriched the treasury.

Abolition of feudal tenures.

The ancient feudal system of military service, though long in a moribund state, still survived in law. Under it every tenant-in-chief of the crown was obliged in time of war to furnish one mounted soldier for each knight's fee that he held ; but while the methods of warfare had long since outgrown that primitive form of service, the institution of scutage had not become general or obligatory, and the nobles were exempt from taxation. The King, therefore, resolved, on the advice of the privy councillor Katsch, an official of the treasury, to relieve the knights of this purely theoretical military burden, and substitute for it a fixed and tangible pecuniary tribute. An arbitrary edict announced the intention of the King to change all feudal into allodial tenures; to renounce, therefore, his own rights of service, aids, wardship, escheat, forfeiture, and the like ; and in return for these sacrifices the knights were required to promise a permanent contribution to the treasury, and were invited to a conference upon the amount, but only the amount, of such contributions. The King demanded, originally, fifty thalers yearly from each knight's fee ; a compromise was finally effected with most of the provinces on a basis of forty thalers. But insubordination was shown in some quarters, especially in Preussen and Magdeburg ; the nobles of the latter province appealed to the Empire ; and

1717.

the support which was accorded them by the imperial tribunals, and at Vienna, was one of Frederic William's grievances against the Emperor.

The reader will naturally contrast this abolition of Bearings of military tenures by the absolute king, Frederic the measure. William, with their abolition by the English Parliament, against the wishes of King Charles II. In the one case the measure was forced by the lord upon the tenants ; in the other, by the tenants upon the lord. The feudal incidents had become onerous in England, and the knights were strong enough to shake them off. In Prussia the same incidents had ceased to be useful to the King, and he replaced them by something more substantial. As regards the constitutional aspect, also, the two reforms are radically opposed to each other. In England the permanent feudal revenues of the crown made it to that extent independent of parliamentary control, and their abolition was, therefore, a victory of the nation over prerogative. But in Prussia the privileges of the knights stood in the way of the King's political and military schemes, and their downfall was a triumph of prerogative over the nation. Yet the nation was probably more directly, and more generally a gainer by the Prussian than by the English legislation. In Prussia the compensation to be given the crown was furnished by the knights themselves, while in England it was put upon the whole country in the shape of an excise, so that in this respect the autocrat was more just and liberal than the Parliament.[1] As another point of difference may be mentioned the fact that the tenures of the Prussian knights were made allodial, while those of their English brethren became tenures in common socage. The theoretical distinction here is

[1] From another point of view the " canon " of forty thalers from each knight's fee in lieu of military service may be regarded as a species of compulsory scutage, like that introduced by Henry II. of England.

important, though the lawyers hold that for practical purposes tenure by socage is as good as allodial tenure. The political bearings of the reform were not, however, to the King the most important. He probably knew no more about allodial tenure than about the Platonic philosophy; but he could see that the old system of knight's service had lost its military value, and was become a mere fiction, while a knight's contribution of forty thalers a year was something which he could touch and count and use. It was, therefore, with him chiefly a fiscal measure, and as such was eminently successful. It yielded about 65,000 thalers a year, — a sum sufficient for the purchase of many grenadiers.[1] Frederic's national militia was at the same time disbanded, and there remained a single uniform system of service for the whole army.

This was, however, only one of many expedients by which Frederic William increased his revenues. The attention which he gave to the crown domains has already been mentioned ; and the re- Increased profits of the domains. sults of his improved methods are shown by a comparison of the first and the last year of his reign. In 1713 the domains brought in 1,800,000 thalers ; in 1738, 3,300,000.[2] And this prosperity gave rise to a change which is characteristic enough to be mentioned. In the preceding reign the palace and the civil service had frequently drawn on the military fund for aid, but now the civil revenues were able to make liberal contributions to the army.[3] Nor is this fact wholly explained by the suspension of the foreign subsidies which Frederic I. had been accustomed to receive, but which were discontinued on the peace of Utrecht. The great increase of the army under Frederic William is also not alone a sufficient explanation. Both

---

[1] Riedel, *Staatshaushalt*, p. 64.

[2] Ibid. p. 61. The precise figures are, for 1713, 1,890,613 thalers; for 1738, 3,300,940. Comp. Droysen, IV. iii. 415, iv. 506–509.

[3] Ibid. pp. 62, 65.

these circumstances must undoubtedly be taken into account; but when full weight is allowed to them, the fact
remains, first, that the profits of the domains greatly increased under a better system; second, that the costs of
the civil establishment were measurably reduced; and
third, that the two kings had widely different notions of
the relative importance of the two branches of the service.[1]

At the same time the military revenues were not neglected. They, too, were gradually raised by
economy, by better administration, and by the
elevation and simplification of existing imposts. The general excise, previously enforced only in the
Mark and Preussen, was extended over all the territories,
except in the new district of Guelders, where vested
rights, secured by the Treaty of Utrecht, made their introduction impossible. The absurd wig tax was abolished
in 1717, but the rate of the excise was raised, and the
stamp duty was made more general. Still, although the
military tributes gradually rose, the rate of progress was
not quite as rapid as in the civil revenues, since the increase during the twenty-seven years of this reign was
only 1,200,000 thalers. The receipts for the fiscal year
1739 were three millions and a half, while the outlays
were a million more. This deficiency was supplied from
the civil fund.[2]

An important change was made in 1722 in the administration of the revenues. This, too, was in the
direction of unity and centralization. It has
been stated that in the very year of his accession the King

*Of the
military
revenues.*

*General
directory.*

---

[1] The system of loans, and that of head-money, or capitation tax
(Kopfsteuer), were also abandoned in this reign. Ranke, iii., iv. 167,
quotes, without refuting, an argument of the King that a large standing army was a blessing, because it consumed the surplus products
of the land. The vicious circle is, however, obvious.

[2] Riedel, *Staatshaushalt*, p. 65. The appropriations for invalids,
hospitals, etc., amounted to half a million more.

tried, with good results, the experiment of uniting the privy purse and the civil list in a single department.[1] But the military fund and the civil service fund were still treated as separate interests, each with its own revenues, officers, and accounts ; and this dual administration was at once costly and illogical. In the course of a decade the King had made so much progress in the art of government that he was able to take a further step forward in the path of simplification, by uniting the war commission and the finance directory in a single board, the general directory of finance, war, and domains.[2]

This was the most important administrative organ in the state. The King announced himself, characteristically, as its president ; and under the president were placed five ministers, as heads of departments, unity and system in action being secured by an elaborate code of instructions, drawn up by Frederic William, and promulgated January 19, 1723. This instrument was ex- humed by Foerster, and published by him for the edification and delight of all Prussian antiquaries.[3]

Members and func- tions.

The five ministers were Grumbkow, Kraut, Kreutz, Görne, and Katsch. The jurisdiction of each of the first four seems to have included both civil and military revenues for certain provinces, while Katsch conducted questions of law and justice from all the provinces. Associated to this ministry was a considerable force of councillors, each group or section having its special sphere of duty; but there was this difference, that while the ministers had a joint responsibility for everything, the councillors were responsible only for matters which belonged to their own jurisdiction.[4] The next lower lines in the scale were the provincial boards, namely, the commissariats for mil-

---

[1] Supra, c. ix. p. 342.
[2] General-Ober-Finanz-Kriegs-und-Domainen-Directorium.
[3] In vol. ii. 173–255.
[4] Art. I. 3 and 4.

itary affairs, and the "chambers" for the domains, which were also consolidated. Lesser officials aided these in the several districts and cities.

The full spirit and scope of the "instruction" is, how-
The in-
struction. ever, less apparent in these general features than in the more minute and detailed regulations which it contains. It was nothing less than a complete code of rules for the government of the administrative service; justice, diplomacy, and the army were alone untouched; and it may therefore properly be regarded as the basis of the Prussian bureaucratic system. It was even, in one sense, considerably more than that. The King made laws; and the directory, which furnished the material for the laws, and often submitted schemes for approval, was accordingly a species of legislature, or at least a legislative council. But the instruction is nevertheless chiefly remarkable as a reform of the civil service, and it is in this light that it deserves the attention of the historian. The administration of the Great Elector had employed many useful men, and recognized some wholesome principles; but it was essentially wanting in system and unity. Frederic I. retained the same men and affected to respect the same principles, and, whether this was from indolence and inertia or from intelligent conviction, little progress was made during his reign. But Frederic William had a masculine sense of order; and in his quaint, coarse, brutal manner built up a machine, which his successors long continued to work to their own and the state's advantage.

Some of the maxims announced in the instruction re-
Its prin-
ciples. veal the stern not to say the stoical integrity of a Roman censor. One of the most infallible criterions of a wise civil service is found in the tests which are imposed upon candidates for office; and while these must always depend in part on the honesty of those who administer them, the chances of dishonesty, or even of honest error, may be greatly lessened by the character of

the tests themselves. It is true that in the scheme devised by Frederic William there was nothing resembling competitive examinations, and even when an appeal was taken, by an unsuccessful candidate, to the King himself, the decision was still an arbitrary and irresponsible one. But the right spirit is shown in the homely language which declares that minor appointees must be the cleverest persons who can be found in the whole length and breadth of the land ; who are true and honest; who have " open heads ; " who understand political economy ; who know something of commerce, manufactures, and such affairs ; who write a good hand ; above all, who are Prussian subjects, — though exceptions were to be made in the case of specially capable foreigners.[1] Similar conditions were applied to the provincial boards. And in respect to these local officials there is a further provision, at once novel and suggestive. It was ordered that when vacancies were to be filled in a provincial council or chamber the ministers should propose candidates to the King, but only from the other provinces, in such a manner that Preussen would be served by Pomeranians, Rhinelanders, Brandenburgers, and not by Prussians; Cleve only by Prussians, Pomeranians and Brandenburgers, and, in short, each province only by natives of other provinces.[2] The object of this rule was evidently to prevent local partiality from warping the administration at any point, and at the same time to break the force of provincial prejudice and jealousy. As such it was profoundly wise, from the King's point of view.

The order of business, both in the directory and the local boards, was defined with the most exact precision, and no excuse was left for delay or disorder ; but these articles, except as they illustrate the King's methodical mind

[1] Art. I. 7.

[2] Art. I. 2. A similar principle was announced in regard to the inspectors of excise. Art. X. 9.

and habits, are not now of importance. And even the King's characteristics are perhaps more graphically shown in the arrangements for securing industry and fidelity.

The directory must meet at seven in the summer and The discipline. eight in the winter, one day being assigned for the affairs of each province; and the session shall continue until every question is settled. If the work is finished in an hour or sooner, the college may adjourn. Otherwise it must sit until two o'clock, or until the dinner hour; and in urgent cases, when an afternoon session is necessary, the King undertakes to give the members a hasty dinner from his own kitchen, economy of time being so scrupulously considered that half the members of the council eat while the other half continue to labor, " in order that our service may be regularly and faithfully conducted."[1] In a special order to Printzen, the grand marshal of the court, the King disposes the details of the official banquet.[2] It is to consist of four courses, one soup, one entrée, one fish, and one roast; and each person shall also have a bottle of wine. Service at the table is to be performed by a single waiter, " in order that the room may not be filled with attendants." The meal is further to be expedited by placing four plates at once before each person, together with a basket in which he can deposit the empty plate after every course! The minister who comes late in the morning is to be fined one hundred ducats; absence without leave from an entire session, except in case of sudden illness, costs the delinquent half a year's salary; and two offences lead to dismissal cum infamia. By such rigorous rules the King held even ministers of state to their duty, "for," said he, "I pay them to work." And in another place the heads of divisions and bureaus are enjoined to learn the capacity and character of their sub-

[1] Art. II. 19.
[2] Foerster, ii. 255, 256. Order dated January 20, 1723.

ordinates, exactly as a captain in the army knows the men of his company.[1]

The colonel of this singular regiment, to continue the military figure, was the King himself; and he was a colonel fully conscious both of his power and of his responsibility. In a great number of places he explains the one and the other with exasperating yet highly characteristic emphasis. Thus the instruction gives an example of the form in which questions are to be submitted for the King's decision. A horse is, perhaps, offered for sale, says his majesty, at one hundred thalers; the directory reports that the beast might be a good bargain at eighty thalers, but no more, and for such and such reasons. In short, continues the royal legislator, "we desire our ministers always to submit with their recommendations the reasons for them, since we remain in the end king and master, and can do what we will."[2] A horse-trade thus illustrates a far-reaching maxim of state. But sometimes the principle is set forth in worthier and more agreeable terms. In the same article his majesty declares, "we will, above all things, have no flattery, but the whole truth shall be told us at all times, without concealment, without evasion; for we are king and master, and can do what we will." There is something rather impressive in the stern candor of this passage, or would be, if it were not known from other evidence that Frederic William was in fact extremely susceptible to flattery and attentions of certain kinds, and was not always tolerant of the truth. The idea of absolute, unconditional supremacy is, however, expressed in terms which leave no room for doubt.

The King's sense of his own royal responsibility is shown by the time and care which he himself devoted to business, and by the liberal yet somewhat arbitrary views

The King's own part.

---

[1] Art. I. 19.
[2] Art. XXXV. 4.

of justice and public spirit which he announced. He imposed no hardship upon his servants which he himself
was not willing to endure. He required his ministers to
His in-   meet at seven o'clock in the morning, but he
dustry.   was also dressed, had breakfasted, and was ready
for work at the same hour. The four courses which he
served the directory from the palace kitchen were his own
daily fare. And no minister, no privy councillor, no secretary even, could apply himself to petty details more pa-
tiently and conscientiously, with less perception of the
ridiculous, than this robust and masculine prince. It is
not wholly an agreeable spectacle, that of the head of a
state, who ought to be engrossed in great affairs, poring
over the accounts of a royal tenant, cutting down the estimates for a new chimney, wrangling over the price of
meat to be cooked for his famished ministers, and avarice
was, perhaps, often as strong a stimulus as zeal. But in
this peculiar system of paternal government it was politic
for the King himself to set an example of industry and
application.

In respect to the other point, Frederic William's regard
for the public welfare, it must be said that this is announced in many parts of the instruction, and doubtless
sincerely. There has never, perhaps, reigned a king who
carried his own personality over so completely into affairs
of state. He was a man of strong convictions, strong
prejudices, strong passions ; and it was beyond his power
to suppress or even conceal them. Yet, aside from the
grenadiers, his one great weakness, he consulted conscientiously, and not always unwisely, the welfare of the state ;
and even in his most arbitrary moods and measures he
kept steadily in view on the one hand the interests, on the
other the capacity, of his people. The directory, says the
instruction, are expected to have a sharp eye for the welfare of our subjects, and to see that they, as well peasants
as burgesses, are not overburdened with taxes.[1] The scu-

---

[1] Art. VII. 1.

tage of the knights must be levied as strictly as the plebeian tributes, without the least consideration for any one,
however exalted. The King's own vehicles shall not be
exempt from visitation for tolls and excise. And finally,
toward the end, in the form of a recapitulation, the instruction protests that in thus establishing the general directory, his majesty " has in view only the welfare of himself and all his faithful subjects," to which end he counts
on the zealous coöperation of the ministers.[1]

By coöperation the King really meant, however, prompt
and slavish obedience. For, although the instruction contains many exhortations to frank and fearless veracity on
the part of the ministers, requests even for suggestions in
regard to details of the instrument itself, there are other
paragraphs in which the officials are informed in unequiv-
ocal terms that discussion of the principles is forbidden,
that they are to be accepted without argument, and that
the slightest infraction of them will be promptly and
sternly punished.

The new directory, being a rough union of many strag-
gling bureaus, divisions, boards, and departments,
had of course a multitude of interests under its
charge; and an enumeration of some of the
Scope of the
directory's
duties.
more important of these will show the range of its activity. It combined, generally speaking, the functions of
the two earlier ministries : domains, and army revenue.
These, again, included a variety of subordinate charges,
each of which has an article, or a chapter, in the instruction. Such are quarters and subsistence for the
troops, the contribution, scutage, excise, tariff and commerce, manufactures, the stamp tax, municipal affairs,
police, lease of the domains, the currency, the post, the
salt monopoly, and many lesser details, some of them
rather trivial, such as the extirpation of wolves, buildings, repair and construction of bridges, and the preven-

[1] Art. XXXV. 6.

26

tion of cattle disease. Careful provision is made for
systematic and correct book-keeping by the chamber of
accounts, an institution founded in 1714. And in the
same spirit of order and method, the King lays down precise rules for the preparation of the annual budgets, rules
which he says " the gentlemen will pronounce impractica-
ble, but we command them to put their heads to the work,
and without any discussion to make them practicable." [1]

Such were the outlines of this characteristic code, — a
code curiously compounded of wisdom and folly, of sound
political principles and grotesque fallacies, of maxims of
the most enlightened justice and outbursts of the most
heartless cruelty, — a code of which every line is marked
by the idiosyncrasies, good or bad, of its author, and
which nevertheless, in its leading provisions, was not ill-
conceived, and in its general purpose and character was
far ahead of the intelligence of the age.

Frederic William was not, however, satisfied merely to
secure a better administration of the existing revenues
and sources of revenue. It was his policy also to stimulate and enrich the industries of the state, to introduce
new branches of manufacture, and thus, by increasing the
productive resources of his people, to increase the receipts
of the public treasury. The instruction announced this
general purpose; but previous measures had already
made a beginning, and later edicts gave the purpose a
more extensive and methodical application.

The basis of this policy was a most shallow and mis-
Mercantile chievous, yet in that age widespread and popu-
system. lar error, the "mercantile system." Roscher
even calls Frederic William the German Colbert; [2] and

[1] Art. XXXII. 28. Die Herren werden sagen: es wäre nicht
möglich, aber sie sollen die Köpfe daran stecken, und befehlen Wir
ihnen hiermit ernstlich, es sonder Raisoniren möglich zu machen.

[2] *Geschichte der National-Œconomie in Deutschland* (Münich, 1874),
p. 360.

it is certain that the fundamental delusion of that great minister was nowhere else more completely and unhesitatingly adopted than in Prussia. During a whole century it and the band of allied fallacies held absolute sway over the minds of philosophers, statesmen, and princes. Pufendorf defended monopolies against current prejudice; Leibnitz called the Spanish-American colonies " the source of wealth." Some of the schemes of the Great Elector for bringing gold into the country and keeping it there have already been described; and Frederic the Great, in spite of his acute intelligence, never wholly shook off the authority of Colbert. But the Great Elector's labors in this field were capricious and unsystematic, and Frederic II. only took up and expanded the policy of his father. In respect to Prussia Frederic William was the undoubted author of the system. The merit, if there be any, of its introduction, on a large scale, and according to a well-defined theory, must be ascribed to him.

The theory was admirably suited to the traditional policy of the Prussian state, and to Frederic Wil- Its fitness liam's own peculiar tastes and capacities. The for Prussia. policy was this : to improve the condition of the people not by lightening their burdens, but by increasing their capacity for bearing the burdens. To reduce taxes was an unknown expedient, even to Frederic William, for the retrenchments which he made, especially at the beginning of his reign, were only in appearance, not in fact, a relief to the subject. He cut down salaries in the civil service, but he created a multitude of new places in the army. He swept away sinecures and pensions, and thus effected vast savings, which were either used immediately in equipping and supporting additional regiments, or were hoarded up for future emergencies. No essential abatement of taxation took place during his whole reign. The tendency was rather toward an increase, either directly or indirectly ; either by actually raising the rate, or by a more rigorous and unsparing enforcement of the existing rate. It is clear, therefore, what Frederic William meant when he expressed, as he so often did, his wish that the taxes might not prove too great a burden to his people. He meant not that the burden, if too heavy, should be lightened, but that means should be devised for increasing the strength of those who had to bear it. Such a remedy would even make it possible for him to realize a larger absolute income without making relatively any higher drafts upon the capacity of the land. This remedy was the mercantile system. To facilitate exports and discourage imports, to stimulate weak industries and found new ones, to increase domestic production, and to convert material articles as swiftly as possible into gold, — such a policy has many apparent and some real merits, and the essential sophism which it conceals was not laid bare until later times.

This system was peculiarly fitted to impress a strong yet rude understanding like Frederic William's. For everything except the tall grenadiers he believed that a country ought to depend on itself alone, ought to yield in sufficient abundance the necessary articles of life, and ought to be assisted to produce even articles which were more complex and not indigenous. If a surplus for exportation could be obtained, that was an advantage or not, according to the nature of the return commodity. To sell native products abroad for money was profitable ; but to exchange them for other products was, in the view of Frederic William, and many wiser men of his time, a false and pernicious policy.[1] It followed, then, that the

[1] Comp. Stenzel, iii. 430. Ranke, *Pr. Gesch.* iii., iv. 163, note, quotes the following from the King's own hand: Vor diesem schickten wir das Geld ausser Landes, und itzo kommt aus anderen Länden Geld im Lande. Manufacturen im Lande ein recht Bergwerk genannt werden kann. Ein Land ohne Manufactur ist ein menschlicher Körper sonder Leben, etc. Comp. Droysen, IV. ii. 19.

chief end of economical legislation was to create and maintain what was called "a favorable balance of trade." But this depends in great part on the amount and variety of home production ; and these may be promoted in two different ways. The one consists in putting discriminating duties and other restrictions on foreign products, or protection proper. The other consists in actively encouraging home production by bounties and other devices. Of these the former is now the favorite method ; but Prussia in the eighteenth century tried both, at the same time, and with the same thoroughness.

The method of protection was not difficult for any absolute prince, and Frederic William could not claim much originality for this part of his performance. The general rule is enunciated in the instruction. "The articles produced in our own land," says the King, "shall pay a reasonable tax, but imported products, such as corn, barley, wheat, hemp, flax, etc., shall be rated so high in the tariff, that our subjects can compete in the market, and their wares be sold always cheaper than foreign wares of the same class." [1] The importation of salt, in which the crown had a royalty or monopoly, was forbidden "on pain of the gallows." [2] In order to control the traffic on the Saale he planned a canal, which should cut off the detour that the stream made in Saxon territory, and throw its whole navigable course within Prussian jurisdiction. The introduction of all foreign woollens was absolutely prohibited by an edict of 1719, and the exclusive use of domestic cloths enjoined, "without distinction of class," on every subject ; and in 1721 the use of East Indian calicoes, linens, and ginghams was forbidden on penalty of one hundred ducats fine and loss of the goods. These are specimens of the measures by which Frederic William attempted to destroy, or at

Protection and prohibition.

[1] Art. XI.; comp., also, Art. XXX. 12.
[2] Art. XXXII. 2.

least control, the import trade into his dominions; they show at once the influence of the age in which he lived, and his own highly arbitrary methods.

It must, however, be said that he rose superior to one delusion, which was extremely powerful at the time. He was a firm disbeliever in the colonial system, in which so many states found a useful ally of their export trade; and after hawking the African station, established by the Great Elector, about Europe for several years, he finally and wisely sold it to a Dutch company for seven thousand guldens.

It was, however, in the other, or positive system of encouraging home industry that the peculiar gifts of Frederic William show to the best advantage. To this cause he brought the same robust though narrow understanding, the same tireless energy, the same imperative will, the same mastery of details, which the army was feeling in every fibre and muscle of its system; if he worked on the military establishment like a drill-sergeant, he cared for the national industry like a household steward. He spared no labor, he let nothing escape his notice. His eye took in the whole range of industrial interests, from the most trivial to the most imposing, from the construction of a village pump to the erection of vast manufactories or the re-peopling of a waste province. The zeal of his officials in the same cause was sharpened by successive edicts, and want of zeal made an unpardonable offence. The relief of some suffering industry, the establishment of some new form of production, the endowment of mills and factories, the importation of skilled foreign artisans, — this class of demands was one of the very few to which the usually close and thrifty King would open his purse; or rather it was one of the few which showed him how to reason from the present to the future, from a temporary outlay to an eventual return, from the loan of money for public improvements to the ample

Measures of positive encouragement.

interest with which in the end the loan would be repaid.
It is true that the ultimate object even of this policy was
to strengthen the army, to obtain larger means for military
ends. But, incidentally at least, it was a general benefit
to the people and the country.

With Frederic William the improvement of the national industries meant, as it means with modern protec-
tionists, first of all, the improvement of the national manufactures. And in a still narrower sense the most important manufacture seemed to be that of woollen fabrics.
Here again, indeed, the prevailing motive was military,
that is, the desire to have the soldiers — the King's " dar-
ling blue children " — clad only in domestic clothes, but
the good effects of such an achievement would not the less
reach every class in society, and also benefit the public
treasury. Hence a series of measures intended to aid this
purpose were taken by the Prussian Colbert.

The introduction of foreign woollens, we have seen, was
absolutely and ruthlessly forbidden. As a nat- The wool
ural corollary to this the exportation of native industry.
wool was likewise prohibited, and with the usual Draco-
nian threat of the gallows in case of infraction.[1] The
same policy had been announced in an edict of the year
1719, an edict provoked by the natural reluctance of the
great landlords to see one of their chief products thus
shut out of foreign markets ; but as compensation to the
temporary sufferers, or as a further part of the general
scheme, the King undertook to create a better home market by the establishment of Prussian factories. The most
important of these was the so-called Lagerhaus, or royal
woollen manufactory.[2] It became a flourishing institution ;
in 1738 is reported as employing nearly five thousand

[1] Instruction, Art. XII. 4. Wer nur einen Stein von einheimischer
Wolle auszuführen sich unterstehet, soll den Galgen verdient haben.

[2] Founded originally in 1713 as a manufactory of cloth for uni-
forms.

men, and producing four thousand pieces of cloth ; and even as having over and above the home consumption a large surplus for exportation to foreign countries, especially Russia.[1] Smaller establishments of the same kind were founded in the various provinces, for the convenience of the neighboring wool-growers, and, as it appears, by a system of partnership between the King and the wealthier nobles, the profits, which were considerable, being divided among the partners, according to their contributed capital. In order to retain in the country the skilled weavers, whom the conscription was driving away in large numbers, its rigor was modified for their benefit. The recruiting officers were warned to treat them with leniency. Support from the privy purse was even promised to such as, having emigrated, would return, and to encourage skilful workmen prizes were offered for the finest productions of the national loom. Nor was this all. The standard of the Prussian goods was raised by obtaining the choicest specimens of foreign manufacture as models, and a body of specially accomplished weavers was imported at considerable expense from Flanders. Protestant exiles from Bohemia and South Germany were also welcomed, not more, perhaps, for their religion's sake than for their technical skill at the loom.

The instruction of 1723 contains explicit and stringent orders to the ministers in respect to the part which they are to have in the application of the mercantile system. They are to take an exact inventory of the annual yield of wool in each province, and the annual consumption in factories; where the consumption does not exhaust the supply new factories are to be established ; and weavers to man them may if necessary be engaged in foreign countries. The King shows how this last-named policy may be worked. The directory hears of a good weaver, invites him to Prussia, buys him a loom, and gives him a German

[1] Foerster, ii. 280.

girl for a wife; the Lagerhaus advances him the wool; and he is thus insured his bread, establishes a family, and soon becomes an independent man. The tenants and peasants are also to be encouraged to spin their own wool, instead of sending it to market in the fleece. Finally, sheep-grazing is commended to the crown tenants and the whole agricultural class.

In this way, slowly and painfully, in spite of much opposition and some failures, but on the whole surely and successfully, the Prussian wool indus- *Apparent success of the policy.* try is built up. The King's indomitable will at length overcomes all obstacles; and he has the satisfaction of looking forward to the time when every farm shall have its flock, every province its factories; when soldier and civilian shall wear nothing but domestic cloths; and when the public manufactories shall yield a handsome surplus for the state.

In some other schemes of a kindred character, such as linen and silk factories, and tobacco warehouses, the King was, however, less successful. These were too great innovations; and they failed to overcome the competition of older and more powerful rivals in neighboring states.

The interests of agriculture were, in the mean time, not neglected, but enjoyed, like manufactures, the zealous, intelligent, though peculiar patronage of *Agriculture.* the King. A long series of edicts and decrees, running through his whole reign, touch upon nearly every subject connected with country life. New mills are to be opened in Brandenburg in order that the peasants may not have to take their grain over into Saxony to be ground. The breed of cattle and horses is to be examined by state inspectors, and the aid of the treasury is promised, when necessary, to measures of improvement. The culture of bees was earnestly recommended. For the purpose of promoting the dairy interest the King caused peasant girls to be sent to Holland to learn how to make butter and cheese, and offered a prize of twenty-four thalers to each one who returned with a good specimen of her work, which dazzling sum, it was thought, would make the possessors attractive candidates for matrimony. The same wise solicitude was shown for the preservation of natural forests, the planting of fruit-trees, the destruction of wolves, the working of peat-beds, the drainage of wet and the irrigation of dry lands, and the recovery of marshes, which were abundant in many parts of the country.

In Preussen especially the widespread desolation left by the plague of 1709 called for the most earnest efforts of the statesman, and it is gratifying to know that Frederic William was sensible of his responsibilities. As crown prince he had been shocked by the flippant indifference with which his father's court beheld the progress of the disease, or rather by the heartless manner in which the treasury met all applications for relief; his hatred of the Wartenberg-Wittgenstein clique is attributed largely to this circumstance. It may, indeed, be a question whether his anger was inspired by the sympathy of the philanthropist, or the cold calculation of a practical economist. But in any event he saw the necessity of a reform, and on his accession at once applied himself to the subject.[1]

State of Preussen.

The first measures were tentative, and were nearly frustrated by one of Frederic William's sudden outbreaks of violence. He had introduced into the province, from 1713 to 1716, small groups of colonists, some going from more prosperous districts of his own land, others being strangers, such as Swiss, Mennonites from Russia, and Protestants from various parts of Catholic Germany; but, owing to ill success and discouragement, or on the expiration of the terms for which special

Its resuscitation.

[1] On the "reëstablishment," as it was called, of Preussen, there is an interesting essay by G. Schmoller in the *Historische Zeitschrift* for 1873, vol. XXX. p. 40 et seq.

exemptions had been accorded them, they frequently deserted their new homes, and fled with their goods over the frontier into Poland. The King tried to arrest the exodus by a ferocious decree, which declared that the fugitives, if caught, should be hanged as thieves and perjurers.[1] This, of course, had the opposite effect to what was intended. None of the traitors returned to be hanged; and other parties, who had been looking toward Preussen, were deterred from accepting such precarious hospitality. The next year, therefore, a new invitation was issued to settlers, and still more liberal terms were offered, extending in some cases as far as complete exemption from all taxes and other public burdens for nine years, with only moderate duties, and those chiefly in the form of service or labor, after that time. Foreign colonists were permitted freely to depart if their new homes proved unsatisfactory. The relations of the native peasants on the royal domains were also meliorated by the abolition of serfdom, or rather its conversion into a scarcely milder form of villenage.[2] Some good effects followed these measures; but they were often crossed by others, contradictory and vindictive, so that the experiment needed further measures to make it successful.

The King's purpose was fortunately aided by a foolish and cruel persecution begun by the Catholic archbishop of Salzburg. The Protestants in that rich and beautiful country were counted by thousands, many of them tracing their faith back to the times of Huss; and though regarded with an evil eye by the dominant clergy, their inoffensive manners, their sober habits, their intelligence, thrift, and industry, and their excellent qualities as citizens, had long secured them immunity from open persecution. But on the election of a certain Baron

Salzburg Protestants.

1 Stenzel, iii. 410.
2 That is, "Leibeigenschaft" was changed into "Erbunterthänigkeit." Edict of March 22, 1719.

Firmian as archbishop, in 1727, this wise policy of toleration was at once changed. The Jesuits were introduced, brutal edicts of conformity were issued, and when the Lutheran peasants appealed to the imperial Diet, the remonstrances of the Protestant princes were treated with contempt and insolence. The most that could be obtained from the oppressor was a vague promise that the Protestants who were unwilling to conform should be permitted freely to emigrate.

But this concession was practically annulled by frivolous charges of sedition brought against all who made preparations to leave; troops manned the frontiers; the prisons were filled with innocent victims. Such an impudent violation not only of the rules of humanity, but even of the plainest provisions of the Treaty of Westphalia, was of course intolerable. The language of the evangelical princes grew more and more emphatic; Frederic William's envoy at the Diet hinted at reprisals on the Prussian Catholics; and even the Emperor was forced to send the archbishop mild protests against his rashness. That prelate responded by a singularly barbarous measure, which converted the permission to emigrate into a decree of exile.

The order, made public on the 11th of November, 1731, forbade the exercise of any religion except the Catholic, and required all dissenters under twelve years of age, unless owners of land, to leave the country within eight days. Peasants were allowed, " out of the archiepiscopal grace," a term of one, two, or three months, according to the value of their property, in which to sell it. Then they, too, must go, or in case of delay be forcibly expelled by soldiers. This cruel edict was enforced in the most heartrending manner. Dragoons scoured the country, armed with lists, treacherously obtained, of the offenders, collected them like cattle in droves, made no distinction of age, sex, or condition, listened to no appeals for mercy, but marched them by thousands, half-dead, penniless, infirm, and sick, to the Bavarian frontier. By a refinement of cruelty the archbishop had taken no steps to procure the consent of the Elector of Bavaria to the passage of the exiles through his territory. The Bavarian officials accordingly stopped them; and for a whole month, in the middle of winter, the suffering fugitives were compelled to await the tardy permission to proceed.

All Europe was aroused by this inhuman measure. Even the iron heart of Frederic William was touched by the hardships of his fellow Protest- ants; and their necessities suggested also, in a more practical sense, a solution of the Prussian problem. He caused it to be announced, therefore, that he was ready to offer them an asylum.[1] He sent agents to meet them, furnished each person a stated daily allowance, and with this encouragement the pilgrims took up their weary journey toward the land of religious freedom. The story of the exodus is one of the most pathetic in the annals of Germany. The genius of Goethe has immortalized it in the poem of Hermann and Dorothea; but more prosaic writers, as well Catholic as Protestant, have naturally furnished the detailed accounts of the sufferings of the exiles, and of the sympathy and relief extended by their Protestant brethren along the route.

In the mean time the peasants, to whom as land-owners the archbishop, by an "act of grace," had granted a slightly longer term in which to prepare for exile, were in nearly as great distress, since the time was wholly insufficient for the sale of their land and effects. For them, too, the King of Prussia interfered. He insisted on the Treaty of Westphalia, which in such cases granted a period of three years for the change; pronounced all intending emigrants to be his subjects; and threatened dire re-

Are invited to Preussen.

---

[1] Edict of February 2, 1722, Stenzel, iii. 426. I have chiefly followed Stenzel, whose account is in vol. iii. pp. 414–430, and Droysen, IV. iii. 152–163. See a Catholic version in Mailáth, iv. 573–575.

prisals in case their rights were violated. Catholic princes in whose breasts humanity was not wholly dead joined their protests to those of their Protestant colleagues, and the archbishop was forced to retract some of his more odious measures.

The end of it all, as regards Prussia, was that great numbers of the Salzburgers, from twelve to fifteen thousand, according to the most authentic reports, were formally colonized in Preussen.

And settled in their new homes.

The peasants were assisted to establish themselves in agricultural pursuits, the artisans settled in the towns. The minister Goerne, to whom the affair had been intrusted, reported frankly that the immigrants were, as a class, far superior to the native Prussians. Many of them had succeeded in saving some part of their capital; and Frederic William's energetic representations caused the archbishop to restore large sums seized in the form of confiscation for pretended offences. It is estimated that the colonists thus obtained some four million guldens, and that the King's own outlays for Preussen were six million thalers. He succeeded in bringing sixty thousand hides of deserted land again under the plow, and in re-peopling fifty-nine royal domains, three hundred and thirty villages, and six cities.[1]

Not satisfied merely to draw, and by various devices to increase the regular revenues, the King also laid his hand on all other moneys which there was a good or bad pretext for seizing. A fund, known as the Rekruten-Kasse, was ready to receive any irregular contribution, without inquiring too closely into its source. Every new incumbent of an office was required to pay into the recruiting fund a certain proportion of his first year's salary in the form of a premium; and as it was soon discovered that the chances of a candidate rose in the ratio of his contribution, the traffic in offices became a regular

Recruiting fund.

[1] Stenzel, iii. 430; Schmoller's essay above mentioned.

system. Appointments were practically put up at auction, and conferred on those who bid the highest. Seniority and even pledges were disregarded. In 1725 the directory asks for a decision between a man who had paid one hundred thalers for a petty office, and received the promise of it, and another who had subsequently offered three times as much; and the King replies, "Give it to the one who offers the most." A widow whose husband had died in office, and left her a large family of children, prays that her son may succeed his father on payment of two hundred thalers; but others offered more, and Frederic William says, "He who promises six hundred thalers or more shall have the place."[1] This was nearly his invariable answer. The Jews were also heavily taxed for the benefit of this fund; they could not marry without first showing a receipt for money paid into the Rekruten-Kasse. And other sums of an even more dubious character — such as hush-money, the price of compromises in civil and criminal suits, arbitrary fines and confiscations — were likewise made available as bounties for desirable soldiers.[2]

Yet Frederic William laid great stress on the pure administration of justice, as well as on the necessity for an honest, efficient, and impartial civil Justice. service. In respect to the latter he took little account of birth, rank, or social standing. He insisted only on capacity and character; and more than once rebuked the pretensions of the nobility to special consideration in the choice of members of the public service. It was the same with regard to justice. The King often did acts of the grossest injustice, but it was rather from impulse and passion than moral callousness; at heart he was a just man, and fully appreciated the importance of an equal administration of the laws. "Bad justice," shouted he once, in an

---

[1] Foerster, i. Urkundenbuch, p. 78.

[2] Comp. Riedel, *Staatshaushalt*, p. 67.

outburst of rhapsodical commonplace, "is an offence which cries to heaven." Hence he seldom interfered with the course of private or civil suits; and though he watched more sharply the progress of criminal cases, his chief solicitude was lest too much leniency should be shown, or useless delays weaken the effect even of severe punishment. The power of pardon was sparingly used. The King believed in capital punishment for capital crimes; and the term "capital crimes" included many acts for which now a short term of imprisonment or a light fine would be considered an adequate penalty. The "gallows" was not a mere empty threat, a mere phrase, by which the King bullied and frightened his subjects into obedience, but an active punishment, provoked by the most trifling misdemeanors, often such as only crossed the King's humor, without being in any sense offences against public morality or public policy.

It has already been shown how the death penalty was made to serve the mercantile system. Deserters lost their heads as a matter of course; but so did citizens who harbored deserters, who, knowing, neglected to reveal their hiding-places, or who failed to join actively in the search for them. Advocates who caused their petitions to be handed to his majesty through tall grenadiers — a common device for securing a favorable hearing — were declared liable to the gallows, and to share the gallows with a dog.[1] Theft by domestic servants was made punishable by hanging the offender, whether man or woman, before the house where the crime was committed; and this sentence was actually enforced in a number of cases.

Capital crimes.

These edicts, though savage and cruel, were at least published before they were put in force,

Arbitrary judgments.

[1] The officials having reported the abuse to the King, and asked for a remedy, his majesty replied by painting on the wall the picture of a lawyer hanging side by side with a dog on a scaffold. This symbolical answer was duly incorporated in an edict. Foerster, ii. 263.

and every man is supposed to know the law. But the King now and then ordered men to the scaffold for acts which were not forbidden by law, or arbitrarily raised the penalty decreed by the courts. A hasty scrawl on the margin of a judge's decision, or of an officer's complaint, might cost a poor wretch his head. Thus a poacher was commanded by the court to the ordeal by oath or torture. The King ordered him to hang. A Jew suspected of theft protested his innocence even on the rack; the King said he would take the responsibility for the wretch, and sent him to the gallows. A poor quartermaster in the army was convicted of defalcation, and although his bond covered the deficit, which he offered to make good, his majesty wrote, " I forgive the debt, but let him be hanged." [1]

From such judgments there was no appeal. Even delay was dangerous, and, as the King's handwriting was nearly illegible, the most unfortunate mistakes occurred. A tax-receiver was once hanged for some apparent irregularity in his accounts, but a second revision of his books, after his death, showed that the first suspicion had been unjust. General Glasenapp, the commandant of Berlin, reported to the King, at Potsdam, that a party of masons had made riotous demonstrations on being compelled to work on a holiday, and his majesty scribbled a reply which the general read as an order " to hang Raedel at once without waiting for me." The commandant was in great perplexity. The order was peremptory, but none of the rioters was known as Raedel, and the only person of the name was a lieutenant of the garrison. The innocent officer was, however, arrested, the order read to him, and a clergyman summoned to prepare him for the scaffold. Fortunately, before the sentence was carried out the order was submitted to an official more familiar with Frederic William's hieroglyphics; and he deciphered them in a different way. The order was " to hang the ringleader."

[1] Foerster, i. Urkundenbuch, p. 51.

27

Even this was difficult, but the general finally selected a bricklayer who had red hair, red being notoriously a seditious color.[1] A mild judgment the King abhorred rather more fiercely than a corrupt or unjust one. But an unjust judgment was sometimes rebuked ; and on one occasion, when the sentence failed to meet his ideas of propriety, his majesty summoned the whole bench of judges to his room, and assaulted them furiously with his cane, knocking teeth out of one, and sending them all flying down the stairway.

It was with Frederic William a rule of conscience never to pardon or commute the death penalty for murder. As murderers he wisely reckoned men who killed their antagonists in duel ; and he issued stringent edicts against " affairs of honor," even between officers, while in their cases the modern military jurisprudence of Prussia looks on duelling with indifference, or even to a certain extent positively encourages it. Suicides were denied Christian burial. Theft and fraud of every kind were peculiarly obnoxious to the King's sense of integrity, and were cruelly punished. Poachers on the royal preserves were summarily hanged.[2] Bankruptcy was a crime, whether fraudulent or not ; and the crown officials were to proceed against an insolvent debtor without any complaint from the creditors, and even if the creditors interceded in his behalf. The laws against witchcraft still disgraced the statute-book. That the rack had not been abolished is shown by incidents already related, and the most that Frederic William attempted was to restrain the brutality of the officials who were charged with its application.

Severity of criminal justice.

[1] The blunder is only explicable in German. What the King wrote was " Du musst den Raedelsführer hängen lassen ehe ich komme," but the general read " Du musst den Raedel früher hängen lassen," etc.

[2] A comparison with chapter viii. will show how Frederic William sharpened the already severe penal legislation of his father.

The general spirit of penal justice during this reign was thus sanguinary in the extreme. The King not only accepted fully the prevailing theory that the efficacy of laws against crime depended on their severity, but he was also by nature hard, cruel, implacable, vindictive; suffered no mitigating circumstances to interrupt the fulfilment of a sentence; and probably took a sombre delight in asserting his power even at the cost of human life. Yet it does not appear that this severity served its object, for crimes were frequent, and the criminal class was large.

It was inevitable that Frederic William's love for order and system should lead to attempts to simplify both the law and the administration of the law. *Legal reforms.* The very year of his accession he ordered the official jurists to prepare a uniform code for all the provinces which had a mixed system of law, that is, part Roman, part Saxon, part customary; but nothing, or very little, seems to have come of this. A number of special codes were, however, drawn up and promulgated. Such were, for example, the penal code of 1717;[1] the mortgage and bankrupt act of 1722; and various edicts regulating judicial procedure, the qualifications of judges, and the inspection of the courts. The organization of the chamber was also improved; and its methods of business, which under the influence of the previous reign had become slovenly and negligent, were made more regular and expeditious.[2]

Justice was one of three interests, foreign affairs and finance being the others, to which full ministers of state were assigned.[3] There was, furthermore, a judicial committee of the privy council, to *Judicial organization.* which was, however, denied the right of hearing appeals;[4]

[1] Comp. Roenne, *Staatsrecht*, ii., under the title, "Die Strafrechtspflege."

[2] The judges in the chamber were already distinguished as "adlige" and "gelehrte," or lay and professional.

[3] Droysen, IV. ii. 23.

[4] Cosmar and Klaproth, *Der Geheime Staatsrath*, p. 197.

a body of jurists in each province, called the Regierung, or government, and charged to watch over the crown's interests in litigation; and lawyers assigned to the provincial boards of finance to give advice on points of law.

The King did not like the gentlemen of the gown. To a man of his blunt and straightforward nature the arts of the lawyer seemed low chicanery; and he charged the conflicts and obstructions, which before 1723 were frequent in the civil service, in great part to the tricks of meddlesome attorneys. If a worthless ignoramus had claims for an appointment the King would assign him with contempt to the legal service. The new system, he says in the instruction, will "put an end to litigation between the rival boards, and those poor devils, the jurists, will become as useless as the fifth wheel in a wagon." [1] To hang an advocate in company of a dog was not exactly to express a high opinion of his worth; and there are many other recorded proofs of his majesty's hatred of lawyers as a class and of their profession. It must be said, however, that there was at the time much to warrant this sentiment. The quality of the lawyers, like the administration of the law, had greatly depreciated during the reign of Frederic I.; and the son found the bar not only destitute of respectable jurists, but even in full possession of a race of ignorant, corrupt, and unscrupulous pettifoggers. [2]

A semi-judicial body which had the most dangerous powers, and enjoyed great popular opprobrium, was the Fiscalate. Its duties, so far as they were publicly defined, were to organize and conduct a complete system of espionage upon all classes of public servants, to scent out delinquencies and report them to the King, and even to administer itself a sort of star chamber justice. It happened, too, or rather was inevitable, that the in-

The King and the lawyers.

The Fiscalate.

---

[1] Instruction, Art. XXVI. 2.
[2] Comp. Foerster, ii. 262, 263; Droysen, IV. ii. 11.

stitution, already odious on account of its functions, fell into the hands of tyrannical and unscrupulous men, and through them was made an instrument not of justice, but of terrorism and oppression.

Among the leading jurists whom Frederic William put in ministerial positions were Katsch, Plotho, Marshall, and Cocceji,[1] the latter being also president of the chamber. The two last named were also trusted servants in the next reign ; and Cocceji especially made himself deservedly famous by his share in the great legal reforms of Frederic II.

The foregoing pages will already have explained under finance or justice many functions, which, in a system where more respect was paid to the division of labor, would belong properly under civil administration in the narrower sense. Out of the extremely complicated machinery which was set up it is often difficult to select the leading motives of power and methods of action.

The King's service.

The main circumstance to be kept in view is that the system was thoroughly collegiate ; that boards instead of individuals did the work, and bore the responsibility. Of these boards the first in dignity and importance was the privy council. But as this body stood nearest the King, it was the one in which he first perceived the wisdom of concentrating functions in the hands of a few men, with individual responsibility. There was formed, accordingly, within the council, or rather out of its members, much as in England, a smaller body, known as the cabinet. These officials were called councillors of state. Their number seems to have been variable ; in 1724 five appear in the budget.[2] The

Its collegiate organization.

---

[1] Originally written Coccejus. But after the family was ennobled, and acquired the particle "von," it put itself in the genitive, and wrote Cocceji.

[2] Comp. Foerster, i. 179. The five were Dohna, Ilgen, Metternich, Plotho, and Knyphausen. But their functions are not described, and there is no uniformity in their salaries.

cabinet had nominally the general supervision under the King of the three interests, foreign affairs, finance, and justice. In immediate daily intercourse with the King stood as the representatives of the cabinet two cabinet councillors.

The departments of justice and finance had, of course, their subordinates throughout the country. The administration of justice was in the hands of boards, the " Regierungen " or governments on the one hand, and the courts on the other. Next under the minister of finance or under the King himself, if there were no minister of finance, came the general directory, which, as has been stated, undertook many of the charges of civil administration. Below the directory stood the provincial chambers for war and domains,[1] and these again were served by war councillors,[2] who administered the excise, as well as police and many civil functions in the cities, and the landraths[3] who in the same manner superintended affairs in the rural districts.

Hierarchical descent.

It would necessarily result from the singular position of the war councillors in the cities that they would be in a constant state of conflict with the magistrates. The disputes were, however, chiefly over the question of quarters for the troops.[4] The magistrates and councils, at least in the smaller cities, were now practically reduced to the purely local duty of keeping the streets paved, cleaned, and lighted; of maintaining schools and churches; and managing other petty municipal interests. Their place in the general system was filled by the agents of the crown.

But the landraths of the counties were at once royal officials and local representatives, a fact which must be ascribed to the circumstance that the

The land-rath.

----

[1] Kriegs-und Domainen-Kammern.

[2] Kriegsräthe.

[3] Landräthe. Comp. Stenzel, iii. 342.

[4] See Foerster, ii. 283 et seq., for some illustrations.

landed gentry had more successfully resisted the process of centralization. Both the title and the office had, however, undergone strange vicissitudes.

In the early part of the seventeenth century the landraths seem to have been deputies sent by the local estates, in the recesses of the Diet, to advise the margrave in political affairs, while in their respective counties they were coördinate to the crown commissioners. The former had charge of police and justice; the latter called out the levies, and collected the public taxes. In the course of the Thirty Years' War the two offices were merged into one — the war commissioners already described. These were nominated by the estates and confirmed by the elector. But in 1701 the commissioners of the Mark petitioned for the restoration of the more euphonious title of landrath, and the petition was granted.[1] The oath then taken gives a reasonably clear idea of their duties.[2] Although the local gentry continued to have influence in the selection of the landrath, who was generally one of their own number, the officer himself gradually lost his character as the organ and defender of self-government, and under Frederic William became a direct servant of the crown. His duties thenceforth may be summed up as police, taxes, levying, quartering, and provisioning troops, and the care of the local interests of the county.[3]

Educational and ecclesiastical interests had no separate representative in the cabinet, and did not in fact acquire one until the early part of the present century. They received shelter as a rule in the department of justice. But special bureaus conducted details, and the provinces had each a consistory, where local

Educational and ecclesiastical administration.

---

[1] Isaacsohn, ii. 312–319.

[2] Ibid. p. 317. Comp. also Mascher, *Das Institut der Landräthe in Preussen* (Berlin, 1868), p. 4.

[3] See the title, "Die Kreislandräthe," in Roenne's *Staatsrecht;* Isaacsohn, ii. 318.

theologians found their field of battle, both for church and for school affairs. The president of each consistory was also its executive officer; and he was aided by inspectors whose duty it was to visit parishes and schools, and report on their condition.[1] In each commune, rural or municipal, the civil authorities were required to provide churches for public worship, and schools for elementary instruction. This authority was, in the immediate cities, the magistrates and councils; on the domains, the crown bailiffs; and in manorial communes, the lord himself. But each parish, at least each free parish, had in the local "presbytery" a body which was charged with something like a moral censorship, and through the consistory could report grievances to the central organ at Berlin. By it everything of importance was referred to the King.

In closing this sketch of Frederic William's legislation one remark ought to be made by way of anticipating criticisms which will naturally occur to the reader. It will perhaps be objected that the system as described does not justify the praise usually accorded to its author. It will be said that the collegiate organization tended to obscure the point of responsibility; that the machinery was intricate, cumbrous, slow; and that its defects were shown by the later modifications which it suffered. This is true, but it is not the whole truth. It is by comparing his achievements with his opportunities that the merit of a statesman must be determined; and while a despot has facilities which are denied to the head of a limited monarchy, these facilities are not the same in all despotisms. A legislator coming like the first Napoleon after a revolution, which has overthrown all the ancient bases of social, legal, and political order, can use his materials with a high, and often a very useful degree of discretion. He can reconstruct, and even recreate, with very little regard to precedent and prejudice. But this

Defects in the system explained.

---

[1] Stenzel, iii. 406.

was not the position of Frederic William. Although his views of the prerogative were sweeping, not to say revolutionary, although organized checks and formulated restraints hardly existed, although some of his measures were extremely radical in manner and purpose, there were nevertheless many and formidable limitations upon his freedom of action during the whole course of his reign. One of them was that inherited respect for the past, which was not wanting even to him, and which forbade him to depart too widely from existing models. Another was the force of local preference, which it was inexpedient wholly to disregard, and the variety of local customs which it was impossible in the space of one life to reduce to a common standard. A third obstacle, finally, is to be found in the nature of the King's own peculiar gifts.

He had neither been granted originally by nature, nor encouraged by his education to acquire the capacity for a broad, comprehensive, and systematic view of political institutions. He was essentially a man of details. His measures, instead of conforming to an elaborate scheme, carefully and logically framed in his mind, were fragmentary, tentative, contradictory; were modified and superseded; gave to his policy a character of vacillation; and left his work at his death unfinished and imperfect. Yet the frequent changes which he made in his legislation show, also, that he possessed one of the very highest qualities of a statesman, the willingness to learn from experience. Even the directory itself was in great part a reorganization of existing materials and systems, which had been found by trial to need amendment. The same holds true of many of his other reforms, provincial and national. He proceeded cautiously, felt his way as he proceeded, and often retraced his steps when he found himself in the wrong path. He was sure of his general goal, but the way to the goal was in the nature of things to be learned only by slow, frequent, and patient trials. It is for the fidelity with which he pursued this task, and not for the possession of a penetrating and comprehensive genius, that he deserves to be ranked among the great legislators of the world.

Between the different social orders Frederic William held the balance impartially, and assailed one or another only when its pretensions came into conflict with those of the crown. In a vague way he assured them from time to time that he had no desire to abridge their fundamental rights. But charters and franchises, written or unwritten laws, were little security against a ruler who was a despot alike by inheritance and by nature; who was an active man of affairs, and had sweeping reforms to accomplish. Hence town, and knight, and peasant, and priest felt alike the pressure of his heavy hand.

King and people.

In the cities it has already been shown that the police, with all which that term implies, was administered by the military authorities;[1] the burgomasters were mere creatures of the crown; the councils had little real authority. Taxes were levied, garrisons were introduced, municipal ordinances were changed or revoked by the arbitrary act of the King. If a grievance was redressed the royal grace alone received the credit; for the towns, though sometimes querulous and even turbulent, had lost their original sense of municipal dignity, and the art of effective resistance. Each sought to make the best possible terms with a wilful and impatient master.[2]

The towns.

But the King was not more tolerant of aristocratic opposition. The summary manner in which he swept away the tenures in chivalry, in spite of their venerable character, in spite of the protests of the knights, has already been described. For the privileges

The nobles.

---

[1] See the Instruction of 1723, Art. XVI.

[2] Comp. Stenzel, iii. 281 et seq.

of birth he had a healthy contempt, which he often expressed, not always in the choicest, yet sometimes in quaintly effective terms. An official at Cleve, belonging to the older nobility, complained that one Pabst, a colleague of plebeian extraction, took a place above him in church, "which presumption he held to be prejudicial to his majesty's highest interests." But Frederic William, with a curious mixture of sense and platitude, pronounced the complaint folly. "In Berlin there is no rank," said he; "in Cleve there must also be none. If Pabst sits above me in church I remain still what I am."[1] Thus this stern iconoclast denied the nobles both the power which comes from a favored system of land tenure, and the power which comes from superior birth. As rich and influential country gentlemen they necessarily continued to enjoy a certain consideration, but not as a political estate.

It might now be expected that the King, having crushed the two upper classes, the nobles and the bur- The peasgesses, would find it expedient to attach at least ants. the peasants firmly to his cause and person. But he was strong enough to neglect even this precaution. He took, indeed, a keen interest in the material condition of the peasantry; and by various edicts secured them against extortion and oppression, even from officials who were in his own employ, and who excused their tyranny by the plea of zeal for his service.[2] Yet little was done to improve their social state or their agrarian relations. The slight reforms in the province of Preussen were required by exceptional circumstances. Elsewhere the servitude of the peasants — not uniform indeed, throughout the country, but cruel and oppressive in all its phases — was sanctioned in the general confirmation of the charter of 1653, and by many edicts issued to meet special cases or emer-

[1] Foerster, i. Urkundenbuch, p. 74.
[2] See Foerster, ii. 273-275.

gencies.[1] Wanton mistreatment of this helpless class the King sharply forbade. But as it was part of his mission to establish respect for authority, and as he tolerated no disobedience of his own orders, he was bound in consistency to require of every man who owed any service or any subjection to another, through all the grades of society, to fulfil the obligation promptly, efficiently, and uncomplainingly.

The clergy in this reign, though a powerful social class, were in politics the servile defenders of prerogative, and could not be counted on for any effectual resistance to tyranny. They had scriptural texts, and unctuous moral phrases for the most arbitrary measures.

The clergy.

In passing to the estates as a body or corporation it is necessary to call attention to an important distinction. The truth does not hold good in politics, as in mathematics, that the whole is just equal to the sum of the parts; it is sometimes more, sometimes less. It is more when the union of different elements, individually weak, gives to each a new confidence, and to the whole a strength much beyond a mere addition of the separate forces. Such was, for instance, the effect of the admission of the boroughs to the English Parliament. It is, on the other hand, less when the previous rivalry of classes or elements is embittered instead of allayed by an attempted fusion or consolidation. Brandenburg furnishes an example of this kind. When harmony prevailed the estates were irresistible; but from the middle of the seventeenth century downward discord was more frequent than harmony, and of this circumstance the electors took advantage. From the time of the Great Elector

The estates.

---

[1] Such for instance as the "Gesinde-und Bauern-Ordnung" of 1722. It even permitted the transfer from one landlord to another of peasants who were serfs, i. e. Leibeigen. They were such in Pomerania and in the Uckermark, but not in the rest of the Electorate, in Cleve, or Magdeburg.

the separate estates had hated one another more bitterly than they hated the common foe, the crown. Frederic William I. had, therefore, practically to deal only with the several orders, not with a united Diet. The opposition which any order offered was all that remained of the former vigorous and formidable parliamentary opposition ; for although he nominally confirmed the "recess" of 1653, which acknowledged the right of the united Diet to at least a consultative voice, no such Diet was summoned, as none had been summoned, since that memorable year.

Under Frederic William the only collective insubordination was shown by the knights, yet even this was provincial, not national. In Magdeburg it took the form of a protest against the transformation of the tenures ; in the Electorate it was aroused by the prohibition against the exportation of wool ; in Preussen the grievance was the introduction of a uniform landtax. Yet in each case the King carried his point, and in Preussen the resistance called forth one of his most characteristic utterances. A leader of the local nobility sent in a remonstrance against the measure, declaring in French that if it were introduced "the whole country would be ruined." Frederic William mockingly replied, in an extraordinary jargon, composed of Latin, French, German, and Polish, "The whole country will be ruined ! I believe nothing of the kind ; I only believe that the authority of the junkers will be ruined, for I intend to make the prerogative as solid as a block of bronze." [1] This

The decree of absolutism.

---

[1] " Tout le pays sera ruiné. Nihil Kredo, aber das Kredo, dass die Junkers ihre Autorität nie pos volam wird ruinert werden. Ich stabilire die Souveraineté wie einen Rocher von Bronce." Marginal by the King, January 31, 1717 ; in Foerster, i. Urkundenbuch, p. 50. But see Droysen, IV. ii. 198, n., for a slightly different version, and especially a worse orthography. Droysen prints, " Curios. Tout le pais cera Ruine. Nihil Kredo. Aber das Kredo, das der Junker ihr ottoritet niposwollam," etc., etc. The " Nie pos volam " was intended to be the " Nie pozwalam," by which in the Polish Diet a single no-

declaration expresses clearly and tersely the whole aim of
the King's constitutional policy.

Nor did it remain a mere declaration ; it was realized
in practice as fully as even Frederic William
could desire. He sometimes consulted the wishes,
and always affected to consult the interests, of the different classes ; now and then a scheme was modified in deference to advice and protests; but the ultimate right of decision was asserted, and successfully asserted, in every
case. A more complete despotism was not to be found in
Europe.

The foregoing description may, and may not, probably
indeed not, have given the reader an intelligible
view of the system of government which Frederic William slowly and painfully organized. Yet a
writer is entitled to say in his own defence that the obscurity in the presentation of the system is in no small part
due to the system itself. It was strictly peculiar to Prussia. It cannot be painted in the colors of modern political science, nor in those which were used at the time in
other countries. It can in fact be understood, if at all,
only by keeping in mind the circumstance that at its head
stood a single man, who not only had the power, but the
will, and not only the will, but also the intelligence, to
direct its daily operation, and to supply from his own resources any defect in its details. A skilfully organized
and well administered despotism is the phrase by which it
must be designated.

It was, moreover, not one of those despotisms which iso-
late themselves at the summit of the political
scale and are content merely to vindicate their
authority in the last resort, but it descended to the very

Its execution.

Personal government.

Conclusion.

ble exercised the liberum veto. The term Junker, it can scarcely be
necessary to explain, designates a narrow, obstinate, pretentious
country squire, and Junkerthum may be rendered by the English
" squirearchy."

units of the system, and made itself felt directly, positively, and efficaciously throughout the whole range of public affairs. A tide-waiter on the Baltic was as much under the King's eye as a minister of state, or a general of the army, at Berlin. A new lock could not be put on a treasury safe, or a pane of glass set in a palace window, without the King's consent. He looked upon himself as the owner of a vast property, over which he had absolute control, but which he was bound to administer as a trust in a frugal, careful, and conscientious manner, and turn over unimpaired to his successor. In this respect, therefore, the absolutism founded by Frederic William deserves to be honorably distinguished from contemporary systems in other countries. His personal faults, not less than the extreme rigor of the system itself, made it indeed odious ; it was an object of horror to all liberal and high-spirited men ; Winkelmann, the historian of ancient art, and a native of the Old Mark, fled in despair to Dresden, whence he wrote that it was the most degrading despotism which the world had ever seen ; that it was " better to be an eunuch in a Turkish harem than a Prussian subject." Yet as a machine it was wonderfully adapted to its purpose ; and much that there was of good in the later civil service of Prussia — its honesty, discipline, and efficiency, its unobtrusive devotion and noiseless regularity — must be ascribed to Frederic William the First.

CHAPTER XI.

SOCIAL AND DOMESTIC RELATIONS UNDER THE SECOND KING.

IT is a reasonable rule of the literary art, that the historian of a state shall not stray too far from the broad path, along which the great interests of a people advance or retreat, in order to pursue the career or paint the features of individuals. This rule is not indeed, in the case of Prussia, specially irksome, nor are the temptations to violate it frequent. The early annals of the state are rarely biographical; and the bureaucratic system, which grew up on the downfall of the Diet, was singularly fitted to discourage talent, repress individuality, and reduce all persons to one dull, uniform, mechanical level. But if the members of the public service were only parts of a living machine, the head of the service, the engineer of the machine, had a broad and uncontested field for the exercise of his powers, and the display of his characteristics. Some of the princes, too, who have held this position — one at least of the electors, and two at least of the kings — were men of marked individuality, were pleasingly or odiously picturesque, and have, therefore, a power of fascination, against which the historian must be constantly on his guard.

This is peculiarly true of Frederic William the First. The King in biography. In writing of his reign, it is always difficult, and sometimes impossible, to separate history from biography; to describe the leading events which clearly influenced the fortunes of the state, without including many details, which a stern criticism might say concerned only the King himself. His strong, angular, aggressive personality forces itself upon the most unwilling writer. Even his moral hideousness — a compound of low cunning, coarse animal tastes, and brutal ferocity — was in its way unique and unparalleled; while his undoubted talents are scarcely less striking to the artistic eye. It has already been shown, too, that Frederic William's eccentricities were not reserved for the domestic circle, but penetrated into, and influenced every political measure of his reign. The history of his administration must, therefore, include a somewhat fuller account of his character, personal habits, and family life, than would be necessary, or even proper, if he had been a man of less emphatic individuality, or if his individuality had forced itself less persistently into the current affairs of state.

Frederic William was not one of those despots who, though severe in their official relations, are tender and affectionate in the domestic circle. His faults became rather more pronounced and more odious in the presence of his family. He was a tyrant as king; but as a father he was both a tyrant and a brute, a savage and unfeeling brute, without the deeper abiding emotions of paternal love.

A domestic tyrant.

It is probably true that his wife, Sophie Dorothea, was not, like some of her children, an object of original and unbroken aversion. For one thing, as she was a large, stately, and handsome woman, the King may have been impressed at times even by her presence, and have respected her in spite of himself; while in his earlier years, before disease and disappointment had completed his ruin, he frequently showed her a coarse, clumsy, bearish kind of affection. There is no evidence that the King's marriage vow was not religiously kept. He boasted, indeed, of his constancy; and such a boast, if supported by facts, implied, to an extent which it is now

The Queen.

28

difficult to conceive, power of self-restraint, victory over temptations, and even, owing to the spirit of the times, a considerable degree of moral courage.

The Queen's life was, nevertheless, a hard and cruel one.

Her trials. If her husband observed one of the proprieties of life, he daily violated all the rest; and gloried not less in his many social crimes than in his single social virtue. He had hardly a taste, a recreation, a passion with which the Queen could sympathize, while the interests which she tried to cultivate were quite as foreign to him. But the relation was still not quite the same as that between the equally unsympathetic pair who preceded them on the throne. Sophie Dorothea abhorred the King's parades, his wild-boar hunts, his nightly orgies with Grumbkow and others, and was only anxious to escape in peace from the tumult, and cruelty, and drunkenness. But Frederic William was not equally tolerant of her matronly and decorous pleasures. What he disliked, he also suppressed; and the Queen saw herself, in the end, compelled to abandon her attempts to cultivate literature and art, to give a softer tone to some phases of court life, and even to assert by her own fireside the authority of the domestic graces.[1]

It was probably, however, not as a wife, neglected and mistreated by her husband, but as a mother, daily witnessing the torture of her children, that the Queen's keenest sufferings were felt.

She bore the King no fewer than fourteen children, — of whom four died in childhood. The oldest of those who survived, and second in order of birth, was Wilhelmina. The third child died like the first, in the cradle, and then came Frederic, born the 24th of January, 1712, two and one half years after Wilhelmina. The other children who reached mature years were Louisa, who married the Margrave of Anspach; Charlotte, who

The royal children.

[1] Comp. Ranke, iii., iv. 242.

became Duchess of Brunswick; Maria, Margravine of
Schwedt; Ulrica, afterwards Queen of Sweden; August
William, founder of the cadet line which continued the
succession after Frederic II.; Amelia, later abbess of
Quedlinburg; Henry, the favorite brother of Frederic;
and August Ferdinand, father of the Louis Ferdinand who
fell in the campaign of 1806 against Napoleon. These all
probably carried with them to the grave the marks of
their father's ready cane, though some of the later ones
were more pliant to the King's moods, and learned to
avoid his worst displays.[1]

Wilhelmina, as the oldest child, was the earliest object
of his peculiar treatment. She herself naively
records, and of course from personal experience, *Wilhelmina.*
the ungracious reception which, on account of her sex,
she suffered at her birth, yet the subsequent arrival of a
prince failed to appease the exacting father, and brought
little mitigation of her own lot. But in the young Frederic she had a devoted brother and a sympathetic companion. The strong affection which bound these two together, not only while they were common victims of their
father's brutality, and were forced as it were into a league
for self-defence, or at least mutual consolation, but also
after the enemy had disappeared, and life began to widen
out before them both, is one of the few sunny and genial
rays which stream across the annals of the time.

The well-known Memoirs of Wilhelmina are a vast store-
house of information on the period which they *Her*
cover.[2] The trustworthiness of this sprightly *Memoirs.*

[1] Preuss, *Friedrich der Grosse* (Berlin, 1832), i. 31. He mentions
August Wilhelm and Ulrica as being specially favored.

[2] *Mémoires de Frédérique Sophie Wilhelmine de Prusse, Margrave
de Bareith* (Brunswick, Paris, and London, 1812. 2 vols. 8vo.).
This is commonly called *Mémoires de Bayreuth.* I have used the English version, also in two volumes (London, 1812). The translation
well preserves the spirit and vivacity of the original, but is careless,
and makes wretched work with German proper names.

and malicious work has indeed often been questioned; it contains internal evidence of exaggeration, though not of deliberate mendacity. Carlyle humorously proposed to deduct twenty-five and sometimes seventy-five per cent. of it as false.[1] For an estimate this may serve as well as another; but if a distinction is to be attempted, it would probably be safe to assume that the later part, where Wilhelmina describes what occurred after she reached years of discretion and could see with her own eyes, is more likely to be accurate than the earlier part, which treats of the period of her childhood, and largely repeats only the complaints of her mother, the tattle of nurses, and the gossip of waiting-maids. Her remorseless candor may create a presumption for or against her truthfulness. Stenzel seems to think that filial respect would have led Wilhelmina to understate rather than overstate the case against her father; but another view is that, instead of feeling restraints of such a kind, she really suffered her loathing for her father to carry her to the extreme of injustice. No one can say positively where, as between these two theories, the truth lies. It is, however, not at all hazardous to use the memoirs as contemporary evidence, and evidence furnished by one who had unusual facilities for learning, often, indeed, through the most cruel personal experience, the state of things which they describe.

The Mémoires de Brandebourg of Frederic II. contain little that was not already known, and are written throughout in a tone of reserve which is in singular contrast to his sister's reckless loquacity. But in his private correspondence the anguish of a sufferer sometimes breaks through the restraints of filial decorum.

---

[1] i. 293. See also Ranke, *Pr. Gesch.* iii., iv. 96. Droysen, IV. iv. 33–96, has a searching examination of the Memoirs, and reaches the conclusion that as an authority for political events they are absolutely untrustworthy. But it is Droysen's habit to accept no statement which cannot be officially verified from the archives.

In Frederic's early education two rival elements made themselves felt, though not in the same way or with equal success. Stout, pompous, brave German officers received the titles of governor and sub-governor, were responsible for the prince's general conduct, and tried to interest him in grenadiers; [1] but Madame de Roucoulles his governess, and Duhan his tutor, both French, were the real powers, the former by reason of her fine womanly qualities, the latter through his intelligence, energy, and sympathetic tact. Duhan gave Frederic's studies an exclusively French turn, and did perhaps more than any other person to form his mind and literary tastes.

Crown prince Frederic.

The diligent labor of antiquaries has exhumed two "instructions" — one of 1718, one of 1721 — which the King issued to the governors and teachers of his son. Both are interesting, alike as literature, as schemes of discipline, and as systems of education. It is impossible here, however, to do more than briefly summarize their contents.

The order of daily life required the prince to arise at six, to study until eleven, to be with his father until two, then to resume his studies until five, and to enjoy the remainder of his time in his own way, until the arrival of the hour for retiring. His studies included nearly everything except Latin. The true Christian religion was to be taught, and the errors of atheism, Arianism, Socinianism, and Catholicism exposed. French and German were to be pursued in order that the prince might learn to write a good style in either. The instructor, it will be remembered, was Duhan, and Frederic spoke and wrote German like a Frenchman to the last day of his life. Of history there was a fair allowance,

His education.

[1] General Finkenstein as governor, Colonel Kalkstein as sub-governor. See Wilhelmina, *Memoirs*, i. 47, for the influences which controlled these appointments.

especially of the history of Brandenburg and allied states,
care being wisely enjoined that their extent, population,
and resources should be thoroughly mastered. But Latin
was absolutely prohibited. An instructor who was caught
expounding the Latin text of the Golden Bull of the Emperor Charles IV. was nearly brained on the spot by the
indignant father.[1]

This does not appear on the surface to be a very severe
course of discipline; it may even excite surprise at the
King's mildness. The trying time was, however, the
three hours which, according to the schedule, the prince
was to spend with the author of the "instructions." This
was not, as might be supposed, a respite from labor, and
a term of pleasant intercourse with an affectionate father,
but a trying ordeal, which was awaited each day with the
gravest apprehensions. It was the interval during which
the prince was more than likely to be abused by the
King's brutal tongue, and beaten with his heavy cane.

Frederic William was apparently cruel by nature, as
well as by impulse. He took delight in the suf-

The King's
cruelty.
ferings even of his own kindred; and sought,
rather than avoided, provocation for showing his perfect
heartlessness, his contempt for the amiable virtues of his
race, his systematic inhumanity. He threw plates at his
children's heads, or chased them out of the room with his
crutch, when such demonstrations were neither required
by any offence that had been committed, nor excused by
the defects of an infirm temper. They too often seemed
parts of a deliberate system of domestic tyranny.[2]

Of this system Frederic, the crown prince, was the
favorite victim. Wilhelmina, whose sympathy with her

---

[1] The first "instruction" is in Preuss, i. 24; the second, in Preuss, i.
19–21; Foerster, i. 356 et seq. But Ranke, *Pr. Gesch.* iii., iv. 81, note,
says that the date of the latter should be 1725, instead of 1721, when
the crown prince would be therefore thirteen, not nine years old.

[2] See one instance among many, in Wilhelmina, i. 147.

unfortunate brother seems to have been regarded as a species of treason, paid the full penalty of her crime, was coerced by blows and hunger into occasional submission, and took her revenge afterwards, by describing her father in the Memoirs.

His antipathy to Frederic.

But the crown prince was nobler game, and Frederic William was a keen sportsman. It is difficult to explain his treatment of Frederic, except on the theory of an original aversion, fostered by the discovery of what was regarded as the prince's unfitness for his mission, and cruelly confirmed by a belief in the superior qualifications of the younger sons.[1]

The King's disappointment had especially two bases, one positive, one negative.

The first was found in the actual preference of the prince for poetry, music, art, and generally for the graces, elegancies, and amenities of life.

Its causes.

Frederic was fond of the flute, and played it clandestinely, in spite of his father's prohibition. He persisted in composing French verses, which the King condemned, not because they were bad, but because they were in French and were supposed to be poetical. And the prince, who was a handsome young fellow, took great pride in his appearance, dressed his hair carefully, and wore an abundance of gold lace on his coat, — all of which his father regarded as low vanities of the world, and hated accordingly.[2]

Again, while chasing these forbidden pleasures, the prince neglected and even ridiculed others to which the King himself was partial, and the taste for which ought, in his opinion, if not natural, to be strenuously acquired by a youth who was destined to become a ruler of men.

[1] Wilhelmina attributes the King's prejudice, in part, to the reports of Kalkstein, the sub-governor. *Memoirs*, i. 47.

[2] For less venial transgressions on the part of the prince, see Wilhelmina, i. 104, 106, 123, etc.; Preuss, i. 29.

But the father's recreations were odious to the son. Frederic took no delight in shooting wild hogs at Wusterhausen, or in smoking cheap tobacco and drinking sour beer, or, worst of all, in drilling grenadiers of any stature. Nay, he had too much honesty, or too little tact, even to affect an interest in the grosser of these diversions. This was bitterly resented by Frederic William, and the prince was taught in daily lessons the price of his insubordination.

The double marriage project, which fills so much space in the Prussian chronicles, and in Carlyle, would not now justify the same attention even if it had succeeded. But since it failed, it may be dismissed with a few words.

Double marriage scheme.

It was originally a scheme of the Queen's. Like a prudent mother, she was anxious to make a good settlement for her children; and family interest as well as ambition led her to look toward the House of Hanover with a view to a twofold connection. She proposed to have Wilhelmina espouse the Duke of Gloucester, grandson of George I., and afterwards father of George III., while Frederic was to wed in the same manner the duke's sister, princess Amelia. It was, therefore, to be a double marriage of cousins; and the vicissitudes of the intrigue are delightful to all lovers of scandal.

Frederic William was not at first, it appears, heartily in favor of the plan, but seeing no great objections, suffered the Queen to open negotiations.[1] Wilhelmina's violent aversion to her intended husband was not a serious obstacle. But the Hanover potentates, father and grandfather, while affecting compliance, evaded on various pretexts a formal engagement; the Prussian

Its difficulties.

---

[1] He did not object to an English husband for Wilhelmina, but saw less advantage in the other half of the scheme. It was, however, on the union between the princess Amelia and Frederic that the court of Hanover insisted as a condition. See Ranke, iii., iv. 18, 95, 99.

King, though acquiescing, gave little positive aid; until the affair finally became involved with questions of diplomatic policy, and thus passed beyond Sophie Dorothea's control. The imperialist party was naturally averse to any closer union of the Houses of Prussia and England. It was the duty of Seckendorf to prevent the marriage, not less than to overthrow the Treaty of Hanover; and with the aid of Grumbkow and other upright courtiers he completely succeeded.

From time to time Frederic William threatened or proposed other candidates for Wilhelmina's hand. Such were the King of Poland, the Duke of Weissenfels, the Margrave of Schwedt, nephew of the Dessauer, and the Margrave of Anspach, her own kinsman. Wilhelmina disliked all of these with or without cause, and the last two eventually entered the family by marrying younger sisters. As a last resort, the King suggested to her the young prince and heir apparent of Bayreuth. Wilhelmina now thought it prudent to yield. The proposed suitor was not specially obnoxious; and in spite of the intrigues and denunciations of her mother, who thus saw slipping away her last grasp on the Anglo-Hanoverian project, the princess felt it unsafe longer to tempt her father's humor, at the risk of even a worse fate than that which opened before her at Bayreuth.[1]

She had, besides, a strong motive for compliance, in the opportunity which it afforded of doing her brother Frederic an urgent service. His misfortunes had finally culminated in a crisis, which was believed to threaten even his life.

As Frederic grew in years, he grew also more attached to his own pleasures, and more hostile to the pleasures of his father. His two favorites, lieutenants Keith and Katte, were brave, clever young fellows, fond of good living, willing to facilitate the

Wilhelmina is assigned elsewhere.

Reasons for her assent.

Frederic's troubles.

[1] *Memoirs,* i. 302 et seq.

prince's liaisons; yet warmly and perhaps unselfishly attached to him. The King looked upon all this with abhorrence. At times indeed, according to Wilhelmina, he maliciously tried to entrap the prince, by the aid of his own dissoluteness, into some indiscretion, which would afford a pretext for disinheriting and disowning him; the depths of baseness to which she describes him as descending almost transcend human belief.[1] But a policy of this kind, if ever seriously entertained, required more adroitness than the King possessed. A prolonged and subtle course of intrigue, espionage, and treachery was beyond his powers; he was himself an easy victim rather than a master of these arts. But in the two other more honorable and yet more brutal methods of coercion, outbursts of savage fury with personal violence; and schemes of deliberate cruelty, such as locking a child up in his room, mocking him with foul language, forbidding him food or sending him filthy and nauseating dishes, — in these he had nothing to learn, even from a Caligula or a Caracalla.

Many of these penalties Frederic early suffered, and his trials increased from year to year. But there was one thing, to which he assured Wilhelmina he would never submit. Bad food, confinement, insult, he could bear, however unwillingly. But the paternal cane he repeatedly declared should never disgrace his shoulders a second time.[2] Blows he did eventually receive, and in abundance, but they completed the work of alienation, and the prince's resolution to escape soon took a positive form.

His revolt.

Flight was, however, made the more difficult, and pun-

---

[1] *Memoirs*, i. 114, and elsewhere. More prudish historians of the other sex omit these details. But see for evidence in Frederic's favor, Ranke, iii., iv. 87, and the note.

[2] Wilhelmina, i. 162–164. See especially, p. 163, Frederic's letter to his mother.

ishment after the attempt at flight was made easier, by
the very circumstance that Frederic had in one particular
endeavored to meet his father's wishes. He had conquered or dissimulated his original dislike for military
life.[1] He not only submitted to prosaic lessons in the science of war, but even accepted the command of a battalion
of cadets, from which he was later transferred to a regiment. In 1730 he was a full colonel in his majesty's
service. But this made him liable to military discipline,
and in case of any offence to the rigors of military law.

Under military law, desertion is always one of the
greatest crimes. If committed in the face of the enemy,
it is punishable, even in the most humane of modern codes,
with death; but a century and a half ago Frederic William's legislation made it a capital offence in any circumstances.[2] The attempt of the crown prince to Attempt
escape to France, which was made during a tour at flight,
of the Rhine territories with his father, belonged, 1730.
therefore, in the category of unpardonable crimes. As
such, the King did not shrink from punishing it with his
own hands. When the unlucky prince was brought into
his presence after his arrest, his father rushed upon him
with drawn sword, and would have killed him on the
spot, if the interference of intrepid officers had not prevented. He was with difficulty persuaded to allow him to
be confined in a fortress, and to undergo a regular trial
by court-martial. Of Frederic's two accomplices, Keith
received timely warning and escaped, but Katte was apprehended.[3]

The prince was sent first to Mittenwalde, and after-

[1] Comp. Ranke, iii., iv. 82.

[2] See supra, p. 416.

[3] Ranke, iii., iv. 112, accepts the version which describes another
Keith, a page, brother of the lieutenant, as revealing the scheme.
Lieutenant Keith fled to Holland, whence he was aided to escape to
England by Lord Chesterfield, English ambassador at the Hague.

wards to the fortress of Cüstrin, where by the King's or-

The prince
in prison. ders he was closely confined in a cell. If his majesty had been strictly obeyed he would have had no books, no writing materials, no companions, no food even, except the meanest prison fare;[1] but he fortunately found friends among his jailers, who risked their own lives by secret attentions to the prisoner, and thus softened considerably the hardships of his lot. He even managed to send notes to his sister Wilhelmina; one of them is given in her memoirs.[2]

Wilhelmina was not, however, to escape without her

Rage of
the King. own trials. The King returned to Berlin in a frame of mind more than usually violent, even for him, and yet not without a certain feeling of malignant exultation. He was naturally of a suspicious nature, and Grumbkow had convinced him of the existence of a widespread conspiracy of the "English party." What this party was, except that the Queen was at its head, he scarcely pretended to know. He was equally uninformed as to its designs. But that a plot existed, he was thoroughly persuaded; and he connected with it as well Frederic's attempted flight as every other disagreeable event which had lately happened. And now he was resolved to probe the mystery to the bottom.

His first visit was to the Queen's apartments, where

Violence
toward
Wilhelmina. he found the Queen herself, Wilhelmina, other children, and several ladies - in - waiting. His eyes glared, his chest heaved, he fairly foamed at the mouth with rage. "He had no sooner cast his eyes upon me," says Wilhelmina, "than anger and fury overpowered him. 'Infamous baggage,' said he to me, 'dare you show yourself before me? Go and keep company with your rascally brother.' In uttering these words, he

---

[1] The order is in Foerster, i. 372. See also the curious details in Preuss, i. 46, 47.

[2] Vol. i. 265.

seized me with one hand, and struck me several times in the face with his fist: one of his blows fell upon my temples so violently, that I fell backwards, and would have split my head against a corner of the wainscot, had not Madame de Sonsfeld broke my fall by seizing me by my head-dress. I remained senseless on the ground. The King, no longer master of himself, strove to renew the blows, and trample upon me; but the Queen, my brothers and sisters, and all who were present, prevented him; they all surrounded me; which gave Madame de Kamken and Madame de Sonsfeld time to lift me up. They placed me in a window-seat which was close by; but seeing that I continued senseless, they sent one of my sisters for a glass of water and some salts, with which they insensibly recalled me to life. As soon as I was able to speak, I reproached them for the pains which they took with me, death being a thousand times more agreeable than life, in the situation in which we were. To describe its horror is impossible." [1]

After this affectionate display, the King instituted a systematic inquiry, and, naturally enough, Grumb- Further measures. kow was placed in charge of it. The papers — such as had not been prudently destroyed — of all suspected persons were seized.[2] The Queen was isolated. Wilhelmina was shut up in her apartments under guard, and permitted to see only her governess, one or two domestics, and such officials as the King from time to time sent to interrogate her, and to betray or intimidate her into a confession. But the inquisition yielded few trophies. Nothing like a general conspiracy, or a plan at all resembling high treason, was discovered.

The examination of the crown prince himself was scarcely more fruitful. He frankly confessed, what was

[1] *Memoirs*, i. 247. The translator is responsible for the English. See also Carlyle, ii. 205–208.

[2] See Wilhelmina, i. 232 et seq.

already known, that he had found his life intolerable; and, preferring exile to curses and blows, had tried to escape. He was even willing to waive his hereditary rights as the price of liberty. But from life imprisonment, which he had heard was to be his fate, he begged to be spared; he would rather suffer immediate death.[1]

The case was thus reduced to Frederic's simple attempt at flight, of which the evidence was clear, and Katte's knowledge of the prince's general purpose, which was also proven; though, as he was at Berlin at the time, he could at most be accused only of a constructive participation in the crime itself. But his own intention to fly was reasonably suspected, and he, too, was therefore arraigned as a deserter.

The court-martial met at Cöpenick, near Berlin, General Schulenburg being president,[2] and in six days completed its work.

Court-martial, October, 1730.

In the case of Frederic the tribunal pleaded want of jurisdiction. His offence was pronounced a family affair, an issue between father and son, for which the articles of war made no provision; though some of the members of the court added inconsequently other considerations, such as that the intended flight was not desertion, that the prince himself had expiated his offence by the disgrace of an arrest, and that he had, besides, sued for mercy.[3]

These representations seem to have been received by the King, who in the interval had become somewhat cooler, without any strong expressions of dissent. But that for some time the worst was apprehended for Frederic is evident from the action of foreign courts. England, Holland, Sweden, the Empress of Russia, the King of Poland, the Emperor himself, sent in remonstances, some of them phrased in very energetic terms,

Alarm for Frederic.

---

[1] Ranke, iii., iv. 116.

[2] But Grumbkow was not one of the members, as Carlyle, ii. 220, erroneously states.

[3] Ranke, iii., iv. 117; Droysen, IV. iii. 110.

against the supposed, and in the King's humor not improbable, intention to take the prince's life. Even Grumbkow and Seckendorf, who began to be alarmed at the possible completeness of their own triumph, and felt that the defeat of the "English party" was assured, interceded for their victim. Seckendorf contrived, however, to have it appear that the King really intended to send his son to the block, and was only diverted from the purpose by the Emperor's intervention.[1]

The case of Katte had a more tragical ending. The court, by a bare majority, refused to pronounce the full penalty for desertion, and recommended, *Case of Katte.* for what, if not desertion, could be only a boyish indiscretion, dismissal from the army, and imprisonment for life.[2] On a second hearing, ordered by Frederic William, it rendered the same verdict. But this did not accord with the King's views ; one victim he was determined to have. He took therefore the grave resolution of changing the penalty to that of death, and, with an exquisite sense of cruelty, ordered that the execution should take place at Cüstrin, before the window of Frederic's cell, and in his presence.[3]

The intercession of Katte's friends and relations, some of whom had high places in the public service, *His execu-* was without effect.[4] The barbarous decree was *tion.*

[1] Ranke, iii. iv. 117, 118; Seckendorf's memorial in Foerster, i. 375–377; the Emperor Charles' autograph letter in Preuss, i. appendix, p. 440; Droysen, IV. iii. 111 and note.

[2] Ranke, iii., iv. 119. According to the practice of the times, the court-martial consisted, besides the president, of three representatives, each of the ranks of major-general, colonel, lieutenant-colonel, major, and captain. The vote of any two determined the vote of the class, and a majority of the classes, that of the court. The president had ex officio a vote equal to that of a class.

[3] See the royal order with its unctuous casuistry in Foerster, i. 309, or in Preuss, i. 43.

[4] The correspondence between Field-marshal Wartensleben, Katte's grandfather, and the King is in Foerster, iii. 13, 14.

literally carried out. But some humanity was left in the breasts of the officers; and they ventured to require of Frederic no more than to appear at the window of his cell, as the procession arrived, and see his friend mount the scaffold. Touching recognitions were exchanged between the pair as their eyes met. Frederic in his anguish could only cry out for pardon. "It is sweet to die for such a prince," replied Katte, and went bravely to his death.[1]

The peril in which her brother stood, and the privations to which, even after his life had been spared, he was forced to submit, filled Wilhelmina with the liveliest solicitude. She lost all thought of herself; her only concern was to relieve the crown prince. When, therefore, a deputation with Grumbkow at the head waited upon her in her apartments, now become her prison, and proposed the hereditary prince of Bayreuth for her hand, dwelling especially on the probability that a compliance with the King's wishes would be of great advantage to her brother,[2] she no longer hesitated to yield. She gave her consent, and the betrothal was duly announced.

Betrothal of Wilhelmina.

This decision was in fact followed by some relaxation of the rigors which Frederic had hitherto suffered. He was not indeed permitted to attend the wedding; but he came to Berlin during the later festivities, and astonished Wilhelmina by the coldness with which he treated her.[3]

November, 1731.

[1] This is the general account. More details are given by Wilhelmina, i. 278 et seq. But this part of her narrative is full of inaccuracies. Comp. Ranke, iii., iv. 120, 121, for a slightly different version, based on the reports of Lepel, the commandant. Also, Preuss, i. 45. It may be added that the corps of governors, tutors, and friends of Frederic was broken up, some of the members, as Duhan, being banished. Ibid. i. 63, 64.

[2] Memoirs, i. 302 et seq.

[3] Ibid. i. 357–360.

From this time the relations between the King and the crown prince began to assume a better shape. The King had conquered and could afford to be merciful. The prince had been defeated ; but even from defeat he learned wisdom, and began to apply himself with prudent resignation to the work which his father prescribed. As he had disgraced his military uniform, he was adopted into the civil service ; and it must be said in justice to Frederic William that the experiment was eminently wise, and explains in large part Frederic's subsequent success in administration. The prince was compelled to take a new and peculiarly stringent oath of loyalty and obedience, which a special commission went up from Berlin to administer.[1]

Frederic enters the civil service.

The pleasures which had the King's sanction at this singular court were for the most part coarse, brutal, and degrading. Backgammon was indeed innocent, though not exciting; and Frederic William's fondness for that game is one of the startling contrasts which so often meet us in his character. Military drill was a pleasure, though it had a serious object, and is rather to be called work, than recreation after work. The two amusements which strictly deserved the name, and were most highly characteristic of the King, were the chase and the tobacco parliament.

The King's pleasures.

In regard to the chase it must be confessed that it differed from the chase of modern Prussian kings only in the degree in which Frederic William himself differed from them, and the manners of his age from theirs. It was not gentle or merciful, required neither skill nor courage, and was little less than heartless, wholesale slaughter of innocent game. The proceeds of a morning's sport were often counted by hundreds.[2] This

The chase.

[1] Mental reservations were excluded on the King's intimation that they were not recognized by Prussian law. See Ranke, iii., iv. 122.

[2] Comp. Foerster i. 334. The latter author gives, p. 351, a sug-

22

alone shows its singular cruelty ; but other emotions than pity are aroused by the fact that his majesty was accustomed to sell such of the game as could not be consumed at his own table to the marketmen of the capital.

The favorite hunting-ground was Wusterhausen, where there was a noble forest, still in part preserved, and still scoured every year by royal sportsmen. The " castle " is also yet in existence, and is perhaps the most curious monument of the king to whom it owes its origin.   It is a plain, substantial building, something like a respectable farm-house of the second class, contains many relics of Frederic William, and is shown to tourists with the most touching gravity by its guardians.   The rooms are hung with remarkable paintings, portraits by the King's own hand.   He was in fact an industrious dauber in oils, though contemporary writers are singularly silent about the fact, and Stenzel hints, — apparently without any suspicion that he is releasing the King from a grave artistic responsibility, — that his canvases were all touched up by professional painters.[1] The session chamber of the " tabagie " has also been religiously preserved. A long, plain oak table, chairs of the same material and style, beer-mugs, pitchers, tobacco-jars, and pipes make up its equipment.

The King with his family and leading favorites was in the habit of spending a few weeks every autumn at this unattractive resort.   It was the one season in which he gave himself up most completely to recreation.

In the morning at daybreak, if the weather was fair, a hunting party was formed, and pheasants, grouse, rabbits, sometimes nobler game, like deer and wild boar, were

gestive statement in tabular form of the King's achievements during the years 1717–1738, inclusive. The totals are 25,066 grouse, 1,455 pheasants, and 1,145 hares. Larger game is not included in the census.

[1] *Gesch. des pr. Staats,* i. 514.

massacred until noon. The family dinner was served at twelve. On pleasant days the table was spread in the open air, under such shelter only as the trees afforded; and after the meal his majesty stretched himself out on a wooden bench, and slept until three. The family in the mean time were not allowed to leave their seats. The sun might emerge from the trees and pour its scorching rays upon them, gnats might tease them into desperation, even a rain-storm might drench them to the skin, — there was no relief. It was as much as the life of the Queen or a child was worth to stir from the place until the King's slumber was over.[1] At five o'clock the tobacco parliament was opened.

The guests who were invited — and no others could appear — sat about the great table, which was well supplied with Swedish beer, tobacco, and pipes. On a sideboard near by stood coarse sandwiches, brown bread, and cheese. Every person was expected to drink, and to appear to smoke, though some like Seckendorf and the Dessauer, to whom tobacco was intolerable, only put an empty pipe in their mouths, which the host was pleased to regard as a constructive obedience to the rule. No ceremony or order of ranks was observed; the proceedings were strictly democratic. The King made jokes and suffered retorts with the same grim and vulgar humor; and toward the end of the session, when the party were heated with liquor, every appearance of reserve and propriety was thrown off; freedom passed into license; the banquet became an uproarious drunken carousal.

The tabagie.

It was at this stage of the proceedings that Frederic William's essential heartlessness became apparent. There was a certain homely independence in the general plan of the tabagie, in the King's willingness to discard the stiff rules of court etiquette, and meet a few friends of an evening over a pipe and a mug of beer. But the gather-

---

[1] Wilhelmina, i. 337, 338.

ing too often lost even this merit as the hours passed by.
A person who is fond of practical jokes needs a butt for
his ridicule; and when the joker is a king like Frederic
William he is likely to command the services of his victims, and there is no escape. His majesty did not hesitate
to select even his own children for this humiliating office.
The crown prince especially, being by nature the most
averse to the orgies of the tabagie, was of all the sons the
one upon whom the King took most delight in forcing its
odious hospitality. The poor youth was ordered into the
room for the mere amusement of his majesty's guests;
forced to smoke a filthy pipe until the tears came into his
eyes, and to drink beer until his stomach rebelled; his
father all the time watching his anguish with ironical delight, teasing him with coarse pleasantries, and chasing
him out of the room with bitter maledictions when his
spirit broke down under the trial.

There were, however, other court fools, not perhaps
permanently engaged but regularly present, who
were more docile and serviceable than Frederic.
The most famous of these was Gundling. He has not the
slightest resemblance to the fool of King Lear, or to the
characteristic jester of history and romance. He was
privileged indeed to bear his breast to his master's jokes,
but not to retort with wholesome truths or merry puns.
He was only a passive agent in the pleasantries. Yet
Gundling was in his way a learned man. He wrote pon-
derous histories of the early Hohenzollerns, and otherwise
vindicated his claim to be considered one of the erudite
men of his age.[1] It was indeed his learning, or rather
his pedantry, which first recommended him to Frederic
William as a useful person in the tabagie; for the King
despised culture, and Gundling, a dull, meek, servile
creature, was sufficiently flattered by invitations to the
tabagie, and was not unwilling to repay his host for the

The learned fools.

---

[1] A list of his works in 21 titles is in Foerster, i. 255, 256.

invitation by maudlin demonstrations, which entertained the other guests. With him may be ranked, in the same order of usefulness, Fassmann and Morgenstern. They were also scholars, and both of them left memoirs of their patron.

But Gundling and his learned colleagues were not the only dupes in the tabagie. Two far more subtle humorists than the King plied their trade in that boisterous assembly, and of them he himself was unconsciously the victim. It was the place where Seckendorf and Grumbkow were most successful in surprising the King's watchfulness, and leading him into their treacherous schemes.

The tabagie, wherever it might be held, was, more than any other institution of the time, the real parliament of the kingdom. The programme was not all comedy. The most momentous affairs of state came up for discussion, and that kind of informal discussion, too, which while best suited to the King's own humor was also most favorable to the schemes of ambitious servants and secret enemies. The men who had standing invitations to the tabagie early became the most powerful persons in the state. Such were Leopold of Dessau, General Derschau, even Gundling in his way, but especially Seckendorf and Grumbkow. The treaty of 1728 was really negotiated in this way, by the aid of beer and tobacco. The tabagie killed the double marriage project. It was there that the plot against the crown prince was matured; and there, too, that, after the plot had done its work, the King was induced to relent by the very men who had worked him into his original fury. His majesty had ministers of a more serious turn of mind, for whom the tabagie had no attractions and never opened its doors. Such were apparently Ilgen and Cocceji. Yet their recommendations had not the less to pass the ordeal of its criticisms, and sometimes emerged with radical changes from a body in which the authors were not accorded a hearing.

The two leading actors in his majesty's company of evening players were by nature wholly dissimilar, and took widely different yet correlative parts.

Seckendorf, though in the service of the Emperor, was a Protestant by religion and affected to be a singularly firm and devout Protestant. He lived an ostentatiously decorous life ; kept a frugal household ; avoided all excess ; and laid great stress upon the necessity of straightforwardness, honesty, and candor in political dealings. But this did not prevent him from having a remarkably keen eye, from using against Frederic William the arts which he knew were the most effective, and from serving his master with perfect fidelity. His ability is proved by the fact that he succeeded in carrying nearly every point with Frederic William, while really having a strong aversion to the King's peculiar tastes and occupations.

He would not have succeeded, however, without the aid of Grumbkow, who supplied the qualities which Seckendorf was unable or unwilling to acquire. Grumbkow was not driven to feign an appreciation of the bowl and the pipe, of coarse jokes and vulgar stories. The taste with him was natural ; for although he was a person of considerable culture, a favorite in salons, and popular with the ladies,[1] he entered heartily into the King's grosser pleasures, was a good liver, and kept his head steady under incredible quantities of liquor. He was a consummate master of intrigue, and through his spies, male and female, knew all the secrets of the capital. His wit and address made him a favorite with those whose paths did not cross his schemes; yet, although he was hated as much as he was feared by all others, the King seems never to have suspected his mendacity, corruption, and perfect unscrupulousness. That he was the paid accomplice of Seckendorf is now universally believed, and

Seckendorf.

Grumbkow.

[1] Even Wilhelmina admits this. *Memoirs*, i. 3.

the belief is fully warranted by the revelation in the latter's own correspondence, and the admissions of Grumbkow himself.[1]

It was said above that Seckendorf was nearly always successful in his diplomatic measures. He made, however, one ignominious failure; and that too was on the question of the marriage of the crown prince, the question on which turned so large a part of the politics of Berlin.

We left Frederic copying rent-rolls and balancing ledgers in the government office at Cüstrin. In the interval father and son have, however, gradually drawn nearer to each other; and mutual explanations, facilitated by Grumbkow, have not only established a fairly good understanding between them, but have led also to sensible modifications of the prince's discipline. He was restored to the rolls of the army, and in 1731 had an interview with the King at Cüstrin. *The crown prince again.*

In 1732 he was permitted to give up his civil apprenticeship, and enter, or reënter, upon his military career. He was placed in command of a regiment, with headquarters at Ruppin, a town northwest of Berlin near Fehrbellin; and here he spent most of his time until his father's death. *Is transferred to Ruppin.*

In the mean time the question of the prince's marriage did not slumber. He had caused it to be intimated to the King, of course under the pressure of necessity, and knowing that his marriage was regarded as a mere affair of state, in which his own preference was to count for little or nothing, that he was prepared to obey his father's commands. His father commanded the Princess Elizabeth of Brunswick-Bevern. She was not Frederic's first choice, nor even his second, or third. She *His betrothal.*

---

[1] See, for instance, Foerster, ii. Urkundenbuch, p. 197, iii. 350–352 ; Seckendorf's budget for 1733, ibid. iii. 231–234 ; Grumbkow to Seckendorf, September 3, 1735, in Droysen, IV. iv. 435. It is painful to find Eugene engaged in such business.

is described by the King and by Frederic himself as being neither handsome nor ugly ; it appears that she was morbidly pious, timid by nature, and nearly destitute of social and intellectual gifts. The betrothal was nevertheless celebrated with the usual ceremonies, and as the princess was niece of the Emperor, and candidate of the court of Vienna, Seckendorf congratulated himself with reason on his triumph.

But circumstances afterwards led the imperial court to take a different view of the alliance. A change in the aspect of European politics caused the Emperor to desire the Anglo-Prussian marriage as ardently as he had once opposed it ; and though Wilhelmina's fate was already settled, Frederic was only betrothed, not married, and a betrothal could be revoked without any greater difficulty than a breach of faith. Seckendorf was, therefore, charged to undo the very work which he had labored so long to complete. But the attempt was an utter failure. Grumbkow foresaw the perilous nature of the scheme, and, though still devoted to Austria, avoided taking an active part in the business. It is to his pen that we owe an account of the effect produced upon the King's mind by Seckendorf's treacherous proposition.[1] His majesty utterly and indignantly refused to break his word ; suppressed peremptorily every attempt of the envoy to re-open the subject ; and the next year placed himself beyond the reach of temptation by causing the crown prince's wedding to be celebrated.

His marriage, June 12, 1773.

Thus the great marriage question was put to rest. The next year Seckendorf obtained a command on the Rhine, and left Berlin forever. But his policy was represented for a time by his nephew, another Seckendorf, who succeeded him as envoy.[2]

[1] See Foerster, iii. 135, 136 ; Droysen IV. iii. 201, 202.

[2] Various publications, historical, biographical, and autobiographical, throw light upon the career of Seckendorf, and his relations with

The crown prince and his bride repaired to Ruppin, which, however, was soon exchanged for the castle of Rheinsberg in the same neighborhood. A Rheinsberg. petty court was there established; and Frederic was permitted, with few restrictions on the part of his father, to live in his own way and gratify his own tastes. His character had, however, undergone a great change since his imprisonment. From an ingenuous, high-minded though impulsive youth, he had become a selfish, cynical, heartless man of the world. He had learned that it was politic to comply outwardly with his father's wishes; but his frantic expressions of filial devotion, of almost slavish submission, could have deceived nobody except the King. His real sentiments are better revealed in the flippant letters which he wrote, and especially those to Grumbkow before his marriage. He treated his wife with public respect, for unlike his father he had some of the instincts of a gentleman; but she never acquired her husband's affection, and finally became little less than an exile in her own household.

Frederic William's method of work was scarcely less novel than his method of recreation. He rose very early in the morning, and, after a short The King's "mar-ginals." Scriptural exercise and a hasty breakfast, began the consideration of affairs of state. These were, indeed, for the most part matters of internal administration, often of the most trivial character; for the larger political questions were treated in a different, and some of them in a far less effective manner. A secretary or two aided to assort and interpret the multifarious papers which came in from the directory and other administrative boards, or from single ministers. The King heard everything, read much, and decided with amazing promptness. As a rule he wrote his decision, in a chaotic handwriting

the Prussian court, but the more important evidence is in Foerster, and, especially for his negotiations, in Droysen.

and a wild dialect, on the margin of the paper which contained the case. Foerster has collected a large number of these "marginal resolutions" in the appendix to his first volume. Some fac-similes of the royal hieroglyphics are also given by the same industrious compiler. The writing is illegible, and the printed translations are not much better, but they furnish, nevertheless, a complete picture of Frederic William's singular system of government, of his unwearied attention to details, his abrupt and insolent manner, his lamentable parsimony.

A certain receiver of taxes having died and left his accounts twelve hundred thalers short, the directory submits a proposition of the landrath to save the widow from absolute destitution by remitting, on account of the husband's long service, a part of the deficit; but the King replies: "Not a penny shall be remitted. Let them take away house, furniture, and everything that remains." The ministry transmits a complaint of the town of Treuenbriezen, that its trade has fallen off since the neighboring Saxons are forbidden to bring their grain there to market. Reply of the King: "Don't trouble me with such things." It is proposed to construct a stone wall to secure the town of Reppen against floods. The King: "I have no money." [1] The city of Schievelbein asks for aid to buy a fire-engine, but his majesty retorts, "No money, it is a royal borough." [2] Another town begs through the directory for a bridge, which will not cost the treasury over five hundred thalers. "Fool's nonsense, fool's nonsense, fool's nonsense, fool's nonsense!" scrawls the royal pen all over the page, and the document is returned to its authors. [3]

There is an infinite variety of these pointed, terse, and emphatic responses. The bluntest refusals are provoked

---

[1] Ich habe kein Geldt.

[2] Poin dargent ist immédiatstaht.

[3] Narren Possen, four times.

by demands for money, and "I have no money," or "Not a penny,"[1] are phrases which frequently occur. But there are also cases covering every form of public interest, and on these, too, the King's decision is not less swift and summary. As he made it an almost invariable rule to refuse, or cut down a proposed grant from the treasury, his penuriousness must sometimes have worked mischief. He must likewise have made unjust, if only because rash decisions in other matters. But the general impression left, after a study of the printed records and other evidence of the King's ways, is that he had both an unusual capacity for work and a high degree of executive ability; power of endurance, penetration of view, and promptness of judgment.

It must be said, however, of his avarice that it was manifested not the less in private than in public affairs. There was, indeed, a certain policy in this, for it enabled the King to point to the frugality of his own household, and the meanness of his own fare, as evidence that the rule of thrift was impartially applied and made no distinction of persons. The rate of pay in the public service was disgracefully low; and only the strictest economy enabled the poorer officials to maintain their families. But the head of that service himself ate brown bread and pickled beef. The royal children were granted no better food than those of any decent burgher, and were granted it far less graciously. Frederic the Great was accustomed to state in later years, that he was brought up on beer soup. Wilhelmina and her sister Amelia once sent in a timid petition to the King, complaining not only that their food was poor, but that there actually was not enough of it, and that they often left the table hungry. The King counted, in fact, the cost of the simplest gratification which was proposed for his family; entertained guests reluctantly and shabbily; and

His avarice and meanness.

[1] Nit ein pfennig.

thus gave no occasion for invidious comparisons between the trials of an overtaxed people, and the luxury of the court establishment.

Yet in spite of all this, the favorite picture, which represents Frederic William as a modern Spartan, with a simple, manly, and sincere indifference to the world's comforts, is grossly overdrawn. Luxuries which were to be paid for out of his own purse he indeed abhorred. But luxuries which could be obtained at the expense of other people were always welcome; and there was no surer way to his favor than to invite him as a guest, and set a well-spread table before him.[1] The institution and fabulous extravagance of the grenadiers would have been impossible under a prince who was systematically economical. He had also a fancy for elegant plate, and in its gratification no expense was spared.[2] In short, he was recklessly prodigal in the pursuit of pleasures personal to himself, and not to be enjoyed by others, but meanly and brutally penurious in regard to outlays which would affect a circle of friends or relations, and thus diffuse their kindly benefits among many persons. The most that can be affirmed in his behalf is, that he was willing to dispense with some of the elegance and ostentation of royalty; and that his thrift, though heartless and cruel in many of its forms, was on the whole advantageous to the state.

Like all tyrants, Frederic William was extremely suspicious. This did not, indeed, prevent him from
His suspicious nature.
being the victim of intrigues during his whole reign, and apparently without ever suspecting their existence. But for intrigues which did not exist except in his own fancy, or in the fictions of base adventurers, he had a

---

[1] See Foerster, i. c. IV. passim. He compelled the leading generals and ministers to hold "assemblies," one each week, and at their own expense.

[2] The value of the silver which he accumulated in the palace is estimated at over one million thalers. See Foerster, i. 327 and note.

watchfulness that was almost painfully keen. The ambiguous hint of a malicious servant could lead him to doubt his wife's fidelity. He detected from time to time, or was persuaded to believe in imaginary plots to dethrone him in the interest of the crown prince. The pretended revelations of one Kléement, a perjured Hungarian, though implicating his highest and most confidential councillors, found ready belief; made him apprehensive even for his life; gave rise to the most extraordinary precautions; and filled the palace with a dense atmosphere of jealousy and distrust, which made life nearly intolerable to its inmates.

It will now necessarily be inferred that the general tone of society in the time of Frederic William was one of profound depression. The popular feel- *Trials of the people.* ing was doubtless correctly expressed in the remark of Winkelmann.[1] An oppressive system of taxation, which harshly and greedily searched the pockets of every subject; an enormous and costly army, which failed to justify its existence even by the poor logic of victorious wars; a vicious policy of state patronage, which deranged the laws of productive industry; a centralized civil service, which hourly intruded upon the most sacred private interests; the nearly complete obliteration of the Diets, which had once spoken to the prince with the voice of the people; the unrelenting severity of the laws and the courts, which the King still found inadequate to the ends of justice; a widespread network of police, and spies, and informers, against which the purest citizen was not secure; and at the summit of all this, a monarch whose tastes were low, passions coarse, and nature cruel, who valued the material above all other interests in the state, and who strode about among his subjects with uplifted cane, ever ready to strike, — such, though very imperfectly described, were the elements of a social condition, in which the people of Prussia

[1] Supra, c. X. p. 431.

vainly struggled to be contented, cheerful, and happy.
The King took his own pleasures; chased deer through
the forest of Wusterhausen, or smoked with Grumbkow
and Gundling in the tabagie. But it is beyond doubt
that during this reign the general feeling of the people
was one of sombre, yet helpless discontent.

The income of the state does not indeed seem, when
Pecuniary
burdens. looked at superficially, to indicate an exorbitant
rate of taxation. In the last year of Frederic
William's reign, it represents only an average imposition
upon the people of three thalers per capita. In the Prussia of the present day, it is five times as much.[1] But in
estimating the relative weight of these burdens, several
things must be taken into consideration. The thaler itself means less than it did one hundred and fifty years
ago; the tax-paying capacity has greatly increased; a
much larger share of the public burdens is now borne by
the rich, and by travelling or domiciled aliens; and, finally,
the state now gives the subject, in the form of protection
and comforts, a much better return for his taxes. If these
distinctions are just, and be taken into account, they will
perhaps enforce the conclusion that the subjects of Frederic William were required to bear unusually heavy burdens. That they were heavier than the regular expenses
of the state made necessary, is evident from the fact that
the King annually put aside a large surplus.

Frederic William, with all his faults, had a wholesome
The royal
task-master. sense of the dignity of labor. He himself
worked, required his ministers to work, and en-
forced upon every person, of whatever condition, the value
of industry. His own talent, it has been shown, was
chiefly that of capacity for hard work; some of his exhortations read like those of Poor Richard's Almanac. He

---

[1] An approximate estimate; on account of the greater complexity
of modern financial systems, and especially of the fiscal relations of
Prussia to the Empire, it is impossible to make an exact comparison.

even commanded the apple-women of Berlin to knit while sitting at their stalls in the market-place ; and his tours of inspection through the streets of the capital were occasions of terror to all persons who wanted a regular occupation, or having one were neglectful of its duties. An idle vagabond he regarded as a traitor to the state. But the punishment for that sort of treason, and for many other light crimes, was an order to work on a new church, or other building, or on public improvements of any kind. The population was, therefore, an industrious one. It is, indeed, impossible to determine in how far this result was due to a healthy improvement in the spirit of the people, and in how far to the stern necessities of daily life, or to fear of the royal lash. The King's policy was undoubtedly associated in public thought with an obnoxious system of government, and was proclaimed in tones which were better fitted to coerce than to convince. A slight relapse was sure to follow the removal of the King's iron grasp. But, on the other hand, there is evidence that Frederic William's example, precepts, and measures gradually worked a beneficial change in the habits of the poorer classes, that idleness came to be regarded as a vice, and that a resolute and fruitful, though perhaps sullen, spirit of labor animated the plow, the loom, and the forge.

But it was not enough that the people were trained by this rigorous policy to have little disposition to be merry. Some sense of humor, some longing for social pleasures might still break through the general gloom ; and further measures of the King seemed to put even the opportunity for diversion out of the reach of the public. He made war upon the innocent amusements, as sternly as upon the positive vices, the idleness or profligacy, of the people.

The theatre hardly received decent treatment until the last decade of this reign. Even then it was sub- Music and jected to a rigid censorship, and barely dragged the drama.

out a feeble existence. The inspection was intrusted for some years to General Dönhof, who had also charge of certain military interests; and Foerster reproduces a novel report to the King, in which the general requests a pardon for a condemned deserter, announces the restoration of a clown improperly dismissed by his manager, and submits a scheme for engaging a ballet girl for the approaching festivities of the crown prince's marriage.[1] Music fared a little better. Military airs were of course encouraged, and his majesty was not averse to the tragic opera; but the finer instruments, like the violin and the flute, were heartily despised, and, in the case of Frederic, even prohibited. A still harsher, and for a military king less intelligible interference with the popular amusements, was the suppression of the target clubs in 1727. The royal decree withdrew the prizes for marksmanship established by Frederic I.[2] In Berlin all the coffee-houses except two were summarily closed. At Potsdam the King went about one day in person, and broke up all the bowling alleys, driving the players away with his cane.[3]

In these and kindred measures there was indeed professedly a moral object. Rifle-matches, beer-gardens, and play-houses, argued his majesty, take honest fellows away from their work, encourage dissipation, disorder, and licentiousness, and thus corrupt the habits of society. In harmony with this view, he issued an order closing all public houses at nine o'clock on week days, and entirely on Sundays. Even the guests as well as the proprietors of taverns which violated this ordi-

Sumptuary restrictions.

---

[1] Foerster, i. 310. The King dismissed the first part of the petition with the "marginal," soll vor dem Fest hangen. It is further characteristic of Frederic William's ways, that being once singularly attracted by a low comedy troupe, he issued an order that every evening one member from each of the government boards should buy a ticket.

[2] Stenzel, iii. 516.

[3] Foerster, i. 237.

nance were seized by the police, and shut up in the watch-house,[1] fortunate if they escaped with only a night's imprisonment. Crimes against decency or the marriage relation were even more sternly punished. Frederic William himself set the example of conjugal fidelity, and exacted the same degree of virtue from all whom he could control. He once became involved in a serious difficulty with the Emperor, because, in his zeal for correct conduct in this regard, he had seized and shut up in a fortress an imperial baron, who, having abandoned his wife, was living openly at Berlin with a mistress. It was no uncommon thing for the streets of the capital to be scoured at night by details of police or soldiers, and all suspicious persons of either sex swept into the guard-house. That the law codes were burdened with a mass of petty sumptuary regulations is a proposition which suggests itself, and needs no evidence.[2] In this policy Frederic William was not, however, a pioneer.

If the cheap pleasures of the common people were thus either forbidden, or jealously controlled, what treatment could be expected by the higher intellectual interests of the select few?

The two academies had not been efficiently supported even by Frederic himself, their founder, especially after the death of Sophie Charlotte. But they were not openly attacked, and on their meagre incomes managed to keep alive from year to year. Frederic William, however, on his accession, at once took the offensive.

One of his first acts was to reduce the annual allowance of the academy of arts from one thousand to Academy of three hundred thalers; and he even proposed to arts. have the institution pay fifty thalers rent for the rooms which it occupied over the royal stables. The functions

---

[1] Stenzel, iii. 518.

[2] Such, for instance, as the edict of March 31, 1718 " Wegen, Abstellung des Voll-sauffens und Gesundheit-Trinkens.

6

of the associated artists in organizing fêtes and pageants were no longer required.   Even individual artists were employed in no more dignified service than touching up the King's own canvases, in painting favorite grenadiers, or hewing them in stone for the façades of public buildings. By a touch of dry, though perhaps unconscious humor his majesty heard the encomiums which flatterers lavished upon his paintings, appraised them accordingly, and then compelled the victims to buy them at this exorbitant valuation.   The artist Mark painted all of the tallest grenadiers, and the portraits were hung in the royal galleries. The grenadier Jonas having died, a sculptor was commissioned to reproduce him in marble, with uniform and arms complete; and this singular statue was added to the art treasures of the capital.   Art, in the true sense, was of course impossible in such circumstances.   The only painter of the age, whose name has deservedly come down to posterity, is Pesne ; and to him the world owes its gratitude especially for the admirable picture, The Little Drummer, which furnishes the first pictorial representation of Frederic the Great.

For science, so far as the term meant the pursuit of
Academy of   truth for its own sake, the King had a con-
sciences.   tempt even greater than for art.   But the academy of sciences was charged with certain interests which had a practical side, — the training of surgeons for the army, and the improvement of agricultural methods — and on account of these it was not at once rudely attacked like its sister institution.   But the pension of Leibnitz was cut off, and he retained only a nominal connection with it after the accession of Frederic William.   On his death in 1716 the King did not scruple to insult his memory by appointing the court fool, Gundling, to the presidency. Gundling, though a learned was anything but a scientific man, and his appointment was merely a flippant joke, which duly amused the tabagie.   The vice-president, one

Graben zum Stein, was a mere drunken clown. Yet the academy was required to pay him a salary of two hundred thalers yearly out of its slender revenues. Jablonski, who became president in 1733, was a scholar, and gave the institution more dignity; it continued in spite of all depressing circumstances to pursue its learned labors, issued in 1723 the second, and in 1737 the third volume of its publications. But it took, during this reign, no hold upon the popular respect. The example of the King himself taught the public to regard it as a society of worthless visionaries, who wasted time that might otherwise be employed in plowing the soil, or drilling with the soldiers, in vain searches after the secret of matter, or the law of planetary movements, or the mathematical possibilities of the circle.

It might be supposed that at least the royal library would have some chance to survive the general wreck of learned institutions. The reader will recall the liberal treatment which it received from the Great Elector, who, though a rough soldier of the camp, was not indifferent to the value of education; and respect for the example of an ancestor, who resembled himself in many traits of character, ought to have led Frederic William to spare such an establishment. Until 1722 it did indeed enjoy its modest income undisturbed. It is true, the income barely sufficed to pay the salaries of the librarians, and left little or nothing for the purchase of books. But in 1722 even this support was withdrawn. The King suddenly cancelled all salaries, and diverted nearly the whole amount of the revenues to the benefit of General von Glasenapp. The next move was to make a certain Hakemann chief librarian, and Hakemann was another of the learned fools. He was finally detected in embezzling what funds were left, fled from Berlin, and the library then took a further step downwards. At the death of Frederic William its collection of books is thought to have numbered only seventy-two thousand.

The universities suffered at once from the aggressions
The univer- of the recruiting officers, from the poverty of
sities. their resources, and from the King's heartless
schemes for bringing them into contempt. It is difficult
to say which of these misfortunes worked the greatest evil.

The annual allowance for Halle was slightly increased
in 1733, so that it amounted to seven thousand thalers ;
Königsberg was helped in a negative sense by a decree of
release from certain taxes. The professors of law and
medicine derived a second income from the practice of
their professions. But the faculties of theology and philosophy were confined to such slight payments as might
be made to them out of the state subvention, and their
share of the students' fees. All representations to the
King were without result. He announced the maxim that
a university chair ought to support itself, and a despot's
maxims require no explanation. It followed, of course,
that the professorships were frequently given to ignorant
and worthless vagabonds, merely because they had, in the
King's view, the grand qualification of taking them without salary, trusting to their ingenuity to make them profitable. One of these worthies, Bartholdi, was forced into
the university of Frankfort, in spite of the protests of the
faculty, and after a short career, full of scandal, ended in
the madhouse. Another favorite, Arnold von Dobrslaw,
after vainly trying to teach in the same institution, was
put back into a gymnasium to acquire a common school
education. Even Hakemann, the defaulting librarian, was
restored to favor, and installed as professor in Halle.
But his licentious life was not changed by academic honors, and going from bad to worse, he was finally sent to
the whipping-post, where he terminated his public career.

The university of Frankfort had steadily declined since
the establishment of a rival at Halle, and was in a peculiar
degree the object of Frederic William's antipathy. By
arbitrary edicts, issued from time to time, he had not only

diverted its income to other ends, but had even robbed
it of a good part of its funded capital. In a satanic
spirit of malice he finally planned and executed, in 1737,
a culminating insult to the institution.

The instrument in this disgraceful scheme was Morgenstern, one of the "learned fools," but the
most learned and least foolish of all. Mor- Morgen-
genstern had found his way to Berlin in the stern and
the univer-
sity of
character of a strolling pedant, holding wild dis- Frankfort.
courses at the gates and in the market-places; and the
watchful officers at the capital had quickly detected in
him a desirable man for the tobacco parliament. In the
tobacco parliament he was therefore duly installed, and
satisfactorily earned a liberal salary. But so erudite a
man deserved even higher honors. In 1737 the King
nominated him vice-chancellor of the university of Frankfort, and prepared by the ceremony of installation to
gratify his peculiar sense of humor, and show his contempt
for academic learning. Master and fool and a party of
kindred spirits repaired, therefore, to Frankfort. The
next day after their arrival, it was announced that Magis-
ter Morgenstern would hold a disputation in the public
hall of the university, on the subject, "Rational thoughts
about folly and fools." [1] He was clad in clown's dress,
with an enormous wig, a fox-tail for a sword, and a plume
of rabbit's hair. The faculty and students were summoned, and the debate began. The King himself took
the chair, prodded the disputants when their zeal flagged,
applauded the good points, bandied epithets with the
students, and from time to time hurled coarse insults at
the mortified professors. "What will you?" shouted this
royal patron of letters, "A pound of mother-wit is worth
a ton of university wisdom." Fools, pedants, hypocrites,
were terms which he applied to the faculty. The scene
finally ended in a great tumult, and the rector was forced

---

[1] Vernünftige Gedanken von der Narrheit und den Narren.

to put on a sergeant's cap before he could restore order.
And this scandalous scene was witnessed by Professor
John Jacob Moser, founder of the positive school of international law, and one of the most meritorious publicists of the eighteenth century.

An earlier victim, and a victim not of the King's ridicule but of his bigotry, was Christian Wolf, professor of philosophical jurisprudence at Halle.
No one now reads his massive quartos, and the substance
of his system has been incorporated in the more practical
treatise of Vattel. But in his day he ranked as one of
the most eminent publicists, and one of the most popular lecturers in Germany. He belonged essentially to
the school of Thomasius, and like Thomasius taught in
German, with a wholesome degree as well of intellectual
vigor as of intellectual courage. But such qualities were
dangerous in an age when theological passions still ran
high. The Lutherans and the Pietists forgot their hatred
of each other in their common hatred of Wolf, and joined
hands in an effort to precipitate his fall. In Frederic
William they found a ready ally. The more subtle theological points involved in the dispute were of course beyond his grasp; but reckless and sweeping charges of im-
piety were fatally effective with so pious a king. Besides,
the complaints were basely supported by a pretended
practical inference from Wolf's teachings. It was insinuated to the King that Wolf's doctrine of fate or necessity
would justify any of the grenadiers in deserting, or at
least would make it unlawful to punish such a deserter.
This was enough for Frederic William. An order was
issued requiring Wolf to leave the Prussian dominions within forty-eight hours, on pain of the
halter.

In later years the King repented of this brutal act of
folly. An invitation was even extended to the exiled professor to resume his chair, but he wisely refused to put

Case of Wolf.

1723.

himself again within the reach of such a tyrant. On the accession of Frederic he was promptly reinstated.

The King's hatred of learning was chiefly felt by the academies, the libraries, and the universities. Common schools. The gymnasiums were not disturbed, and the common schools taught those elementary branches, which even his majesty held to be not only proper, but even necessary. Hence, while he ridiculed the professors, and discouraged the studies of the universities, he made attendance in the primary schools obligatory on all children between the ages of five and twelve.[1] Thus two of the most characteristic features of Prussian polity — universal military service, and universal common school education, the fundamental bases of the present state — may be traced back to this far-seeing though narrow-minded king. Even the soldiers were required to have regimental instruction in reading, writing, and the Christian religion.[2]

This wise policy was, however, carried out, like everything that Frederic William undertook, in a harsh and arbitrary manner, which robbed it of half its merits.

The greatest ignorance prevailed in the extreme eastern provinces, as a consequence of the plague and the general poverty. It was dense and widespread enough to shock even the King's sensibilities. But he hesitated to give out any money for the purpose of reform, and was reckless enough to suppose that a population whose ignorance was largely due to its poverty could be enlightened by means of new taxes laid upon itself. Even the Prussian officials protested against such a scheme. The King made, therefore, reluctantly a small grant out of the treasury. With more propriety it was then ordered that the local population should contribute to the extent of its means, and by the end of this reign the number of village schools in Preussen and Lithuania was increased by over eleven

[1] Edicts of 1717 and 1736.
[2] Droysen, IV. iii. 420.

hundred.[1] But in other parts of the monarchy Frederic William was content to reform only by mandates and edicts. No money could be extorted from him, and local resources were inadequate to the work.

The only branch of higher education not immediately and purely practical — such for instance as medi-
Theology.
cine — which the King encouraged, was theology. Students of divinity were reasonably secure against the recruiting sergeant, and their teachers were held in some esteem. Yet even here the King fell into an error nearly as great as that which led him to ridicule jurisprudence and philosophy. It is now very well known that the excessive refinement of theological distinctions, and the sharp antagonisms of the ecclesiastical doctors, were the reverse of favorable to true piety. It was, however, in the interest only of practical religion, and not at all of theological science, that the King encouraged the study of divinity. The metaphysics of Christianity were hateful to him.

But here again, by another of the startling inconsisten-
Doctrine of cies of his character, he threw himself with great
election. ardor into one of the most abstruse of all theological disputes. A Calvinist by inheritance and profession, he had a violent repugnance to the Calvinistic doctrine of predestination. That he really understood what the doctrine meant is of course improbable. But he fancied that it was a restraint, in some mysterious way, upon his freedom of action as an absolute monarch, while excusing at the same time, acts of negligence on the part of his officials, or of insubordination on the part of his subjects. It is easy, therefore, to understand why the suspected adhesion of the crown prince to the seditious dogma was one of the offences alleged against him.[2] In an edict of 1719 he even forbade the defence of the doc-

[1] Stenzel, iii. 511; Droysen, IV. iii. 420.
[2] Stenzel, iii. 472, 474.

trine in the Calvinistic pulpits, although the Lutheran clergy were likewise warned to avoid polemical preaching.[1]

If the theory of predestination separated the King in a measure from the Calvinists, the ritualistic cere- The Luther-ans. monies and general formalism of the Lutheran worship were not less obnoxious. This evil he also undertook to correct, partly by arbitrary decrees, partly by conferences with the Lutheran clergy. In 1733 appeared a royal order regulating the service of worship in St. Peter's church at Berlin. This swept away a large number of usages which the Lutheran church had retained from the Church of Rome, such as the sign of the cross at baptism, auricular confession, chants in the service, the use of Latin, of candles on the altar, and of priestly robes. A little later the King summoned all the clergy of the Electorate to an inspection and conference at Berlin, called popularly at the time, the "clerical review." On this occasion, too, the King, or officials in his name, called attention to the obnoxious rites of the Lutherans, and asked them to abandon their rigid insistence on unessentials. The royal purpose to extend the reformed system of St. Peter's over the whole monarchy was immediately afterwards proclaimed. To this a stubborn resistance was naturally made. In the district of Magdeburg, now part of the province of Saxony, many of the Lutheran clergy gave up their livings rather than obey, and many were also suspended by the King himself for offering the most deferential protests. A further difficulty arose from the adroit use made of this policy by the Catholic authorities of Silesia. They declared that the King of Prussia had violated the religious treaties by suppressing the Lutheran church, and made the charge a pretext for similar measures within their own jurisdiction.

It must be admitted that on the whole these schemes for uniting the two Protestant sects, or rather for tempering

[1] Comp. Ranke, iii., iv. 124.

the differences between them, met with very little success.

A few liberal preachers at Berlin supported the King's efforts, but the great body of the clergy of both denominations remained suspicious, critical, and obstinate. Bigotry and intolerance, rather than charity and forbearance, marked the character of the age. Frederic William was unwilling to be guided by the advice of more learned and more adroit negotiators than himself, and his own temper and methods were obviously unfitted to carry out a reform which required patience, a conciliatory manner, and unruffled diplomatic tact.[1]

The King professed and in general practised toleration. But in special emergencies, or in the case of particularly offensive individuals, he departed from this rule; and planned reprisals upon sects, or disciplined offensive preachers. The persecution of Protestants in the Palatinate, and later in Salzburg, led him to measures of retaliation upon his own Catholic subjects, which were however suspended as soon as they had effected their purpose. One of his diplomatists, Metternich, who had been an envoy at Utrecht, and on other important missions, became secretly a Catholic, and just before his death sent a notice of his treason to the King, saying that his new religion justified him in abusing the confidence of a Protestant prince. The King was greatly alarmed by this cynical confession.[2] He issued a series of decrees forbidding the Catholic clergy to exercise the right of ecclesiastical discipline and visitation, and even of making converts from the Protestants.

Minor sects outside the three recognized churches were

[1] More or less authentic statistics from the year 1722 report in Prussia 302 clergymen of the Calvinistic faith, 2,993 Lutherans, and 398 Catholics, with a total of 4,321 churches. This is not a good showing for the Calvinists, but it must be remembered that some provinces, as Preussen and Pomerania, were nearly destitute of them.

[2] See his letter to Seckendorf in Foerster, iii. 255, and Seckendorf's reply; also Droysen, IV. ii. 449.

treated capriciously, but always with suspicion, and sometimes with cruelty.   The Mennonites were at
first kindly received on their expulsion from   ^{Dissenters.}
Russia, and in 1722 were colonized in Preussen on very
liberal terms; but when the King became better acquainted
with their peculiar belief, and especially with the fact that,
in spite of their excellent husbandry and generous contributions to the public purse, conscience forbade them to
serve in the army, their privileges were revoked, and the
local authorities were ordered to re-colonize their lands
with good Christians who were not averse to bearing
arms.   The edict even ordered them to leave the province
within three months.   But by a later mitigation of this
cruel sentence they were, however, permitted to live in
Königsberg, on condition of founding woollen and other
factories.   A few Socinians in the same province were
guaranteed against persecution by a decree of Frederic I.,
but Frederic William interpreted this strictly, and forbade the sect to hold any public religious services.   The
writings of these two sects were suppressed with those of
infidels and atheists.

The contemporary biographers relate a story which
well illustrates Frederic William's ignorance, and the extravagant character of his prejudices.   A certain pastor,
Baumgarten, in Halle, was reported as being a Socinian,
and was summoned to Berlin with a view to placing him
in the grenadiers; for the King naively supposed that a
man who was bold enough to attack, as he thought, the
whole foundation of the Christian religion, must of course
be of heroic stature.   But when there appeared not a
giant, but a man much below the average height, frail and
timid, his majesty was amazed.   "Go back," he cried,
"in God's name, and keep up your preaching; you are no
Socinian; you are too weak to overthrow the Christian
religion."

The abatement of theological strife, the union of the

two Protestant churches, the toleration of Catholics, the
Frederic suppression of dissenting sects, and the general
William's encouragement of piety, were the main objects
ecclesias-
tical policy. of ecclesiastical policy in this reign. But the
facilities for public worship were wholly inadequate, and
the King's rigid parsimony denied the means for increasing them. He did indeed grant funds for rebuilding the
Berlin church of St. Peter's. But an incident connected
even with this church shows how, in an unguarded
moment, the King revealed his relative estimate of religious institutions. Some persons came in upon him one
day with the announcement that a grave calamity had
happened. " What ! " gasped his majesty, sinking into a
chair. " Yes," continued the messengers, " the tower of
St. Peter's has fallen in." "Oh!" replied the King, re-
covering himself; "I feared the grenadier Glasenapp
might be dead."

A creative, or even an imitative literature, was in the
reign of such a king almost an impossibility.

It was not, indeed, an age of great productive activity
in any part of Germany. The ruling literary
State of
literature in magnate was Gottsched, of Leipsic, a person who
Germany.
held a position not unlike that of Pope in England, and who indeed represented Pope's artificial theories
of poetical composition, though wholly destitute of the
Englishman's wit and even of his skill in versification;[1]
a passionate defender of the French school and the three
unities ; a narrow, lifeless pedant, whose arrogant yet not
unhandsome face is familiar in German print-shops. He
defended against Bodmer and the so-called Swiss school
the negative of the question, whether Milton could be
called a poet. Gottsched's influence was at this time
paramount in Germany, and current literary productions
were merely servile, and withal poor imitations of the
French.

[1] Gottsched's wife even translated Pope's *Rape of the Lock*.

But the Prussian muse was not privileged to enjoy even this limited freedom. The success of literary works, except those of the very highest order, was still held everywhere to depend on the support of patrons in high station. But in Prussia there were not only no patrons to whom ambitious poets could dedicate their odes and satires, but there was rather an official tone unfavorable to literature, and at the head of the state an ignorant and arbitrary royal censor. It is, therefore, not surprising to find that the literary records of Germany for this period contain not a single Prussian name of eminence. Such works as the histories of Gundling, the theological tomes of Rheinbeck, Franke, and others, or the voluminous treatises of Wolf, hardly belong to literature; were addressed to scholars not the public; and were likely, if widely read, to deepen rather than dispel the general gloom.

In Prussia.

The residence of the crown prince at Rheinsberg was indeed a centre of literary effort, if not of literary production. Enabled by distance to elude his father's vigilance, Frederic gathered about him at his retreat by preference men who were interested in letters, and who if not themselves poets, were at least friends of poetry and of all the liberal arts. Some of these were soldiers, some painters, some musicians; but all were required to have at least a general interest in the various departments of human culture. Educated tourists, especially those of literary reputation, found a warm and somewhat eager reception. Preuss enumerates among these Lord Baltimore, sixth of the name,[1] though it is not known to English readers that he had ever successfully scaled the heights of Parnassus; another guest, Algarotti, an Italian, had a less spotless reputation than Baltimore, for he had written many works. Frederic fell also early into correspondence with distinguished foreigners, and notably, in 1736, with Voltaire.

The muse of Rheinsberg.

[1] Vol. i. p. 77.

The literary tone which prevailed at Rheinsberg was of course exclusively French. In this respect, indeed, it went far beyond the precepts of Gottsched. What Gottsched demanded was not the adoption of the French language, but the adoption of French canons of literary criticism, and French rules of poetical composition. At Rheinsberg, however, the vehicle itself was foreign, as well as the road along which the vehicle moved. But the cargo was not valuable. Four of Frederic's literary products were written at Rheinsberg, but none of them were published until after his accession.[1]

For hospitals, asylums, and other benevolent institutions many and fairly liberal measures were taken in this reign. The orphan house at Potsdam was founded by Frederic William, chiefly for the children of soldiers, and endowed in part by money contributed outright from the treasury, in part from the proceeds of certain fines, and other incidental revenues.[2] The Charité, the great Berlin hospital, arose about the same time. In Halle an entensive orphan asylum was established through the efforts of Franke, the theologian, and was justly associated with his name. Other private persons were persuaded or compelled by the King to apply their fortunes to such beneficent uses; and institutions of relief or support sprang up in many of the larger towns. The Jews often purchased immunity from open acts of persecution by contributing to such humane enterprises. The end did

Benevolent institutions.

---

[1] The four were, " Considérations sur l'état présent du corps politique de l'Europe," written 1736 ; " Sur l'innocence des erreurs de l'espirit," 1738 ; " Avant-propos sur la Henriade de Voltaire," 1739 ; and the Anti-machiavel. Comp. Preuss, i. 77. Under this period would doubtless fall many of the so-called poems, as for instance this one, written in the imperial camp, 1734.

> " Ah ! Mortels, quel est votre erreur,
> De prêter vos mains meurtrières,
> Et vos talens, et vos lumières,
> Au meurtre, au carnage, à l'horreur ! "

[2] Comp. Riedel, *Staatshaushalt*, p. 69.

not indeed justify the means ; yet, since the means were likely to be employed in any event, public compassion for the victims was doubtless modified by the keen sense of benefits received.[1]

In another part of his policy Frederic William also bore hardly upon this unfortunate people. Their favorite occupation was attacked in severe laws against usury, and measures of various kinds against borrowing money at any rate of interest. Difficulties having arisen in the case of a foreign envoy, who attempted under cover of his diplomatic privilege to leave Berlin without repaying his loans, an edict was issued making it a penal offence to lend money to that class of persons. The same severe prohibition was enforced in regard to minors, and to the royal princes of any age. Frederic's large secret debts were one cause of his troubles. In spite of the death penalty attached by the edict to such transactions, rich bankers and merchants were not unwilling to secure the favor of the future king by timely aid to the embarrassed prince; and when Frederic's affairs were laid bare after his arrest the stern old father found that his victim was a considerable debtor. Payment was of course forbidden, and one at least of the creditors had to save himself from a worse punishment by flight and exile.[2]

It is probably not so much to any general increase of wealth as to the deliberate extortion of money from rich citizens, and to other grossly tyrannical measures, that must be attributed the remarkable growth of the cities. Potsdam and Berlin especially grew during this reign with almost tropical rapidity.

The Jews.

Growth of the cities.

[1] It is computed that the number of Hebrew families in all Prussia in 1728 was only 1191, and that they paid yearly 15,000 thalers for " protection." See Pierson, *Pr. Gesch.* p. 176.

[2] See Preuss, i. 64 ; Foerster, i. 364 ; Foerster gives the total amount of Frederic's debts at the time of his arrest at nearly 15,000 thalers.

Potsdam was indeed created by Frederic William. At the time of his accession it consisted only of a few squalid fishermen's huts, half immersed in the swamps. The tall grenadiers were garrisoned here from the first; and it was the desire to provide comfortable quarters for them, as well as the King's own original fondness for the locality, that led to successive measures of enlargement and improvement. New sections were opened in 1717, 1733, and 1737. Some of the streets were built up at the King's own cost, and some at the cost of private individuals, to whom aid was afforded in the form of free building materials. It was required, however, by his majesty's artistic sense that the houses should all be of the same height, and in the same style, even to the doors and windows. The public edifices which arose under his auspices were especially the garrison church and St. Nicholas, a gun factory, a set of barracks for married soldiers, and the great orphan asylum. The population of the city increased from some four hundred to twenty thousand during the time of this energetic king.

Potsdam.

The population of Berlin in 1713 is estimated at about sixty thousand, while in 1726 it numbered, including indeed the large garrison, seventy-two, and in 1740 ninety-eight thousand. It nearly doubled, therefore, in size within the twenty-seven years of Frederic William's reign. One large section of the city, — the Friedrichstadt, the present modern quarter of Berlin — though laid out as its name implies by Frederic, was almost entirely built by Frederic's son. He encouraged architectural zeal by measures from which the gentler father would have shrunk.

Berlin.

Certain sums were indeed assigned from the treasury for building purposes.[1] Stone, wood, and lime were often furnished free by the King to encourage the work. But there was a more sweeping

How building zeal was stimulated.

---

[1] In 1721, for instance, 10,000 thalers. Stenzel, iii. 406.

and effective policy of enlarging the quarter by compel-
ling rich citizens, or even those vaguely suspected of
wealth, and even those whom influential persons in a spirit
of malice chose to report as wealthy, to build houses at
their own, which often proved a ruinous, expense. The
organ of this policy was General Derschau, a leading
member of the tabagie. His method of procedure was extremely simple. He would report to the King that a certain man had money, and ought to build a house in the
Friedrichstadt. The man might not have a penny of capital, yet the King generally acted on Derschau's advice;
and the poor wretch would be forced to borrow money
at fabulous rates in order to escape a cruel punishment.
This happened in the case of a petty official, who drew
only two hundred thalers salary. He pleaded his poverty,
and his superiors confirmed his statement. But Derschau
insisted on obedience, and the King decided, "The fellow has money, and must build." [1] The minister and jurist, Marshall, sharply remonstrated with Derschau on his
arbitrary course, and the reply was an order " to build "
addressed to a number of his personal friends, and a little
later one for himself, all of which were approved, although
Marshall was a man whom the King held in high esteem.
Nussler, a titular privy councillor, had rendered the state
important services without pay, and was poor. Yet Derschau commanded him to put up a house, and even assigned him a lot in a swampy quarter, which would first
have to be reclaimed from the water. Frederic William,
on appeal, replied that he must obey Derschau's order
" without argument." The result was that this unpaid
servant of the crown had to borrow money, and build for
twelve thousand thalers a house, which when finished was
worth only two thousand.[2]

The vanity and special taxes of Frederic, the foresight

[1] Der Kerl hat Geldt, soll bauen.
[2] Stenzel, iii. 408.

8

and open robberies of Frederic William, coöperated to
lift Berlin rapidly upward during these reigns.   It was
paved and lighted; and was as far ahead of the other
cities of the kingdom in the comforts of civilization, as it
was behind cities of the same class in the rest of Europe.
In fact one of the great problems which vexed Frederic
William's practical mind was that of finding a chimney
which would carry the smoke up into the air, instead of
distributing it through the houses.   Domestic architecture was evidently in its infancy.

It is probable that in spite of the grossly oppressive
burdens of the public there was during this reign
a gradual increase in the extent of industrial
production, in the value of property, and in the
prosperity of the laboring classes.   There are no statistics
which afford conclusive proof, but there is valuable evidence of an indirect kind.

Growth in
wealth and
prosperity.

The steady growth of the royal revenue warrants strong
inferences as to a corresponding growth in the taxpay-
ing capacity of the land.   It is true that this increase, if
compared with the preceding reign, must be ascribed in
part to better administration, and also that Frederic William himself frequently raised the rate of contributions.
But there are other considerations which may be set over
against these.   A stricter management did undoubtedly
in the first few years yield abundant results ; but the
severe tension introduced at the outset was necessarily
somewhat relaxed with the progress of time, and of the
King's own infirmities, so that the element of economy was
relatively less active in the years when the revenues were
largest.   Again, the mere raising of the rate of imposts
was not, under a well-known rule of political economy,
any assurance of a corresponding increase of aggregate
receipts.   The opposite result might indeed follow.   The
revenues were chiefly indirect, and as rates rose, and with
them prices, consumption would naturally diminish, and

the treasury might suffer through its own unwise cupidity. But if the rate of taxation and the returns of the revenue increased side by side, there would be a fair presumption that the people were also improving in respect to the power to purchase luxuries.

Further evidence, though also of an indirect kind, is found in the King's frequent injunctions to the officials, not to tax his subjects beyond their capacity to pay. The fact that humane considerations probably had no place in this policy strengthens rather than weakens the argument. The King was greedy of money, and was indifferent to human suffering; but he was too good an economist recklessly to destroy the permanent sources of income in order to fill his treasury in a single year. He aimed to have the revenues increase steadily, as in fact they did, and yet relatively, as they also probably did, to the increase of public prosperity.

Then, finally, his own measures of improvement, harsh and arbitrary though they often were, seem fitted to enlarge both the productive resources and the actual wealth of the country. The growth of Berlin, Potsdam, and other towns must have raised the value of city property. The colonization policy in Preussen, and other provinces, raised in the same way the value of land, and the aggregate of agricultural production. The protective system multiplied the number of Prussian looms. Some of these measures had, of course, their counteracting evils, but these were not immediately felt. The first results were beneficial. And as a further circumstance likely to affect favorably the value of land, may be mentioned the King's policy of buying large estates for the crown; for since the purchasing power of the royal treasury was great, and its desire to purchase keen, the owners of farms would of course appraise their property with reference to that state of things.

In view of these considerations, it seems reasonable to

conclude that the taxable wealth of Prussia increased both relatively and absolutely during Frederic William's reign.

The population of the state in 1740 is variously esti-

Population and area. mated, and absolute accuracy is out of the question. But taking account of the two extremes it is probably safe to say that the kingdom contained between two million four hundred thousand, and two million eight hundred thousand souls. This was a considerable increase over the number left by Frederic I.; and although it is in part explained by the addition of new territories, such as Stettin and Guelders, there is good reason to believe that there had also been a steady growth in the original provinces. The area of the kingdom was about fifty-six thousand English square miles.[1]

The finances were left in a flourishing condition. It

State of the finances. had been Frederic William's purpose to set aside seven or eight hundred thousand thalers yearly as a reserve fund; and this rate ought to have produced a surplus in 1740 of some twenty millions. But this treasure was frequently opened by the King in special emergencies, such as the marriage of a child or the distress of a province, so that at his death it amounted only to eight millions. But this was for the times an enormous sum, and the heir to whom it fell knew how to use as well as to save money.

During the later years of his life the King was a con-

Infirmities of the King. stant sufferer from a complication of diseases. His excessive corpulency was itself an evil. Although he had always spent much time in the open air, taken violent exercise, and lived with great regularity, his enormous consumption of food and drink finally conquered his robust system, brought on the dropsy, swelled him out to incredible dimensions, and in the end prostrated him with a malignant form of the gout. In 1734 a sudden and severe illness forced him to leave the army on the

[1] 2,275 German Quadratmeilen.

Rhine, and return to Berlin. His death being feared, the crown prince was summoned. He survived this attack, indeed, but never fully recovered; and for a good part of the time afterwards had to be wheeled about in an arm-chair, a helpless physical wreck.

A morbid apprehension about his future led the King, as his end drew near, to look back over the past *His mental* with occasional feelings of remorse. He insisted *depression.* always on the rectitude of his intentions; the most rigid self-examination never found any flaw in them. But he was not equally sure about the infallibility of his judgment. He learned to doubt the wisdom of some of his arbitrary measures, of his persecution of individuals, of his gross excesses in the tabagie; discussed them with preachers; tested his conscience with almost pathetic solicitude. And he had to bear this heavy burden alone. It is a stern law of retribution in political ethics that sweet as are the pleasures of arbitrary rule, the ruler cannot at the day of reckoning appeal from his own conscience to the advice of responsible ministers.

Under the influence of this depression even his prejudices lost some of their original violence. The zeal of the recruiting officers was restrained. Reparation was offered to Wolf by the invitation to return to Halle. The crown prince was treated with more and more forbearance. Frederic himself was gratified by this apparent change, and in letters to confidential friends describes not only his father's improved humor, but also, as something almost miraculous, his willingness to speak of science with respect and even interest. But these were evidently slight concessions made under the pressure of spiritual anxiety. In all the essential traits of his character, Frederic William continued to be the same man who had ascended the throne in 1713. He frequented the tabagie down to the last evening that his enfeebled body could bear its fatigues. The day before his death he was wheeled out to the parade ground to see his "beloved blue children," the grenadiers, once more march in line and wheel by companies, shoulder arms and fix bayonets. One of the last remarks which he made as he took a final look out of a palace window, was a regret that he could not go down and flog a groom, who had committed some trifling mistake. "Go out there," said he to an adjutant, "and horsewhip the rascal for me."

Yet the death scene itself was not without a certain dignity.

The King had some days before bidden farewell to Berlin, preferring, as he said, to die in Potsdam. It was early in the morning of the last day that the incident at the window occurred. After that he collected the leading officials, civil and military, about him; thanked them for their services; exhorted them to show the same fidelity to his successor, whom he formally presented; and then proposed to resign the government at once to Frederic. But this required a written renunciation over the King's own signature, and in the interval he was overcome by weakness and carried to his bed. When a little later he regained consciousnesss, he saw around his couch his weeping family, a clergyman kneeling in prayer, a surgeon trying his pulse. Between one and two o'clock in the afternoon, in full control of his faculties, he quietly passed away. "He died," says Frederic, "with the firmness of a philosopher, and the resignation of a Christian; preserving a wonderful presence of mind down to the last moment of his life; regulating his affairs like a statesman; examining the progress of his malady like a physician; and triumphing over death like a hero."

His death.
May 31,
1740.

Although Frederic William was only fifty-two when he died, he had outlived nearly all the servants and favorites of his earlier years. Fuchs, Kraut, Ilgen, Printzen, Blaspiel, and Grumbkow were gone;

Conclusion.

Leopold of Dessau alone survived. Most of the men who held leading positions in 1740, such as Podewils, Marshall, Cocceji, Thulemeier, and Borcke, were either new men, or men who had risen from the ranks in the course of the twenty-seven years reign. They naturally represented the King's views and methods better, therefore, than ministers who had carried into his service the looser habits of the previous reign.

The machine of state had learned to work so smoothly and regularly that the King was relieved of the anxiety which he had once felt about its future behavior, and turned it over finally to a successor of whose fitness he had also, after long and painful doubts, become fully convinced.

Thus, on the last day of May, 1740, at the age of twenty-eight years, Frederic II. was King in Prussia.

GENEALOGY OF THE HOUSE OF HOHENZOLLERN IN BRANDENBURG–PRUSSIA.

I. The Electoral Line.

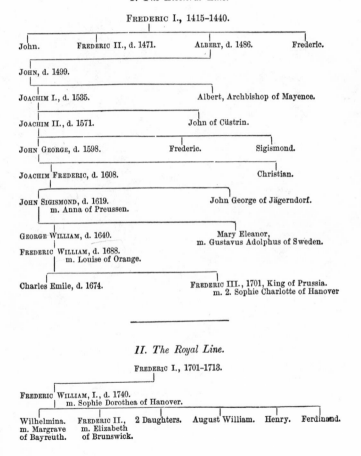

FREDERIC I., 1415–1440.

John. FREDERIC II., d. 1471. ALBERT, d. 1486. Frederic.

JOHN, d. 1499.

JOACHIM I., d. 1535. Albert, Archbishop of Mayence.

JOACHIM II., d. 1571. John of Cüstrin.

JOHN GEORGE, d. 1598. Frederic. Sigismond.

JOACHIM FREDERIC, d. 1608. Christian.

JOHN SIGISMOND, d. 1619.
m. Anna of Preussen. John George of Jägerndorf.

GEORGE WILLIAM, d. 1640. Mary Eleanor,
m. Gustavus Adolphus of Sweden.

FREDERIC WILLIAM, d. 1688.
m. Louise of Orange.

Charles Emile, d. 1674. FREDERIC III., 1701, King of Prussia.
m. 2. Sophie Charlotte of Hanover

II. The Royal Line.

FREDERIC I., 1701–1713.

FREDERIC WILLIAM, I., d. 1740.
m. Sophie Dorothea of Hanover.

Wilhelmina. FREDERIC II., 2 Daughters. August William. Henry. Ferdinand.
m. Margrave m. Elizabeth
of Bayreuth. of Brunswick.

INDEX.